PELICAN BOOKS

A CONCISE HISTORY OF
EAST ASIA

C. P. Fitzgerald was born in London in 1902, and
educated at Clifton College, Bristol. He lived in
China, with brief breaks, from 1923 to 1939, and for
four years after the war, from 1946 to 1950. He
held the Leverhulme Fellowship for anthropological
research in China from 1936 to 1939 and worked in
Tali, in Yunnan province. After the war, he was
the representative of the British Council in North
China. He then became Professor of Far Eastern
History in the Australian National University,
Canberra, and is now working on a Contemporary
China project, supported by a Ford Foundation
grant, in the same university.

C. P. Fitzgerald is the author of *Son of Heaven*,
China: A Short Cultural History, *Tower of Five
Glories*, *The Empress Wu*, *Floodtide in China*,
Barbarian Beds, *The Third China*, *Chinese Communities in S.E. Asia*, *Des Mantchous à Mao
Tse-tung*, and *Classical China*.

A CONCISE HISTORY OF

EAST ASIA

C. P. FITZGERALD

PENGUIN BOOKS

Penguin Books Ltd, Harmondsworth, Middlesex, England
Penguin Books Australia Ltd, Ringwood, Victoria, Australia

—

First published by Heinemann Educational Australia 1966
Published in Pelican Books 1974

—

Copyright © C. P. FitzGerald, 1966

Made and printed in Great Britain by
Richard Clay (The Chaucer Press) Ltd
Bungay, Suffolk

Set in Linotype Pilgrim

Contents

List of Illustrations

List of Maps

Note

IN the original edition of this book the story of the nations of East Asia was brought down to the time of writing, 1967–8, in outline. The post-war period, however, not only differs widely from the earlier ages, but is not yet 'history' in the full sense of that term, because archives and confidential state papers have not yet been made available to students and scholars. It has therefore seemed more appropriate, in a history of these nations, to conclude at the point, usually some three or four years after the end of the Second World War, when profound changes occurred constituting a sharp break with the past.

Independence for the former colonial possessions of the European powers, and for Korea, the advent of the Communist régime in China, the post-war era in Occupied Japan, were all nearly contemporary events, except in Malaysia where the full independence was not attained until a few years later. The developments of the past twenty years, so largely affected by the war in Vietnam, have been the subject of other books devoted to this period, and not concerned with earlier history.

C.P.F.

PART ONE

CHINA

CHAPTER ONE

The Classical Age

(1700–200 B.C.)

THE phrase 'China's four thousand years of history' is often used in speaking of China, but it is an exaggeration. Four thousand years ago, that is about 2000 B.C., is a period well before we can speak of Chinese history. All that we know of that time is that the people of China were still in the New Stone Age, and had certainly not devised a written script nor learned to keep any record of events. The actual evidence of archaeology, of inscriptions, city sites and bronze vessels does not appear till about 1200 B.C., but the Chinese records, compiled in their present form hundreds of years later, do speak of the Shang kingdom as existing from 1700 B.C. and have preserved a list of the names of the kings and some brief accounts of what went on in their reigns. For a long time Western scholars used to treat this as legend: but some forty years ago it was found that inscriptions carved on bones which were excavated at the site of the Shang city of Anyang in the north China province of Honan really did mention the same names as the traditional list of Shang kings, with two exceptions, and these missing names were precisely those of the kings who had reigned later than the inscriptions on the bones found at Anyang.

This is the kind of luck which does not often come the way of historians or archaeologists. But it conclusively proves that there was more truth in the traditional Chinese histories than modern scholars had supposed. Therefore it is worth taking into consideration what these histories do relate and then comparing it with what archaeology can confirm. According to the Chinese traditional history the world began under the reign of Sages, ideal rulers who taught their people all the arts, governed with perfect justice, but were not incarnate gods, as so many of the legendary heroes of other lands were thought to be. It is an interesting early example of the practical character of the Chinese people that they thought of these first hero kings as mortal men even if they were also more than human in their wisdom and moral perfection. Even these legends seem to have admitted that the rule of the Sages did not cover the whole earth. There are references to barbarians, whom the Sages tamed or repelled, more by using mercy and benevolence than by force of arms. It is also worth remarking that the Sages are not represented as military heroes and great warriors. Theirs was a rule of peace.

There were five Sages who ruled before the first founder of a dynasty. These, who have always been honoured by the Chinese as the true founders of civilization, were Huang Ti ('The Yellow Emperor'), Chuan Hsu, K'u, Yao and Shun. The Five Sages were not fathers and sons. In each case we are told the son of the Sage ruler was not judged worthy to follow his father: in some cases a grandson was chosen, but in others the next ruler was not any relation of his predecessor. This also is an interesting point, because in all later Chinese history down to the Republic the throne was hereditary and went by primogeniture – the eldest son succeeding his father. But the founder of the first legendary dynasty, Yu, was a descendant of Huang Ti, and from his time onward hereditary succession was the rule. Yu founded the Hsia dynasty, which according to the two conflicting chronologies used by the traditional histories, ruled from either 2205 B.C. to 1766 B.C. or from 1989 B.C. to 1557 B.C. These dates have been translated into the forms of the Western calendar.

In truth nothing is known about the existence of a Hsia dynasty from archaeology. Not a single inscription, site or artifact exists which can be certainly attributed to such a dynasty. Yet the tradition of its existence, and that it came before the Shang, is very old and was never questioned in China. It is always possible that archaeological work, which is proceeding very actively in China today, will bring to light some piece of conclusive evidence proving that a Hsia dynasty, or kingdom, did exist and that it was either prior to the Shang, or perhaps contemporary in another part of the country. One belief of the old historians is certainly wrong. Neither the Shang nor the Hsia nor any other government in China in the most ancient period controlled all the present land of China, or, indeed, any region of great extent. We know nothing of the Hsia : but we do know something of the Shang, and it is clear that it covered at most the present provinces of Hopei and Honan, about a third of the basin of the Yellow River. Practically nothing is known of the history, or prehistory, of south and west China. In these provinces neolithic sites have been found in large numbers, but they can be roughly dated to about 3000 B.C. and cannot be linked with any historical dynasty. They have provided clear evidence that the inhabitants of prehistoric China were, to judge from the bone structure of skeletons, hardly at all different from the present people of China living in the same areas.

This indeed is not the only reason to think that the Chinese people evolved from the neolithic population. Among the types of pottery found at neolithic sites there is one which is peculiar to China, and never found in any other part of the world. It is called a *li* and really consists of three pots joined at their mouths so that the pot has three large hollow legs and can be placed over a fire in such a way that three different liquids can be cooked at once, one in each leg. It would seem that the Chinese skill in cooking goes back a very long way. *Li* have continued to be made, and used, right down to modern times; later, metal being often preferred to earthenware. There is thus this certain link between neolithic culture in China and later civilization.

In the traditional histories the events told about the kings of Hsia or of Shang are really moral tales; virtue rewarded and vice leading to disaster. From what archaeology has to show we know that in Shang times there were still many savage customs in use. At the burial of kings, servants were slain and entombed with him, together with his chariots and horses and their charioteers. Fiercesome weapons, axes for decapitating men – with grim little pictures of the process engraved upon them – have been dug up. The first inscriptions were made on bones to record the consultations of oracles, and it is clear that it was believed that the royal ancestors were the spirits who gave the answers. It is due to this fact that we have the list of the kings preserved. The oracles were taken by 'reading' the cracks made in the shin bones of oxen or the shells of tortoises when a hot metal rod was held against the bone or shell. There is no positive evidence, but it seems very probable, that the true origin of the Chinese script came from this practice: certain kinds of crack were interpreted to mean this or that, and later an ideograph or 'picture' was made representing this pattern, and came to have a fixed meaning. We do know from finds on early Shang sites, especially at Chengchou in Honan province, that about the middle of the second millennium B.C., say 1500 B.C., the practice of taking oracles in this way was in use, but the ability to write the answers down in primitive script does not appear. It may be that we should therefore date the invention of the Chinese written script to some period between 1500 and 1200 B.C. This is of course very much later, two thousand and more years later, than the beginnings of Egyptian hieroglyphs or the cuneiform inscriptions of ancient Mesopotamia. It used to be thought that such an invention was never really made twice, and that therefore the Chinese script must have derived from those of the Middle East or Egypt. This view is not held today. There appears to be no connection, except the general one that both are the work of the human imagination, between Chinese writing and Egyptian or Sumerian scripts.

The principle of the Chinese script is often misunderstood; there are not 'thousands of letters in a Chinese alphabet'. The system is exactly the same as we now use for figures. If we write '5' any reader, no matter what language he speaks, can understand it, but when he pronounces the sound he may say *five*, *fünf* or *cinq*, etc., in a great number of different languages. But '5' has no sound, only meaning. This is the system of all Chinese writing, the characters, or ideographs, as they are sometimes called, have, strictly, no sound. They are ideas, like our numerals, which every reader can sound according to his dialect. Thus the Chinese character meaning Sun is pronounced in the northern language, which is nowadays the standard form of Chinese, as something like *ir*, but in Cantonese as *yat* and in some of the lower Yangtze dialects as *lap*. In this way the sound and the meaning are quite separate in Chinese, and as the written form does not indicate the sound in any dialect, the sounds have changed very much faster than is the case in languages written in alphabetic scripts. Even in these scripts parts of the word have often become silent. For example, in French *avait* the t is not now sounded and the word is almost identical in sound with *avez*. This kind of transformation has gone very far in Chinese: we know that in ancient Chinese there were many final consonants but these are no longer sounded in modern Chinese, except to a limited extent in the Cantonese and other southern dialects. An example of how a Chinese word can be changed by not being tied up with an alphabetic script is the word 'Buddha'. This is now pronounced in standard Chinese as *Fo*. This would make one think the word can never have been Buddha at all, but it was. First, the second syllable was dropped off – a common Chinese habit, for the tendency of the language is always to shorten words. Thus it came to be pronounced as *Bud*. But then the final consonant went, and it was just *Bu*. The B then changed to F, and the vowel sound to O. All this has happened in less than 1500 years.

Consequently we have no real idea how Chinese was pro-nounced in the earliest times: when a character is found on an early inscription which stands for a place name it is often quite impossible to tell how it should be pronounced. Yet it is pre-cisely this feature which makes early inscriptions readable. It was found that the most ancient oracle bones already used a system of dating the days of the month which has endured until modern times; these characters could be recognized by scholars in their primitive form, and from these it was possible to read more and more of the early forms until whole inscrip-tions can be deciphered. But no one knows how these words were pronounced in antiquity. Chinese writing is thus very largely independent of time; ancient books can be read as eas-ily as modern ones, which has, of course, kept literature in circulation far longer than in any other culture. Style has changed, and words have gained new meanings, but the oldest works written about 1000 B.C. can be read as easily as English scholars can today read the works of Chaucer.

Being independent of sound, like the numerals, Chinese is also just as comprehensible to foreign peoples who have learned the Chinese script, even though they cannot speak Chinese. An educated Japanese can read Chinese without being able to speak a word of it; so can Koreans and Vietnamese. Southern Chinese who do not speak the northern dialects, or northerners who know no spoken Cantonese can write to each other, or read the same books and newspapers without any obstacle at all. This has been a great bond of unity in the Chinese civilization; indeed, some scholars think that without the Chinese script the unity of Chinese civilization over so great an area could never have developed. There are about four thousand characters in common use, although the great dictionaries list many hundreds, indeed thousands, of variant forms etc. An educated man would probably be able to read up to five thousand without using a dictionary. Ordinary literate people can manage very well with three thousand or so. For popular education the Chinese have now produced a system which brings the number of essential characters down to about one thousand, or less. In modern times there has been a movement to simplify the forms of the more complicated ones, and this has already happened more than once in past history.

The Chinese system, once invented, developed rather quickly. By the time of Anyang it had reached a stage when it is now possible for specialist scholars to read most of the bone inscriptions – which are quite short – and usually take the form: 'The king asked (so and so, one of his ancestors) shall we go hunting? What spoil shall we win?' The oracle replied, 'Favourable: four deer, twelve boar, many hares', or words to that effect. Sometimes the oracle said the prospects were unfavourable. The oracle was also asked about war. 'Shall I attack the X tribe (we usually cannot read the proper names, which have not survived in any other literature)?' The oracle replies,

'Favourable: you will take many prisoners.' The prisoners, we know, were made into slaves, and also used for human sacrifices. All this gives rather a different picture of the real life of Shang times from that which the traditional histories presented. We see a primitive society just emerging into the first stages of civilization, inventing a script and soon making superlatively fine bronze ware.

This is another interesting question about early Chinese history. Where did the Chinese obtain the knowledge of working metals and casting bronze? It used to be assumed that they must have got these arts from western Asia, where they are many hundreds of years older than in China. But recent work has cast a great deal of doubt on this. To begin with, it does not appear that any place on the very long difficult route across Asia which links China with Persia and Iraq had any such early knowledge of metal work. It seems unlikely that so fine and skilled an art could have been brought all this great distance and then only developed in distant China. Secondly, it can be shown that the Chinese method of casting in the early times was not that which the western Asians and Egyptians used, and further, that it gave the Chinese products a far higher technical quality of precision, enabling them to decorate their bronze vessels in a most elaborate way with intricate patterns, knobs, handles and decoration in relief. The fact that pottery vessels showing the same skilful decoration are now being found in Shang sites suggests that it was from their advanced skill in pottery and ceramic work that the Chinese invented metal smelting, possibly as an accidental consequence of using metal-bearing clays. It is known from finds that the Chinese furnaces were able to produce much higher temperatures than those known to the western Asian nations.

The tendency of modern scholarship, backed by archaeological evidence, is towards the view that Chinese civilization did in fact originate in China, and nowhere else. This does not mean that the earlier neolithic culture had not many features which are found in every part of the world at the same stage; but the steps which lead upwards to a true civilization, a system of writing, metal work, social organization and religion, seem to be in every case of Chinese origin and not borrowed. The Shang worked stone for sculptures, carved bone and ivory, very finely, but seem to have built in brick, no doubt because the region where they lived, the Yellow River basin, has much good clay but very little stone, and none of the easily worked sandstones or volcanic lavas which early builders found easy to handle. The rocks of north China are limestone, which flakes, but is hard to cut and shape.

Owing to the fact that all the written information about Shang culture dates from centuries later, except the brief oracle bone inscriptions, it is not possible to know very much about the way they organized their society, nor about their religion. The government was a monarchy: there is some reason to think that they followed fraternal succession – that younger brothers succeeded the dead king before his sons or son. But we do not really know whether this was a rule or just exceptional cases. It is clear that there were slaves, prisoners of war in the main, and also free men and certainly nobles or heads of clans. The Shang kings worshipped the spirits of the great dead, but whether the humble people did so also we cannot tell. Many Shang bronzes are dedicated to the use of the ancestral temple 'to be used by sons and grandsons for ten thousand generations'. Sometimes the name of the ancestor in whose rites the vessel will serve is mentioned. But these valuable and beautiful things must have been made only for the rich and powerful.

To judge from the greater knowledge which exists concerning the next age in China, the Chou dynasty, the people, rich and poor alike, worshipped many nature gods, local gods, and above all the Sky God, who came later to be known simply as T'ien, which means 'Heavens' or 'the Sky'. In later Chinese civilization this Sky God or T'ien became the Supreme Being, whom the Emperor worshipped as chief priest, and who was thought to control the universe. It does not appear that the Chinese ever worshipped the Sun as such: the Sun was part of T'ien, but so was the Moon, and at a very early period the idea that the harmony of the universe was controlled by the balance of the forces of nature, wet and dry, cold and heat, male and female, earth and sky, sun and moon, took shape. These twin forces were known as Yin and Yang. Yin was wet, female, dark, cold and the moon; Yang, dry, male, light, heat and the sun. But the Chinese did not think of these forces as conflicting and at war with each other. They pictured them (as they still do) in the diagram made up of a circle, equally divided by a curving line typifying the idea that these forces constantly acted upon each other, fluctuated, but remained in equal strength and should be in harmony. There is no doubt that this, in whatever primitive or sophisticated form it appears through the centuries, remained one of the basic concepts of the Chinese mind.

Unlike most other peoples the early Chinese did not habitually make images of their gods in human shape. They preferred abstract shapes, circles with a round hole in the middle, the emblem of T'ien, and other shapes whose origin is not so obvious, but which we know stood for Earth, the points of the compass and other natural features. These emblems were made of jade, considered a very precious substance (probably because it was rare, coming from the deserts of Central Asia), and they have not only been found in early tombs but are referred to in the earliest literature.

The Chou Dynasty and the Period of the Warring States (1050 or 1122–221 B.C.)

One of the first events which can be said to be truly historical was the overthrow of the Shang kingdom by the founder of the next dynasty, the Chou. The date is not certain, either 1050 B.C. or 1122 B.C. depending on which of the ancient chronologies is followed. In either case there is reason to doubt whether it is exact. The course of events, as told by the traditional history, makes the last king of Shang a tyrant of the worst type who tortured his nobles, slaughtered his people, engaged in every sort of debauch and vice and was finally defeated and slain by the noble ruler of the Chou, who had been one of the Shang king's principal vassals, ruling the western region, as far as the modern province of Shensi. This is clearly a very streamlined version, which probably only touches truth at a few points. The Shang kingdom was replaced by the Chou. The nature and cause of the crisis which brought this change cannot be known, but we do know from bronze inscriptions that several years after the victory the Shang people were still at war with Chou vassals, under a king who finally himself became a vassal prince of the Chou king. These facts are not consistent with the old view that the people revolted against a tyrant and willingly accepted the rule of his conqueror. On the other hand, Western historians of China used to favour the idea that the Chou were an invading people from western Asia who conquered China (the Shang). This is not supported by evidence, and is now discarded. The Chou chief was the ruler, under the Shang, of the western part of the kingdom, but there is no reason to think that either he or his people came from some distant country.

In some ways the Chou seem to have been rather behind the Shang, at least at first. Bronze vessels of very early Chou date are less fine than late Shang, but this soon changes. The written script remained the same, but before long developed rapidly. Bronzes were inscribed with long dedicatory pieces, praising ancestors and recording the services of descendants, and the glory of the noble house. From these inscriptions it can be confirmed that the institutions of the Chou dynasty were of a feudal kind. Nobles were awarded fiefs for war services; they had the duty to raise men to serve the king; there were grades of nobility which have been given Western equivalents, duke, marquis, count and baron. Beneath these was a large class of gentry, the 'sons of lords', to give an exact translation, who served both the king and their feudal chief. The whole country was divided into fiefs great and small. There seem to have been a great number, but no accurate record remains. There were some very large fiefs, under dukes, which were given – in theory – only to the sons and brothers of the founder of the dynasty, King Wu. But it is clear that in some cases this pedigree is a fiction, and that some of the great fiefs were ruled by chiefs who had no relationship at all to the king, but were more probably either former vassals of the Shang, or lords of independent tribes.

By the time that history was written in a systematic way, at the end of the Chou period, more than six hundred years from its foundation, many records had been lost, and the men of that time did not clearly understand the differences between their own age and that of their ancestors. In their day feudalism was collapsing, and large kingdoms, only nominally under the suzerainty of the King of Chou, were fighting each other in incessant wars. Late Chou historians deplored their own chaotic times and believed that in the golden age of the great King Wu all had been harmony and peace. The contemporary records from bronze inscriptions do not bear out this idyllic belief.

Yet it is probable that at the time of the foundation of the Chou, Chinese civilization was greatly extended over peoples hitherto barbarous. The coast of north China, including Shantung, became a fief of Chou; we hear for the first time of the Yangtze valley region and later of the south-east coast, although both areas were not then considered to be part of the Middle Kingdom, the name by which already the Chinese knew the land over which the Chou king claimed overlordship. The precise limits of that kingdom cannot be defined; it certainly covered north China, the Yellow River basin up to the mountains which divide China from Mongolia, along which the Great Wall was later built. Westwards it included Shensi province, and perhaps parts of Kansu, the great fief of Ch'in. This fief later conquered and colonized what is now the western province of Szechuan, in which there were early states outside Middle Kingdom control. Perhaps it would be true to say that about half the area of modern China formed, very loosely, the group of fiefs and territories owing some sort of allegiance to the King of Chou. That is a very large region, and though we cannot guess at its population, it must have already numbered several millions.

In 771 B.C. the ninth ruler of the Chou kingdom was driven from his capital, which was near the modern Sian in Shensi, by an invasion of barbarians, mounted people from the Mongolian steppe. This was the first of many such invasions of which we have some record. The Chou kings moved east to Loyang, where their city has recently been located and excavated, lying on the outskirts of the modern Loyang. This catastrophe probably weakened the central power, and led to the slow rise of the great fiefs, especially Ch'in, which inherited the old western territory.

In 841 B.C. a revolution at court leading to a regency marks the beginning of accurate dated history, for from that time the divergent chronologies coincide, and history, or annals, begins to be written in consecutive form with remarkably accurate dating.

The beginning of Chinese literature is supposed to come from a somewhat earlier age, the first years of the Chou. The famous classical books, the Book of History, the Book of Changes, the Odes and a few others are alleged to be the compositions of this time. How far they are really so, or how much of these texts can be considered so old, is an intricate scholarly problem on which generations of Chinese scholars and later Western sinologists have laboured. The Chinese revere an ancient book and copy it faithfully, difficulties and all. No people has preserved its literature so carefully. But they did not inscribe on stone or write in baked clay like the Egyptians and Mesopotamians. They wrote on bamboo slabs, with a stylus. Bamboo rots, and the cords which hold the strips together rot also. Ancient books have been found, but often the order of the strips of bamboo is confused, and this has led to endless problems. It is on the whole probable that much of the Book of History is really early Chou, most of the Odes are early Chou, but some of the other works are certainly much altered by later additions.

Confucius and his followers revered these ancient texts. They became in later centuries classics, almost sacred writ. But no one ever claimed them as the revealed words of a god. It was accepted that they were the works of men, the famous heroes of early Chou, King Wu and his brother, the Duke of Chou. The Odes are the most ancient Chinese poetry, and it is now thought were composed at the court of the western Chou kings, between 1000 and 700 B.C. These books formed for the next two thousand years and more the basic texts of Chinese literature and scholarship. Every educated person knew them, they were quoted, commented upon, and studied by generation after generation. It is in this sense that the Chou period is the real beginning of the Chinese culture, the age of the first literature, whose continuing influence has lasted to modern times.

The great age of the philosophers came in the second part of the Chou period, from the age of Confucius (died 479 B.C.). In the lifetime of Confucius the feudal system of the Chou kingdom was already breaking down, and in the two centuries after his death it wholly collapsed. The kings became powerless, if still revered, rulers of an isolated capital. The great fief holders made war upon each other, seized the territories of lesser rulers, and incorporated them in even larger states. Wars were incessant. At first they were fought under rules of chivalry which were often carefully observed. Nobles fought in chariots, the common people swarming round their leaders on foot. It was considered ungentlemanly to strike down a noble if his chariot was disabled and he was on foot. You should wait until he found another chariot and then resume the fight. It was wrong to attack the enemy by surprise, or before his battle line was formed: it was also indecent to seize his territory, you should only raid it. When, in the year that Confucius died, the southern kingdom of Ch'u in the Yangtze valley, always considered rather beyond the true pale of Chinese civilization, actually conquered and annexed one of the old fiefs of the Middle Kingdom, this event was considered as an international outrage marking a sad decline in conduct. But the King of Ch'u did not relax his grip, and before many years passed others followed his bad example.

One great difference between the Chinese feudal age and that of Europe, centuries later, was that the nobility in China were not only the warriors and rulers but also the scholars. Only the nobility were educated: there was no priesthood outside the class of the nobility, who themselves performed the rites of religion whether public, such as the worship of regional and nature gods, or private family worship of ancestral spirits. Consequently the great division between religious and laity, between Church and State, which existed in the ancient Near East as well as in later Christian Europe, had no place in China. This meant that literature was far more concerned with politics, history and war, and also with romance and arts, than in other cultures where religion and an organized priesthood dominated the early culture and wrote its literature. The Chinese have no great religious epics like the Indian Ramayama, but they do have a dated and often very well told history at an age when no other people had invented this form.

History was not only to be a record of events, it was designed to point a moral, to be a mirror – the expression is constantly used by the Chinese – in which later rulers could see their defects, and correct their mistakes. 'See what happened to King so-and-so, who governed so foolishly, but note, too, how the wise King such-and-such consolidated his realm by clever moves, and above all by righteous conduct.' Confucius and his school firmly believed that history should teach these lessons, that this was its purpose. Therefore it must be accurate. Vice must not be hidden under flattery, nor folly excused because it was the action of a king. Virtue could be recorded equally, and should be, but it was as true then as now that virtue in political life is rarer than folly and wickedness. Consequently Chinese history is plentifully supplied with records of treasons, stratagems and cruelties.

These historical records, growing fuller and more detailed as the centuries went by, give us the real background to the world in which the great Chinese philosophers lived and taught. It was a world in which it was no longer possible to believe in the old order which was falling fast; in which kings sought cunning counsellors rather than sages as their advisers, where nobles began to betray their feudal lords, or tried to usurp their fiefs. The Golden Age of the Five Sages of myth was remote and unreal, but the philosophers believed that it was the ideal which should be restored. Various conflicting ideas on how to achieve this end were put forward. Confucius believed that the virtues of loyalty, filial piety, respect for antiquity and observance of the old chivalric code was the foundation on which everything must rest. Another school, later called Tao ('The Way'), taught that the world was hopeless : the sage should withdraw from it to the peace of the hills, and show by his example how to live, not strive to convert others. Example was all-important, teaching was useless. There were many variants of these two main divisions : Mo Tzu taught that only univer-sal love could save society, but did not believe in Confucian love of antiquity nor in Taoist withdrawal from the world. Strangely, his doctrine, in some striking ways a forerunner of Christian ethics, did not gain great power and later faded away.

There was another school, the School of the Law, who were harsh realists. They believed that only the power of the king kept the peace or enforced good conduct. So law must be made terrible, and men would not dare to break it. Only warriors and peasants were useful citizens – the first to fight the wars of the king, the second to grow food for the soldiers to eat. The rest, scholars, merchants, were useless folk who should be discour-aged, if not actually exterminated. These doctrines were not of course completely put into practice, but they did become the ruling ideas of the state of Ch'in, the great fief of the far west, which was ultimately to prove the victor in the long drawn out wars. Much of the literature of the philosophers survives. Con-fucius and his followers preserved not only their own works but a great deal of what was left by their opponents, perhaps to show their pupils what they should oppose. Very much more would still be extant if Ch'in, when it conquered all China, had not destroyed what it could in the great Burning of the Books.

The question of how far there can be said to have been a real Chinese nation, rather than a number of different kingdoms inhabited by people of much the same race, is still rather de-batable. We have no maps dating from the classical age, and the limits of the different states in late feudal times are not clear. It is evident that some were much larger than others, and that there were also a number of quite small fiefs scattered about between and in the midst of greater neighbours. The location of some of these has been proved by archaeological discoveries, but usually all that is known of them is some passing mention, or the record that in such and such a year the little state was annexed by a powerful neighbour. In the hill country, and also probably in marshy areas, there were still pockets of 'barbarians' whom the Chinese knew by various names, but whom they clearly regarded as primitive savages. We have really no knowledge at all of who these peoples were, what race they belonged to or whether they were aboriginals inhabiting the land before the Chinese came, or simply very backward groups of much the same stock as the Chinese themselves. On the whole, the last alternative seems the most probable. During feudal times they were gradually conquered and absorbed by the Chinese neighbouring states.

This is one of the first glimpses we get, in history, of a process which has gone on for the past two thousand years and led to the expansion of China to her present frontiers. For there is no doubt that it was in much the same way that the south – the vast region making up more than half the present China, which lies south of the Yellow River basin – was slowly incorporated into the Chinese civilization and empire of later times. In the feudal age, from about the seventh century B.C. onward, more and more is heard of kingdoms in the Yangtze valley which the Chinese of the older northern states still looked upon as rather barbarous. It is clear, too, that the language of these southern states, Ch'u in the middle and lower Yangtze valley, Yueh along the south-east coast, differed from northern Chinese, which seems to have been a common language to all the northern region (as it still is). Mo Tzu, wishing to illustrate his doctrine of universal love by a striking example, declared, 'A man of Ch'u is my brother.' This clearly had much the same force as the nineteenth-century missionary's use of the term 'black brother' to proclaim his full Christian charity. No one else thought of men of Ch'u as brothers or even, perhaps, as fully human.

Archaeology has recently shown that the northern Chinese had very little reason to take up this superior attitude. At Ch'angsha, now the capital of Hunan province, in the south, and once the capital of Ch'u (it is a very ancient city), tombs of

Ch'u date have been found which contain very finely worked articles of gold, remains of silks, bronzes, carvings and the first known examples of lacquer ever found in the Far East. Ch'u may have been foreign, but it was not barbarous. Yueh, along the south-east coast, seems really to have been more backward. In any case, archaeological discovery has not yet thrown much light on the culture of this period in the region. It is also very probable that the Yueh people were of a different stock to the northern Chinese. They were sea-going folk, and there is some reason to think that part of this people later, or at this time, settled in Japan and made up one of the elements from which the Japanese people were formed. The name Yueh, in its southern pronunciation as *Viet* still appears in 'Viet Nam', which northern Chinese would pronounce as *Yueh Nan*, and testifies to the fact that the coastal peoples long believed that they all belonged to one people, the *Yueh*. (Viet Nam means Southern Viet, or Yueh.)

Ch'u, and later Yueh, came under strong Chinese influence from the north, partly because Ch'u conquered the more southerly of the Chinese states of the Middle Kingdom, partly from trade and travel. It is clear that these southern kingdoms learned the art of writing from the north. No trace of an alternative script has been found in the south. This influence in itself was enormous, as it brought with it the literature and traditions of the north and thus steadily converted the Ch'u and Yueh into Chinese only differing from their northern neighbours in speech, as, to some extent (especially in the ancient Yueh area) they still do. From the time of Confucius onwards the southern states played a major part in the wars and statecraft of the old Middle Kingdom, and the fact that they never seem to have been true vassals of the Chou king lost all importance when the former vassals had all repudiated allegiance and claimed to be kings themselves. Ch'u from the fifth century B.C. onwards was clearly a major competitor in the growing power struggle which now began to have as its conscious objective the unification of the Chinese world under one single ruler.

Had Ch'u been opposed only by the old Middle Kingdom

states, such as Ch'i in the east and Tsin in the centre, there is little doubt that Ch'u would have been the ultimate victor, for these northern states were themselves competing for the chance to conquer and absorb other, smaller, northern states. In some ways the situation of China resembled in this age the almost contemporary situation of Greece. In China, also, ancient and cultured states, which had carried civilization to new heights, were menaced by simpler, larger, more backward or foreign states, Persia and Macedonia in the west, Ch'u and Ch'in in China. For Ch'u had a deadly rival, the great northwestern state of Ch'in. Ch'in's territory (our word *China* comes from the name of this state) lay west of the Yellow River in what is now Shensi province. It had expanded both westward into what is now Kansu province, and south-westward across the mountains into the then remote lands called Shu and Pa, which together now form the great province of Szechuan, an area larger than France and Germany together.

This conquest of Szechuan was crucial: the area is very fertile, easily defended, especially from the east, where the Yangtze gorges bar the way, but controls the upper Yangtze, and thus turned the flank of Ch'u. Szechuan had developed a local civilization of which we know very little from history, but are learning more from archaeology. Skilled engineering and water control were among its marked features, and what has been found of the art, even from some centuries later, shows strong local character differing very sharply from that of the old Middle Kingdom. The country must have had, even then, a large population, and it added hugely to the resources of the Ch'in kingdom, whose original territory was much smaller and not so productive. The Ch'in state was hardly accepted by the eastern Chinese of the Middle Kingdom as a true member. It claimed to have been a fief of the Chou king, but it had absorbed so many 'barbarians', was so remote and cut off, that it had evidently not kept pace with the civilized eastern kingdoms in any art but that of war. In this way, also, it resembled Macedonia in the Greek classical age.

Unfortunately this means that we know very little about it until the last years of the Chou period, when Ch'in was rapidly gaining ascendancy. The earlier history of Ch'in is sketchy; even the conquest of Szechuan is but briefly recorded. But one very significant fact emerges: the ministers of the kings of Ch'in were rarely natives of the state. They came from the eastern countries, and the probability is that they found opportunity and careers in Ch'in precisely because they were literate, educated and civilized, and the nobles of Ch'in were not. The men whom the kings of Ch'in came to favour were those who followed the hard-hearted School of the Law, believed in severe punishments, iron discipline, despised the arts and set their policy on conquest and war. What we know of the School of the Law is indeed the writings of these men themselves, or at least, the books now extant that are attributed to them. Gradually they reorganized Ch'in as a state planned only for war and conquest, and then the plans were put into action.

The Period of the Warring States (481–221 B.C.)

This last age of the Chou period, the Period of the Warring States, ended in the unification of all China, the first foundation of the real Chinese Empire. But for two centuries there was almost ceaseless war between the rivals, of whom there were seven: 'Ch'in, the western power, Ch'u the great southern power, Ch'i the power on the north-eastern seaboard including the Shantung peninsula, three central states Han, Wei and Chao, which had formerly been united as the big kingdom of Tsin, but had broken apart – and by doing so, opened the road for Ch'in to advance eastward – and Yen, remote in the north-east, with its capital on the site of modern Peking. The main lines of statecraft and strategy were the rival 'Horizontal' and 'Vertical' policies. 'Horizontal' meant an alliance across the country from west to east, from Ch'in to Ch'i, to stop the northward advance of southern Ch'u. 'Vertical' was the opposite policy of an alliance from Ch'u to Yen (from south to north) to stop the eastward advance of Ch'in. The central states tried to keep influence, and survive, by balancing between these rival policies, first joining one alliance, then breaking off and joining the other. Their interest was to frustrate both plans, and also keep eastern Ch'i from growing too strong. There is a certain resemblance in this situation to that of Europe in the sixteenth and seventeeth centuries when France and other middle powers sought to frustrate the ambitions of Austria in the north-east and also those of Spain in the south-west. The outcome was different. It was not the middle powers who won the wars, it was Ch'in.

Ch'in had one advantage which was possibly the conclusive cause of her ultimate victory. She had no enemy behind her. Ch'u had Yueh, the warlike coastal state, to harry her flank. The central states feared each other, and also Ch'i. Ch'i herself had Yen to worry about; but after the conquest of Szechuan Ch'in could drive eastward without fear of attack from the rear. There is also some archaeological evidence, not yet too positive, that Ch'in began to use steel weapons before her rivals. Iron working had been known for several centuries before this date, but all the earliest finds are agricultural implements, not weapons. It seems as if bronze had a prestige, an almost mystical quality, which, perhaps on account of the antiquity of bronze casting, gave bronze weapons the preference. It is also probable that the art of making iron into steel was late.

This age of the Warring States has become very famous in Chinese literature: the stratagems, intrigues, wars and revolts in the various kingdoms are the subject of a long series of tales, half historical, and, in later centuries, of some of the most famous plays on the Chinese stage. As it was also the age of the later philosophers, such as the Confucian Mencius, the Taoist Chuangtzu, and the writers of the School of the Law, such as Han Fei Tzu, it is a very important period in the development of Chinese thought. The philosophers were also politicians, or at least hoped to be employed by some king as his close adviser. Some, such as Mencius, sought to influence their patrons to govern wisely and humanely, others sought power and domination, such as Wei Yang, Lord of Shang, chief minister of the King of Ch'in. Chuangtzu, the Taoist, proclaimed the vanity and folly of all this warfare and statecraft, and urged his contemporaries to forsake the world. The kings gave power and confidence to the men of action.

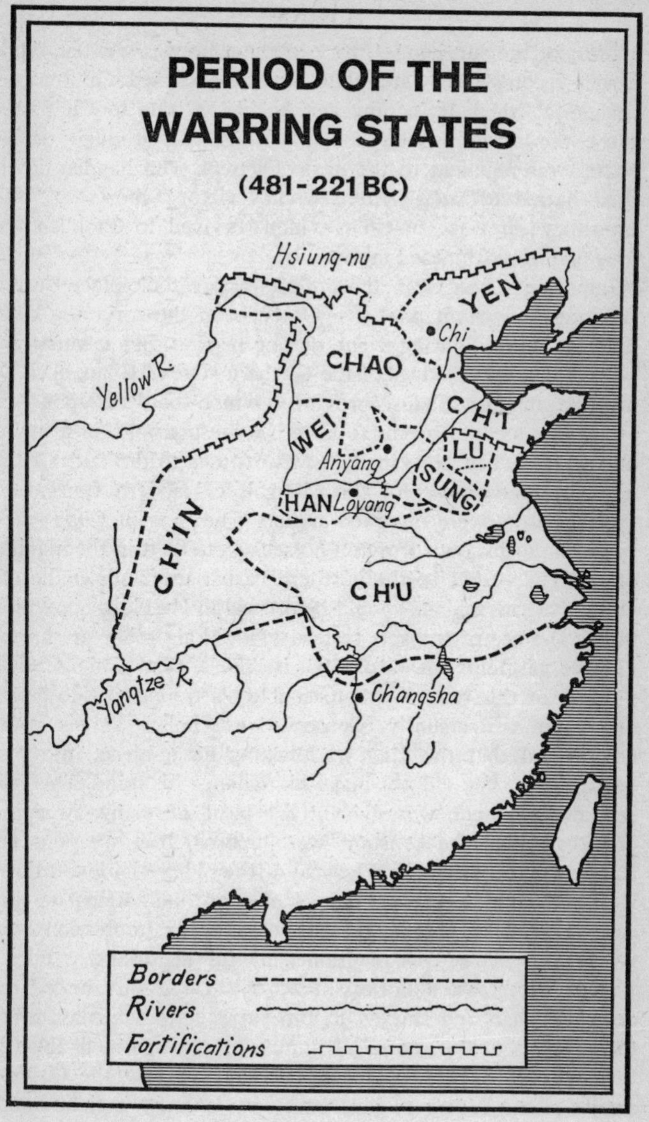

PERIOD OF THE
WARRING STATES
(481-221 BC)

Hsiung-nu

YEN

Chi

Yellow R.

CHAO

CH'I

WEI

LU

Anyang

SUNG

HAN Loyang

CH'IN

CH'U

Yangtze R.

Ch'angsha

Borders
Rivers
Fortifications

Map 1

Most of the surviving history of the time was written, from earlier records, at a later date, after the unified Empire had been established. It is, however, hostile in tone to Ch'in, because the ruthless policy of that kingdom, although triumphant, was repellent to the men of letters, who handed down their hatred to later writers. Ch'in's victory, moreover, was transitory: it was not Ch'in which survived to establish the long enduring Chinese Empire.

Important changes in the art of warfare took place during the long drawn out final struggle between the surviving kingdoms. Chariot fighting went out of fashion and cavalry appeared. One of the kings of the northern state of Chao, occupying the modern Shansi province, which borders upon the Mongolian steppes, seems to have been responsible for a major change in tactics. His kingdom was exposed to the raids of the nomads, predecessors of the Mongols of modern times, and these enemies were mounted archers. The King of Chao (325–299 B.C.) put his own army on horseback, to fight in the manner of the 'Hu' – that is, the northern barbarians. Further, he decreed that the soldiers should be dressed in Hu clothing, which meant the use of trousers instead of the long robes or shorter kilt-like garments hitherto worn by the ancient Chinese. The purpose of this reform was to enable his troops to ride better and more conveniently. Conservative scholars at his court complained that the king was making his subjects into barbarians, but they did not make him change his mind. This one recorded incident was evidently typical of many sweeping changes which the constant war imposed. Iron weapons became more prevalent, and instead of the old feudal levies there were now huge organized armies of conscripts, almost on the scale of modern forces. This, at least, is the impression conveyed by the numbers mentioned by the historians as taking part in the greatest battles. In 259 B.C. Ch'in surrounded the army of Chao and starved it into surrender, then massacring the captives to the enormous number of 400,000 men. Even if this figure is divided by ten it still suggests that the Chinese armies of the Warring States were very large by ancient standards, and implies that the population was also numerous.

24

Ch'in was certainly a ruthless enemy: this is not the only example of wholesale massacre recorded in the final years of the struggle; often it is stated, after a victory of the Ch'in armies, 'a hundred thousand heads were cut off'. A later historian who wrote the story of these wars compares the advance of Ch'in to a silkworm devouring a mulberry leaf, steady, inexorable and final. In 256 B.C. the nominal king of the ancient Chou dynasty was dethroned and his small territory seized: ten years later the new King of Ch'in, later to unify the whole country and reign as First Emperor, ascended the throne, and within twenty-five years had accomplished his ambition. Between 230 B.C. and 223 B.C. Ch'in successively conquered and annexed the central and eastern states, Han, Chao, Ch'i and Wei. In 223 B.C. the conquest of the great rival Ch'u marked the end of the struggle. Remote Yen, in the north-east, fell the next year, and all China down to and including the Yangtze valley and much territory beyond was brought under the rule of Ch'in.

The Ch'in Dinasty (221–207 B.C.)

Until the foundation of this Ch'in dynasty ruling all China it is not correct to speak of the monarchs as 'Emperors'. This Western word is a translation of the Chinese *Huang Ti*, a title which was first used by the King of Ch'in to show his supremacy over the kings (wang) whom he had dethroned. Henceforth the ancient title Wang came to mean, first under-king, later simply prince. It seems probable that the new title of *Huang Ti* had anciently been a style used for gods, not men. The King of Ch'in further decreed that he was to be known as First Emperor (*Shih Huang Ti*), his successor would be Second Emperor, and so on down the generations for 'ten thousand years', which meant, forever. This was by no means the only innovation made by the new government. All feudal states and kingdoms were abolished and the whole vast realm reduced to administrative areas, under military governors, which did not correspond with the old boundaries of the states. These divisions are called 'commanderies' as the best translation of the Chinese term; they were much smaller than the provinces of modern China, which did not come into existence until the seventh century A.D. and later.

The aristocracy of the former kingdoms were transported to the old kingdom of Ch'in where they had no following, and thus could raise no rebellion. Ch'in garrisons were set up throughout the country, ruling harshly by the doctrines of the School of the Law. The First Emperor refused to make feudal fiefs for his son and relatives, arguing that the existence of such fiefs was the first cause of the divisions and wars which had plagued China for so long. Finding that these new measures were opposed and criticized by the scholars, particularly those of the conquered countries, he decided to put an end to their teaching and ordered the burning of all the books in existence except those dealing with technical subjects like agriculture and building. He hoped in this way to destroy the various schools of philosophy and force all educated men to follow his own policy, based on the hard teaching of the School of the Law.

There is no doubt that a great number of books were destroyed: some were lost forever, and many others only survived in fragmentary form. But the plan really failed: scholars hid their books, at great risk, and some, with that marvellous Chinese memory which still marks the people of China, memorized whole texts before yielding up their books to be burned. Later the greatest part of the Confucian literature and much else besides was recovered from the memories of old men and from hidden books. Inevitably these texts were defective: some parts had been forgotten, or differently remembered. Some books hidden in caves and walls had suffered from weather, and the order of the pages (bamboo slips) was confused. For centuries, and still today, scholars have disputed about the authenticity of some of the reconstructions.

In some very important respects the foundation of the Ch'in unified Empire was a real revolution. The ancient social system was largely destroyed: feudal privilege vanished, soldiers of any origin became the new ruling class, the old feudal clans were merged in the general population, and a new kind of name, the surname, begins to appear. It is an interesting fact that only in China and the western part of Europe has the true surname been evolved. Elsewhere, until very modern times, men were known by given names with the addition of 'son of so and so'. This form, (Johnson, Thomson, etc.), is still visible in many of our present surnames. In China this form is so rare as to be negligible. Surnames as they came slowly into use were taken from places, or from occupations and ranks. Many common names are those of large areas, the ancient kingdoms (such as Chao and Wei), others are simply ordinary occupations or ranks. Chang means 'headman', no doubt the village headman. Wang, which is the word for king or prince, seems to have been given to the very large number of men who were serfs on the royal lands, hence it is very common. There are also names taken from the rank of some ancestor, such as Shang-Kuan, which means 'high official'. It is clear that this change reflects a great social upheaval. The ancient peasants certainly used only a personal name, the aristocracy both a personal and a clan name, but no true surname. The clan name disappeared, and this must be due to the elimination of the aristocracy themselves. In later times many old families claimed descent from great officers or generals of the early unified Empire, but none do so from the ancient feudal aristocracy.

Not all the reforms of the First Emperor were cruel or harsh measures. He is said to have unified the currency system (not coined money, but weighs of silver), he standardized measures, and abolished varying forms of the written script, which he also reformed in a simpler style. He even went down to details such as standardizing the length of the axles of the two-wheeled Chinese carts so that all could travel on the same rutted roads. Roads were built throughout the Empire, for the swifter movement of troops. He also built the Great Wall of China : or rather, he linked up a number of stretches of wall built by earlier kings of the northern states, and continued the line far to the west to guard the whole northern frontier, for fourteen hundred miles from the sea to the deserts of the north-west. The wall is built for the most part along the crest of high and rugged mountain ranges: the passes are heavily fortified with gates and strong castles. It is about twenty feet high and broad enough to drive a cart along the top. Much of the present wall is later repair, but the core of it is still the Ch'in wall, and it follows the ancient line.

The building of the wall, although intended to give the country security against nomad raiding, was very unpopular owing to the enormous death rate among the conscripted labourers, many of them prisoners of war from the defeated states. Popular belief claims that a million men died in the cold inhospitable mountains where the wall is built. The rule of Ch'in was indeed as cruel and tyrannous as the conquest had been. So long as the First Emperor lived, no rebellion broke out. When he died after eleven years as sole ruler of China he expected to be succeeded peacefully by his son as Second Emperor. But a fatal intrigue, which had implicated the Crown Prince a short time before the death of the Emperor, had caused the First Emperor to execute this son, and promote his younger brother, who was both too young and also incompetent. He had hardly come to the throne before rebellion broke out, and at once spread to all parts of the Empire. The armies of Ch'in were not now concentrated in the west, they were dispersed in garrisons all over the realm. Some of these, led by their commanders, also revolted. Chaos engulfed the Empire, the capital was taken and the Second Emperor slain. The Ch'in dynasty was at an end after only twelve years (rather than 'ten thousand'), but no clear successor emerged.

A complex civil war broke out among the contending leaders, who at first pretended to restore the old kingdoms. But the kings whom they put on these ephemeral thrones were only the puppets of self-appointed generals and rebel leaders who were really interested in winning power for themselves. The attempt to restore the old system collapsed almost at once, and the struggle became an open contest to secure the vacant throne of the Ch'in, and the dominion of the whole Empire.

It was a long war: although the final victor and founder of the Han dynasty dated his reign from the capture of the Ch'in capital and the destruction of the Ch'in dynasty in 207 B.C., he had then to struggle for several years against a formidable rival who had gained control of the old kingdom of Ch'u and much other territory. The two rivals were very different both in character and origin. Liu Pang, who founded the Han dynasty, was apparently the son of a village headman. It is not very easy to establish just how obscure his family had been, as they naturally tried to claim better origins when they had won the throne. But it is probable that they were of peasant stock, and had risen but little above the level of the ordinary countryfolk. His opponent, Hsiang Yu, was on the contrary a descendant of an aristocratic family from Ch'u, and thus won the support of men of similar background who hoped to restore their fallen fortunes. Hsiang Yu was brave, handsome, courteous and a poet of renown: Liu Pang was cautious, rather cowardly, very seldom won a battle, but never lost a campaign. He was also certainly illiterate. At first he was frequently defeated, but he had the ability to rise again, to gather followers, while Hsiang Yu alienated allies by his ambition and arrogance. It was the tortoise and the hare, and the hare lost the race.

At last Hsiang Yu, deserted by the followers from his own country whom he had alienated, found himself surrounded by the armies of Liu Pang. At night he heard their camp songs, and they were the songs of Ch'u, his own land. Realizing that all was lost, he composed a famous poem (still recited on the Chinese stage when this scene is played) and cut his way out of the besieged camp to take his own life when capture was certain. Liu Pang, the peasant soldier, had won the Empire. Probably few contemporaries believed that he would keep it long, but in fact the Han dynasty which he founded endured for four hundred years, with one short break, and is one of the most famous and formative periods in Chinese history. It lasted about the same length of time as the Roman Empire, although founded two hundred years earlier than the reign of Augustus, and in the Chinese world the role of the Han is very similar to that of Rome in the West. For the first time the whole civilized world of China (and there were then no other civilized states or countries within her range) was brought under a stable and long-lasting regime. The institutions of Han, the art, the literature and indeed the language, became the models for later ages, just as Roman law and Roman order became the inspiration for later European states to copy if they could. All this prestige of the Han dynasty was not acquired at first. Liu Pang had to face revolts from his chief generals, but he always forestalled the rebels and emerged triumphant. The country, exhausted by a terrible series of wars for more than two centuries, was not willing to back rebels who had not the harsh spur of oppression to goad them on.

The Han Dynasty (207 B.C.–A.D. 221):
Historical Introduction

Liu Pang and his successors ruled carefully and skilfully. Fully determined to uphold the supreme imperial power, they pretended to revere ancient ways and made a show of restoring feudalism, to satisfy conservative opinion. Fiefs were granted to close relatives of the Emperor. But they were cleverly intermingled with commanderies ruled by the imperial generals, and their capitals had to be placed on the border, near to an imperial stronghold. Fiefs were inherited by and divided among the sons of the prince, so that before long many very small fiefs succeeded the early large ones, and their power for rebellion became quite insignificant. After a century or so they ceased to be of any importance, and became nothing but large estates to which a title was attached. Although illiterate himself, Liu Pang did not persecute the scholars; he allowed the books to be produced and reconstructed. He did not employ many scholars, preferring his military followers, but his successors gradually began to favour the educated class, and among these the followers of Confucius were the most numerous and influential. It is in the Han period that Confucianism as an organized system of ethical and political doctrines really takes shape.

The dynasty reigned for four centuries, during which there were many changes of ruler, and different developments. It was only gradually that the distinctive character of the new world of a unified China became apparent, but as the dynasty grew stronger, and the country recovered from the devastation of the wars, a new outlook on the world, a new interest in history, in foreign lands, in strange religions and new forms of literature and philosophy arose. The intellectual climate of the first two centuries B.C. was stimulating, reflecting the creation of a new kind of society, differing profoundly from the feudal age. Ancient family counted for little when the Emperor himself was a peasant by birth: merchants became rich and prominent, and there was clearly much more social mobility – people were able to rise in the world – than had been the case in the feudal period.

The foundation of the unified Empire of all China, first by the conquests of Ch'in and then consolidated by the great Han dynasty, marks one of the main turning points in Chinese history. The ancient China was not really one country, but a loose group of states inhabited by people of the same ethnic origin – or 'race' – speaking very similar dialects of one language, and gradually spreading their culture into regions further south and west which had been more or less separate centres of civilizations, of which we know very little so far. It is clear that, for example, Ch'u, the Yangtze region, was not 'barbarous' but was different in many ways from the northern Middle Kingdom. The same is certainly true of the ancient kingdoms in Szechuan which Ch'in absorbed. But we have no real knowledge as yet of how these separate centres of culture developed in their earliest phases. Archaeology is beginning to fill this gap, but it still remains. The social system of ancient China was quite unlike that of the later Empire, but much more closely resembled other ancient societies in western Asia. One of the great differences between Chinese society and other parts of Asia, and Europe also, was that in China a priesthood never developed as a distinct class. The work and duties of priests were performed by the aristocracy, who were also the only literate class. This also marks the main difference between the Chinese feudal system and the feudalism of Europe many centuries later.

The union of all the Chinese world under one monarch has earlier been compared with the Roman Empire which, about two hundred years later, brought all southern and western

Europe and also north Africa and the western part of Asia under one government. In many very important respects, however, the situation in China was different. First, China is a geographical whole. There is no natural division between north China and south China, the climate gradually changes from cold to warm, the crops differ, but the large intermediate region of the Yangtze valley has characteristics common both to the colder north (winter can be snowy and cold) and to the warm sub-tropical south, the Canton region, such as rice growing, a high rainfall and a moist, very hot summer. There is no sharp difference between regions, they merge.

Secondly, no part of China is cut off from any other region by the sea. This has meant throughout history that land armies can conquer the whole country. Travel and trade also can be carried on by land, or by rivers, so the sea has never been of great importance to the Chinese as a means of communication or defence. The Chinese peoples of antiquity were not very different in speech or in customs. There was nothing to compare with the differences between Greek, Egyptian, Syrian, Latins and Celts which continued beneath the surface of the Roman government. Therefore true unity was easier to attain in China. There was only one language used in written records, which meant that there was only one culture, and this became the great unifying force in China. In the West, Greek and Latin remained both alive and distinct, and there were also the ancient languages and cultures of Syria and Egypt.

The comparison between the Chinese feudal kingdoms with their wars, jealousies, and also with their philosophers and politicians, and the Greek city states, is attractive and can be illuminating, but it must be remembered that the Chinese kingdoms were very much larger than any Greek city state. Kingdoms such as Ch'u or Ch'in were much larger than any modern European state except Russia. Even the small fiefs in China were larger than all of classical Greece combined. This is one reason why democratic forms of government never arose in ancient China. A Greek city could be governed by an assembly of all its citizens, but in the ancient world there was no means of consulting the whole population, or even all the literate nobility, of a state bigger than France and Germany together. Consequently monarchy was the only form of government known to China, and no philosopher ever questioned it. What they did consider was how to secure wise rulers, how to make sure that kings governed sanely and did not oppress the people. Naturally they did not succeed in finding any safe rule to ensure this, but they did succeed in limiting the power of kings in other ways.

In China, unlike most of the western Asian countries, kings were never gods. No Chinese monarch ever claimed to be divine – the idea of the god-king, so important in western Asia, and later borrowed by the Roman emperors, was quite absent. The kings and princes of the ancient Chinese states all claimed to be the descendants of the heroes of the legendary age, Yao, Shun or Yu. This was a claim to be 'royal' – not divine. In the feudal world of China only families who could claim this ancestry were considered fit to rule, but even this did not always apply. After the earlier Tsin kingdom broke up into the three states of Wei, Han and Chao, the new kings of these states were the heads of three great noble families, not members of the ancient royal house of Tsin. In Ch'i, the eastern state, the throne was usurped by a great noble family, also not connected with the ancient ruling house. So already in the feudal age the possibility of non-royal families ascending a throne existed.

Another distinctive aspect of ancient China was its isolation. The Chinese were not in touch with any other people even partially civilized. Their neighbours were the nomadic tribes of the Mongolian steppes to the north, the ancestors of the Tibetans (wild mountain peoples) on the west and primitive forest tribes in the south, all of whom they gradually absorbed. All of these foreign peoples were backward or primitive, none had any great contribution to make to Chinese civilization. Beyond them the Chinese knew nothing of the rest of the world. They were not in touch, either, with any people beyond the sea. Japan was at this time unknown to the Chinese, and very little indeed is known about the condition or inhabitants of prehistoric Japan. It seems probable that the Ainu people, who are not Japanese, and now live only in the extreme northern island, were then spread all over the Japanese archipelago. It is clear that in remote antiquity, the neolithic period, some foreign influences reached China across the land route through central Asia. Chinese neolithic pottery has some patterns common to pottery found in western Asia and in eastern Russia. There are a few other evidences of similar transfers, although we do not know which way the transfer went, or whether it was both ways. It was in any case slight, and did not bring any knowledge of western Asia to the Chinese of the feudal age.

This isolation during the early formative period of Chinese civilization has had profound importance for the whole of later history. Unlike Egypt, Babylon, Crete or the Syrian and Hittite civilizations of western Asia, the Chinese were wholly out of touch with neighbours of similar levels of development for the first thousand years or more of their recorded history. Chinese language and script, literature and religion arose and developed without any foreign influence, and so did the art of China. It was therefore inevitable that during this long period the Chinese thought of themselves – the Middle Kingdom – as the only part of the world which was civilized, had writing, art, advanced crafts and political institutions. This was then true within the limits of possible communications, and it remained a firm belief among the Chinese for many centuries after it ceased to be true. Another very important difference in China's story from that of almost every other part of the world is that China was never conquered and ruled by an alien civilized people. This happened to Egypt, to Babylon, western Asia, Greece, but not to China. The only foreign conquests were made by barbarian peoples, nomadic tribes from the steppes of Mongolia, who could only supply military power, but were dependent on the conquered Chinese for every art, craft and institution, and also relied upon Chinese officials to govern the country, keep records, maintain the irrigation and drainage systems, write their history and supply their literature.

These foreign conquests by the nomadic peoples were also relatively short, the numbers of the invaders small, and their influence on the Chinese consequently very slight. On the contrary, it was the invaders who soon lost their own language, intermarried with the Chinese, gave up their own costume, learned to read and write in Chinese and in a few generations were almost completely absorbed. For a very long time, close on two thousand years since the first records of the Shang dynasty, China had really no contact with any other civilized people, either by peaceful commerce or conquest. It was during this age that the Chinese civilization developed its peculiar forms, and such marked differences from any other culture: these chracteristics became so much a part of Chinese life and thought that when foreign influences such as Buddhism from India finally did penetrate to China, they could not really prevail against the Chinese ways of thought and life: it was the foreign influences which were more changed by China than China was by any foreign idea or religion.

The fact that Alexander and the Greeks, and later the Romans, made great and long-lasting conquests in Asia and Africa, has left Europeans, throughout subsequent history, with the strong belief that they were the destined rulers of the world, superior, particularly in arms, to all other peoples. Such a 'Europe-centred' view of the world is still very prevalent. In the same way the Chinese, for many centuries the only civilized people of eastern Asia, and unaware of any other rivals, became convinced that civilization and China were one and the same thing. All the foreign peoples they had known were barbarians, far below their own level of achievement; therefore all foreign peoples must be barbarous – and those that were in fact not backward lived so far from China that no one knew of their existence. It is this background which has coloured all Chinese thought and still today remains a very powerful unconscious force shaping the outlook of the Chinese people.

CHAPTER TWO

The Rise and Fall of the First Empire

(200 B.C.–A.D. 600)

ALTHOUGH Ch'in first unified China, the dynasty founded by
the king of that country, who became the First Emperor (Shih
Huang Ti) hardly endured beyond his death in 209 B.C. After
the struggle between many contending rebels had ended in the
outright victory of Liu Pang, founder of the Han dynasty, his
descendants occupied the throne of China for 427 years, briefly
interrupted by an interval of fifteen years (the usurpation of
Wang Mang, A.D. 9–25). The two periods of the Han dynasty
are known as the Early (or Western) Han from 206 B.C. to A.D.
9, and the Later (or Eastern) Han from A.D. 25 to A.D. 221. It is
therefore the Han dynasty which consolidated the new form of
government, the unified Empire, and remained a model which
all subsequent dynasties strove either to restore or uphold. In
place of the group of feudal states under the suzerainty of one
high king, which had been the Chou system until it broke
down in the Period of the Warring States, the Han established a
central monarchy which increasingly governed the whole Empire through officers appointed and removed at the pleasure of
the throne.

As was pointed out in the last chapter, this pattern did not at
first become uniform. In the early days of the Han dynasty
there were feudal states given to close relatives and sons of the
Emperor. But they were all smaller than the former states of
the Chou period. They were intermingled with commanderies
under the direct rule of the Emperor's officers, and by making
the succession to any state pass to all the sons of the prince,
not solely to the eldest, the number of states was soon greatly
increased while their size and importance diminished propor-
tionately. In less than a century they ceased to have any im-

portance as political units, becoming merely large estates. In place of the feudal nobility the Han rulers had now to find a new class of men to act as provincial governors and officers. Their system was to fill these posts by recommendation : leading governors, high officials and other prominent people recommended their clients for posts in the government. The candidates had to be educated men, and as the sponsor was held responsible for their conduct and efficiency, there was a real check on the appointment of favourites who would prove useless in office. Naturally favouritism and influence counted very strongly in these appointments, but inefficient or corrupt and worthless officers were a danger to the man who had recommended them. Among the many clients who sought the favour of a high official he tended to pick out men who would do him credit, or at least would not involve him in scandals and accusations which would endanger his own career, and probably his life also.

The Han Empire was not very much troubled, until towards the end of the age, by rebellions which aimed at changing the dynasty. The Liu family had enormous prestige. Court intrigues and plots were common, but their object was to control the regency when an infant was on the throne, to advance the cause of one son of the Emperor rather than another, or to promote the fortunes of a family allied to the throne by marriage. This last ambition was the most troublesome danger the dynasty had to contend with, and it was caused precisely by the supreme position which the monarch now occupied. In feudal days the various kings used to seek their brides from the family of another king, ruling a different state. This had two advantages : such a marriage paved the way for an alliance between the two states, and the new queen, being a foreigner, had no followers of her own, and no relatives, in the country into which she had married. Therefore she could not become the centre of a dangerous faction. In this way the motives of the royal marriages were very similar to those of European royal marriages in the Middle Ages and Renaissance centuries.

With the coming of the unified Empire all this was changed. There was now only one imperial family, the Liu, and no other foreign royalty with whom they could intermarry. Chinese custom, still prevailing today, absolutely prohibited the marriage of persons of the same surname (originally of the same clan) who were considered to be in a wide sense of the same family. This is called the 'rule of exogamy' by anthropologists and is found in many parts of the world. Marriage is only possible to a woman outside the line of paternal descent. Thus the Liu imperial family of the Han dynasty could not marry into the collateral branches of this family, which in time became very numerous. These collaterals might at first be feudal princes, and thus in rank suitable to provide brides for the Emperors, but they were of the same family and the same surname, and so ruled out. The Emperor had to choose his wife among his subjects, of another surname to his own. No foreign people were considered civilized, so foreign marriage was out of the question also.

When the Emperor chose his bride she was likely to be the daughter of a high official, a great general, or provincial governor. These people were already powerful; when their daughter became Empress, and the probable mother of the next Emperor (who, when he succeeded, would be the grandson of the general or minister), it is obvious that the family which had provided the Empress became the second family in the Empire, and enormously influential. Inevitably they filled the civil service and army with their clients and relatives. Everyone who hoped to get on sought their protection and help. If the ruling Emperor died before his son was of age, as often happened, it was the Empress who became principal regent, and it was her brothers, or her father, who really controlled the government and exercised the whole power of the throne. But when he grew up, the new Emperor must also marry : if he married a girl from another family, this new 'Consort Family' would soon inherit all the influence of the former one, try to put their followers out of office so as to promote their own relatives, and thus a violent and often murderous political struggle began. To avoid this fate the family of an Empress hoped to find one of their own relatives, a niece or grand-niece, to be the next Empress, as this would secure the continuing power of their family. Naturally all other prominent families opposed such a plan. They argued that the power of the Wangs or the Lus was already too great; another marriage to the next Emperor would make them virtually supreme, and established forever.

Therefore no effort was spared to interest the young Emperor in some girl from a fresh family. The most certain way of doing this was to find him an outstanding beauty. This plan usually was successful. But beauty does not always go with rank and position. Very often the beautiful bride turned out to belong to a comparatively unimportant family, the more often as those who had put her forward were not interested in installing a new powerful Consort Family, but on the contrary, in finding one which would not be too influential. The very fact that the new Emperor had married for love, rather than for policy, made the new Empress all the more powerful with him. Soon her rather obscure family was rising fast, occupying the most powerful positions at court, obtaining the most important army commands and before long was intent on getting rid of the family of the Emperor's mother and seizing its wealth and power. As long as the Emperor's mother remained alive they often had to hold their hand. Filial piety is one of the principal virtues taught by the Confucian philosophy, and the Emperor owed this duty to his own mother, even if he was not naturally affectionate. But once the Empress Dowager was dead, the new family of the Empress could move in to the attack. They would accuse the Emperor's uncles, or cousins on his mother's side, of ambitious plans, of disloyalty and conspiracy. Often enough there was some substance in these charges. The old Consort Family was in a desperate position, running the risk of losing all, wealth, power, even life. Under these circumstances it was not surprising that they very often did plot to destroy their rivals, or even to get rid of the Emperor, and substitute another.

So the conflict went on from one generation to the next. It began in the reign of the founder himself, Liu Pang, who is known to history by the reign title of Kao Tsu, which means 'high Ancestor' – a title often given to the founders of dynasties after his time. His wife, a most ambitious woman, exercised the regency for her son, but when he grew of age, he married into another family, who brought about the downfall of that of the Empress Lu. The pattern was repeated. Some Emperors, seeing the danger, married the daughters of very powerful men in the hope that the great eminence of the Empress's family would put them above greedy ambition. But this usually meant that other families feared them all the more, and sought in every way to make sure that the next Empress was not one of their relatives. Other Emperors tried the opposite plan of marrying rather obscure girls, in the hope that their family would never be influential enough to become a menace. This also failed: once a family had provided an Empress who was the mother of the heir to the throne, nothing could prevent them acquiring power, and nothing stopped them from abusing it.

The sixth monarch of the Han dynasty, the great Emperor Wu (which title means 'the Warrior'), who reigned from 140 to 86 B.C., more than fifty years, was the only Emperor who solved the problem, but by a peculiarly ruthless plan. Having chosen his Empress, he had her entire family put to death. Thus there was no Consort Family during his long reign, and no court intrigue arose to displace a family already dead. Later successors were more merciful or less farsighted: less than a century after the death of the Emperor Wu one Consort Family, having provided Empresses for two successive reigns, and thus grown all-powerful, actually usurped the throne rather than yield power to newcomers. The Wang family, headed by the usurping uncle, held the throne for fifteen years, but at his death, after a long civil war, a collateral branch of the Liu family, the imperial house of Han, regained the throne. It might have been expected that after this experience his successors would find some way of avoiding this persistent danger: they did not. Throughout the second period of the Han dynasty – the Later Han – the problem of the Consort Families and their ambitions recurred regularly, reign by reign. In the end it was this problem which led to such disorders that the dynasty itself was overthrown.

The ambitious plots of the Consort Families were strictly a

THE RISE AND FALL OF THE FIRST EMPIRE

court matter. In the provinces of the vast Empire these sanguinary events made little impression. The provincial officers might be dismissed or replaced, but the system of government went on, and on the whole worked very well. There is no doubt that as the country recovered from the devastating wars of the last age of the feudal period China became very prosperous. All the arts flourished, and archaeology has brought to light abundant evidence of the high quality of Han art, craftsmanship and skill. Many tombs of rich men were decorated with bas relief sculpture showing scenes of daily life, or historical episodes, and from these it is possible to get a vivid idea of the life of the times – at least as led by the ruling classes. Gentlemen ride in elegant light chariots, or on mettlesome horses, go hunting, hold banquets at which jugglers and dancers perform, while servants in the background cook vast quantities of food. Houses, too, are shown, having in many respects the same style as has lasted down to modern times. There are scenes of religious rites and ceremonies, not all of which are now to be understood.

Literature also revived. The Han writers not only re-edited the classical books after the Ch'in proscription, but wrote themselves on a great variety of subjects: philosophy (Confucianism mainly), religion, poetry, the first dictionaries and above all history. The first great Chinese historians were Han period writers, and they set a model which later ages copied. Chinese histories were not written in the way which the Greeks and Romans used, and which European writers have largely followed. In China history was very accurately dated, but the main record, the day to day or month to month annals of the court, is simply a dry brief chronicle of events without comment or explanation. For that one turns to the large section of biographies of famous men of all kinds, generals, princes, ministers, rebels and also writers and artists. In these sections there is less accurate dating, but much continuous narrative, full of incident and sometimes even recording speeches and dialogue. Each biography deals only with the life of the subject. Matters with which he was not concerned are not mentioned. So to get a rounded picture of just what happened in some important event, a conspiracy, a military campaign or the workings of a new policy, one must read all the biographies of those in any way involved in this affair, and also the main records of 'original annals', as they are called, which provide the dates.

History was also meant to serve a purpose. It was written to guide future rulers into wise policies and help them to avoid mistakes. This would not lead to any distortion if the historians had not had very definite ideas about which policies were wise and which doctrines were false. But historians, always Confucians, believed that those acts which could be considered as conforming to their doctrines were virtuous, and those doctrines which they did not support were wrong and foolish. Consequently Chinese history is not as objective as it seems. Facts were not suppressed, even if they were interpreted in a special way. The modern reader who does not always agree with the Confucian point of view can therefore find the facts, and interpret them in a new way. This is important, because in the Early Han period the country was faced with economic problems of a new kind, for which the government had no ready solution. The unified Empire was vast. The Emperor was responsible for governing a huge area, of very different climate, produce and resources. Feudal kingdoms had been much smaller. If a neighbour suffered from famine, it was no concern of the king of a feudal state. But the Emperor had to take responsibility for all calamities, and try to mitigate them. Some regions might be prosperous, and at the same time others stricken with drought or suffering from floods. Money economy was coming in, as a widespread commerce replaced the old local trade. This was a new problem, and at first the court had no idea how to manage it. Rich men were allowed to coin their own money. Soon the economy suffered from what would now be called inflation.

Salt and iron workings were granted as monopolies to great courtiers. The result was rising prices, distress and widespread smuggling. In the end the Emperor Wu called in the aid of the merchants, who understood something about economics. This met with the stern disapproval of the scholar officials, and the historians who wrote for them. The merchants are condemned as false scheming fellows only out to get rich. No doubt they had that end in mind, but they also did suggest and carry out many reforms which put things to rights. Money was made a government monopoly, only to be coined by the state. An ingenious system of collecting taxes in grain and storing the produce in government granaries made it possible for the court to alleviate famines and keep the price of grain steady. This was called the 'equalization' plan. Salt was also made a government monopoly, as it still is. Iron working was freed from any control, and soon found its rightful place in the economy. The story of these economic crises, and the cures suggested and tried out, not always successfully, are told by the great Han historian, Ssu-ma Ch'ien, and as he disliked the Emperor Wu and his policies, the story is told with much prejudice. Yet the facts are there, and it is now possible to see what the problems were, and how the court and the merchants who advised the Emperor grappled with them.

Chinese historians, being scholar officials and trained in Confucian philosophy, did not understand much about trade and finance, nor did they care for these matters. Their accounts are partial and prejudiced. They particularly opposed government interference in these questions, although they do not conceal the fact that the economic troubles were serious and had to be solved in some way. From the arguments they record it is possible to get some understanding of the great changes which were taking place in the China of their time: the growth of the use of iron tools and implements, the wider flow of goods and produce, the problems of raising revenue from a huge Empire and financing a large government which also engaged, before long, in foreign wars. Perhaps it is fortunate that the Confucian historians so thoroughly disliked the policies of the Han Emperors in these affairs. If they had approved them they would have written less about them, and we should be without valuable knowledge of the development of the Chinese economy in the first age of union.

For sixty or seventy years after the foundation of the Han dynasty, until the accession to the throne of the Emperor Wu in 140 B.C., the Empire was too worn out by the long wars of the previous century to do more than defend its frontiers against the nomad peoples beyond the Great Wall, and to maintain internal peace. After two generations of peace and increasing prosperity the young Emperor Wu found himself ruling a strong state, with great resources. He began a policy of expansion. This had two aspects; first, to find a lasting solution to the threat of nomad invasions from the Mongolian steppes beyond the wall, and secondly, to conquer and colonize the south of what is now China, but which was then a region inhabited by backward peoples, not very different from the Chinese themselves, but less civilized. Throughout his reign the Emperor pursued these two objectives, and it must be recognized that he achieved great and lasting results.

The two frontiers, north and south, were quite different both in their geographical character and in the kinds of enemies to be resisted. The nomad people then dominant were called by the Chinese Hsiung Nu. It has been suggested by many historians in the West that these people were the ancestors of the Huns who broke into Europe in the late Roman period. Remote ancestors, if so, for the Hsiung Nu whom the Emperor Wu finally defeated after long wars were occupying the southern part of Mongolia in the second and first centuries B.C., but it was not until the fifth century A.D. that the Huns appeared in Europe. It is true that the Chinese describe these ferocious and dangerous mounted bowmen in very much the same terms as the Roman and Greek historians speak of the Huns. But Herodotus, centuries before the Huns, described the Scythians of south Russia in similar words. The truth is that mounted nomads lived and fought in much the same way in all ages. The conditions of their country forced them to be nomadic, following their herds from pasture to pasture. Lack of a fixed dwelling place made them unable to manufacture complicated weapons, or mine for metal. They relied on the bow and arrow, and they always rode horses, as foot travel is too slow and exhausting in their vast open deserts. Their armies were wholly cavalry, very rapid in their movements, unencumbered by baggage trains and heavy equipment.

These qualities always made the nomad horsemen formidable to an infantry force. They could surround foot soldiers, shoot them up at long range, retire if charged, reform and harass the weary infantry till they were exhausted and unable to defend themselves. Greeks, Romans and Chinese all encountered such enemies along their frontiers, and naturally held them in fear and hatred. The nomadic raiders were cruel and ruthless: as they did not usually intend to occupy a country, only to raid it, they spared no one, spread terror, burned and looted, then retired with their plunder. To check these raids and give some security to the farmers of the northern provinces the Ch'in Emperor had linked up the older local walls into the immense Great Wall of China, covering the whole frontier from the sea to the deserts of Sinkiang (Chinese Turkestan). Strong garrisons held the passes, which were the only places through which a large mounted force could advance or withdraw. A wall twenty to thirty feet high built on the top of steep mountain ridges cannot easily be crossed by horses. The difficulty was that the cost of guarding so long a fortification was very great. But if the garrisons were reduced, sooner or later a strong raiding force would break through.

The Emperor Wu conceived the idea of breaking the nomad power in its homeland, invading Mongolia and destroying the enemy before he ever entered China. The Chinese had some cavalry, but relied for remounts on horses traded from the Hsiung Nu themselves. They could not expect to get these if they were at war with the Hsiung Nu. But the Chinese also had a new weapon, and this proved decisive. The crossbow, invented by the Chinese at some time late in the feudal wars – evidence is lacking as to just when this occurred – was developed by the Han armies. Crossbows (the string being drawn back by a winding mechanism and released by a cocking piece – all made of bronze in Han times) are much more powerful than ordinary bows. They have a greater range and more penetrating power. But they are heavy and cumbersome to use in combat. The Chinese tactics were to put the crossbowmen in the centre of a square. When the Hsiung Nu charged and started to shoot into the Chinese squares, these formations

45

opened, the crossbowmen stood forward and poured in a devasting flight of their bolts. The square then reformed while the crossbowmen reloaded. Such tactics did not always meet with success, and in any case the history of the nomad wars is rather badly described by historians who were not soldiers. Yet it does become clear that the crossbow was the real foundation of the military supremacy which the Han armies gradually acquired.

The wars in the south were very different, and far less dangerous to the Han Empire. Beyond the former kingdom of Ch'u, in the middle and lower Yangtze valley, there was no strong state. Ch'u, after conquest by Ch'in, was inherited by the Han. The frontier was thus already well to the south of the Yangtze valley. But the most southerly of the great rivers of China, the West River and its various large tributaries, lie beyond a high and rugged range of mountains, which today forms the boundary between the provinces of Kiangsi and Hunan to the north and Kuangtung to the south. Canton was then the capital of an independent kingdom, under some Chinese influence, but how deep this influence was, and how long it had prevailed in the far south is still obscure. The southern kingdom – called by the Chinese Nan Yueh (southern Yueh) – does not seem to have had any written records, either in Chinese script or any other.

It had paid tribute to Ch'in, probably to avoid attack, but fell away in the troubles when Ch'in was overthrown. The Emperor Wu, using the pretext of the ill-treatment of some of his envoys in Canton, and intrigues at the court of Canton, made a sudden swift invasion which was completely successful. Nan Yueh was incorporated in the Han Empire. It is not very clear how far inland the Han authority reached. Certainly it did not cover the present south-western provinces, Kweichow and Yunnan. It probably was effective as far up the West River valley as navigation reached. The conquest of Nan Yueh brought Chinese civilization and rule down almost to the frontiers of modern North Vietnam, but it was many centuries before this remote province was really absorbed. It remained in Han times a colonial region on the edge of the known world, valuable for its southern produce which does not grow farther north, a place to which political exiles were banished, and, rather later, a link in the first sea route opened between China and the west of Asia. The Han court also learned much about the southern region which had been but vaguely known to the northern Chinese before this time. Gradual colonization and penetration were quickened.

There was no real obstacle to this process. The southern peoples, or tribes, were small, their organization weak, their military skill slight. They were readily absorbed by Chinese settlers, and assimilated after conquest. There was not for many centuries yet any serious opposition to Chinese advance in the southern provinces. As there was nothing spectacular about this Chinese advance, it is not well recorded in history. No dramatic events occurred, wars were small border affrays, and it is mainly through the increasing mention of settlement and cities in the south that the steady advance is revealed.

The long war with the Hsiung Nu, on the contrary, is very fully recorded, and some of its consequences are of great interest. For it was as a direct result of this struggle that the Chinese discovered first western Asia, then Europe. The Emperor Wu wanted an ally who could take the Hsiung Nu on their western flank, from the deserts of Sinkiang. He sent an envoy to find a tribe called the Yueh Chi, a people who had long been hostile to the Hsiung Nu, and could be expected to welcome an alliance with the great Han Emperor. But his envoy, Chang Ch'ien, was captured by the Hsiung Nu. When after ten years of captivity Chang Ch'ien escaped, he fled westward, still searching for the Yueh Chi, rather than return to China to face the disappointed Emperor. The Yueh Chi had migrated far to the west, and when Chang Ch'ien finally found them, they had no desire to return to fight with the Hsiung Nu. But by this time Chang Ch'ien had found a new world, which when he returned to China (after a further captivity of a year with the Hsiung Nu) greatly excited the Chinese court.

The country where Chang Ch'ien found the Yueh Chi is now called Russian Turkestan, the old kingdoms of Bokhara and Samarkand. It had been, only a few years before the Chinese envoy reached it, one of the furthest provinces of Alexander's Asian empire, and later ruled by Macedonian dynasties descended from his generals. The Greeks had been conquered by the nomadic peoples, such as the Yueh Chi, but many of their cities still remained, inhabited by the Greek settlers. This fact, the existence of a settled urban population, 'cities, mansions and houses as in China' as he put it in his report, was the great new discovery. There was another civilized world, beyond the nomad steppes. Chang Ch'ien learned much about it. He heard of Persia, then under the Parthian rule, he learned of India, and conjectured, rightly, that it should be possible to get there from China by a southern route, avoiding the nomads and their steppes. He believed that he had seen Chinese silks in India. It is quite possible that he was right, and that a primitive trade route already existed across Yunnan and Burma. But this route is very difficult, even today, and the trade must have been by barter, from tribe to tribe. The Emperor Wu later sent envoys to try to find the way, but none survived to report.

What most interested the Emperor was the report of fine horses which Chang Ch'ien had seen in the kingdom he called Ta Yuan, the modern Bokhara. The Chinese lacked cavalry; the Mongolian pony, which is the only horse bred in the steppes north of China, is small and cannot carry a heavily armoured man. Large horses which could supply this need were infinitely precious to the Han. The Emperor Wu determined to secure a breeding stock and build up his own herds. He probably had no clear idea of the immense distance between China and Turkestan, nor of the difficulties of the road. Chang Ch'ien was sent back to Central Asia, better guarded this time, with the duty of persuading the King of Ta Yuan to sell horses to China. The king, however, absolutely refused to part with any of them. One later Chinese envoy tried to carry some off by force, but was pursued by the king's men, killed and the horses recovered. The Emperor Wu decided that he must send an army to teach Ta Yuan a lesson. In 104 B.C. this astonishing expedition set out, surely one of the most remarkable military feats in ancient history. It was commanded by one of the Emperor's favourites, the brother of a concubine. The general soon discovered what a task he had been set. Each of the oases in what is now Chinese Sinkiang was then an independent state; all resisted the approach of a large Chinese army which would eat up their scarce supplies of grain. The general had to capture each of thirty-six cities, or settlements, to get supplies, but fought his way with an exhausted army right through to Ta Yuan, where he was completely defeated. Nevertheless he managed to withdraw nearly two thousand miles back to China.

The Emperor refused to give up. He sent a reinforcement of sixty thousand men and ordered a new invasion. This time it was successful. The Chinese besieged the capital of Ta Yuan until the king agreed to part with a large number of his best horses and three thousand of lesser value. The Chinese marched back, the King of Ta Yuan was styled a tributary, and many embassies and horse-buying expeditions followed. Thus the Chinese for the first time penetrated Central Asia and developed, in consequence, a relationship with that region which has persisted to modern times. In 51 B.C. the war with the Hsiung Nu ended in a Chinese victory. The Hsiung Nu split into two tribes, one migrating westward, while the other paid tribute to China and ceased, for a time, to be a threat. For many years Chinese interest in the far west diminished with the fear of Hsiung Nu invasion, but it revived in the Later Han period, and led to direct Chinese rule over the great area now known as Sinkiang.

The second important phase of Han discovery and penetration of the western region took place nearly one hundred years later, in the years between A.D. 73 and A.D. 102, the career of the famous viceroy and general, Pan Chao. In the course of thirty years spent in these countries Pan Chao brought the entire area under Chinese authority, finally advancing to the shores of the Caspian Sea with an army of seventy thousand men. From his camp at this point, to the Chinese the very end of the world, Pan Chao sent out envoys to the neighbouring countries to learn the nature of these hitherto unknown lands. It is certain that one of these visited Persia, and returned with a detailed report. This envoy, named Kan Ying, was also charged with the task of visiting the country which the Chinese named Ta Ts'in (or Ch'in), which is the Roman Empire. When Kan Ying reached the sea coast he was put off by tales of the distance and perils of the crossing, and after collecting what information he could, returned. The question of which sea coast he reached is much discussed and still uncertain. It was long believed by Western scholars that it was the Persian side of the Persian Gulf, but recent work by Chinese scholars puts forward the suggestion that it may have been the Black Sea coast on the southern side of the Caucasus range. It is also possible that the long sea voyage against which Kan Ying was warned (three months with a favourable wind) can only mean the coasting voyage down the Persian Gulf, round Southern Arabia and up the Red Sea. But there is some reason to think that the information he was given was false, intended to put him off making the journey.

It is in any case very probable that later envoys from China, whose names have not been recorded, actually did reach the eastern provinces of the Roman Empire. One of the great dynastic histories of China, *The History of Later Han*, compiled in the fourth century A.D. from original materials preserved in the court archives, gives a long and quite detailed description of Ta Ts'in (the Roman Empire), but owing to the very great difficulty in fitting the Chinese names of cities to Greek equivalents, it is still debated exactly which places are mentioned. An Tu is the name the Chinese give to the 'capital' of the country. This was long taken to mean Antioch, the chief city of the eastern provinces at that time (before the foundation of Constantinople). But there are linguistic difficulties in accepting this identification. It has been suggested that by the time the Han history was written Constantinople was already the capital of the Eastern Empire, and that the Chinese were still using for that city an older name for the Roman colony on the same site, which bore the name of Augusta Antonina until Constantine renamed it and made the city his capital. This view agrees with the theory that the sea which Kan Ying reached was the Black Sea. Antioch was not, at any time, the capital of the Roman Empire, and it seems somewhat unlikely that a Chinese envoy could have made the mistake of thinking it was. This is supported by the fact that the Han history records some facts about the government of the Roman Empire, clearly taken from information derived at different times, as it refers to the temporary nature of the Consuls' power but also mentions other facts which can only refer to the later Empire.

In A.D. 166 the Chinese record the arrival of an envoy in China sent from Rome, by the 'King of Ta Ts'in, An Tun'. This person can be certainly identified as the Emperor Marcus Aurelius Antoninus – 'An Tun' representing the first two syllables of the last name. But the Chinese themselves suspected that this embassy was not really official, but consisted of traders who passed as envoys to get a better reception. The presents they gave were recognized by the Chinese as the products of India and south-east Asia, not of 'Ta Ts'in'. This fact at least proves that the sea route had already been opened up, for the merchants or envoys, whichever they were, must have been Greeks from Alexandria or some other large city of the Roman orient, who had embarked at a Red Sea port in Egypt. Several years later another embassy, which the Chinese accepted as official, arrived in A.D. 226, shortly after the fall of the Han dynasty. The Chinese give the name of the chief ambassador as 'Ch'in Lun', but this has never been identified in Greek or Latin form. The Chinese court intended to send an ambassador back with 'Ch'in Lun', but he died before embarking. It is recorded that the ambassador was closely questioned by the Emperor concerning his country, its customs and people, and it is more than probable that much of the information on the Roman Empire in the Han history comes from this source.

There can be no doubt that the discovery of western Asia, and to a lesser degree the new knowledge of Europe also, made a great impression on the Chinese of the Han period. This was the first time that any other civilization had been known to them, and they freely recognized that it was in many ways, though different, the equivalent of their own. In the event the troubles of China after the fall of the Han, and the declining power of Rome from much the same period, prevented the early contact from developing into a regular intercourse. The land route fell back under nomad control, and the sea route, which certainly continued to be used, was always dangerous as well as very long. After the rise of the Arabs in the early seventh century A.D., this trade fell entirely into their hands. To the Chinese these distant lands had always something of a fairy tale character : only a very few people ever visited them, they could have no importance in the affairs of state or government policy, even such trade as went on was in luxuries, and certainly passed through many intermediaries. We know that Chinese silk was imported to Rome, and fetched high prices. Roman glass (a substance hitherto not known in China) was brought eastwards, and archaeological discoveries have shown that Roman and Greek gold coins, lamps and some other objects are to be found in scattered sites in China.

About the time of the alleged embassy of Marcus Aurelius Antoninus the Han dynasty began to decline. The old trouble of the powerful Consort Families grew menacing, and in an attempt to offset their power the later Han Emperors gave more and more power to court eunuchs. From the Emperor's point of view the palace eunuchs were a very useful group. They knew him intimately, and he could see and talk with them at any time, without the formality of regular court audiences. They came from obscure families, and had therefore no political following outside the court : and they could not found a new family which would, like the families of the Empresses, seek to monopolize all power and promote their own relatives to every important post. So in A.D. 159 the reigning Emperor used his eunuchs to carry out a *coup* against the all-too-powerful Consort Family of the Liang, who had poisoned his predecessor, as dangerous to their ambition, and had dominated the government for thirty years, providing three Empresses, three commanders-in-chief, and no less than fifty-seven ministers and provincial governors.

The Emperor succeeded with his eunuch support in destroying the Liang family, and thenceforward he and his successors relied on the eunuchs to curb the power of any other Consort Family. Unfortunately this meant putting as much, or more, power into the hands of the eunuchs themselves. Had the Emperors been strong rulers they could have checked the growth of eunuch power, but in the thirty years between A.D. 159 and A.D. 189 the throne was occupied by foolish or weak sovereigns who simply relied on their eunuch advisers in all things and let them have their will. The eunuchs abused their power in every way. They sold public appointments, promoted men for bribes, had those who did not satisfy their demands dismissed, and thus corrupted the civil service and weakened the army. An association of the scholar officials, formed to oppose eunuch authority and restore the old system of administration, was represented to the Emperor as a treasonable body, and all its members exterminated. This blow at the real core of the Chinese government, the civil service, hastened the collapse of the dynasty.

In A.D. 189, on the death of the weak and foolish Emperor Ling Ti without a direct heir, a violent struggle began between the army, led by the commander-in-chief, a brother of the Empress, and the palace eunuchs. The general obtained an order from his sister the Empress, bringing the élite troops to the capital. Believing that with this backing he was safe, he attempted to persuade the regent to dismiss the eunuchs. They retorted by assassinating him in the palace to which he had been summoned on a false order. If the eunuchs thought this act would overawe the troops, they made a fatal mistake. The infuriated soldiers attacked and stormed the palace, slaughtering all the eunuchs. The child Emperor fell under the authority of a soldier of fortune, whose power was immediately challenged by other commanders. A complicated civil war broke out, during which the unity of the Han Empire, and ultimately the dynasty itself, collapsed.

The Period of the Three Kingdoms (A.D. 221–265)

The Han dynasty nominally endured until A.D. 221, but for thirty years before the last shadow Emperor was dethroned, the country had in effect been divided between three main contending factions, established in the north, south-east and far west of China respectively. After the dynasty was finally over-thrown the ruler of the northern kingdom claimed the imperial throne, but his rivals did so also, and Chinese historians have never agreed as to which was 'legitimate' – or rather, have agreed that not one of the rivals could rightly make such a claim. The period is thus known as the Three Kingdoms, and it lasted from A.D. 221 to A.D. 265, although in actual fact the division of the Empire had occurred as early as A.D. 190. It was a period of constant warfare between the Three Kingdoms, each striving for supremacy, sometimes two briefly combining against the strongest, but without stability or good faith.

In Chinese literature the Three Kingdoms has a different importance. The period has become a romantic age, of heroes and adventures, the subject of one of the most famous Chinese novels, and of very many plays and folk tales. The popular version of events is certainly not strictly correct – there is a division into villains and heroes which sober history cannot really endorse – but there is no doubt that this version is so well known that the real character of the period is almost obscured. Every Chinese child knows that Ts'ao Ts'ao, the ruler of the northern kingdom of Wei, was a double-dyed traitor, that the Sun family who ruled the eastern kingdom of Wu, were wily and faithless, and that Liu Pei, who claimed to be a distant collateral of the Han imperial family, and his two friends Kuan Ti (now deified as the Chinese God of War) and Chang Fei, were pure-minded patriots and heroes. The reason for this choice of 'goodies' and 'baddies' is that centuries later, when the story of the Three Kingdoms came to be written in the form of novels and plays, the authors were intent to drive home the lesson that the unity of China was the true aim of all good men and true, and those who disrupted the country for selfish ambition were traitors. Liu Pei, as the heir of the Han, was in their eyes 'legitimate' – the real Emperor (although his was the weakest of the Three Kingdoms). Ts'ao Ts'ao, who de-throned the Han Emperor, must be the traitor disrupting the Empire. The Sun family, carving out a kingdom for themselves in the chaos after A.D. 190, were simply selfish adventurers, faithless to the real Emperor. It is in the field of literature, and the development of political ideas at a later time, that the Three Kingdoms period has real significance in Chinese history.

The Tsin Dynasty and the Age of Confusion
(A.D. 265–589)

In A.D. 265 the Empire was reunited for a short period of fifty years under a dynasty called Tsin, which was itself the successor of the Wei or northern member of the Three Kingdoms. The Tsin lasted only until A.D. 316. In that year a great invasion of the nomadic peoples swept into China and the Tsin lost the whole of the northern half of the country. They fled south to Nanking, on the Yangtze, where they managed to set up a new government controlling the Yangtze valley and those parts of south China which had by that date been settled and colonized. This period, during which Chinese dynasties ruled at Nanking over the south, and the north was divided between dynasties founded by the invading Tartar peoples, lasted from A.D. 316 to A.D. 589, 273 years. There was now no central unified Empire. In the south the Tsin dynasty lasted another century but was followed by four others, all of short duration. In the north, after fifty years of great confusion and the rise and fall of several small kingdoms, a new Tartar invasion by the Toba tribe unified the whole north under the Wei dynasty which lasted for one and a half centuries (A.D. 386–A.D. 533). The last half century of the Period of Partition saw the north under the control of four short dynasties, none of which controlled the whole region.

This 'Age of Confusion', as the Chinese historians call it, was not so chaotic as they sometimes tend to suggest. There were relatively long periods in both north and south when the regimes were more or less stable and arts and culture flourished. Border warfare between the two regions was frequent, but serious attempts by one or the other to reunify the Empire were few, and all failed. The Chinese considered the Southern Empire to be the legitimate heir to the Han dynasty, and denied the title of Emperor to the rulers of the north. In reality the country was for much of this time divided between several kingdoms, both in the north and in the south.

The period has sometimes been compared with the Dark Ages in Europe, after the fall of Rome and the invasions of the barbarians from northern and eastern Europe. There are some similarities, but also very great differences. In China the age was not 'dark'. The art of writing and the records of history were never lost either in north or south. Arts, architecture and literature not only flourished, but acquired new forms. The old language did not die out, or become transformed, as happened to Latin, but continued very little affected by the languages of the invaders. This was undoubtedly because these were few in number compared to the large native Chinese population. The north, the region occupied by the invaders, was at that time by far the most populous part of China. It may have had about thirty million people, perhaps more. The south, which Chinese dynasties ruled, was still largely a thinly-inhabited country, with perhaps less than twenty million people, occupying a vast region. We do know that 150 years after the Empire was re-united the whole country, north and south, did not have a population of more than sixty million. It had undoubtedly increased greatly during that century and a half.

The invading peoples established their rule in the north and north-west of China, and it was from the north-western provinces that contact with western Asia, first made under the Han dynasty, was carried on. Therefore it was this region which was most closely in touch with India – by the land route across Central Asia and modern Afghanistan – and came under the strongest Buddhist influence. The new rulers had been illiterate warriors when they conquered north China. They were easily converted to Buddhism, and in the works of art made during these first centuries of the nomad rule great Indian influence is visible, but much less Chinese tradition. At Yun Kang, a famous cave temple dating from the fourth century A.D., which was close to the capital of one of the northern kingdoms, there are very fine bas-reliefs dealing with Buddhist subjects. But in the earliest carvings there are no Chinese inscriptions, and the style is rather alien to Han art. Later, the Chinese influence grows stronger, and is finally quite dominant. Thus this archaeological monument illustrates what was happening over the whole field of culture and civilization in north China under the nomad dynasties.

As they became established and secure they had to turn more and more to their Chinese subjects for assistance in governing the country, and rely on Chinese skills and arts. Buddhism gave them a new religion, but the Chinese educated class was Confucian, and this class was essential if orderly government was to be maintained. Chinese became, or rather continued to be, the only written language for business, government and literature. Sanskrit might be the sacred language of Buddhism, but very few could read it, and the conquerors found it more convenient to learn the language of their subjects. Many of the nomad warrior kings were illiterate; this meant that they relied the more heavily on Chinese ministers. When, in a few generations, the descendants of the nomad warriors themselves began to speak and read Chinese, they in turn became Chinese in outlook and in thought. In the fifth century the Emperor of Wei ordered his Tartar subjects to give up their national dress, and learn Chinese. It is said that fourteen thousand people obeyed his decree. It must be assumed that this means the heads of fourteen thousand noble families, for although the conquerors were not numerous they were certainly a much larger group than this handful.

The nomad warriors formed a military class, but they soon had to admit Chinese to it. Many of the old powerful Chinese families had migrated to the south when their country was conquered, but others held on, submitting to the invaders, and later became closely related to the invading nobility. As the conquerors lost their language and adopted Chinese customs, the difference between them and the Chinese tended to disappear. The weak, disturbed kingdoms were always at war with each other, and in these conditions a military class of all origins rose to power and wealth. Chinese commanders serving a northern dynasty were the companions of officers of Tartar descent. They frequently intermarried, and after two or three centuries the class of warrior nobles was really an indistinguishable group of related families. Yet no true return to ancient feudalism occurred. The new nobility of alien and native origin were the servants of the various dynasties, usurped the throne frequently, but had no long-lasting local power. Their influence was not so much territorial as military. It was the number of troops a noble commanded, his power to raise an army, not his local ownership of great territories, which made him powerful. He could place his clients and relatives in the civil and military service, secure his influence at court by giving his daughter in marriage to the sovereign, take as his own wife a princess of the imperial family. This mattered much more than local territorial power.

In the southern Chinese Empire, the heart of which was the great Yangtze valley, the old families who had migrated from the north did have much greater territorial power. They had been granted huge estates to compensate them for what they had abandoned in north China. Often these estates were in areas of the south which were only recently colonized by the Chinese. The northern emigrés brought with them many hundreds of servants and followers, and settled them on these new lands. But although their local power was much more feudal in character than that of the northern nobility, the southern Chinese aristocracy were also the heirs of the Han imperial tradition. They longed to restore the unified Empire, and they took pride in carrying on, in a much weakened form, the imperial civil service of the former Empire. Rank at court, high office as a minister, were the prizes they esteemed. Local feudal power gave them wealth, and sometimes armed followers also, but this power was used to win influence and position at court, not to set up local sovereignties. Like their northern counterparts the great families frequently usurped the throne. The dynasties were all short, and rarely lasted beyond the lifetime of the founder. Other families were too jealous of their power, no one imperial family had the prestige of long tenure of the throne, any noble felt he was as much entitled to the throne as the ruling dynasty. A web of relationship joined all these families together, so that the usurper was usually a close relative of the Emperor he dethroned, and had most to fear from other relatives who might do the same to him.

Society in the Period of Partition, in north and south alike, had thus developed a character unlike either that of the unified Empire of the Han, or the feudal age which came before the Han. The new nobility might be, often were, descendants of the high officials and generals of the Han in the south; of the Tartar invaders and local Chinese grandees in the north; in both regions this class monopolized both civil and military power. The wider choice of men for the civil service which had prevailed under the Han Empire was now much more restricted to a narrow class of aristocracy, in which the influence of a few great families was dominant. These great families could not be kept in loyal obedience to a monarch who came from just such a rival family himself. The throne had no continuing prestige, it was the biggest political prize, but every noble family thought itself entitled to compete for it. None ever held it for long. Dethroned monarchs and their relatives retired to distant areas, where they sometimes rebuilt their power, or were reduced to the status of subordinate nobles; but as they were related to other noble families they could always find support and protection against the worst calamities. These conditions prevented any solution to the political problem of the division of the country for three hundred years.

Neither side was strong enough to conquer the other. After the defeat of a great northern invasion in A.D. 387, no later northern attack came near to victory. The southern Empire was usually on the defensive, lacking the cavalry which was needed to win battles on the northern plains. On the other hand, they had strong naval power on the Yangtze which the northern invaders wholly lacked, and the southern commanders were expert defenders of fortified cities, which Tartar horsemen could not capture. This military stalemate could have led to a final division of China into two or more countries, and as this is just what did happen to the Roman Empire after the very similar barbarian invasions at much the same period, it is important to see why the story of China was different.

The Roman Empire had no ethnic or cultural unity. It was fundamentally divided into a Greek-dominated eastern half and a Roman-dominated western half, apart altogether from the minority language and culture groups within these areas. Nor had it a real geographic unity, despite the efforts of the road-builders to overcome the barriers of sheer distance. Roman success lay in imposing political unity upon the disparate groups which made up the Empire; once this political structure collapsed, there was nothing left to hold the Empire together.

China, however, has both geographic and ethnic unity. The border of the two Empires in the Period of Partition was not the Yangtze River, but the watershed between the Yellow River basin and the Yangtze valley. This is a very indefinite line, and for much of it, in the east, it is far from clear-cut. Here there is a large area of flat marshy country with a very complicated river system, making communication easy between the Yangtze and the rivers of the north. In the western part of the Yangtze valley there is a range of mountains separating the two river systems, but these mountains are neither high nor hard to cross. Armies have always been able to pass from north to south, or vice versa, without finding great geographical obstacles. Cultivated and inhabited country continues from one zone to the other. So the conquest of the north could not make this country into a separate land, breaking its links with the south.

Further, the north of China was the most populous area, had the oldest tradition of civilization, and was the real stronghold of Chinese culture at that time. The barbarians were unable to change this, unlike the western European barbarian invaders who changed the languages and character of the old western Roman provinces. On the contrary, the overwhelming Chinese majority absorbed the invaders and soon taught them Chinese ways and converted them into Chinese. As soon as this transformation had reached the point where there remained no obvious difference between a man of Tartar ancestry and one whose descent was from pure Chinese, the last reasons for separation disappeared.

Intermarriage among the ruling aristocracy of both races helped to remove the old distinctions and the ancient quarrels. The main reason why this reunion was so long delayed was political, the instability of the dynasties in both north and south; as soon as one strong power arose, in the north as it happened, the reunion was certain to follow. In A.D. 581 a revolution in the north produced this situation. In that year a Chinese general, Yang Chien, who was the son-in-law of the Tartar monarch of a short-lived dynasty called Northern Chou, dethroned his young cousin, the Emperor, and seized the throne. He was partly of Tartar blood himself, like so many other members of the northern aristocracy, and he had no difficulty in making himself master of all north China. Then he invaded the south, which was at the time under the weak rule of another brief dynasty, the Ch'en. Resistance was slight, because as the invader was not a Tartar, but a Chinese, there was very little reason to oppose a reunion of the Empire which all professed to wish for. In A.D. 589 the new Sui dynasty re-established the united Empire. The ease with which this great change was brought about – so different from the vain efforts of Western rulers like Justinian and later Charlemagne to re-unite the Roman world – proves that in China the union of the country was natural, whereas in the West it had always been artificial.

But just as the first Empire of the Ch'in and Han, which brought the feudal period to an end, was a great turning point in Chinese history, the second reunion achieved by the Sui, and a few years later consolidated by the T'ang dynasty, was an even more important historical crossroads.

The fact that after three hundred years of division the Chinese people had not lost their identity, but preserved the tradition of unity and a common culture, made it very unlikely that this fate would ever befall them in the future. The population had grown, the south was now colonized and brought fully into the mainstream of Chinese life. The long period when the capital had been at Nanking had spread Chinese civilization as well as settlement deeply into the southern provinces. Although the new dynasty set up its capitals at Loyang and Ch'angan (the modern Sian) which had been the capitals of the Han Empire, and were in the north, there was no sign that the south was discontented or hoped to secede. In later Chinese history periods of division were always short 'ages of confusion' caused by the collapse of a dynasty and the struggle to set up a new one. Rivals fought for the throne, but the prize was the Empire of all China, not a separate kingdom in some part of the country. Foreign invasions led to the loss of some northern provinces, but even these were relatively short breaks in the long-lasting united empire which was set up by the Sui and T'ang in the late sixth century A.D.

Unity came to be regarded as right, and normal; division as wrong, brief and bad. It is sometimes said that before modern times the Chinese did not have any idea of national patriotism, and in one way this is true. As, in their view, there was only one civilized state in the world, it was natural that all men who were civilized regarded it as their homeland, but did not feel that it was 'their country' as opposed to some other country, which other men, equally civilized, cherished as their own. The other countries known to the Chinese were inhabited by barbarous tribes, who certainly had no sense of nationality beyond tribal allegiance. No Chinese wished to be a barbarian, and would never have been accepted by the tribes. So if you were Chinese you belonged to civilization, which was China. It went without saying. We do not think of ourselves as Earthmen, because we do not know of any beings in another planet. So the Chinese did not think of themselves as Chinese in the modern national sense, they thought of themselves as members of the civilized world.

In later centuries men looked back upon the Period of Division as one of calamity, the destruction of the unified Empire, and this was thought to be due mainly to the invasion of foreign peoples. In truth this was rather a consequence than a cause of the collapse of the unified Empire after the Han dynasty, but most Chinese did not see it this way. The nomad invaders had destroyed the Empire, so they were a danger which must always be watched, lest they come again with similar disastrous results. In this sense the Period of Division undoubtedly did sharpen the Chinese sense of exclusiveness.

One important consequence of this outlook was a change in the attitude to war and the military profession. In ancient

China the feudal nobility were warriors as well as courtiers and governors. In Han times there was no clear division between civil and military service. Every minister might command an army, generals could be governors of provinces, men changed from one occupation to the other. War in the Han period was mainly war against the nomads of the north until the troubles at the end of the dynasty. But in the Three Kingdoms, and later in the Period of Division, the military group among the officials and ruling class came to be dominant. The nobility of the north and south alike were primarily commanders, and only secondarily ministers or officials. Military power was essential to win political influence. Wars between north and south and between rival dynasties in both north and south were frequent, almost continuous. As there was no one central government these struggles were not those of rebels against loyalists, but contests for leadership among groups of rival aristocrats. War was honourable, military ability was admired, all leaders were warriors.

After the reunion of the Empire all this gradually changed. War now meant either rebellion against the unique Emperor – which was treason and endangered the unity of the Empire; or it meant frontier defence against barbarian raids – which was necessary, but not particularly important or politically significant. Frontier commanders tended to be professional soldiers, often barbarians in Chinese service. They counted for very little in the administration of the Empire or its politics. So war became no longer honourable, but evil: the military were a necessity on the frontier, but a danger elsewhere, and not admired. Rebellion was the only form of civil war, and rebellion was morally wrong unless it could be shown that the Emperor had 'lost the Mandate of Heaven', that is, was no longer fit to govern, incapable, tyrannous or the helpless plaything of factions. Then the rebel hoped to found a new dynasty and restore the Empire – not to destroy it. But this new outlook reflected social changes which only began to appear after the new reunited Empire had been established for several years.

APPENDIX

The Introduction of Buddhism

The official date at which the Chinese histories record the introduction of Buddhism is A.D. 65, in the early part of the Later or Eastern Han dynasty. As this is the date at which the court decided to recognize the new religion, and send an embassy to India to collect Sanskrit books and bring back Indian scholars to translate them, it is clear that the Indian religion had reached China many years earlier than this. It is possible that archaeological discoveries will reveal an early Buddhist site, but at the present time there is no such evidence available. When it reached China, some time in the first century A.D., Buddhism was already an old religion. It is believed, without direct evidence, that Buddha lived in the first half of the fifth century B.C. The split between the two branches of Buddhism, *Mahayana*, 'The Greater Vehicle', and *Hinayana*, 'The Lesser Vehicle', had already occurred probably shortly before the introduction of the Mahayana doctrine to China. In general terms the Mahayana system now prevails in China, Japan, Korea and Vietnam; Hinayana is practised in Burma, Thailand, Cambodia and Ceylon. In India itself, Buddhism is very nearly an extinct religion, except in so far as it has merged with Hinduism.

Many scholars believe that the Mahayana system has incorporated ideas derived from Greek philosophy (through the contact between India and the successors of Alexander's empire in western Asia) and also Persian ideas. It is much more complex than Hinayana, which, its own followers claim, maintains the simple unchanged teaching of Buddha. Hinayana, however, has not been influential in China, and as an intellectual force in the Chinese Buddhist tradition it is not important. Mahayana, which teaches that the historical Buddha was only one in an almost infinite series of reincarnated Buddhas, covering an unimaginable period of millions of years, and living in many other worlds than ours, has also paid great veneration to Bodhisattvas, or saints, who have in the course of time become popular deities. Differences at least as great as those dividing the Roman Catholic and Protestant churches separate Hinayana from Mahayana Buddhism, and a further difference is found in the Buddhism of Tibet, which is unlike either. The unity of the Buddhist world, at least in matters of faith and religious practice, is largely a myth.

In China the great importance of Buddhism is that it was, until very modern times – the nineteenth century – the only important foreign influence, deeply affecting the whole culture and life of the Chinese people, which took root in China. Its growth was slow: it was nearly four hundred years after the official introduction of Buddhism before it became a really widespread popular religion. One reason for this was the fact that to understand the new religion its sacred books, written in Sanskrit, had to be translated into Chinese. This was a very difficult and laborious task. At first no Chinese scholars knew any foreign language, and no Indians knew Chinese. Both sides had to learn to read a foreign language which used an entirely different script from their own. The structure of Sanskrit and Chinese is quite unlike, the sounds of the two languages very different. Consequently the elementary task of rendering the names of Buddhist saints or the doctrines themselves presented great problems. In the end the Chinese versions of these names and words is either a translation such as *Kuan Shih Yin* ('He who Hears the Cry of the World'), or a very free approximation to the Indian name – 'Maitreya' becomes *Mi Lo*.

Several centuries passed before the whole body of Buddhist scripture was rendered into Chinese. Buddhism was therefore at first confined to scholars and a small number of educated people: in time it spread to the lesser educated, and ultimately to the mass of the people, but as they could not read the sacred books (in any language), their understanding of the doctrines was imperfect, and Buddhism was much transformed. Contact between Chinese Buddhist scholars and India was maintained by pilgrimages and by the visits of Indian Buddhists, who spent years, often all their lives, in China translating the Sanskrit texts. But the number of such pilgrims and missionaries was never large; the hazards and length of the journey to India were daunting to most people. In this way the introduction of Buddhism to China was a long slow process which gave plenty of time for Buddhism to undergo changes which made it more acceptable to Chinese ways of thought.

Unlike Christianity, which arose and was preached within the Roman Empire, converting the whole Roman world in just about three hundred years, Buddhism was an alien religion from a distant country, and it never converted the whole Chinese people, nor drove out the creeds which they had followed before Buddhism came. The whole approach was different. The Chinese had not been accustomed to believe that there was only one true faith. They worshipped many gods, depending on their occupation. The educated class were Confucians, but not entirely so. The Taoist teaching was also followed by very many, but it was not felt that because a man was Taoist in his outlook he could not respect Confucius, nor accept Confucian doctrine in many matters. When Buddhism was introduced, the Chinese tended to treat it in the same way. Men studied and accepted the new religion, but they did not on that account give up all their old beliefs – even when these were quite contrary to important Buddhist dogmas. Thus Buddhism teaches that every human being is reincarnated after death in another body, and immediately begins a new life, his new incarnation depending on the manner of life he led in the last one. Bad men will be reincarnated as animals, reptiles or even insects. Some who were wealthy and comfortable, but made poor use of their advantages, will be poor and miserable people in the next life. Those who were virtuous will have a happier life next time, and ultimately, by slow degrees and study, all men will raise themselves to the level of Buddha himself, and escape from the vast chain of reincarnation to merge in the deity itself.

This teaching, fundamental Buddhism, is quite opposite to the beliefs of Confucians or Taoists. They had only rather unclear ideas about any future life, but firmly believed that man's fate on earth was mainly determined by what he did in this life, rather than what he may have done in a previous one. They also believed that the first duty of every man was to revere his ancestors, and provide them with descendants who would carry on the sacrifices and reverence for all ages to come. The happiness of the dead in their shadowy after-life depended on the care and attention which the living paid to them. But if a man is reincarnated in accordance with his previous conduct, there can be no certainty – indeed almost the opposite – that he will be in any way connected with the family to which he belonged in his previous life, or to that which he will belong in his next incarnation. He may not be human at all. Ancestor worship should therefore be meaningless to a Buddhist : and Buddhism should be contrary to all that a Confucian revered.

Some Chinese, at all times, have been very much troubled by these contradictions. Strong Confucians denounced Buddhism for these reasons. Buddhists usually seem to have ignored the problem – possibly because it was always dangerous and unwise to attack Confucianism openly. The less educated people, not too much worried by problems which they found hard to grasp, simply decided that worship was due to all important divinities, Buddhas, Taoist gods, 'Heaven' and 'Earth', alike. Confucianism remained the philosophy of the government, was officially taught in schools and established in the civil service. Most people went to Buddhist monasteries to pray for luck or to turn away bad fortune. Others, or the same people, also went to Taoist temples for the same reasons. Buddhist monks and Taoist priests performed ceremonies at weddings and funerals together. From the point of view of Western Christians the Chinese were neither real Confucians, true Buddhists, nor faithful Taoists. From the Chinese point of view there were 'three ways to one goal' – Confucianism, Buddhism and Taoism. The 'goal' was the good life on earth, virtuous conduct, happiness and long life.

It is not entirely certain how soon this compromise came to be the general attitude of the Chinese people. Buddhism was undoubtedly more active, and more fervently followed, in the earlier centuries of its long sway in China. But it never eliminated Taoism nor replaced Confucianism as the dominant ethical system on which education was based and government conducted. In the centuries after the fall of the Han Empire there were, for political reasons, periods when Buddhism was strongly favoured at the court, at other times periods when it was persecuted, although rather mildly. Nothing in China compared with the great persecutions carried on against Christianity in the Roman Empire. It was never made a crime to be a Buddhist, but at certain times there was much objection to the large number of Buddhist monks and nuns, on the grounds that these people were unfilial, refusing to provide posterity for their ancestors. On some occasions nuns and monks were forced to marry each other. It was very rarely indeed that anyone was put to death for his religion, and when this did happen there were always extraneous reasons for it.

Buddhism had great influence on Chinese art, and there is a sharp difference in the styles of art which prevailed in the Han period, before Buddhism, and the style which arose in the centuries after its introduction. In some ways this is comparable to the difference between classical and medieval art in Europe, although some of the effects were just the opposite to the Western experience. Sculpture in China was almost entirely a consequence of Buddhist worship, especially the portrayal of the human form (as opposed to animal sculpture). In Europe sculpture was one of the great classical arts, but waned in the early Christian centuries. Indian influences in art were at first strong in Buddhist work, but after a few hundred years they decreased and largely gave way to traditional Chinese forms, somewhat changed by new styles. One of the factors in the introduction of Buddhism was that the new religion only became widespread and strong after the fall of the unified Empire, and in a period when foreign invasions had overrun much of the country. This may have helped the spread of Buddhism, as the invading peoples were more easily converted – being barbarians – than the old Chinese population. Certainly Buddhism was favoured in the courts of the conquerors, earlier, though not in the end more, than in the court of that part of China which remained free from conquest.

CHAPTER THREE

The Restored Empire

(A.D. 600–1800)

THE restoration of the Empire by the Sui dynasty in 589 was followed by events strangely like the original unification of China by the Ch'in eight hundred years before. Like the Ch'in, the Sui were short-lived: like the Ch'in also, this was due to the unwisdom and incompetence of the second Emperor of the dynasty, Yang Ti. And just as the Han had won the Empire after a period of confusion following the collapse of the Ch'in, so when the Sui fell, there was a furious civil war from which the founder of the T'ang dynasty emerged triumphant to set up a stable and enduring regime. The downfall of the Sui in the years 615–618 was mainly due to the overweening ambition of the Emperor Yang Ti, who not only spent the revenues on luxurious palaces and extravagant projects but engaged in an unsuccessful and sustained attempt to conquer the northern of the three kingdoms into which Korea was then divided. This kingdom, Korguryo, included not only much the same area as contemporary North Korea but also most of what is now the Chinese province of Liaoning, or South Manchuria. Traditionally the region had been a province of the Han Empire, but had then been an independent kingdom for several centuries, more or less Chinese in culture, although not in race.

The Koreans proved valiant and firm defenders of their country. Yang Ti's armies were caught by the harsh Manchurian winter, their invasions failed and the discontented troops mutinied. Rebellion broke out on all sides, during which the Emperor was murdered by one pretender, while no less than eleven others disputed the inheritance of the Sui. It seemed that the new-found unity of the country was once more to dissolve into chaos and separate, contending states. After six years of

civil wars the founder of the T'ang dynasty defeated all rivals
and restored the Empire. The real victor and founder of the
new dynasty was not the first T'ang Emperor, but his second
son, Li Shih-min by name, later the Emperor T'ang T'ai Tsung,
second of the dynasty. The first T'ang Emperor, his father, had
been a provincial governor. Like so many members of the aristocracy of that age, the Li family, although Chinese on the
father's side, had intermarried with the noble families of Tartar
ancestry. They were related to the former imperial house of
the Wei and to some members of the short-lived dynasties
which had followed the Wei.

The T'ang Dynasty

Li Shih-min was a youth of barely eighteen when he organized
the revolt against the Sui, pushed his hesitant father into supporting it and then led his armies to final victory in six years.
He succeeded his father (who abdicated) after a conspiracy by
his elder brother, the nominal Crown Prince, had been detected
and suppressed.

T'ang T'ai Tsung (the Supreme Ancestor of T'ang, as this title
may be translated) is still generally held in China to have been
the greatest ruler that ever occupied the Chinese throne. In his
youth he proved himself a general of outstanding skill; on the
throne he excelled equally as a wise, tolerant and far-seeing
statesman. His one failure was a renewed attempt to conquer
Korea, but finding this task too great a burden for the Empire,
he refrained from persisting in the attempt. Famous for his
enlightened government, he was also a great patron of literature, personally editing the histories of the previous age of
division, establishing schools and a university – perhaps the
first that ever existed. His handwriting, an art much admired in
China, is still reproduced as the model for school children. The
oldest extant texts of the classical books of ancient China are
those which were engraved on stones set up at his command,
in the Confucian temple at the capital Ch'angan (where they
still remain), and engraved from his own calligraphy.

Among the many reforms which he instituted, one was to prove fundamental: the establishment of an examination system for admission to the civil service. It was not at first made the only and compulsory way of entry. Recommendation, the ancient privilege of the aristocracy, remained a second source of recruitment for a long time, but the examination system grew steadily more effective and finally wholly replaced the older system. There is no doubt that the Emperor devised this revolutionary plan to meet and overcome the principal danger which had afflicted every dynasty in China since the fall of the Han: the power of the military aristocracy, the class from which his own family came. As long as this class dominated the government and had a monopoly of the recommendations for the civil service posts, no dynasty was secure. An ambitious general, often a relative of the sovereign, could raise rebellion with the certainty that a great part of the administration would serve his cause rather than that of their nominal monarch.

The examination system made it possible to recruit from a much wider field – the general body of the literate gentry, including families with no military traditions and little influence. Such men would owe their chance of advancement to the throne alone: their careers depended on the favour of the Emperor and they had no outside backing. During his reign, T'ai Tsung's immense prestige and the respect in which he was held kept the military aristocrats in obedience, and, indeed, even in loyalty. But the Emperor foresaw that this would not be the situation under his successors, who might well be mediocre rulers. The dynasty, the Empire, needed a system which secured the continuing loyalty of a large class of officials who owed allegiance to no one except the Emperor.

The new system was designed to produce such a class of officials, and in time it succeeded in doing so. But it was necessary to go carefully. The founder of the Han had been willing to allow some outward forms of feudalism to survive under close supervision of the imperial court, until any danger from this quarter had eventually disappeared. T'ai Tsung also continued the system of aristocratic recommendation to the civil service and army commands, but created a parallel system under imperial control, which gradually wore down the power of the military aristocracy. Probably neither he nor any of his contemporaries realized what a momentous reform this really was. It was destined to transform Chinese society by creating the 'bureaucratic state' in place of the aristocratic society, thus laying the foundations of a unified Empire based on an institution which was to survive every change of dynasty. Dynasties might decay and fall, military adventurers might found new ones, but the civil service went on, recruited by examinations, manned by members of the literate gentry, 'the scholars', whose continuing tradition, monopoly of power, of education and of literature, made them a cohesive force carrying on the T'ang tradition for fifteen hundred years.

In the long view, the examination system was therefore the most important of the new T'ang institutions: at the time, the reform of the tax system, of land tenure and of the army seemed more important. The creation of a highly efficient civil service to administer all these reforms and execute policies in a huge Empire was another great achievement of the early T'ang period. Proof of this efficiency exists in the surviving records of the dynasty, including the detailed census figures taken in various years. For long Western scholars (perhaps unconsciously unwilling to recognize that seventh century China was so far in advance of Europe till the nineteenth century) treated the T'ang census figures as guesses or fictions. But the discovery of actual census returns in deposits of manuscripts which had been sealed up in caves, has shown that even a discharged soldier occupying a farm in a remote frontier district of the north-west sent in a return giving the names and ages of his family of a wife and three children. This kind of detailed information was not collected by the central government of a great state anywhere else in the world till more than a thousand years later.

These examples of the way in which the T'ang government ruled serve to illustrate the advanced type of administration it developed; it does not follow that all the consequences of the creation of the bureaucratic state were good and beneficial.

Under the rule of the T'ang and the dynasties which followed and imitated the T'ang, China became consolidated into one unitary Empire. Regional differences gradually diminished. The national culture, the peculiar possession of the ruling class of officials – the Mandarins as they were called later by Europeans – became stereotyped. Confucian ethics dominated thought, classical patterns moulded literature, no new political ideas were encouraged or developed. It could be argued that the Chinese civilization would have been more diverse, more stimulating and more creative if China had not been permanently reunited under one imperial rule, but had broken up into rival, but kindred kingdoms, as happened in the European Middle Ages. This is one of history's 'might have beens', and no one can say what the consequences would have been. What is certain is that no Chinese ever regretted the restoration of the Empire, nor thought that at this great turning point in his country's history a wrong road had been chosen. From T'ang times onward the country was united far longer than it was divided by rebellion or partial foreign conquest. Such intervals were treated by Chinese writers as calamities, as inferior ages of confusion, and every restoration of unity was welcomed as a return to the right and normal state of the world. These ideas have outlasted the Empire which nourished them. At the present time the opposition and resentment which Chinese on both sides, Nationalist and Communist, feel to any proposal for perpetuating the separation of Formosa (Taiwan) from the mainland of China spring directly from the ancient view that there can be no two Chinese states, no two legitimate rulers of China, 'no two suns in one sky' as the old saying put it.

It is the continuation of this tradition of unity and central government, meticulous and efficient, reaching to every place and every man (an ideal which, of course, was not often, or even ever, really attained), that is the real importance of the T'ang period for later and modern times. China has been formed on the model of the T'ang dynasty, which itself revived and modernized the more ancient Empire of the Han. Even today, under a Communist regime, many of the basic features of the T'ang Empire continue. It was one of T'ai Tsung's reforms which first created the present provinces of China, very large areas, replacing the smaller commanderies of the Han age. The northern part of the country is still divided mainly on the lines of the T'ang provinces, which retain the names given them at that period. The south, much less populous in the seventh century than the north, was divided by the T'ang into huge areas which were later split up.

It was also in the T'ang age that the division between civil and military first became marked, and later firmly fixed. The military aristocracy of early T'ang were, like their forefathers of the age of partition, both generals and ministers, turn and turn about. This was a dangerous system and the policy of the first rulers of the dynasty was to alter it gradually, by establishing both a professional civil service to supply civil ministers, and a professional army which would have no connection with civil government. This is the universal system now followed by all advanced states in the world today, but in the seventh century it was unique to China, and far in advance of any other country. Many of these changes were begun in the reign of T'ai Tsung, but only completed by his successors.

One of the most interesting features of the T'ang period is that these successors arrived at power in a highly irregular way. Just as T'ai Tsung himself had succeeded his father after the violent suppression of his own elder brother's attempted *coup d'état*, so he had to degrade his own eldest son for a similar attempt, and when he died was succeeded by a younger son, the Emperor Kao Tsung, who proved an incompetent weakling. This might have been, probably would have been, disastrous for the dynasty had not power been seized by a woman, Wu Tse T'ien, who was originally one of T'ai Tsung's junior concubines. She beguiled his son, who – very improperly – married her, and when she had thus become Empress, she acquired complete control over her husband and dominated the government for more than fifty years.

The Confucian historians unsparingly condemn the Empress Wu as an intriguing usurper. It is true that she dethroned her own son after Kao Tsung's death, ruled for a while in the name of a second son – who was virtually kept a prisoner – dethroned him also, and then made the unprecedented act of ascending the throne herself. No woman ever before, or ever since, reigned as sovereign in the Chinese Empire. Many Empresses have exercised hidden or almost open power as regents when children were on the throne. But the Empress Wu alone actually reigned as the sole sovereign. In spite of the ruthless treatment which she gave to all who opposed her, the hostile historians themselves are forced to admit that she governed the Empire with great skill, wisdom and success. No serious rebellions shook her authority: she was largely responsible for overthrowing the power of the military aristocracy, who were most opposed to her rule. She gave a lead to the employment of obscure men of capacity, patronized the arts and literature, consolidated the imperial government in the provinces, reformed the army under professional officers drawn from the ranks – not from the aristocracy – and was even successful in carrying out the conquest of Korea, which neither T'ai Tsung himself nor the Sui Emperor had been able to achieve. At a great age, when sick and failing, she was forced to abdicate in favour of her long-deposed son, who fell at once under the influence of his consort, a woman as ambitious as the Empress Wu, but lacking her competence and character.

From the perils which such a succession was certain to produce, the Empire and the dynasty were rescued by the emergence of the third great ruler of the T'ang, the Emperor Hsüan Tsung, nicknamed 'Ming Huang' – 'the Brilliant Emperor'. He was her grandson, son of her second son, and like T'ai Tsung before him, he restored this nonentity to the throne for a few years, and succeeded to him on his abdication. Like T'ai Tsung again, he was the second son of his father, not the eldest or the Crown Prince, but this time his elder brother yielded his rights without a contest, and lived in friendship with his brother for many years afterwards. It is interesting to observe that, for more than 150 years – the greatest epoch of the T'ang dynasty, covered by these reigns and the short intervals between them – not one of the eldest sons succeeded his father, not one Crown Prince reached the throne. Yet in the T'ang, as in all other dynasties, strict hereditary rules of succession were the law, and these violations of it were all in fact usurpations. But the prestige of the dynasty, the effective administration of the Empire, was hardly at all disturbed by these revolutions at court. No rival family tried to gain the throne through rebellion or intrigue. The nephews of the Empress Wu – on her, the Wu, side – did indeed entertain hopes that she would make them her successors, but she never seems to have really supported this plan, and before her abdication had made her own deposed son once more her designated successor. The contrast between this situation and the constant intrigues of the Consort Families of the Han period is thus very significant. The monarchy under the T'ang was far more secure and safe, even though it frequently violated its own laws of succession. It is curious that although these events clearly proved that some form of elective monarchy, confined, perhaps, to members of the ruling dynasty, would have been more suitable and desirable than hereditary succession by the eldest son, no attempt was ever proposed to regularize the actual situation on these lines. One reason for this was certainly the strong opposition of the ever more powerful civil service, trained in Confucian doctrine, which steadily disapproved of these palace revolutions, even though it loyally served the Emperors who emerged from them.

The reign of the 'Brilliant Emperor' is well remembered in popular Chinese tradition, not for its very great achievements in the arts, literature and social changes, but for its tragic end. At an advanced age the Emperor fell in love with a beautiful concubine, the famous Yang Kuei Fei. She warped his judgement and induced him to foolish policies, including unmerited favours to a barbarian general of the frontier forces, An Lu-shan. An Lu-shan was given the supreme command of the northern army : the court was heedless of his guile and ambition; extravagant, luxurious and idle. Suddenly An Lu-shan seized what he believed to be his opportunity to gain the Empire. He revolted, marched almost unopposed on Ch'angan, the capital, and, as the Emperor and court fled hurriedly to the west, captured it. On the road the imperial bodyguard, demoralized and mutinous, demanded that the beautiful Yang Kuei Fei should be executed as a traitor: otherwise they would join the rebels. The Emperor was forced to consent, and Yang Kuei Fei, as the poet Po Chu-yi wrote, 'perished before their horses'. This event is famous in Chinese legend and literature. It was the subject of one of the very few epic poems in Chinese, Po Chu-yi's 'Everlasting Wrong', written in the generation following the revolt of An Lu-shan. Many plays have taken this tragedy as their theme, and it remains one of the most popular of the tragic stories in Chinese history.

After a long war the rebels were defeated, their leaders killed, and the aged Emperor, who had abdicated in favour of his son, returned to desolate Ch'angan. The T'ang dynasty continued to rule for another 150 years, but the glory had to a large degree departed. There was some revival, and in art and literature the ninth century still ranks very high. But the administrative machine of the early T'ang was irreparably damaged. To suppress the rebels large armies had to be raised, and the war continued for several years at great expense. The army commanders had to be given great provinces to rule as they recovered them, and they raised taxes to pay their men. They became semi-permanent rulers of these regions, hard to dismiss and only to be replaced by others who would act in the same way. Some of them were ex-rebel leaders whose return to true allegiance had been bought at a great price in power and wealth. The policy of the later T'ang Emperors had to be an attempt to strike a balance between these military governors and the power of the court. which was not negligible. In order to enforce their authority the later Emperors turned to the palace eunuchs, as in Han times a subservient body owing all they had to the throne. They became the court's instruments in the tortuous intrigues which played off one great provincial governor against his rival, or against his own ambitious subordinates. Inevitably the power of the eunuchs grew greater, and the control which the sovereigns exercised over them diminished. When children succeeded to the throne, during long regencies, the eunuch power grew fast.

It was no longer the old centrally-governed Empire, but there was no complete breakdown into feudal or military power. For more than a century the dynasty's right to the throne was never challenged, even by factious governors who warred upon each other. The court was still the source of legitimate power. Governors tried to get the backing of the throne against rivals; they did not yet seek to substitute themselves for the dynasty. One reason for the continuing authority of the court, even when its power was fast fading, was the loyalty of the civil service. The scholar gentry who had laboured to pass difficult examinations to enter the service were not willing to see the fruits of all their struggle and study stolen by illiterate army men. They strove to keep power in their own hands, and this they could only hope to do by supporting the Emperor. The outcome of this long political battle was still uncertain when a new factor entered to tip the balance fatally against the dynasty.

The need for money to maintain the huge city of Ch'angan (then certainly the equal at least of Constantinople as the greatest city in the world), with its extravagant court, hosts of pensioners, sinecure holders, greedy eunuchs, clamorous soldiers and courtiers expecting favours, had led to ever-increasing burdens of taxation being laid upon a population which had not greatly increased since the early T'ang times.

Famines and bad years, then as later, came at intervals to aggravate conditions. In A.D. 868 the army on the southern frontier, the present border of North Vietnam with the southwestern Chinese province of Yunnan (then an independent kingdom), mutinied. Their pay was in arrears, and in their isolation at the ends of the Empire they felt forgotten. They started to march home, led by a new type of rebel, familiar enough in later centuries. Huang Tsao was a failed scholar who had not passed the civil service examination, a disgruntled but educated man. He quickly realized that the military governors of the provinces he crossed only cared to get rid of him and his rebel army, not to suppress him. He could bribe his way through if he promised to invade the territory of the next governor, and then repeat the process. He advanced on the capital in this way, while the governors failed to stop him and the imperial forces were hindered by their jealous generals. In

881 he took Ch'angan, and the Emperor fled west. This date was the real end of the T'ang dynasty. It lingered on, nominally, until 907, while China was torn by civil war between the military governors, the rebels and the remnants of the imperial army. Huang Tsao was suppressed, but more by buying off his followers than winning victories. One of these ex-rebels finally dethroned the last T'ang Emperor, sacked and destroyed Ch'angan and set off to found a short-lived dynasty in the district which had been his province.

During the T'ang dynasty, trade and travel with western Asia had revived. The pilgrimages of Buddhist monks to India brought new and more accurate knowledge of these regions, in which, at its height, T'ang military power was sometimes employed. Persia, both before and after the Arab Islamic conquest, was well known to the Chinese. The last pre-Moslem Persian King died in exile in Ch'angan and his son became a Chinese general. The Byzantine Empire was also known to the Chinese and they have recorded in the history of the dynasty a full description of Constantinople as it was in the seventh century. For the first time, as far as can be known, the Chinese learned of Western Europe, in a rather vague way, and there was some traffic with Africa, almost certainly through Arab hands. The Arab traders formed large communities in the southern ports, and have also left some record of T'ang China in Arabic literature. Islam came to China by way of these traders and the mercenary troops which the court employed in the war against An Lu-shan. The two oldest mosques still used in China were founded in the seventh century, one at Canton, and one in Ch'angan, the modern Sian. Other strangers familiar in the streets of the great capital were Nestorian Christians from Syria and the Byzantine Empire, refugees from the Orthodox persecution of their faith. T'ai Tsung had allowed them to build a church and preach their religion, which flourished for a time, as is recorded on the still-surviving stone monument they put up to celebrate the rebuilding of the church after An Lu-shan's rebellion. At that time they enjoyed the favour of the court.

In T'ang times, as earlier, the Chinese were accustomed to bury in their tombs many finely-modelled clay figures of servants,

horses, camels, women, houses and other things which the
spirit of the dead person would need in the after-life. These
objects were supposed to be magical, and would provide their
counterparts as spirits for the use of the dead. Consequently
they form a kind of inventory of what a wealthy man expected to need in the next world, as he had in this one. Grooms
came from Central Asia, dancers and jugglers from India and
probably Syria also. There are certainly Africans represented,
and some others, among them Europeans, from Byzantium. The
fashions of the various periods are shown in the elaborate cos-
tumes, beautifully painted on the clay, worn by the female
figures. Warriors as guards show the armour and weapons of
the age, horses of fine breed, camels for travelling, houses with
watch towers; all are modelled in clay and have been found in
very large numbers by modern archaeologists.

In the arts intended for the living the T'ang also excelled.
Buddhist sculpture of the T'ang period is more human, less
austere than the earlier Wei. Some few rare paintings have been
preserved, but there are many written descriptions of the
works of famous painters, now lost. It was also the greatest age
of Chinese poetry, and the work of these poets has been preserved and many times republished. There was no field in
which the T'ang period did not either break new ground or
carry an old tradition to higher perfection. The Chinese drama
began at the court of the 'Brilliant Emperor', who is still the
patron of actors. The novel also, in the form of short stories,
first appears at this time. In recent times excavation of T'ang
tombs and sites has brought to light exquisite work in gold and
silver, fine lacquer ware and the earliest porcelain, another process which made great strides in this period.

In this sense, just as the Han period produced the real beginning of the literature which has continued to inspire the Chinese tradition, the art of the T'ang has more relation to later
Chinese civilization than to that of earlier times. Buddhist influences had been absorbed, some other foreign motifs came
into use, and it is certain that the lively mind of this dynasty
was more open to foreign thought and foreign influence than
any earlier age could be, or than many later ones were to be.

Yet it was still, essentially, a Chinese civilization, proudly aware that it stood far above that of neighbours near or far, who came to admire and to borrow. Japan, just emerging from its mythical age, was deeply impressed, and the early culture of the newly-established Japanese state was impregnated with Chinese ideas, arts and skills.

The Five Dynasty Period and the Northern Sung Dynasty
(A.D. 907–1126)

The T'ang Empire collapsed, but the traditions of the great dynasty were cherished, and soon the united Empire was once more restored. Fifty years of confusion followed the fall of the T'ang. In north China ephemeral dynasties, ruling but a part of the region, rose and fell within a few years. In the south, the provinces were divided among six kingdoms – all claiming to be the 'Empire', but too weak to do each other much harm, and on the whole keeping an uneasy peace. It was in this region that many of the old T'ang civil officials took refuge, and the culture of the south was thereby rapidly advanced. In 960 a new dynasty, founded by an able general, seized power in the north. Within a few years it obtained the submission of all the southern kingdoms, often by diplomacy as much as by conquest. The Sung, as this new unifying dynasty was called, indeed owed their rapid rise to power as much to the general discontent with division and chaos as to their own power. The T'ang tradition of unity was now the strongest political ideal. When one of the southern kingdoms pleaded for independence to the new Sung Emperor, he answered, 'What crime have the people of Kiangnan committed that they should be excluded from the Empire?' Kiangnan, the 'country south of the River' (Yangtze), was the name for all south China at that time. The Emperor thus expressed the prevailing view that it was a calamity to be separated from the Chinese Empire – the Empire must rightly embrace all China.

Yet in point of fact the Sung Empire never did achieve this objective. During the fifty years of confusion and short régimes in north China following the fall of the T'ang, one of these dynasties had ceded a large tract of the modern province of Hopei, including the city now named Peking, and the passes through the Great Wall. This territory, so vital strategically to the safety of north China, had passed under the control of the Khitan Tartars, a tribe who, having acquired a considerable measure of Chinese civilization when under T'ang suzerainty, now styled their state the Liao dynasty, and claimed equal rank with China. The Sung endeavoured to eject the Liao from this region, but they failed. Nor did subsequent attempts meet with better success. The loss of this region was a grave weakness for the Sung dynasty, perhaps the first cause of the ultimate success of the northern invaders who in the end destroyed the Sung. For in the Sung dynasty (960 to 1126) and the later period when the Sung had lost north China (1127–1278), the main danger to the Empire was no longer internal revolt or insubordinate military governors, but foreign invasion.

Great changes, the origin and cause of which are still rather obscure, had occurred in the steppes beyond the Great Wall during the last years of the T'ang and the fifty years interval – known as the Five Dynasty Period – before the foundation of the Sung. The tribal confederations which the T'ang had easily repelled or contained had been replaced by much better organized kingdoms, under stable and enduring leadership. This was no doubt a direct result of long relations with the great T'ang Empire, which all who came into contact with it sought to imitate. It was, in the result, rather a disastrous consequence of T'ang glory for their weaker successors, the Sung. To the northeast of China (in what is now Manchuria, but also including the ceded area of northern Hopei province), the Liao kingdom had arisen. The ruling group were the Khitan tribe. Their name, transformed into *Kitai*, became the name for China current among the Russian and eastern European peoples, and from this word comes the English poetical name for China, 'Cathay'. It was naturally north China that the eastern Europeans first learned about, by way of the great caravan route across Central Asia, hence they took the name of the local dynasty as the name of all China.

Westward of the Khitan kingdom of Liao there had arisen another powerful state of non-Chinese origin, but deeply influenced by Chinese culture. This was known to the Chinese as Hsia, or Hsi Hsia (Western Hsia) and occupied the extreme north-west of China, modern Kansu province and the adjoining parts of Mongolia and Central Asia. Very little is known about Hsi Hsia. The dominant people were a tribe called Tangut, related to the Tibetans. There were certainly both large numbers of Chinese and also Tartar tribes among their subjects. They had invented a new written script, imitating the Chinese system, but distinct. Owing to the later destruction of this kingdom by Genghiz Khan, the Mongol conqueror, the script cannot now be read, although a number of inscriptions using it still exist.

Both these northern states were hostile to the Sung and endeavoured to profit by any weakness in China to extend their rule farther into the rich lands to the south. The Sung were therefore preoccupied throughout the dynasty by these northern dangers. Perhaps on that account they were not very much – hardly at all – disturbed by internal rebellions. The Sung period in China was a highly civilized and sophisticated age, too sophisticated to live easily with more turbulent and restless neighbours. The rulers of this dynasty were competent, intelligent and moderate men, particularly the first four or five, and their age, the tenth and eleventh centuries of the Christian era, was one of the most fruitful epochs in Chinese history. This was the age of the great painters, largely landscape artists, whose work has come down to modern times: it was the age when porcelain was perfected, and today Sung vases are the most precious and admired of all Chinese ceramics. It was also a great age of literature, of historians, poets, essayists and writers on a wide variety of subjects. One such book contains the first detailed Chinese account of Europe and Africa, as well as the intermediate parts of Asia. It was written by a high official in charge of foreign trade, and he got his information from the Arab merchants who thronged to the southern ports. His work describes the Mediterranean countries – known to the Arabs – with fair accuracy, and refers to north-western Europe as a country where the sun shines all day long. This is because the Arab traders only made the long and hard voyage to the Baltic and Scandinavia in the summer, when the sun hardly sets in these northern latitudes. It was written about the time of the Norman conquest of England.

But the Sung period is mainly famous, in the realm of arts and thought, for the new schools of philosophy which arose and flourished in this dynasty. They were all Confucian, but their interpretations of the ancient writings and the systems of thought which they derived from these interpretations varied widely. Such questions as free will or predestination, whether the nature of man was originally good or bad, or neither good nor bad but dependent on training; whether there was a supreme divinity, and if so, whether He should be thought of as a Person or a Moral Force: these were the great questions which the scholars debated. In the end the greatest of them, Chu Hsi, formed a school which became the orthodox Confucian teaching of later times. It was a great deal more sophisticated than the original thought of Confucius, and it taught that the Universe was ruled by Moral Force, not by – to quote him – 'a man in Heaven judging sin'. From this teaching later Confucians took up an almost atheist position: it would be true to say that in later Chinese thought the deist belief – that there is a God – was weak, and the belief in an impersonal Moral Force was the predominant one. Chu Hsi also maintained that the nature of man was good, and evil only appeared in him through neglect and lack of the right training and education. This concept is still very widely held in China today, and has been given a new, Communist, interpretation.

Sung government was almost, if not quite as elaborate as that of the T'ang. The civil service was now entirely recruited through the examination system, but this, even so early, began to be very formal, relating to literature and philosophy, not to practical questions, as had been the case in the T'ang period. The scholars dominated government as much as literature and philosophy. Some of the greatest names in Sung literature are also the highest officials, the best known statesmen. They tended to divide not only into rival philosophic schools but also into rival parties, or factions. There was a conservative group, and an 'innovator' group. The latter tried to introduce new laws designed to meet some of the problems of the time: the provision of adequate defence against the northern dangers, the equalization of taxation, relief of famines and price control over basic necessities – all very modern problems, which were real enough to the Chinese of the Sung age. Their opponents disliked these measures, which they said had no foundation in the teaching of the early sages. Which was, of course, true, but not a very helpful criticism. The Emperors of the early Sung gave their confidence first to one party, then to another, or tried the ideas of both. Unlike earlier and later periods, those who fell out of favour were only banished to be provincial magistrates in some remote district, not put to death as traitors. The Sung were unusually humane for their age.

The peaceful, civilized conduct of affairs at home, where the pen was the weapon rather than the executioner's sword, reflected the pacific, even pacifist attitude of the Sung government in foreign affairs. After the failure of early attempts to reconquer the north-east, the Sung seemed content to keep peace, even to buy it, by 'gifts' which their northern rivals might well regard as something not far from tribute. The policy worked well enough for 150 years.

Calamity came in the reign of the Emperor Hui Tsung, who is also remembered as one of the greatest patrons of art in China and was himself a painter of the highest quality. He was not, perhaps on that account, a good ruler. He could not be bothered with the tiresome affairs of state. He was guided into foolish and provocative policies which brought a new invasion into China. In 1119 the Liao dynasty, reigning in Manchuria and the north-eastern corner of China, had been overthrown by a new power, the Nuchen tribe, who, arising in northern Manchuria, defeated the Liao and conquered their kingdom. They named the new state Chin, a Chinese translation of their word for Golden, and they also seized upon the north-eastern territory which the Liao had held. The Sung decided that if they had had to renounce this land to the Liao, it did not follow that they should leave it to the new Chin. An army was sent to recover the region. The Chin considered this area as their own, defeated the intruding Sung forces, and then followed up with a massive invasion of the Chinese Empire. The Sung defence collapsed, the capital, the modern K'aifeng in Honan province, was besieged and taken, and the Emperor died a captive in Manchuria. It was at this siege that the use of gunpowder is mentioned for the first time in Chinese history. It is not certain how many years earlier than this the invention had been made, but it would appear that the siege of K'aifeng in 1126 is the first recorded use of gunpowder in warfare.

The Southern Sung Dynasty (A.D. 1126–1279)

After the fall of the capital one of the Emperor's sons was able to set up the government in the south, choosing the city of Hangchou, now capital of Chekiang province, as temporary capital. The Sung hoped to recover the north, and the war continued for several years, but although they did recover the whole of the Yangtze valley, they were never able to drive the Chin dynasty out of north China. The war was finally brought to an end by the policy of a minister who has in later times been regarded as a traitor. This is because he made the peace policy prevail by bringing about the downfall and death of the hero of the Chinese resistance, the General Yueh Fei, whom later generations have glorified as the type of true patriot. The Sung held south China for another century and a half, and the traditions of the earlier period continued to be upheld. In art the 'Southern Sung', as this period is called, is just as renowned as the 'Northern Sung': it was also in the later period that the philosopher Chu Hsi lived and taught. The Chin, like other nomad invaders of the earlier centuries, very soon absorbed Chinese civilization, and in this respect there was little difference between north and south. From the cultural point of view, the Chin dynasty is simply rather provincial Sung; there is no essential difference in art, letters or thought.

But beyond the Chin a new, much more ferocious and formidable power was soon to appear, Genghiz Khan, the founder of the Mongol nation, was originally an obscure petty chief. By skilful wars against neighbouring tribes he built up a confederation of many tribes in the semi-desert region of Mongolia, and this name, and that of the Mongol people, derives from the name of his own small tribe, which after his victory became that of the whole people. In 1206 Genghiz became Great Khan of the Mongols; four years later he attacked and overthrew the Chin, taking Peking, their southern capital, in 1210. It was not until 1235, some years after the death of Genghiz Khan in 1227, that the Mongols, already masters of north China, invaded the Sung Empire in the south. They had destroyed the other northern state, Hsi Hsia, in 1224, devastating the land so utterly that it has never recovered, and the culture and even the language of the Hsi Hsia people was obliterated. The invasion of the south was fortunately less catastrophic – partly, no doubt, because a few years of experience of ruling vast areas of China inhabited by millions of people had taught the Mongols that the savage manners of the steppes were unsuitable for the government of civilized peoples. The dead can pay no taxes. Another reason was the difficult character of the southern countryside. The Mongols were essentially a nomadic horse-riding people, and south China, cut up by mountains, forests and waterways, is not suitable country for cavalry tactics. These reasons had hitherto prevented any nomad people from conquering the south, both in the early invasions of the fourth and fifth centuries, and in the recent Chin invasion. But the Mongols were far more powerful and persistent; they continued the war year after year, for more than forty years, until the Sung, driven even farther into the south of China, were finally annihilated in a sea battle off the coast of the present Hong Kong. This event, the final end of the Sung, occurred in 1279.

The Mongol Dynasty (A.D. 1279–1368)

The Chinese historians always count the years of a dynasty until the last year of the Emperor whom they regard as legitimate ruler. Thus the Sung are counted as lasting until A.D. 1279, and it is only after the death of the last of the Sung that the Mongol Emperors are acknowledged as legitimate rulers. In point of fact the Mongols had been masters of north China since 1206 – seventy years earlier. Their Empire had comprised the major part of China since the middle of the thirteenth century, and Kublai Khan, who was reigning when the Sung was finally defeated, had been on the throne at Peking for twenty years before the event. Thus when the Chinese historians claim that the Mongol rule only lasted eighty-eight years, this is only true if all China is meant; their rule in China, beginning in the northern half, endured for one and a half centuries.

The Mongols were an alien people, savage nomadic warriors when they first entered China, but, like all other invaders, they were rapidly influenced by their contact with the Chinese. At first their invasions were marked with enormous massacres, and the flight into the mountains of thousands of refugees. North China was laid waste; but before long the Mongols themselves began to understand that these conditions were doing them more harm than good. Slaughtering the Chinese and destroying cities and villages did not turn north China into good grazing land, as the Mongols seemed at first to expect. It turned it into a wilderness full of starving multitudes who wandered despairingly from region to region. They could not be taxed, for they had nothing to give; they could not be governed, for they had nowhere to live. Under the advice of a wise statesman who was himself a former official of the defunct Chin dynasty and a descendant of the royal house of the Khitan Liao dynasty, Yehlu Ch'u-ts'ai by name, Genghiz was persuaded to allow the Chinese peasantry of the north to settle down and cultivate the wasted lands, so that they could be taxed. His successors followed this policy, but their rule was alien and unwelcome to the Chinese.

Unlike all previous invaders, the Mongols, who ruled vast territories in Asia beyond China, did not employ the Chinese scholars as officials, or only to a limited degree. They preferred to enlist their subjects from distant countries, and even to employ foreigners from beyond their Empire. Thus China was governed by Persians, Central Asian Moslems, and other foreigners, including one famous in the West, the Venetian Marco Polo, who held provincial office under the Mongol Emperor for nearly twenty years. During the early Mongol period China was in fact only one very large province of a Mongol Empire which included all Central Asia, Persia, much of what is now Turkey, north India, and most of Russia. At their furthest, the Mongols invaded Poland, overran Hungary, and would have swept into Germany but for the fact that the death of the Great Khan recalled their generals to take part in the choice of his successor. Such was the terror that their invasions spread that the English merchants of the east coast resolved not to sail that year for the Baltic ports, lest they find the Mongols already there. The death of Mangu Khan marked the end of Mongol expansion (1260). The vast Empire covered so many races of mankind, with differing religions and customs, that the Great Khans had been compelled to appoint their sons and relatives to rule different parts of it. The western Khans, ruling in Persia, Turkey and Russia, became converted to Islam, the religion of most of their subjects. Some for a time seemed about to become Christians, and the Western Europeans had high hopes that they would be their allies against the Moslem powers in the Crusades. Meanwhile the eastern Mongols became Buddhists, including those who governed China. When Mangu died, the western Khans were unwilling to acknowledge the authority of the Buddhist Kublai who ruled in China. So the Mongol Empire was divided, and the further history of the western Khans had nothing to do with China.

Kublai, who ruled in Peking, is perhaps the best known name to Western people of any Emperor of China. 'Xanadu' has made his name a household word. Marco Polo was one of his officials, and his book, immensely popular in later centuries, and still well known, helped to make Kublai known to the peoples of Europe. Yet he was not a Chinese, and to the Chinese his reign was not so glorious as those of many of his T'ang or Sung predecessors. Marco Polo was tremendously impressed by the wealth of such cities as Hangchou, the former southern

Sung capital – far outstripping at that time any city of Europe. But in China Kublai was ruling over a defeated people, decimated by terrible massacres and governed by foreigners ignorant of their language, literature, religion and art. Marco Polo was a provincial governor, yet he clearly knew no Chinese although he did speak Mongol. His statements about Chinese customs are very inaccurate, his transcriptions of Chinese names come from Mongol. He knew nothing about Chinese history and called the south part of the country, the former Sung Empire, 'Manzay', which is a corruption of the Chinese word 'Mantzu', meaning a non-Chinese tribesman from the backward hill country of south China.

The examination system was discontinued, the Chinese scholar class was out of office, and the Mongol Emperors gave their favour to Buddhist monks from Tibet who introduced the Lamaist form of Buddhism, hitherto unknown in China. Under these conditions it is hardly surprising to find that the Chinese regarded the Mongol dynasty as alien and barbarian, and longed for a deliverance. After the death of Kublai in 1297 the Mongol dynasty produced no capable ruler. His successors were feeble and short-lived, until the last, who ruled for thirty years over an Empire rapidly sinking into great disorder.

Perhaps the most lasting contribution made by the Mongol dynasty was to fix the capital of China at Peking. In earlier times the capital, when the country was united, had been at Ch'angan, which is in Shensi province, or later at Loyang and K'aifeng, which are both in Honan province, in the middle basin of the Yellow River. It was the Liao and Chin who first made Peking one of their several capital cities. Kublai made it the sole capital of the Empire. Situated in the north China plain close to the three main passes through the mountain chain on which the Great Wall is built, and also commanding the old road to Manchuria (which avoided the then marshy coastal region where Tientsin now stands), Peking had, and has, great strategic importance for the control and security of north China. It had been the headquarters of the Northern Frontier Command in T'ang times. From the point of view of the Mongols it was close enough to their homeland to give them a sense of security: from the point of view of their Chinese successors it was essential to keep the main forces near the threatened northern frontier, and the government in touch with its problems. In modern times, the development of Manchuria and Inner Mongolia as the main industrial region of China makes Peking, which controls the access to this region from the rest of China, an even more important strategical centre. The Peking of Kublai Khan was built on almost the same site as the later city rebuilt by the Ming dynasty, but it was not quite so large. Some small remains of Kublai's palace and some of the city walls were incorporated by the Ming when they moved their capital, at first at Nanking, to Peking in 1405.

The Ming Dynasty (A.D. 1368–1644)

In the middle of the fourteenth century the Mongol rule, grown very corrupt and inefficient under the successors of Kublai, began to collapse. Rebellions broke out on all sides: the Chinese leaders of these movements did not agree together, and at first the Mongols were able to suppress the risings. But presently there arose in south-east China a leader of real capacity who step by step built up his power, defeated the rival rebels and enlisted their men, beat off the Mongols and finally captured Nanking. He then proclaimed himself Emperor of the Ming dynasty. Chu Yuan-chang, who founded the Ming, was a man of very obscure origin. His parents were famine refugees who sold him to a Buddhist monastery as a child to save his life. Later he fled from the monastery, became a beggar and then a bandit. From this he graduated into the ranks of rebellion, where he made his mark, culminating in the capture of Nanking in 1356. Twelve years later, having overthrown all competitors, his armies advanced on Peking, from which the last Mongol Emperor fled without offering resistance (1368). The Chinese historians count the Ming dynasty from this date.

When he died, thirty years later, Chu, who is known to history by his reign title of Hung Wu, left a China once more united under one dynasty, ruling from the Great Wall to the distant southern frontiers, now farther south than before. His generals had added the province of Yunnan to his realm, and established the frontier of China on the line at which it has subsequently remained. Annam, or Vietnam as it is now called, was a tributary: so was Korea. The Mongols had been pursued even into Siberia, and their power broken. Chinese rule was re-established in part of Central Asia, although, perhaps because the sea route had largely replaced the old caravan route to western Asia, the Ming never occupied the western part of what is now Chinese Turkestan, or Sinkiang. 'Rule like the T'ang and Sung' was the injunction to his successors which Hung Wu had engraved on a great stone at his tomb in Nanking. In the sense that the Ming restored the Chinese unitary Empire, they succeeded in following this counsel: but in many other respects it is doubtful whether the Ming achieved their aim. Their government was less humane than the Sung, and less efficient than the T'ang. They were unlucky in that after two reigns the throne was often occupied by children, which meant regencies and the growing power of the court eunuchs. But for more than half a century until the death of the Emperor Yung Lo in 1425, the power of the Ming was truly impressive.

Yung Lo, a son of the founder, and a very experienced general, dethroned his nephew, the son of his elder brother, who had died before Hung Wu. He moved the capital back to Peking, his own headquarters, and rebuilt the city. The present palace is his work, and so is the general plan of the old city, the walls and many of the famous buildings and temples. It is said that he employed a million men to build Peking and gave them ten years to do the job. They completed it in five. Even in Ming times the Chinese people could make 'Great Leaps' if sufficiently stimulated. Capable, autocratic, a magnificent and profuse builder, Yung Lo ruled his Empire with common sense and hard ability. He also undertook a new form of activity which previous Chinese Emperors had never considered. He built up a sea power. The story of the Ming overseas expeditions is a strange one, very little noticed in the Western world. There were altogether seven major expeditions sent out from China between 1405 and 1433. They were very large, carrying a force of seventy thousand men in specially built great ships, very much larger than the ordinary Chinese junks of commerce. The purpose of these voyages was to impress the kings of South-East Asia with the power of the Ming, to collect strange and curious treasures for the court and, it would seem, sheer interest in exploration.

The whole series were commanded by a certain Cheng Ho, who was a court eunuch, but a navigator of great skill and a commander of high competence. The first voyages, to what is now Malaysia and Indonesia, established Chinese suzerainty over these countries. The local kings paid tribute; some were brought back to do homage in Peking. Kings who refused were dethroned and subservient rivals installed in their places. These voyages were then extended to Ceylon, up the coasts of India, to Burma, and later to the Persian Gulf and Red Sea; finally to the east coast of Africa. It is at least possible, but not proved, that some of the Chinese ships touched the northern coasts of Australia. One object found near Darwin many years ago suggests that they did so. They certainly visited Timor, the nearest island of Indonesia. From Africa Cheng Ho brought back a live giraffe, the first ever seen in China. It was taken to Peking, where an artist painted its picture, and this work still survives. The flattering courtiers told Yung Lo that it was a Chi Lin, a fabulous animal said only to appear when the Empire was ruled by a sage. But Yung Lo, a hard-bitten old general, would not hear of such stuff. 'I am not a Sage, so this animal is no Chi Lin,' was all he replied.

Thus, sixty-four years before the Portuguese sailor Vasco da Gama rounded the Cape of Good Hope and discovered the Indian Ocean – with all the consequences this had for Europe, Asia and later Australia – the Chinese had made themselves masters of the Indian Ocean and could easily have established lasting and strong bases on its coasts. Had Chinese sea power been then maintained, it is very unlikely that the Portuguese could have challenged it effectively. The whole course of Asian history would have been very different, and the 'colonial era' in south and south-east Asia might never have come about.

The Chinese withdrew from this promising venture, which

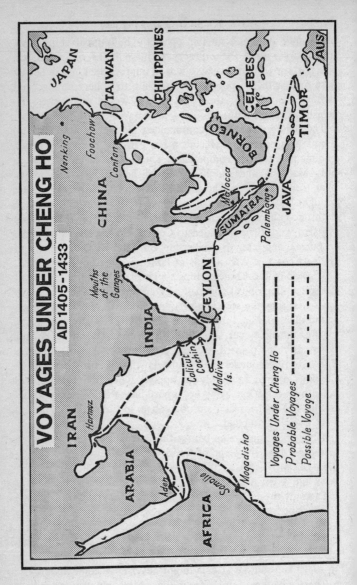

Map 2

they had begun so well, for reasons which now seem very insufficient. One of these was the jealousy of the civil service. The sea-borne expeditions were commanded by a court eunuch, and were outside the control of the regular civil service and the regular army. There was no such service as a regular navy, which might have established the maritime policy. So when Cheng Ho died, the pressure on the court to stop sending expeditions was very strong. The civil servants managed to lose (or more likely, to destroy) the sailing directions and other papers left by Cheng Ho. The court was preoccupied by new frontier troubles, and the revenue used for the expeditions was failing.

It had been argued that one reason why the court of Yung Lo could afford these huge expeditions, at a very great cost, from which there was little return in treasure, was that the Ming court had taken from the Mongol Emperors very great areas of land in eastern China which the Mongol rulers had kept empty and uncultivated as hunting grounds. The early Ming could settle farmers (and ex-soldiers) on this land, and sell it at a good profit. When this source of revenue gradually dried up, the expeditions had to be financed from the ordinary revenue over which the civil service had control. Thus their objections to the whole policy became more powerful and carried weight which could not be ignored. The expeditions were discontinued, the great ships were allowed to decay and never replaced, and Chinese sea power, for a while so formidable, disappeared. The Ming themselves, and later generations also, had cause to deplore the unwisdom of this withdrawal, which was not at that time due to any competition or opposition from foreign maritime powers.

It is in the Ming period that for the first time the problem of pressure upon the land by rising population begins to appear. By the zenith of the Sung dynasty, in the early twelfth century, the population was counted as about one hundred million. The Tartar and Mongol invasions probably checked the rise, if they did not positively reduce the total: Mongol administration was not good enough to return an accurate census. By the middle of the Ming period, the late fifteenth century, the population of the Empire was double that of the Sung (the area was also somewhat larger) and numbered some two hundred million people, by far the largest national community in the world. At this same time France, the most populous state in Europe, had probably not more than fifteen million inhabitants at the outside. The Ming, as has been mentioned, found large tracts of land held empty by the Mongol rulers. These were quickly settled, for the huge armies of the Ming had to be disbanded after the war was won. Hsu Ta, Hung Wu's general who took Peking, led a quarter of a million men on that campaign. The newly-conquered province of Yunnan, which in former dynasties had been an independent kingdom, received large numbers of Chinese settlers, whose descendants today form the basic Chinese population of the area. The fact that it was necessary to settle the ex-soldiers in special regions, not then fully inhabited, suggests that the ordinary provinces from which the soldiers had originally come were already finding land short. South Manchuria, which was part of the Ming Empire, also now received its first strong Chinese settlement. It is certain that in the later years of the dynasty, population pressure, and consequent famine and distress when bad years came, were among the main causes of the unrest which disturbed the Empire.

The Ming dynasty ruled China for 276 years: this is a long period, and because it is necessary to cover it in a short chapter it is easy to get the picture out of focus. The troubles of the later decades came slowly; for several generations China flourished and the achievements of the Ming in art, letters and the graces of civilization were very great. The porcelain industry, begun in the T'ang period, developed in the Sung, now became one of the major achievements of the Ming. It is not only because so much more Ming porcelain has survived the passage of time, it is also the high quality of all their work, not only the pieces produced for the court (as in Sung times), that makes Ming porcelain so famous. When the Western nations began to trade with China, they imported Ming wares. China, the land where 'China' came from, was known best to them for that reason, and the name of the country was adopted for its chief product. Very little of the architecture of earlier dynasties survives to the present day, but Ming buildings, from the palaces of Peking to the temples and even the private houses of wealthy men in all parts of China, are common. Consequently Ming architecture is what we now know as Chinese architecture, and there is reason to believe that it was greatly developed during this dynasty.

It has been said that although the Ming achievements in art and literature were great, they were only carrying on a tradition begun in earlier times, without much original contribution of their own. This is certainly to some extent true: Chinese civilization had been cast in a pattern by the T'ang, which the Sung developed and the Ming restored. But much of the judgement which we can make on earlier Chinese culture depends on Ming work. Their paintings are far more plentiful than the surviving Sung and exceedingly rare T'ang pictures; their literature preserved the work of earlier times, and enriched it. It is also true that after the experience of the Mongol conquest the mood of the Ming period was more exclusively Chinese than before: foreigners had anciently been barbarians; the Mongols, the most recent foreign conquerors, were certainly savage and barbarous when they invaded China, alien and hostile while they ruled it. The Chinese in the Ming period became inclined to see all foreigners in their image; dangerous and unwelcome people whom it was best to keep out of China. When, in the middle of the Ming dynasty, Japanese pirates disturbed the coastal provinces, and the rising power of the Manchu people beyond the Great Wall began to threaten the northern frontier, the Chinese were less inclined to give a free welcome to the Western navigators who now for the first time appeared off her coasts and sought to open up trade.

It was perhaps unfortunate that these Western visitors were at first only the Portuguese. That nation had had a long experience of wars against the Moslems of their own country, and later in North Africa and the Mediterranean. They had a strong bias against 'infidels' and when they came into the Indian Ocean, and established bases in such places as Goa and later Malacca, they continued to find Moslems as the main foes. The ancient quarrel continued in a new setting. So the Portuguese had developed a special kind of imperialism: they traded when they were still too weak to conquer, and sought to conquer when trade had given them a sufficient opportunity. In China they at first acted in this way, trying to seize ports and bases. The Ming government reacted strongly, and the Portuguese were driven away. They came back, and were allowed to trade under strict rules and troublesome supervision. This set a pattern which was later applied to other Western foreign peoples as they arrived: first the Dutch, later the English. In earlier dynasties the Arabs, the principal foreign traders, had lived in peace with the Chinese. There had been very large Arab trading settlements, under Chinese rule, in such ports as Canton and Ch'uanchou, in Fukien province. The Chinese histories make little mention of them (which proves that they gave no trouble), but Arab historians have left some record of these settlements. After the Portuguese came, the Arab trade dwindled and disappeared.

It was in the early years of the sixteenth century, between 1517 and 1522, that the Portuguese first touched at the southern ports of China, and came into conflict with the local authorities. Later, incidents occurred throughout the first half of the sixteenth century until in 1577 a solution was found by confining the Portuguese to the single port of Macao, from which they were allowed to trade during some months of the year at Canton, farther up the delta of the Pearl River. It was not until many years after the traders had appeared in China that the missionaries followed in their footsteps. Consequently the first, and lasting, impression which the Chinese received of these 'Ocean Barbarians' was that they were ferocious, untrustworthy and turbulent. The missionaries did not reach Canton until 1575, for St Francis Xavier, the first to try to enter the Chinese field, died on a small island near Macao in 1552 without setting foot on the Chinese mainland. At the very end of the sixteenth century Father Matteo Ricci was able to travel to Peking, present gifts to the Emperor and was permitted to reside in the capital.

A very few years later the Portuguese found their monopoly

of the China trade challenged by the arrival of the Dutch and then the English. These nations were Protestant, and their competition was unwelcome to the Portuguese, who endeavoured, not without success, to give their rivals a bad name with the Chinese. Dutch and English captains were almost as ready to resort to violence, indeed to plain piracy, as the Portuguese themselves, so the Chinese found it easy to believe what they were told. But by the time the English and Dutch were arriving at Chinese ports the Ming dynasty was nearing its final crisis.

After Ricci had arrived in Peking, a number of other scholarly missionaries, all Roman Catholics, reached China, and won a place which was steadily denied to the traders. The missionaries were highly educated men : they had a better knowledge of mathematics than the Chinese scholars, and they gave valuable assistance in correcting errors in the calendar, devising astronomical instruments, and later in casting cannon and training artillerymen. These activities were not exactly the purpose for which the missionaries had come to China, but they were what the Chinese found useful and helpful from these foreigners. In the hope that acceptance as scientists would in time make them heeded as religious teachers, the missionaries were ready to supply these skills. But the Chinese remained as indifferent to their religious message as they were eager to profit from their scientific knowledge. At this time the Protestant nations, although beginning to trade with China, made no attempt to convert the Chinese people. More than a century was to pass before the first Protestant missionaries arrived in China.

The Ming dynasty began to lose strength in the middle of the sixteenth century. Corruption was widespread in the civil service, and the greed and extortion of the court eunuchs magnified this evil. In 1510 one of these, whose wealth excited general envy, was finally arrested by the Emperor and his estate confiscated. It amounted to a vast sum, 251,583,600 ounces of unminted silver, a great quantity of gold, precious stones and a magnificent residence. By any standard he was a millionaire, and his wealth had all been acquired by bribery

CHINA

and peculation. At the same time, the inventory of his estate
proves how wealthy China then was if such a vast fortune
could be acquired by one man. The last effective Emperor of
the Ming was Wan Li who ruled from 1572 to 1620. Proof
exists that the wealth of the Empire was still great even though
during this reign rebellions were beginning to disturb the
peace. Wan Li's tomb near Peking was recently excavated, and
found intact. It contains an enormous treasure of gold, silver,
jade, porcelain and the remains of fine silks and embroidery.
The value of the treasures buried with the Emperor has been
calculated as exceeding half a million sterling. These objects
are now displayed in the Peking Palace Museum.

The death of Wan Li occurred only two years after an important change had occurred in the northern regions beyond
the Great Wall. During the Ming dynasty the area which was
later called Manchuria had been under Ming suzerainty. The
southern part of the country as far north as Mukden was part
of the Ming province of Shantung, now confined to the peninsula of that name on the south side of the Yellow Sea. Northern
Manchuria was inhabited by Tartar tribes, related to the Nuchen of Sung times who had set up the Chin dynasty in north
China until destroyed by the Mongols. The Manchu tribes were
in close contact with China and under fairly close Chinese
supervision. They thus learned to organize, and acquired some
knowledge of Chinese civilization. By the end of the sixteenth
century they were no longer a barbarous people.

The rise of the Manchus in this region is an example of a
slow change in the northern regions which had begun to appear ever since the early Sung period. The north-east – what
foreigners later called Manchuria (the Chinese name for this
region is Tung Pei, the 'North-East') became more important
than the true Mongolian steppe directly north of China beyond
the Wall. It is uncertain whether the cause of this change was
partly climatic, a drying up of Mongolia, or mainly due to the
agricultural possibilities of Manchuria, which the inhabitants
learned to develop from contact with China. Perhaps the latter
explanation is the more probable. It is certain that from the
time of the Liao and Chin formidable states could be organized

100

in Manchuria, while Mongolia remained essentially a country of nomadic tribes. In 1618 the Manchu tribes found a leader of great political skill and military ability, named Nurhachu, who welded them into a unified nation, established his kingdom in the central part of the country, the modern province of Kirin, and declared his independence of the Ming Emperor. Wars followed, in which the Manchus were able to extend their state over the southern part of Manchuria, the Chinese-inhabited region. This greatly added to their strength and to the stability of the new state. By 1629 they had spread their rule right down to the Great Wall, but the formidable character of these defences seemed likely to prevent them advancing farther.

Two Manchu rulers – later dignified with the posthumous titles of Emperor – had ruled the new state, but at the death of the second, the throne passed, in 1643, to his young son, still a minor. This was not the moment when a Manchu invasion of the Ming Empire could be expected. But in the year 1644 the Ming dynasty had been overthrown by an internal rebellion. The rebel leader, originally a bandit, with an army swollen by famine refugees, had long been active in the north-west of China. The court, since the death of the Emperor Wan Li, had been racked with intrigues and conspiracies which had cost the life of one Emperor and finally enthroned a feeble youth who was entirely in the hands of the palace eunuchs. The rebel invaded Honan province in 1640, overran it, and then sweeping north-westward, appeared before Peking which had been left almost undefended, as the main army of the north was on the Manchu frontier. Li Tzu-ch'eng, the rebel, captured the city without a struggle. The last Ming Emperor took his own life in the palace gardens (the spot is still shown), deserted by his faithless court.

The Shun Dynasty and the Manchu Dynasty
(A.D. 1644–1911)

Li at once proclaimed himself Emperor, calling his dynasty the Shun. But it did not last very long. His victory depended on the attitude of the general commanding the main Ming army, stationed on the Great Wall at Shanhaikuan, the gateway to Manchuria. Wu San-kuei, who commanded this force, was not particularly loyal to the fallen Ming. He was, no doubt, like other high commanders and officials, disgusted and weary with the corruption and folly of the eunuch-ridden court. But he was not very willing to submit to the claims of a bandit rebel leader, a man of no education. His doubts were turned to open enmity by the unwise conduct of the rebel, who took into his own harem a concubine of Wu's who happened to be in the capital when it fell. Li Tzu-ch'eng refused to restore the young lady, Wu San-kuei refused to acknowledge the new dynasty: instead he called in the Manchus. It is probable that he believed that this device would simply permit him to withdraw his army, drive out Li Tzu-ch'eng and establish himself as Emperor, after which he could get rid of the Manchus.

It did not work out in this way. The Manchus accepted his offer, and swiftly moved in: Wu defeated Li Tzu-ch'eng, but continued his pursuit after the rebel had fled from Peking, leaving the Manchus to occupy the capital and proclaim their own ruler as Emperor of China. A long and complicated war followed. The Ming were for a time re-established in the south, in Nanking, and perhaps hoped, like the Sung before them, to hold south China even if they could not recover the north. Wu destroyed the rebel Li, but continued, as a prince under Manchu suzerainty, to attack the Ming. Other pretenders arose in various provinces, while the Manchus quietly concentrated on consolidating their rule in the north and then steadily advancing southward, leaving Wu San-kuei to deal with the rebellions in the west of China. After eighteen years of warfare the last Ming pretender was driven into Burma, and the Manchu dynasty was nominally acknowledged as sovereign in all mainland China; but not in Taiwan, or Formosa, where a Ming partisan, the naval commander Cheng Cheng-kung (called by the Portuguese and Dutch 'Coxinga' from a corruption of his title) reigned as an independent king. Thus the separation of Taiwan at the fall of a mainland government – today one of the chief problems of the Far East – has its precedent in what happened at the fall of the Ming just three hundred years earlier.

South China remained under three Chinese princes, one of whom, the most powerful, was Wu San-kuei. The Manchus did not rule directly south of the Yangtze. This uneasy situation continued for several years. It was not until 1673 that the inevitable contest for final power broke out. In that year the southern princes, led by Wu San-kuei, revolted, and a bitter struggle followed. Had Wu himself not died during the war, leaving the leadership to sons far less competent, it is probable that the Manchus would never have conquered south China, and might not have retained the north either. As it was, after nine years the young Emperor K'ang Hsi was able to destroy all his rivals, and in 1682, nearly forty years after their occupation of Peking, the Manchu dynasty at last ruled over all China.

The Manchu Dynasty (A.D. 1682–1911)

This was a foreign conquest of China, and in the south, which resisted so long and so nearly successfully, the Manchus were always felt to be alien and oppressive. In the north this attitude was far less marked. The Manchus had not conquered this area, they had been invited in. Their arrival was not marked with massacres and slaughter to leave an evil memory. The Manchus, also, were already very much under Chinese cultural influence and it was naturally the ways and speech of north China which had prevailed among them. They soon lost the ordinary use of their language, although they made great efforts to preserve it, including the invention of a script derived from Sanskrit. But before many generations had passed, the common speech of Manchus was Chinese, the dialect of the north, which has been usually called 'Mandarin'.

They had owed their rise to a system of military organization called the Eight Banners. Every man was enrolled in a Banner, had the duty to serve in war and the right to rations from his Banner. When the Manchus conquered the Chinese-inhabited area of south Manchuria, they enrolled these Chinese in two new Banners (there were originally six), so that even

among the so-called Manchus of the dynasty there was in fact
a large proportion of north Chinese. This organization was kept
intact after the conquest, and the Bannermen ('Ch'i Jen' in
Chinese) became the common name for Manchus. The Bannermen were settled around Peking to protect the capital, and also
in large garrisons, each with its own inner walled city, in the
principal provincial capitals. They were forbidden to engage in
commerce or agriculture, serving purely as military and civil
officials. This law was designed to keep them as a reserve military force ready to save the dynasty in case of rebellion. In
practice it worked out badly as time went on, for the idle
Bannermen, drawing rations, but doing no work, became sloth-
ful, useless parasites, who even lost their military skill as a
long peace gave them no opportunity to use it.

All this was still far in the future when the young K'ang Hsi
began a reign which lasted for sixty years. The Manchu Empire
which he consolidated, and later extended far into Mongolia
and Central Asia, was in his reign the largest and most populous empire in the world. For nearly a hundred and fifty years,
until the end of the eighteenth century, there was practically
unbroken peace in the provinces of the Empire, a situation
which had not been seen since T'ang and Sung times. The population grew rapidly under these conditions and seems to have
almost doubled until it reached more than three hundred million. But the Manchu Bannermen were only a tiny fragment
of this huge number. It is doubtful whether the Manchus ever
exceeded ten million.

A dynasty supported by so small a minority ran two opposing risks: either it retained its foreign character, relying on its
Manchu followers, and then would certainly, sooner or later,
incur the fate of the Mongols, and rouse an immense, overwhelming Chinese reaction. Or it must accommodate itself to
the views and ways of the Chinese majority: rely on Chinese
officials, adopt Chinese customs, patronize Chinese learning.
The Manchu monarchs made a skilful compromise with these
two policies. They retained their own people in a military
organization, which for some generations really supported
their power. They divided the civil service between Manchus

and Chinese, on an equal basis. This gave the Manchus a great advantage, since they were few and the Chinese very many. It was much easier for a Manchu to pass into the service, and gain one of the reserved places, than for a Chinese faced with tremendous competition. This naturally meant that the successful Chinese were better scholars and better brains than the Manchus. The Manchu Emperors were keen patrons of Chinese art and literature, provided there was no subversive character to the literature. But they exercised a vigorous censorship, and suppressed many books which they deemed anti-Manchu. They also tried to keep their own language alive: all official documents had to be written in both languages, inscriptions were in the two scripts, Chinese works of history and philosophy were translated into Manchu. This continued to the end of the dynasty, but long before that Manchu was virtually a dead language which Manchus themselves had to learn at school.

Every Manchu Bannerman, of whatever rank, was regarded as the personal servant of the Emperor. Chinese officials were, of course, bound by an oath of loyalty also, but they acted as officials; Manchus were also personal followers, in a more intimate relation to the throne. This gave the Manchu Emperors a greater and more autocratic power than had normally been exercised by Chinese Emperors. When the throne was held by men of great ability, such as the three Emperors K'ang Hsi, Yung Cheng and Ch'ien Lung, whose reigns covered the second half of the seventeenth and all the eighteenth centuries, this system worked well enough. The Emperor was all-powerful: the court was less troubled by intrigue than under many Chinese dynasties, and the Manchus avoided one peril by refusing to appoint any son of the ruler as Crown Prince until the Emperor was dying. He then wrote the name of his successor on a piece of paper, which was sealed and opened immediately he was dead. Should he recover, he could destroy this 'Will' unread. No faction could thus be formed round a Crown Prince, no rival faction to promote the cause of another brother. In this way, the Manchu court for long escaped from many of the dangers which had faced earlier dynasties. Had they maintained their own rules, they might have saved the throne.

To keep their armies in battled-trained condition, the first Manchu Emperors undertook extensive wars along the northern frontier, and also to the north-west. Under K'ang Hsi and his two successors, Yung Cheng and Ch'ien Lung, all Mongolia was reduced to Manchu rule; the great region of Sinkiang, which China had not controlled since T'ang times, was conquered and made into a Manchu province; Tibet was invaded and brought under Chinese suzerainty; Korea and Annam were tributaries, as was Burma and even Siam. Late in the eighteenth century the armies of Ch'ien Lung invaded and conquered Nepal. The Chinese Empire had never been so extensive nor so populous. In addition to these large conquests the Manchus also retained their ancestral kingdom, in the north-east, which included what is now the Maritime Province of Russian Siberia, although this far-off country was but sparsely inhabited.

One great consequence of Manchu expansion was the ending, for all time, of the ancient menace of the nomad tribes from Mongolia who had so often invaded China. The Manchus conquered them, while to the north the Russians were occupying Siberia and Central Asia, thus cutting off the nomad peoples from the great steppes to which they had always withdrawn when Chinese power was too strong. With peace established within the region of China itself, and the nomad enemies conquered and pacified, there remained no wars to wage. The army began to decay. Convinced of their own superiority, the Manchu rulers saw no need to modernize, did not appreciate the fact that Western forces were growing stronger and developing more lethal weapons. They took no interest in naval power. The south had always been unrestful and disloyal : it was from the south that naval forces would have to be raised, and this could give rebels an opportunity. It had taken the Manchus many years to gain control of Taiwan (Formosa) defended by the Ming partisan, and later king, Cheng Cheng-kung (Coxinga). Only when his grandsons quarrelled did the Manchus get the chance to intervene and seize the island. A land people, whose warrior Emperors had experience of war only in the vast inland regions of northern Asia, the Manchus neglected the sea and its possible dangers. Japan, in the period of her voluntary seclusion, was no menace. The European nations seemed far away and in the eighteenth century were pre-occupied with their own wars and quarrels. Although the British were then conquering India, the Manchus seem to have ignored the implied threat to their own Empire. Their successors were to pay dearly for this failure to move with the times.

It is an irony of history that the later troubles of the Manchu dynasty were largely caused by the overwhelming successes of their own early Emperors. The long peace bred a huge population which outran the resources of the country, and unbalanced the agricultural economy. The successful wars removed the dangers of the frontier which had kept the armies of earlier dynasties, even of the Ming, in fighting form. The need to keep the Chinese literate class loyal made the Manchus the patrons of conservative Confucianism, and shut their minds to the need for change and reform in a world which was changing very rapidly. They were too successful, too powerful at home, too rich and too self-satisfied. By the end of the eighteenth century, the perceptive Lord Macartney, the first British Ambassador to be received by the Chinese court, could see that behind the façade of the magnificent court and the venerable Emperor Ch'ien Lung, then in his eighties, there was weakness and decay. Macartney, like other Western visitors, was impressed by the power of the throne, its wealth, the range of its control over the provinces; but he equally saw the technical backwardness of China, the lack of modern improvements, the bad roads, the contrast between rich and poor. He saw that under less able successors the Empire would soon develop serious failings. All these things were to come about within a generation of the death of Ch'ien Lung. The end of the eighteenth century was also the end of China's power and the beginning of a swift decline.

CHAPTER FOUR

The Origin and Development of the Chinese Revolution

(A.D. 1800–1950)

THE nineteenth century was in China the exact opposite of what it was to Europe, America and Australia. For the Western peoples it was the great century of progress, when scientific discovery altered the whole condition of mankind, the century which saw the rise of liberty and democracy, the creation of the modern world and the settlement of the empty continents. In China it was the century when the great Empire swiftly and fatally declined, when the ancient codes and ways were proved useless or inadequate but no new ones came to take their place; when order collapsed and famines became frequent, and, above all, when the country was attacked and invaded by foreign powers, lost large territories and suffered great loss of prestige and power. The Empire of Ch'ien Lung (died 1798) was huge, intact, magnificent and apparently powerful. It had just conquered Nepal by a most difficult campaign across the Himalayas. In 1900 it was invaded by the foreign powers, unable to defend its capital, and very nearly suffered complete partition at their hands.

What, then, had happened to China, which made her story so different, her fate so tragic? Many causes contributed to the decline. But it is only since that process has been reversed, and China is once more a powerful and organized state, that some of them have become apparent and the real character of the period can be seen. In modern times men will often first look at the economy of a country to see why things are not going well, or why such a country is strong. The Chinese economy had been purely self-contained until late in the eighteenth century

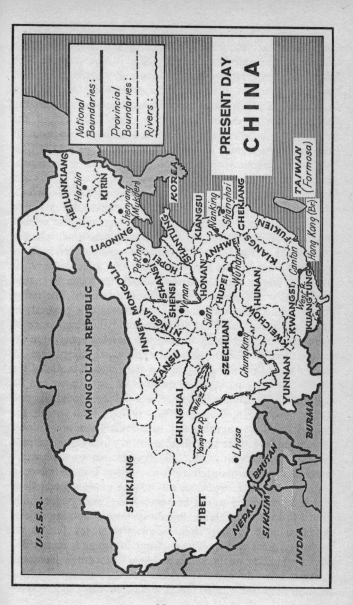

Map 3

and did not become seriously affected by outside factors till the middle of the nineteenth century. But it was stagnant. The population grew rapidly but the area under agriculture could not grow; there was little land left vacant. New crops had been introduced in the previous centuries, such as sweet potato, the ordinary potato, cotton and maize. These had helped the growth of population, but had not led to the development of industry. Foreign trade was restricted to the single port of Canton, hedged about with many obstacles and tiresome regulations. It consisted mainly in the export of Chinese tea, silk and ceramics, and the import of Western cotton and woollen cloth, and, later, opium. Industry was not developing: the invention of steam power was ignored, mining remained simple and shallow, coal was little used for fuel, and handicraft industry remained the only method of producing consumer goods.

Only a few decades before all these conditions were to be found in Europe also, but in the West things began to change very rapidly at the end of the eighteenth century. The ruling classes in the West welcomed and promoted this progress; in China the ruling class neither understood the importance of these questions nor believed that such developments were desirable. The Confucian philosophy, in which they were all trained taught them that China was the civilized centre of the world: the arts and sciences, methods of government and literature of China were the only arts, sciences, methods and letters which counted as civilized – nothing from outside the Empire could be anything but barbarous. Therefore Chinese ways were best, were indeed the only ways that civilized men could follow. Western visitors like Lord Macartney were astonished at the lack of interest shown by the Chinese court in various scientific instruments and other European productions which he presented to the Emperor. The Chinese were conditioned to treat these things as curios, strange, amusing objects produced by barbarians from far-away countries. Just as we might recognize that a poisoned arrow blowpipe is more efficient as a hunting weapon than a shotgun (since it is silent and does not scare the game away) but yet never dream of taking to blowpipes and discarding shotguns, so the Chinese were amused by clocks and chronometers but did not dream of trying to start a precision instrument industry themselves.

The Chinese economy stood in urgent need of reform and progress; had this been undertaken promptly, even if gradually, China would have escaped her catastrophes. But the ruling class were quite unable to see this need, were trained to think on opposite lines, to believe that a return to the past, or at least the preservation of everything ancient and well tried, was the right policy. Reform could only lead to chaos, foreign contact could only lead to unrest and should be shut out as far as possible. In the T'ang dynasty, or even the Sung period, this policy would have made some sense. Then China really was far superior to her neighbours, near and far. Then she had little or nothing to learn from foreign contacts and good reason to keep barbarians out of the country. But that, in point of fact, was not the attitude of the T'ang or even of the Sung. They maintained as wide a contact with the outside world as their resources and communications could sustain; they welcomed and, indeed, recorded information of far-off countries. It is evident that in the nineteenth century the Chinese suffered from something deeper than a mere cultural superiority complex.

The trouble lay in the fact that the dynasty was alien, was Manchu not Chinese. The Manchus feared, all through their rule, that they would end as the Mongols had ended, driven out by a great Chinese revolt. The best way to prevent this, the only way, was to win the approval and support of the Chinese leadership, which might otherwise go over to the ranks of rebellion. They knew that the south was disaffected, had never really accepted the Manchus and had been the last region to submit. The foreigners traded with the southern ports, their contacts were with the southern people, and the court feared that from these contacts the rebellious southerners would draw strength and encouragement. They were, of course, quite right. It was precisely in the south that the influence of Western technology, thought and even religion made its first and deepest impression. It was also in the south that the first great rebellions against the Manchus broke out; the southerners certainly were influenced by foreign ideas. It was there also that the final revolution started.

The Manchus were not imagining a danger, they were trying to counter a very real peril. They believed that the strict maintenance of the old ideas, the Confucian teaching, the imperial system, with rewards for the able Chinese officials and careers for the educated class, would draw this class close to the throne, deprive the rebels of leadership and so contain the dangers of foreign contact. Such contacts, also, must be kept to a minimum. This meant that the whole technology and science of the West must be excluded, for it would let in Western thought and encourage revolutionaries while putting the Confucian gentry out of office and straining their loyalty. So the policy of the government must be rigidly conservative. These ideas were at least logical if one accepted the great first premise – that the Chinese civilization was not only superior to that of the rest of the world, but could continue to flourish without contact, or with very little contact, with the outside world. But that premise was no longer valid.

The Manchus did in fact keep the loyalty of the great bulk of the Confucian-trained Chinese gentry far into the days of their last decline. Among the last most faithful servants of the throne the most distinguished were not northerners, but actually Cantonese, whose fellow provincials were at that very time the chief leaders of revolution. In this sense the ultra-conservative policy succeeded all too well. But what was not understood was the fact that the loyalty of such conservative scholars was no longer a strength but a weakness to the dynasty and to China. These cultivated but completely isolated people had no conception of what policy to propose when crisis after crisis struck the Empire. They could quote the classics, consider the history of the T'ang or the Han, but they had no understanding of the world in which China now lived. They could not appreciate the dangers of estranging powerful maritime nations, nor could they understand that the power of these nations grew from advancing technology and scientific knowledge.

In this age the long isolation of China, her unique standing as the centre of a civilization with no close competitors, which had moulded her thought and institutions, became her greatest weakness. To change needed a violent wrench, a repudiation of the whole background of Chinese life, recognition of facts which the educated class had been trained to ignore or deny. It would have been difficult, but certainly not impossible, to carry out the reforms, change the attitude of the people, and remodel the Chinese system to suit modern conditions if the leadership of the sovereign had been exerted in this direction. Just as was done in Japan, with the Emperor Meiji using his prestige as a semi-divine monarch to carry on what was really a revolution, so a Chinese Emperor of sufficient capacity and strength of will, a T'ang T'ai Tsung or a Han Emperor Wu, could have given this lead. But there was not a Chinese Emperor: the ruler was a Manchu, and he and his dynasty were mortally afraid of revolutionary change. If they took that course, the conservative Confucians would treat them as barbarians, unfit to rule, to be driven out; they would lose all support, and be engulfed. It is possible that they might have been mistaken in this fear, but they certainly felt it and dreaded to make any experiment until it was too late.

The consequence of these fears and hesitations was that the Manchu dynasty rejected reform as dangerous, resisted foreign contacts when they were strong, and gave way only when forced by superior power, and then reluctantly, with ill will and bad faith. It was also perhaps unfortunate for them and China that the dynasty was already well past its zenith when the full weight of the foreign impact came to China. The days of Ch'ien Lung were gone, and his successors were weaker, less intelligent men, ill-fitted by training or mental powers to cope with a dangerous crisis. The extreme centralization of the imperial authority which great and capable rulers like K'ang Hsi, Yung Cheng and Ch'ien Lung had brought about, was a handicap to weak, incapable successors. Nothing could be done without the Emperor, but if the Emperor did not know what to do or had the wrong policy, then everything that was done was mistaken or unwise or just incompetently performed.

The foreign powers were at first only interested in trade.

They wanted more ports open to their merchants, a freer system than the regulated Canton trade, a way of dealing directly with the Chinese government through an embassy in Peking – fair tariffs and freedom to travel in the interior of China. All these things were refused. Such increased contacts would stir up trouble in the south. An ambassador in Peking was unheard of, only tribute-bearing missions came and went after a short stay, loaded with valuable presents to show the Emperor's magnanimous treatment of loyal subordinates.

In the nineteenth century foreign businessmen were not too ready to consider moral restraints on trade. When the British found they were paying out silver for Chinese products, but could not sell their own cloth profitably, they turned about till they found something the Chinese did want and would buy. That was opium. It was produced in India: if it was shipped to China in what were called 'country ships', that is, ships not controlled or owned by the East India Company (the sovereign authority in India at that time), then the East India Company did not have to take steps to stop a trade which the Chinese soon declared to be illegal. This, the British contended, was hypocritical on the part of the Chinese government. They did not care, it was said, about the harm opium smoking might do to the people; they cared about the loss of the silver formerly paid in to buy Chinese silk and tea, now balanced by the sale of opium. The British government did not deny that the Chinese government could prohibit the import of opium; they merely said that the British government could not control what was carried in the free ships of free merchants. The Chinese, with their own ideas on the subject of such freedoms, thought this very hypocritical.

In 1839 the long-smouldering dispute broke out into war. The Chinese sent down an upright official who genuinely believed that opium was a harmful drug and was determined to suppress the trade. He confiscated huge stocks and burned them at Canton. The British merchants demanded compensation, trade was disrupted and the two countries drifted into war. It was disastrous to the Chinese and the Manchu Empire. The Bannermen were shown to be militarily useless, if brave. They defended Canton, but were annihilated. The British also took Nanking. Their ships enabled them to go where they pleased on the sea and the Chinese had no navy in a modern sense. Peace was made which conceded almost all the British demanded. The opium trade was legalized, the Canton system abolished, other ports were opened up, Hong Kong was ceded to Britain as a base, British subjects were no longer to be subject to Chinese law; they were to have a concession area in Canton in which to live, and concessions in other ports as they were opened up. The Chinese still managed to reject the demand for a resident ambassador in Peking. This was the first of what the Chinese came to call the 'Unequal Treaties'. It was a model which other foreign powers, France and the U.S.A., used to win similar privileges from China.

There can be no doubt that the war and the peace treaty dealt a mortal blow to the prestige of the dynasty. Small forces of foreign troops had invaded the Empire at many points; they had taken great, important, cities. The Manchu troops had been unable to defend the country; they had proved useless. The Emperor had had to yield concessions and territory to the invaders. Before long the restless Chinese of the south had absorbed the lesson: the time had come when a great rebellion had a real chance of victory.

The T'ai P'ing Rebellion (A.D. 1851–1864)

The T'ai P'ing rebellion was the most formidable challenge that the Manchu dynasty had to face. In some ways it can be regarded as just another of the long cycle of rebellions which had assailed dynasties in decline. Its leader was a familiar type, the failed candidate for the civil service examinations. Hung Hsiu-ch'uan was also a southerner, and moreover a Hakka, a member of a community believed to be descended from northern refugees who had taken refuge in the southern provinces at the time of the Mongol invasions of the thirteenth century. They had never been fully accepted by the older southern population and remained a rather under-privileged group. The rebellion enlisted landless peasants, famine and flood refugees and gave expression to the deep unrest which a failing agricultural economy had produced in a large part of the country. All this is familiar from earlier times: equally familiar in some respects was the sequel. The T'ai P'ing armies, first taking up arms in the far south in 1851, swept northward through Hunan province, where they failed to take the capital, Ch'angsha, but captured Nanking, the southern capital of the Empire, in 1853.

A determined effort to push northwards might well have driven the Manchus, demoralized by these disasters, out of China. But the T'ai P'ing leader made the mistake of sending only small armies towards Peking, which, lacking support, had to fall back when within a hundred miles of the capital. This gave the court a breathing space in which to organize new forces. A long war followed, ending in the suppression of the T'ai P'ing movement and the recapture of Nanking (1864). A rebellion which had shaken the dynasty, but failed to over-throw it, was usually the prelude to developments which finally brought the ruling dynasty down. Just as Huang Ts'ao's rebellion against the failing T'ang had led to the final anarchy of that dynasty, but had itself failed, so the T'ai P'ing Rebellion ushered in a period of increasing and rapid decline in the power of the Manchus. To suppress the T'ai P'ings they had to raise large new armies, and these armies were Chinese, commanded by Chinese. The Bannermen proved useless and the whole burden of the war was carried by the new Chinese armies. This fundamentally altered the standing of the dynasty: from now on they really ruled by the consent of the Chinese, or at least with the essential support of the Chinese who had raised and commanded the armies which defended the throne. These leaders became the real arbiters of policy: ultimately their successors, the commanders of the Chinese armies, were to be the instruments of the revolution which dethroned the dynasty.

In this sense the T'ai P'ing movement and its sequel were in the traditional pattern of dynastic change. But there were other aspects to the T'ai P'ing movement which were quite contrary to the familiar pattern and which clearly reflected the new forces that Western contacts had brought to China. Hung Hsiu-ch'uan, who was later styled the Heavenly King, was a convert to Christianity: not, indeed, to any regular Western sect or church, but a man who had read the Bible in the early translations made by the first Protestant missionaries, had also, during an illness, experienced visions which he believed confirmed his reading of the Bible and pointed to him as the chosen instrument of God to convert the Chinese people, drive out the Manchus and establish a Christian empire in their place. His movement began as a religious sect and turned into an armed rebellion as it gathered followers and incurred the hostility and opposition of the local authorities. Throughout the decade of T'ai P'ing power in the south and west centre of China, the religious aspect of the movement was the dominant characteristic. It was this which largely caused their ultimate failure: T'ai P'ing Christianity made no appeal to conservative Confucian scholars. This class remained opposed, and rallied to the throne.

The Chinese officials and scholars who raised loyalist armies – Tseng Kuo-fan, Tso Tsung-t'ang and Li Hung-chang – were Confucian scholars: thousands of lesser men of this stamp supported them. The Manchu conservative policy at least succeeded to the extent that when given the choice between a Chinese national rising which was anti-Confucian and an alien dynasty which conformed to Confucian views, the Confucian scholar class as a whole and with very few exceptions backed the throne. The fact that the rebels were a kind of Christian reinforced all the conservative fears concerning the danger of foreign contacts and influence. Here were the fruits of missionary endeavour; rebellion, a new, subversive creed, the destruction of temples, the overthrow of the scholar class. The missionaries themselves were by no means so sure that the T'ai P'ing movement represented the fruit of their labours. Hung had not been baptized or instructed by any missionary: he made claims – to be a prophet in his own right, to have direct inspiration from God, and to vary the teaching of Christianity (of which he had only an imperfect knowledge) – which were clearly unacceptable and highly inconvenient and embarrassing to the missionary churches.

The missionaries found the situation very difficult. They could not but feel encouraged that any form of Christianity had gained so large a following and seemed likely to sweep the Manchus out of China; they were well received, accepted as brothers in religion by the T'ai P'ings themselves. But the claims and assumptions of the Heavenly King were too much. To accept him would involve such sweeping changes in their own theology as well as in their own position in China that it was clear the home churches would never agree. Missionaries who acknowledged Hung as a directly inspired prophet, the adopted 'younger brother of Jesus Christ' as he claimed, would have been treated as deranged by their colleagues at home. The decision to refuse backing to and acceptance of T'ai P'ing Christianity was a turning point in the history of Christian missionary activity in China. This was the only occasion on which the Christian religion in any form made for a short time a mass appeal and gathered in thousands of converts. But this success depended precisely on the fact that under the leadership of Hung it appeared as a national, Chinese, movement against alien rulers. Its foreign origin was partly obscured by its Chinese leadership. If that leadership was rejected, the mass following would never transfer its support to a foreign-directed church. The choice before the missionary churches was to accept Hung, and thus a new kind of Chinese Christianity with which they did not agree, or to reject Hung and lose all chance of ever converting the mass of the Chinese people. They made the latter choice, but certainly did not see the real significance of their action.

The T'ai P'ing movement was crushed. The Heavenly King, a sick man when the final siege occurred, refused medical aid, hoping to die before the city was taken. His religious scruples forbade him to take his own life. He did in fact die shortly before Nanking fell, but the victorious commander of the imperial army, the Chinese Tseng Kuo-fan, falsified the record and reported to the throne that Hung had taken his own life. This fact has been recently proved by the discovery and publication of original documents in the possession of the Tseng family. The foreign powers had taken a hand in the defeat of the T'ai P'ings, even though they had just won another war against the Manchu dynasty. They had imposed peace terms which made China almost helpless. More ports were opened, tariff restrictions imposed, new concessions exacted. The Western powers now believed they had the Manchu dynasty at their mercy. The Chinese market was open to them and secured. It would be highly inconvenient if at this stage the Manchus were overthrown by a new, Chinese dynasty, claiming impossible religious status, and expecting, no doubt, that the Western Christians would accept these claims.

Under the T'ai P'ing régime China might rapidly develop strength, would expect to be treated as an equal, and would not accept the treaty imposed on the defeated Manchu court. There were other, local, reasons why the British and French, and the Americans also, decided to supply officers to organize an anti-T'ai P'ing army in the Shanghai area, commanded first by an American officer, Ward, later by the British General Gordon, who some years later died the hero of Khartoum. The T'ai P'ing movement arose in south China, in the region always disaffected towards the Manchu government. It had little support in the north, and was also firmly opposed in some of the central Yangtze provinces, notably Hunan, from which the successful Tseng Kuo-fan came, and where he raised his victorious army. The Hunan army from that time on came to play a major role in China.

These aspects of the rebellion emphasized an important difference between north and south. The north accepted the dynasty; the south opposed it. In the central provinces, the key to power, for these are the richest and most populous part of China, opinion was still divided. For these reasons, and their own mistakes, and the sincerity with which they held to a religion which was alien to the vast majority of the Chinese people, it is probable that the T'ai P'ing movement would in any case have failed. The fact that the Western powers finally also opposed it did not add to the prestige of the dynasty.

Yet, although in some ways the last example of an old style

Chinese rebellion aiming at a change of dynasty, it was also in other ways the first hint of a new kind of political movement, which sought its justifications in a change, not only of dynasty, but of ideology also. Hung no doubt accepted monarchy as the only form of government. It must be remembered that in his generation this was true of Europe as well as Asia. The sole example of a republic in the Western world outside the Americas was Switzerland. But the T'ai P'ing form of Christianity openly accepted a foreign teaching, recognized that foreign ideas could be and actually were superior to the native Chinese Confucianism and was ready to treat foreign Christians as equals and friends. These were powerful new ideas, hitherto quite unknown in China. Although the T'ai P'ing movement was destroyed, the new outlook it had fostered continued to exist and gradually to grow, especially in the south. Former T'ai P'ing followers fled to Malaya and other foreign countries, where they maintained their anti-Manchu views and passed these on to a younger generation which evolved a new, more up-to-date revolutionary ideal.

The Manchu dynasty had other troubles to contend with as well as the T'ai P'ing rebellion. The second war with Britain and France had broken out in 1858 over disputes concerning trade and shipping in the Canton region. The allied powers this time determined to put pressure directly on the distant Emperor in Peking. They forced the entrance to the Tientsin River, and advanced on Peking, which they captured. The Emperor fled to his summer residence in Inner Mongolia, where he died. His successor and only son was a young child. The era of regencies, prelude to the fall of so many dynasties, had begun. Any prestige which the dynasty might have recovered from the crushing of the T'ai P'ing rebellion was largely, if not wholly, offset by the defeat suffered at the hands of the Western powers, and the fall of the capital itself. The terms of peace imposed made it now an obligation on China to accept foreign ambassadors in Peking. The dynasty relied for support on Chinese armies, commanded by Confucian-trained scholar gentry. As the Manchus saw it, this made it all the more necessary to maintain their conservative policy and keep the loyalty of this powerful class. But in the period following the T'ai P'ing rebellion there was a possibility that China might be guided cautiously into reform by some members of the class which had hitherto most stubbornly opposed all change.

Attempts At Reform

The generation of scholar officials who came to power in the late sixties and early seventies of the nineteenth century had seen at first hand the full fury of the T'ai P'ing war. They had been able, also, to realize that the power of the British and French now far outweighed that of the Chinese Empire. It was no longer possible for intelligent men to take the standpoint which their fathers had held at the beginning of the century. It was all too clear that the 'barbarians' did really have useful arts, advanced sciences and a superior technique of warfare. The leaders of this generation began to consider how China should meet what must now be admitted to be a changed world situation. Many of them devised various ideas, but the policy which came to be identified with this period and these men has been known in China as the 't'i-yung' theory, from the works of a great scholar and statesman, Chang Chih-tung. He advanced the view that whereas none should doubt that Chinese learning and culture should remain the base of all education and culture, Western learning had its uses for practical purposes. So, 'Chinese learning as the substance (t'i); Western learning for use (yung)'. The theory is known by the two key words 'substance' and 'use' – 't'i-yung'.

The idea was that Western science could be useful in supplying modern weapons, some modern means of transport and communication, some other technical processes. But no attention need be paid to Western ideology, religion, political science, art or literature. These were the fields in which the 'base' – Chinese learning – was to remain unchallenged. In accordance with this idea, which was rather grudgingly accepted by the Regent but still regarded with deep suspicion by the more conservative scholars and officials, some progress was made. China built a fleet of modern warships with the aid of foreign experts. An arsenal to produce modern weapons was established at Foochow on the south-east coast. Steamships were purchased to start a commercial line to navigate the Yangtze. Telegraphs connected the capital and major cities and, somewhat later, in the eighties, railways began to be built between Peking and the great centres of the provinces. But these were few. Even the more progressive governors and viceroys of the provinces opposed the opening of modern mines. This was thought to go beyond the range of 'use' – and it upset the prejudices of the common people. The important limitation to this beginning of modernization was that all was governmental enterprise. No Chinese capitalists entered this field, no companies of free merchants or investors put money into such development. The money was either raised from provincial revenue or borrowed from foreign banks. This last development was really an unwise policy since it placed Chinese resources indirectly under foreign control and, as the revenues were insufficient for any large-scale plans, it became more and more common to finance these works with foreign loans.

The other weakness of 't'i-yung' was that it simply ignored the all-important fact that Western technology – the ability to build railways, invent the steam engine, make modern cannon and other weapons – was only the by-product of a wider learning and a more profound, theoretical science. China could buy these products, but unless she could make them herself she remained more, not less, dependent on foreign power. The Chinese scholars stuck to Chinese learning for all their basic culture; they did not study the fundamental problems and theories of science, and had no understanding of the roots of Western technical achievements. No changes in the social or political system were wanted, or started; no reform of agriculture, no development of industry. Above all, the supreme leadership at court remained unaffected by, and positively suspicious of, these modern changes.

When the allies took Peking in 1860, the Emperor Hsien Feng fled to Jehol, his hunting park in Inner Mongolia, and there soon died, leaving only an infant son. He was the third successor of the great Ch'ien Lung, but an unworthy one. His father, Tao Kuang, had been well meaning, personally frugal, but bewildered and unable to meet the changes his reign had witnessed. In a reign of thirty years from 1821 to 1851, the Empire had sustained the disasters of the Opium War, and was about to suffer the T'ai P'ing rebellion. The whole ten years of Hsien Feng's reign had been filled with the troubles of this rebellion and its aftermath. At least these monarchs, although far from adequate to the needs of their position, were grown men, able to act for themselves and take decisions. But the early death of the dissipated Hsien Feng left the throne to a child, under the Regency of his mother, the Empress Dowager Tz'u Hsi. This woman, a Manchu lady of medium rank, had been the concubine of Hsien Feng, but as she alone bore him a son, she was promoted to Empress Dowager by her son's accession to the throne, and exercised the Regency.

Had Tz'u Hsi been a weak character, or willing to be guided by men of more experience and wisdom, this might not have mattered. Among the Princes of the imperial family was one at least, Prince Kung, who, from his experience of negotiating the peace treaty with Britain and France after the fall of Peking, had come to some understanding of the realities of China's situation. But Tz'u Hsi was capable, ruthless, ambitious and strong-willed. She was also quite without any modern education, brought up in the classical tradition as far as such education extended to women (which was not very far), and completely conservative in her outlook. She was determined to rule, and she prevailed. The fact that the Regency was exercised – and with it the whole power of the throne – by a woman who had no trace of modern outlook, deeply suspected every change and utterly distrusted foreign innovations, hindered every timid advance which the more progressive governors and officials might have been persuaded to make. Among the many calamities which assailed the Manchu dynasty and China in the second half of the nineteenth century, the power of the Empress Dowager and her influence on the government was by no means the least.

Unfortunately the young Emperor T'ung Chih was weak and

easily led into debauch by the palace eunuchs. He had barely come of age, the Empress Dowager postponing that event as long as she could, when he fell ill with smallpox, and died after a short illness (1875). This event destroyed the slender hope that, had he lived, he might have come under the influence of progressive ministers and permitted a more liberal and advanced policy. His death, moreover, produced a kind of constitutional crisis. Under the dynastic laws of the Manchu dynasty the Emperor chose his successor, when he was dying, from among his own sons. But T'ung Chih had no children. He had only just married, and although it was hoped by some that his wife, the young Empress, might give birth to a posthumous son, the Empress Dowager had no intention of waiting for this possibility, the more so as she disliked the young Empress, and, had a son been born, it would have been this young Empress, not the Dowager, who would have become Regent. Tz'u Hsi therefore declared that the throne could not be left vacant in such disturbed times, and a prince must be chosen to succeed T'ung Chih. In the event, the young Empress died shortly afterwards without leaving any child, and the common belief, incapable of proof, was that her death was not a natural one.

There was another difficulty : T'ung Chih had had no brothers, so he had no nephews either. The heir would have to come from a collateral branch of the family, and as it was the law that the heir to the throne must belong to a generation below that of the late Emperor, this very greatly limited the choice. The reason for this law was that in Chinese custom and religion, the heir, if not a son, must be adopted as the son of the late Emperor, so that he could stand in the son-to-father relationship, necessary for the rites of ancestor worship. A brother could not be the 'adopted son' of an elder brother, nor could a cousin of the same generation. The only possible younger prince was a distant second cousin of T'ung Chih. The Empress Dowager objected to him on the grounds that his father had been adopted by an uncle who was childless. She claimed that this made him too distant a relation to be eligible for the succession. This was certainly a false interpretation of the law, but her real objection was that this young prince was already some sixteen years old, and if there was to be a Regency at all, it would be very short. K'ang Hsi had assumed full powers at sixteen, and with this great precedent no Regency would be likely. So she forced the reluctant Council of the Princes and high Ministers to accept her solution, which was to choose her own nephew, her sister's son, then a young child – and moreover a cousin of the late T'ung Chih of the same generation, and thus strictly ineligible. But the accession of the infant Emperor Kuang Hsu made a further long Regency under the Empress Dowager secure.

This dynastic intrigue would not be important if it had not been the means by which the Empress Dowager prolonged her power for another twenty years. Yet it had other damaging effects. The manipulation of the succession law in an illegal way shocked the loyal ministers and conservative officials. They felt that such an act was impious and would bring divine retribution upon the dynasty. One such loyal official felt so deeply that he committed suicide at the tomb of the Emperor T'ung Chih, leaving a 'memorial to the throne' denouncing the Empress Dowager for violating the law of succession. His act made a very deep impression on the opinion of the age. Under the second Regency of Tz'u Hsi things went from bad to worse. War with France resulted in the loss of Vietnam (Annam). Russian ambition led to the cession of part of Manchuria (the present Maritime Province), and parts of Central Asia also. Although the rebellions of the provinces were at last suppressed, the dynasty was short of money, foreign loans increased, the new railways were built wholly with foreign capital, and their management remained under foreign control. The foreign powers began to consider that China was ripe for partition : no one believed that the dynasty would long survive.

In 1894 war with Japan broke out over the question of Korea, which had been a Chinese tributary. China was rapidly and completely defeated : she had to cede Korea, Formosa (Taiwan) and even the southern part of Manchuria. The intervention of Russia and France made Japan release this territory, but Russia promptly obtained a lease of it from China as her reward, and built in it the naval base which was named Port

Arthur. When the young Emperor Kuang Hsu was at last allowed to take the reins of power, the state of China was desperate. Kuang Hsu was intelligent and open-minded; he was also clean-living and well intentioned. He had had only a strict classical education, no touch of modern learning had been allowed to come near him, but he realized the urgent need to do something to save the empire and the dynasty. He gave his confidence to a young Cantonese scholar and reformer, K'ang Yu-wei. Under his advice the Emperor suddenly announced a programme of sweeping reforms. The old examination system was to be revised and modernized, the army strengthened, the school system modernized, and many other far-reaching plans were proclaimed. Some of them would have taken years to realize; they have been called utopian and ill thought out, but in fact not one of them was so advanced or radical as the reforms which followed the revolution a few years later, and not one of them has not been put into effect in later times.

The Reforms of the Hundred Days, as they came to be called, were not a clear and consistent plan for China; they were only the first draft of such a plan, the things which Kuang Hsu and K'ang Yu-wei believed were most urgent. In any case, they had no time to try them out. Within three months (One Hundred Days) the actions of her nephew roused the utmost wrath and fear in the mind of the Empress Dowager. She determined to stop the programme, and to do this she realized she must depose the Emperor. He and his friends got wind of her plans. They decided to strike first, and tried to persuade Yuan Shih-k'ai, an officer commanding one of the few modernized corps in the army, to carry out their plans. Yuan pretended to agree, but betrayed the Emperor, assisting the Dowager to seize him and his advisers instead. Some of the reformers escaped, including K'ang Yu-wei, to live in exile for years. Others were at once executed. The Emperor was confined on a small island in the Palace Lake at Peking, and the Empress Dowager returned to full power. Thus ended the last chance of the Manchu dynasty, the last hope of peaceful, orderly progress and reform in China.

Two years later, when the pressure of the foreign powers had grown even more acute, and there was open talk of the impending partition of the Empire, at first into 'spheres of influence' which would be the blue-prints for future colonies, a movement of protest broke out among the peasantry of Shantung province. The Boxers, as this sect or rising came to be called – a pun on their Chinese name, 'The Society of the Harmonious Fist' – were first and foremost an anti-foreign sect. They believed that the foreigners were responsible for all the ills of China. They persecuted all Chinese who had adopted foreign ways in any respect; Christian converts they slew, people who wore foreign articles of dress, or used foreign goods and implements, were forced to burn these things in public, and lucky to escape with nothing worse.

The court was at first uncertain whether this movement was anti-Manchu as well, but presently the reactionary party now in power decided to back the Boxers, and use this popular explosion to drive out the foreigners and destroy all reform movements. The consequences were fatal. The Boxers were allowed to enter Peking, and soon permitted to attack the foreign community which defended itself in the legation quarter, mainly in the stronghold of the British Embassy. The foreign powers intervened to save the lives of their diplomats and residents in Peking. After some fighting, an international force drove off the imperial armies and captured Peking, relieving the siege of the legations. The Empress Dowager, dragging the captive Emperor with her, fled to the north-west.

Meanwhile the great southern viceroys, all disapproving of the mad policy of the court, had in effect declared neutrality. They made a local agreement with the foreign powers to keep south and central China quiet and suppress any Boxer movement there, if the foreign powers refrained from military action in their provinces. This agreement worked, and the war was confined to the north. After the fall of Peking, the court had fled to the far west to Sian, the ancient Ch'angan. There it remained while negotiations for peace were conducted in occupied Peking. By the terms of this peace the foreign powers obtained the right to station troops for their protection in the legation quarter of Peking and to garrison key points on the railway between the capital and Shanhaikuan, on the sea coast. They also obtained some concessions, leased ports and additional territory. A huge indemnity was imposed on China, and Russia occupied Manchuria in order to build a railway to Port Arthur from Siberia.

The restored court came back to Peking, and for another ten years vainly attempted to check the rising tide of revolution by promising reforms which, had they been put into effect thirty years before, might have averted the storm. But they were now too late, and inspired no trust. It was only too clear that they were extorted by fear from weakness, and that the Empress Dowager remained in her heart opposed to all change. When she died (1908), suddenly, and by an extraordinary coincidence the day after the death of the ailing Emperor, she had already put another child upon the throne in whose name she still hoped to rule. This was the last Emperor of China, dethroned four years later by the revolution of 1911. His reign title was Hsuan T'ung, his personal name P'u Yi.

The Republic, the Yuan Dynasty and the Warlord Period

Even before the reform movement of the Hundred Days the new generation of young Chinese, especially in the south, had become convinced that not only the dynasty but the monarchy must be overthrown. They believed that to be modern China must go the whole way and become a republic. Many of them had been educated in America, and it seemed to them that the United States, by reason of its size (roughly equal to that of the Chinese Empire), was a more appropriate model for a modern society than the European countries. There was a further reason for republican feeling. The European powers, with the exception of France, were all monarchies: even the constitutional monarchy in Great Britain did not appear very progressive in the eyes of Chinese who could not fully appreciate the real distribution of power in the British political system. The empires of Germany, Austro-Hungary and Russia were frankly autocratic, in varying degrees, and made no appeal to a generation of Chinese students who were by now convinced that the Manchu dynasty, and thus all monarchical systems, were out of date and reactionary.

From the late nineties onward the revolutionary movement gained ground, and the movement for reform of the Empire without revolution, the ideal of K'ang Yu-wei and the hope of the Emperor Kuang Hsu, lost its appeal. The defeat and dispersal of the reformers of the Hundred Days were fatal to the cause of reform without revolution. If the Emperor himself could neither guarantee the safety of the reformers nor his own liberty, there was clearly little to be hoped from such a movement. The revolutionary party had now a leader, who indefatigably rallied his followers after every check – and there were many – returning again and again to his dedicated task of overthrowing the dynasty.

Dr Sun Yat-sen was a new type of 'rebel' in Chinese history. He was not a failed candidate for the civil service, nor a military leader who had once been a bandit; he was, in education and upbringing, an 'overseas Chinese'. Although born in the neighbourhood of Canton, he had migrated while still a child to Hawaii, where he was educated, and later attended the Medical College at Hong Kong (forerunner of the present Hong Kong University) from which he graduated. His education and training were thus foreign, modern and scientific. Critics later alleged that he did not write good literary Chinese and had only a superficial knowledge of the old classical culture. In foreign countries Dr Sun learned not only how slightly China was then regarded in the Western world, but also how completely the generation of foreigners contemporary to his own believed in the democratic system, and regarded any alternative as outworn and backward. These opinions might not be so widely held today, but at the end of the nineteenth century any other views would have seemed peculiar and reactionary.

In all his writings, therefore, Dr Sun never questioned what to him was beyond discussion, that the only solution for China was to become a democratic republic. There is nothing to show that he ever considered the difficulties of this plan. He did not reflect that the democratic society in the Western states had grown over a very long period from small beginnings : that a system of law was essential to that development, and that China had no such system, nor had ever had anything of the same character. In China, unlike the West, law was either criminal or customary. Criminal law alone was the business of the state; penalties were harsh, the magistrate both prosecuted and judged, there was no system of legal defence, the innocent depended on the justice and perception of the presiding judge. But the state had nothing to do with the whole field of what we call civil law. Disputes about contracts, business deals, property, inheritance, marriage and divorce – all these matters were settled by the arbitration of the elders of a village, the heads of large families, the officers of a merchants' guild, or some other unofficial body of responsible men. There were therefore no written laws relating to these matters, and the criminal code simply stated what penalties would be inflicted for different crimes. The legal profession did not exist.

Yet if there is no such system of law a democratic parliamentary system cannot work. If the liberty of the subject is not defended by laws, political opposition is dangerous and criticism of the government almost impossible. So it had ever been in China. To oppose the government was sedition or rebellion. The only people who could criticize the government were the special group of officials called Censors, who were appointed to do this, but it was none the less a dangerous and thankless task. All this had to be changed if a democratic republican system was to work in China. Dr Sun and his followers do not seem to have realized just how vast the task of making such a change would prove to be.

The revolutionaries made several unsuccessful attempts to raise a rebellion against the Manchus, but when this actually did happen, in October 1911, it came about almost by accident. Some revolutionary conspirators in Hankow accidentally exploded a bomb while they were making explosive weapons in secret. The police raided the house, and found in it a list of revolutionaries which included many army officers of the local garrison. Realizing that this discovery imperilled their lives, these officers raised a mutiny, seized the city, forced their commanding officer to assume the leadership of their movement and proclaimed the Republic. Army officers of the new, modern, armed forces have, in all the countries of Asia, been among the most active revolutionaries. In later times such men as Nasser in Egypt, Ne Win in Burma and Ayub in Pakistan are only following a path marked out more than fifty years ago in China and in Turkey. One reason is that these officers, trained in modern science and technology, are by their education inclined to modern ways of thought and less under the influence of the old culture of their countries.

The Chinese revolutionaries had discovered this important fact and for some years they had turned their attention to propaganda among the officers of the new model armies. There was another reason for this line. Only the officers could find support among men already trained and armed; if a rebellion or revolution was to have any chance of success it must be well supported by armed men, not only by the public opinion of civilians. The winning over of the army was therefore decisive. Throughout south China, within a few weeks of the Hankow outbreak, province after province declared for the Republic, the imperial party made no resistance, the whole of south China simply seceded to the Republic. In the north it was different. There the republican party was weak, and the court, in panic, turned to the general who had most prestige in the army for protection.

Yuan Shih-k'ai had had a distinguished military record in Korea, and he had played the major part in the betrayal of the Emperor Kuang Hsu to the Empress Dowager. He was thus certainly no liberal. But the new Regent, the father of the little Emperor Hsuan T'ung (P'u Yi) was the younger brother of the Emperor Kuang Hsu. He hated Yuan for his part in the *coup d'état* of 1898. When the Empress Dowager was dead, and Kuang Hsu also, the new Regent had at once dismissed Yuan and forced him into retirement. He had not dared to go farther than this, for fear of Yuan's great influence with the army.

Now the only hope for the dynasty, with half China in revolt, was to get the support of this northern army, the best trained and armed force in China; so Yuan must be recalled, made commander-in-chief and given supreme power. But Yuan well understood the reasons for his recall: he also felt sure that the dynasty was finished, but he did not intend to promote the cause of any Republic. He aimed at the throne himself. In previous dynasties the Empire had often changed hands in this way – a decadent, feeble dynasty pushed aside by its own supreme military commander. It would be necessary first to add to his prestige by defeating the revolutionaries. This he at once proceeded to do. His armies retook Hankow, and Hanyang also. Then, at the end of 1911, having proved his power, Yuan was willing to negotiate. The dynasty was forced to abdicate (February 1912). Yuan appeared to accept the Republic, induced Dr Sun Yat-sen, the provisional president, to retire in his favour, arranged for the republican forces to be disbanded or reduced, and announced that, as President, he would uphold the Republic.

At the same time, he managed to avoid moving the capital to Nanking, as had been agreed when he joined the Republic. Before long, after obtaining a large loan from the foreign powers, he dismissed the Parliament and began to rule by decree. Within two years he was openly aiming at the throne, had organized a movement for that purpose, and early in 1915 obtained a vote for the establishment of his new dynasty from his subservient assembly. All this had taken place between 1912 and 1915. The foreign powers were at first ready to welcome Yuan. He was the strong man who would keep the peace in China and protect trade. They had very little faith in the republicans. Most of these, like Dr Sun himself, were returned students who had spent years abroad as exiles. The Parliament, when called in Peking, proved incompetent, corrupt and ineffective. The only bill it ever passed was one raising the salaries of the members. No Chinese had experience of the democratic system in action, and very few had any intention of working it properly. The type of politician who came to Parliament was most often a self-seeking careerist, and the early clashes between the President and the Parliament soon made any organized business impossible. When Yuan dismissed Parliament, the foreign observers thought things would now be better, and no protests were made by them when it became clear that the President would soon be an Emperor.

The First World War had broken out. The European powers were preoccupied by this struggle; they had no time to think about China. They were anxious to win the alliance of Japan, while the German side were equally anxious to keep Japan neutral. Neither side was prepared to check Japanese ambitions. The military rulers of that country saw their chance. They joined the allied powers, and by agreement with them drove the Germans out of their leased territory and the port of Tsingtao in Shantung province. China was not consulted. But the Japanese had further ambitions. They did not want to see Yuan found a strong new dynasty which might become an obstacle to Japanese plans. Moreover, they disliked Yuan, who had for a while, in Korea, successfully opposed them. When Yuan proclaimed the new dynasty, the Japanese presented to China the Twenty-One Demands. These demands would have reduced China to the position of a Japanese protectorate, and no Chinese government could have accepted such an ultimatum and retained any prestige or authority in the country.

Yuan accepted the least offensive Demands, and rejected the most dangerous, after arranging that the news, which the Japanese wished to keep secret, had been leaked to the Western press. He was thus able to gain some support for his stand from the Western powers. The Japanese accepted this situation, but instead started to foment anti-Yuan movements in China and, above all, to buy over his generals and prod them into open revolt against the new dynasty. In this they succeeded. One consequence of dethroning the Manchu dynasty, which perhaps the revolutionaries and Yuan also had not foreseen, was that with the long-established throne went also the only institution which could command the respect and loyalty of officials and officers. The generals of Yuan felt that they themselves, each of them, was just as good a man as he was. They saw no reason why he should be the Emperor, rather than one of them.

The dynasty having fallen, it was normal, in the view of most educated Chinese, to expect a period of confusion before the new, lasting dynasty came to power. The Republic was in their view only one such passing phase, but Yuan Shih-k'ai was not likely to be the final answer either. He had a bad reputation for treachery, to the Emperor Kuang Hsu, to the Manchu dynasty and now to the Republic. He did not command respect or confidence, and he had no able sons to follow him. No one really believed that a 'Yuan dynasty' would last beyond the lifetime of the founder. The generals, therefore, assuming a republican virtue which they certainly did not possess, rose in one province after another. Very soon half China was in revolt. Yuan saw that all was lost. He postponed his accession to the throne, then announced that he had abandoned the plan but would remain President for life. He was now a sick and ailing man; as it was soon realized that he could not live long, the rebel generals, with characteristic Chinese restraint, allowed him to live on as President, almost without power, till he died, a broken-hearted, disappointed man, in June 1916.

One reason for this compromise was that no one could clearly see who or what would follow Yuan. The south had declared for the Republic, and Dr Sun, recently an exile, had been welcomed in Canton and resumed the Presidency. He proclaimed his government there as the only legal one. But in the north, at Peking, the former generals of Yuan, who one and all hoped to succeed where he had failed, had no intention of recognizing the régime of Dr Sun. They made one of their number President, and before long entered into that complicated, wasteful and selfish struggle for power which is known in China as the Warlord Period (1916–26). It would be tedious and unnecessary to follow these minor wars in detail. No sooner did one warlord gain power than the rest combined against him. The government at Peking, dismissed at will by whichever Warlord was for the moment in control, exercised no authority beyond the city, and that only at the sufferance of the military master. Provincial Warlords fought each other, all opposed Dr Sun, who in turn was at the mercy of the local Warlords who controlled the province of Kuangtung, in which Canton is situated. China had fallen into complete disorder; was indeed hardly an organized state.

The only reason for continuing to recognize the Peking government and the pretence of a Chinese Republic was that the foreign powers had loans which were serviced by the revenues of the Chinese Customs administration, which the foreign powers themselves supervised and collected. These were collected in the name of the Peking Republic, and this was the real reason why the powers would not recognize Dr Sun at Canton. It was also under these conditions of chaos and local civil war that the economy of the country began to suffer serious damage. Banditry increased, and assumed formidable proportions. From these unsettled conditions the country landlords and rich men fled for safety to the larger cities and foreign concessions in the Treaty Ports. They left behind them bailiffs to collect their rents. These men could only act if they had the support of the local military or even of the local bandits. They went into illegal partnerships with soldiers and bandits, shared the rent revenue and in order to satisfy their partners and employers, raised the rents even higher. Soon very great distress and increasing poverty became widespread. Throughout the ten years of the Warlord Period these evils grew rapidly; by the middle twenties China was in the mood for a further, and much more drastic, revolution.

With the situation in the interior of the country going from bad to worse, racked by civil wars, plundered by indisciplined armies and bandits, the position of China in the world also declined rapidly. The Versailles Treaty had awarded the former German-leased territory to Japan. This provoked an important political development which was to have far-reaching consequences. On 4 May 1919, when the news that the venal government in Peking was making no protest against this award spread through the students of the University of Peking, they came out in a patriotic demonstration, which soon clashed with the police. Shots were fired, and the houses of some of the corrupt ministers were burned. The agitation was not stopped and spread to other cities and other classes of the population. Finally the ministers responsible were driven out of office, and the Chinese delegation to the Peace Conference refused to sign the Treaty of Versailles. The May 4th Incident, or Movement, as it came to be called, was the first occasion on which the Chinese people (or a large number of them), led by the younger intellectuals, had reacted strongly to a patriotic appeal. The realization of how far the power and influence of China had declined, the fact that the change to a Republic had only made this decline faster, not stopped it; all the disillusion which the failure of the Revolution of 1911 to achieve any useful reform had bred in the minds of the educated class, and the spreading discontent and poverty among other classes, were focused by this relatively minor issue. From this developed a new, more aggressive nationalist movement, which was far less inclined to take democracy as its model or the Western powers as examples. Soon after the May 4th Incident, the influence of the Russian revolution made itself felt in China.

Contact with Russia:
the Kuomintang and the Chinese Communist Party

Russia, before her revolution, was not a country for which the Chinese reformers and revolutionary party had any admiration, or one in which they felt any interest. Tsarist Russia had been among the most greedy and aggressive of the foreign powers who encroached on the declining empire. When the revolution first broke out, no one in China had any clear idea of what was at stake. Civil war followed in various parts of the old Russian Empire for several years. It was only after the final collapse of the White Russian armies in Siberia, and the unification of the whole country under the new Communist government in Moscow in the year 1920, that the Chinese people, or rather the educated class, became aware of what this might mean for China. The new Soviet government at once abrogated all the treaties entered into by the Tsars, and gave up in China the special rights and privileges and the Treaty Port Concessions which Russia, like other Western powers, had obtained in the nineteenth century. The Soviet government declared that they wanted only equal relations with foreign countries. This act made a deep impression on the Chinese. If Western foreigners pointed out that Communism, or 'Bolshevism' as it was then more commonly called, was a system which would destroy freedom, seize property and bring about a social revolution, the Chinese were not much impressed. They had no freedom to be destroyed: they were rapidly losing their property to bandits and corrupt militarists. A social revolution which might get rid of these people seemed positively attractive.

Left Wing ideas spread rapidly in Chinese intellectual circles: long before Marx or Lenin had been translated into Chinese, a considerable sympathy for the Russian revolution and its aims had grown up in China. Dr Sun Yat-sen was then an exile once more, living in the foreign concessions of Shanghai. He had been driven from Canton by the local Warlord. In 1921 a Russian envoy from the new Soviet government, named Joffe, had arrived in Peking, where he was well received by Chinese university circles, and accepted less eagerly by the government. Later that year he met Dr Sun in Shanghai. They held discussions and from these came an agreement by which, while both Joffe and Dr Sun declared that Communism was not suitable for China, Dr Sun accepted Russian aid to reorganize his party and at the same time agreed to collaborate with the new, very small, Chinese Communist Party. Just before this, Dr Sun had appealed for recognition and help from the Western powers, whose form of democracy he still admired. But he was refused on the grounds that his was not the rightful government of China.

Aided by Russian experts and supplies, Dr Sun reorganized his party, which was renamed the Kuomintang or Nationalist Party (the term 'Republican' was disused), and soon returned to power at Canton. There he built up a new model army with Russian advice and arms. He overcame the local Warlords, and accepted the Communists as individual members of the Kuomintang. The reforms in Canton went almost unobserved by foreigners in China, who had no great faith in Dr Sun. But in

China itself they made a deep impression. Before long the Kuomintang and the Communist Party were growing fast in every large city. The Communist Party was founded in China in 1920, and almost at the same time a group of Chinese students in Paris founded a branch of the Party there. These later fused together. The first group, those who met in Shanghai to form the Communist Party, did not number more than twelve or thirteen men (accounts of the exact number vary), but one of these was Mao Tse-tung, a young man of twenty-seven, who had left his native province of Hunan and served for a time in the library of Peking University. He already had become prominent in revolutionary circles as a trade union organizer and writer. The son of a small landholder, or medium-scale farmer, not of a poor peasant as is often claimed, Mao had from childhood attended the old-fashioned country school in his village, where he was grounded in the old classical learning. Later he attended a new modern school in Ch'angsha, the provincial capital, where he acquired a knowledge of the modern world and came under Left Wing influence. He never learned a foreign language, and his only knowledge of Marxism, or Communism, at the time of the foundation of the Chinese Communist Party came from some short translations of a small part of the writings of Marx and Lenin.

Chou En-lai was among the group who founded the Paris branch. A man of a gentry family, whose grandfather had been a high official of the Manchu dynasty, he had been educated at the Nank'ai school in Tientsin, one of the best modern schools in China. He had come under Left Wing influence while in Paris, and had a knowledge of French. None of these early Communists, later to become the chief leaders of the Party and today the rulers of China, had ever been to Russia, understood Russian, or had yet read the full works of the main Communist theorists. They knew very little as yet about the theory of Communism, but they admired the practice of the Russian Revolution, which they saw as the model which China should follow. It is an important fact that it was the example of the Russian Revolution, not the imperfectly known doctrines of theoretical Communism, which inspired the foundation of the

Chinese Communist Party. In this respect, there is a certain resemblance to the T'ai P'ing movement, which was led by men with a sketchy knowledge of Christianity, but undoubtedly inspired by the belief that these doctrines would give their movement a purpose and strength which would carry them to victory. It is also important, in the light of contemporary events, that the early Chinese Communists, who now lead the Party and the country, were all pure Chinese, with very little, if any, direct knowledge of the Western countries, and none at all of Russia. From the first, the Chinese Communist Party had thus a distinctive character, differing from most other Communist parties. It was more national, less under direct foreign influence, less theoretical and more inspired by Chinese aspirations.

It was still very small, and its influence was confined to large cities and student circles. But in the chaotic years in which it came into existence, conditions for rapid growth were very favourable. Only a few years later the Communist Party was almost the equal partner of the Kuomintang, and soon to become its deadly rival. As a result of the agreement between Dr Sun Yat-sen and the Russian envoy, Joffe, the Communist Party joined with Dr Sun's Kuomintang, and the two parties actively co-operated in preparing a new revolution to drive the militarists out of power and reunify China under a Left Wing government. In the year 1925 Dr Sun Yat-sen died, in Peking, where he had travelled in the hope of inducing the Warlord then in power to join the Kuomintang and reunify China. A short time later, on 30 May 1925, an incident between the Shanghai Foreign Settlement Police and Chinese students demonstrating in support of strikers at a Japanese textile mill, resulted in shooting and the death of several of the students.

This incident touched off the explosive mood of the Chinese people. An agitation similar to that of 4 May 1919, against the Versailles Treaty, but this time far more widespread and prolonged, swept the country. The demand was for the abolition of foreign privileges and concessions, which it was claimed had proved to be an oppression upon the Chinese people and an aid to every reactionary régime. There was certainly some substance in the latter accusation. Warlords not only invested the money which they looted and acquired by forced taxation in the safety of foreign banks in Shanghai or Tientsin, but when driven from power they took refuge in these Concessions, where they were immune from any legal process which China could bring against them. The foreign Concessions had thus become a kind of bolthole into which all who wished to avoid the consequences of political plans that had failed, and many elements of a near criminal character, were taking refuge. In any case, the whole idea of foreigners having privileges in China was now repugnant to the aroused nationalist feelings of the Chinese educated class. The Nationalist and Communist parties profited from the wave of indignation which these events provoked. Riots and further incidents occurred in all parts of the country, especially at Canton, where a total boycott of English and Japanese firms and business was enforced. This also spread to Hong Kong. The militarist government in Peking made ineffectual attempts both to protest to the European powers and appease the agitation. They succeeded in neither policy, and only earned deeper contempt from the educated class in China. The situation was thus ripe for a new phase of the revolution, and this opened in the next year, 1926, with the launching of what was called the 'Northern Expedition' from Canton, a military campaign to conquer China and drive the militarists out of power.

It achieved rapid success. Led by Chiang Kai-shek, the commander-in-chief of the Kuomintang forces, the Northern Expedition had, in a few months, overrun all south China and the Yangtze valley. The capital of the Nationalist government was moved from Canton to Wuhan, the joint name of the three cities of Hankow, Wuchang and Hanyang, which form a single urban complex at the junction of the Han River with the Yangtze. Late in 1926 the advancing Nationalist armies approached Nanking and Shanghai. It was at this point that the latent split between the Kuomintang and the Communist Party came into the open. A Communist-led uprising captured the Chinese city at Shanghai before the Nationalist regular forces reached the city. At the same time, the government in Wuhan was coming under increasing Communist influence. Chiang Kai-shek had close ties with the bankers and industrialists of Shanghai, who, although Nationalist, were certainly not pro-Communist, and had become very much alarmed at the turn the new revolution was taking. In the spring of 1927 Chiang staged a *coup* against the Communist Party in Shanghai, drove them from power, with large-scale executions of those members and supporters whom he could catch. Chou En-lai, one of the chief organizers of the movement, had a very narrow escape.

The Kuomintang Period

Chiang then set up a purely Nationalist, anti-Communist government at Nanking. A civil war between him and the original government at Wuhan followed, ending in the victory of Chiang, and the expulsion of the Communists and also of the Russian advisers. The Communists took to the hills of south China, supported by some units of the army. This was the beginning of the Communist Party's guerrilla period (August 1927) which was destined to continue for ten years. In the next year Chiang's Nanking government completed the conquest of the north, drove the militarist government in Peking out of power, and moved the national capital to Nanking, The Japanese, disliking this success, seized Manchuria in 1931 and shortly afterwards installed the deposed Manchu Emperor P'u Yi as puppet ruler of a new state, called Manchukuo, which the foreign powers refused to recognize. The civil war against the Communists continued in south China. The Communists at first, following Moscow's directions, attempted to seize large cities, such as Canton, Ch'angsha and others, but were defeated with heavy loss. The urban population which, according to Communist theory, should have supported the revolution, proved lukewarm and often opposed to their programme. But meantime the peasants of south China had responded to the propaganda drive led by Mao Tse-tung, organizer of peasant revolt. In 1928 he made contact with the remnants of the 'Red Army' – the Communist-led units of the former Nationalist forces – and began to establish a Communist-controlled area in the interior of south China, along the borders of Kiangsi and Fukien provinces, a rural region without railways or modern roads.

For several years Chiang attempted to crush this movement and some subsidiary Communist areas in the provinces of Hunan and Hupei. He failed, repeatedly, and the Communist area spread. Ultimately, in 1935, a new plan of encirclement with blockhouses and the denial of all supples, forced the Communists to break out and seek a refuge in the north-west. This was the 'Long March', by which the whole Communist army and many thousands of its dependants and followers struck out through the encircling lines, and marched by way of south-west China, the Tibetan border, to the north-west of China, where, at Yenan, in northern Shensi province, close to the border of Inner Mongolia, they established a new head-quarters. The Long March covered more than six thousand miles. During this extraordinary operation, the Communists suffered great losses but evaded destruction by the Kuomintang pursuit or the provincial forces in their path. It was also during the Long March that Mao Tse-tung was chosen at the Ts'un Yi conference to be the supreme leader of the Communist Party, a position he has retained ever since.

While Chiang was preoccupied with his vain campaigns against the Communists, Japan had continued to encroach, both in the north and at Shanghai. The Chinese nation saw these invasions with more concern than the government seemed to feel. A popular clamour for resistance to Japanese aggression and peace at home arose and gained strength. In 1936, when Chiang had gone to Sian, in the north-west, to organize a new campaign to 'exterminate' the Communists, he was arrested by his own mutinous army, led by the former Manchurian warlord, Chang Hsueh-liang. They argued that Chiang should agree to negotiate a truce with the Communists and join with them in resisting Japanese aggression. Faced with the choice of death or agreement to this policy, Chiang accepted the terms of the mutineers, met Chou En-lai, and signed an agreement by which the Communist Party nominally acknowledged the Nanking government as the central government of all China, but was itself established as an autonomous government of the 'Border Region'. The Red Army changed its name to Eighth Route Army, but retained its own commanders and separate organizations. Both parties pledged themselves to resist Japan.

The pledge had soon to be honoured. In July 1937 the Japanese forces, after provoking a minor incident near Peking, seized that city and soon attacked Shanghai also. The war this time could not be restricted to a few places, but soon became a general Japanese invasion of all China. The Japanese, better equipped, enjoying complete air supremacy and the command of the seas, had no difficulty in overrunning great areas. They drove the Nationalist government from Nanking to Wuhan, and later far up the Yangtze to Chungking. They occupied the entire coast of China, and pushed inland along the railways. But they found it difficult to maintain control in the hilly regions, and were over-extended in the plains. The Communist forces, from late 1937 onward, began to organize guerrilla warfare against the Japanese behind the lines. Within a few months they had won over to their support the peasants, cruelly oppressed by the Japanese occupying forces, and for the rest of the Second World War the Chinese Communist Party really dominated the rural districts of north China, while the Japanese, occupying the cities, waged a ruthless war against the guerrillas and the peasants who supported them. It was in this period, and for these reasons, that the Communist Party won a dominant and unshakable hold on the rural regions of north China.

After the Japanese attack upon the United States at Pearl Harbour in December 1941 and the subsequent Japanese invasions of Malaya, the Philippines, Burma and the Netherlands East Indies, China found herself a member of the alliance against Germany, Japan and Italy. This did her no good for some years, as the Japanese cut off free China, the western part of the country, from all but air-lift contact with the allies. Relations between the Communist Party and the Kuomintang also deteriorated. There were clashes, and a virtual blockade of the Communist area by Chiang's forces, which prevented the

Communists from obtaining any of the supplies flown in by allied aircraft from India. When the Japanese surrender took place, following the dropping of atomic bombs on Hiroshima and Nagasaki, the Kuomintang controlled west China and the Communists controlled north China, apart from the larger cities which the Japanese had held.

The question of whether the Japanese should surrender these to the Communists who surrounded them, or to Nationalist troops flown in to take them over, was the first cause of the post-war dispute which within a year had flamed up into a new civil war. The United States government tried to mediate between the two parties, but neither trusted each other; their views were not to be reconciled, and the attempt at mediation failed. From early 1947 open civil war had begun, and the issue this time was the survival of the Nationalist government. It was soon clear that its chances were slight. The troops, although better armed with U.S. weapons, had a low morale, and the corruption, incompetence and misgovernment of the Kuomintang had alienated all support. Chiang tried to occupy Manchuria, which the Russians had occupied at the Japanese surrender, and from which they withdrew after looting and stripping the industrial plants. The Communists also organized forces in Manchuria; the war spread to north and central China, where the Nationalists held only the cities and precarious communications between them. These the Communists soon cut. By the end of 1948 the collapse of the Kuomintang was imminent. Their Manchurian armies, the best troops, were besieged and starved into surrender. Peking and the north was lost; late in that year the main forces of Chiang were utterly defeated and dispersed at the great battle known as 'Huai-Hai' to the Chinese, as it was fought on the Huai River and Lunghai railway. Following this, the Communists advanced to the north bank of the Yangtze. In 1949 they swept into south China, took Nanking, Wuhan and Shanghai, and by the end of that year the remnants of the Kuomintang evacuated Canton and withdrew to Formosa (Taiwan), where they have since maintained themselves with U.S. aid.

PART TWO

JAPAN AND KOREA

CHAPTER FIVE

Japan: Early History

(A.D. 400–1333)

IT is often suggested that the history of all the great Asian countries and cultures goes far back into antiquity, and that, in comparison, the European countries are 'young' and their story more recent. This belief in respect of Japan is wrong. Japanese history, as opposed to legend and myth, is roughly contemporary with that of England; indeed, the history of Roman Britain is better recorded than that of Japan at the same period. In Japan, as in Britain, the earliest records are not those made by the inhabitants themselves, still without the art of writing, but by visiting foreigners or in the annals of the near-by mainland Empire. In this way the relation of Han China to early Japan is very similar to that of the Roman Empire to Britain before the Roman conquest. But there was no Chinese conquest of Japan.

The prehistory of Japan is still very obscure, although recent archaeological work has established some certainties. It is not known when Japan was first inhabited, but it is clear that in the neolithic period – the New Stone Age – the whole country was occupied, sparsely, by the ancestors of the people now called Ainu, who today exist in small numbers only in the most northern island of Hokkaido, which for most of Japanese history was really a foreign barbarous land. Approximately 1000 B.C. the country was entered at its western extremity, the large island of Kyushu, by another race, or more probably by migrants of more than one race. Some of these newcomers undoubtedly came from the mainland by way of Korea, the nearest point, and were closely akin to the Korean population of that remote time. The second stream of migrants came from the south, and brought with them elements of an 'Oceanic' culture which has some relationship to that of modern Polynesia. Modern scholars do not believe that on this account the southern migrants really came from such distant countries as the Pacific islands or even Indonesia. They believe rather that the common ancestors of the later Polynesians, some Indonesian peoples and some elements of the Philippine population, all alike came from the south-east of China, whence they migrated in various directions over a long span of time. This origin, although suggested by a number of archaeological finds and other evidence, is still far from certain or confirmed.

The newcomers, of all races, established themselves in the south-western islands, Kyushu and Shikoku, where they developed a culture known as the 'mound building' or 'Tumuli' culture, so called from the fact that it is the large grave mounds of their chieftains which provide almost the only archaeological evidence for this age. It endured for many centuries, and in the later grave mounds Chinese-imported artifacts have been found, proving a growing commerce with the mainland, probably Korea. In the Early Han dynasty, the first two centuries B.C., the Han had a flourishing colony in North Korea, around the modern city of Pyongyang. This area, known then as Lak Lang, enjoyed all the refinements of the Han civilization, and there is little doubt that it was from there that the early Japanese received the Han mirrors and other bronze objects which have been found in the graves.

The first written record of the Japanese appears in *The History of the Later Han* under the date corresponding to A.D. 57. In that year the Chinese record that an emissary of a 'King of the Wa' presented himself at court and was given a gold seal certifying that his master was king of the country (and, in Chinese eyes, thus became a 'vassal' of the Han Emperor). The country from which he came has been identified as the district of Hakata on the north-west coast of Kyushu. The Han records also state that there were 'more than one hundred' kingdoms, or chieftaincies, among the Wa. It can be deduced that the organization of Japan was then in the tribal period, with numerous local tribes independent of each other but sharing a new, bronze age, culture. From the dynastic records of the Wei state of the Three Kingdoms period, which have much more information on Japan, we learn that by A.D. 292 regular exchange of envoys had arisen between the Chinese governor of Korea and the king, or rather the queen, of western Japan. There were now not more than thirty countries, all of which in some degree acknowledged the overlordship of this queen. It would appear that the 'Queen Country', as the Chinese called it, covered northern Kyushu and part of the western end of the main island, Honshu. In the next century the Japanese from this country had established a small colony in southern Korea, and engaged in frequent wars with the Korean kingdoms farther north.

At some date not far from A.D. 350 the rulers of what had been earlier the 'Queen Country' led a great eastward expedition which conquered – from the Ainu – the rich rice basin around modern Osaka, Nara and Kyoto, the land which the Japanese call Yamato, and which now became, and long remained, the real centre of power. Japanese legend ascribes this migration to a much earlier date (667 B.C.) and makes the leader the original founder of the Imperial dynasty, the Emperor Jimmu Tennō. There seems to be some real probability that such a planned invasion of the eastern, or central, part of the island of Honshu did occur, but that it occurred in the fourth century A.D., and may well have been led by a warrior king who was perhaps the ruler of the old 'Queen Country' in Kyushu. Legend also recounts later expeditions to suppress another alien people, the Kumaso, of southern Kyushu. It is thought by many scholars that these Kumaso were the people who had entered Japan from the south, and were probably not closely akin to the migrants who had come from Korea. Japanese accounts of these events date from the compilation of the two quasi-historical works, the *Kojiki* and *Nihon-shoki*, composed in A.D. 712 and 720 respectively, nearly three hundred years after the introduction of Chinese learning to Japan. These books are therefore strongly influenced by Chinese models, and openly aim to glorify the antiquity and claims of the ruling dynasty. The events they record for early times are not historical, but give valuable information on early Japanese customs, beliefs and legends.

At some date between A.D. 265 and 369 the rulers of Japan had set up in the region of Yamato a unified kingdom, exercising control over the neighbouring provinces and more uncertain suzerainty over the western and southern islands. The east and north remained under Ainu occupation. The Chinese southern or Liu Sung dynasty of the Period of Partition between north and south records embassies from this Japanese state in the years A.D. 421 and 479. It was about the year A.D. 400, not very long after the establishment of the Yamato kingdom, that envoys from the King of Paikche, the western of the three Korean states, brought Chinese books to Japan. It was from this time that the introduction of Chinese learning can be dated, and its influence on Japan was profound. Up till then the Japanese had no written script, and therefore no records other than oral tradition. The Chinese system of ideographs ('characters') is not really well designed to fit a polysyllabic language like Japanese, and indeed is very awkward for this purpose. But it was the only system known in the eastern world: the civilization of China was advanced and mature, its prestige great and its literature abundant. It was natural that the Japanese should adopt it, and it is a tribute to their native genius that in a relatively short time they had made an adaptation which provided Japanese with an essential element – that is, a syllabic auxiliary script which enabled the Japanese to render the tense endings and cases of their language, features which do not exist in Chinese. But at first, and for a long time, the Japanese had to write not only in Chinese characters without this aid, but also, as a consequence of its lack, in the Chinese language. Early Japanese literature is in fact written in Chinese.

Inevitably the Chinese learning had an immense impact. It seems to have grown slowly at first, no doubt owing to the difficulty of a new script and a foreign language: perhaps for these reasons many pure Japanese institutions and customs of great importance did not become modified or displaced by the widespread imitation of things Chinese. The two native institutions which showed most power of resistance were the old

150

religion and the clan organization of society. The native religion of Japan is that which is now called Shinto, meaning 'The Way of the Gods'. It was a polytheism – the worship of many gods – in which the forces of nature, prominent natural features and past heroes were personified as deities. It has been compared to the classical religion of pagan Greece, but there is an important distinction. The Greeks thought of their gods as supermen, and their art was inspired by the representation of their gods as divine men, perfect in form. The Japanese never seem to have had this concept. They did not make statues or pictures of the gods; they do not seem to have thought of them in superhuman terms in this sense, but as rather vaguer forces, without concrete shape. The gods and goddesses are at times described as beings, but not very precisely: the main rituals of Shinto were simple, without blood sacrifices, and based upon the idea of ritual purity and an avoidance of everything unclean. Blood was unclean, as were wounds, sickness and death. These ideas directed the development of Shinto away from sacrifices, instilling a simple, almost gentle, religious approach to rather vague gods and divine powers. Such ideas were fertile ground for the new religion of Buddhism which was soon to arrive in Japan.

The organization of Japanese early society was on the clan basis, deriving no doubt from ancient tribal systems. The chiefs of the great clans became the great landowners and developed rapidly into aristocrats enjoying very great power and privilege. There was as yet no feudal system, but there was a strong native aristocracy controlling all the functions of government, and owning most of the good land. The Imperial Family was itself one such, the most powerful, of these clans. There is a good deal of evidence to show that in the early period their preeminence was not everywhere acknowledged, and that other clans disputed for the supreme leadership. The fact that the two most sacred, and probably oldest, Shinto shrines in Japan are associated (the one, Ise, with the Imperial Family, the other in Izumo province, at Kizuki) with a legendary rival of the Sun Goddess, ancestor of the Imperial Family, is clear evidence that the pretensions of some rival clan had to be admitted at least to the extent of paying great veneration to their family shrine. The continuing existence and power of the great clans and their leaders proved to be a barrier against the introduction of Chinese forms of government, and ultimately led to the rise of Japanese feudalism.

A new wave of mainland, alien influence reached Japan in the years between A.D. 552 and 570 with the introduction of Buddhism, which had already spread throughout China about two or three hundred years earlier. It was from Korea, and once again through an official embassy, that Buddhism reached Japan. The King of Paikche, seeking Japanese support, sent an envoy with an image of the Buddha, copies of the scriptures and explanatory documents. Whether the Japanese had had any previous knowledge of Buddhism is not clear, but this official invitation to accept and receive the new faith arrived at a moment which made it necessary for the Japanese government to take the matter up in a formal way. There was already in Japan a party which had begun to advocate reform of the government and state. They had reason to observe and respect the growing and aggressive power of the Korean kingdoms, and had come to realize that superior organization was the main reason for this strength. The reform party therefore welcomed the new faith as likely to promote the wider application of Chinese forms of government, which would, they hoped, strengthen the throne and curb the power of the great clan leaders. On the other hand, these leaders, or some of them, saw this intention, and came out as champions of the old native religion, of which they were the guardians. Power at that time was largely in the hands of the Soga clan, who had intermarried frequently with the Imperial line. They thus had an interest in promoting the authority of the throne, and supported the introduction of Buddhism. Palace intrigues to secure a sovereign who favoured Buddhism were successful, and led to the appointment of a grandson of the Soga chief as Crown Prince and Regent. This was the famous Prince Shōtoku, one of the great figures of Japanese history, and the main architect of the triumph of Buddhism.

Although Prince Shōtoku exercised power for thirty years

until his death in A.D. 622, he never ascended the throne. His life's work was devoted to the promotion of Buddhism and, with it, the further development of Chinese learning. He is traditionally the founder of two of the most famous Buddhist monasteries in Japan, the best known being the Hōryūji, near Nara, which still retains several original buildings of the early seventh century A.D. Shōtoku's work also prepared the way for more far-reaching changes which occurred in the next generation. Known as the Taikwa Reforms, and carried out over a number of years, these were initiated in A.D. 645. At this date the Chinese T'ang dynasty, which had reunited the Empire after the long Period of Partition, was at the height of its glory, under the rule of the great T'ai Tsung. It afforded a dazzling model for the aspiring court of Yamato, which sought to establish a stronger central authority. Power at court was now in the hands of a man who founded one of the most famous families in Japanese history, Fujiwara Kamatari (in Japanese, as in Chinese, the surname comes first). From him descended the Fujiwara family which controlled the government for several centuries, forming a kind of parallel Imperial Family – a feature of Japanese government which now appears for the first time, but was destined to continue until modern times.

The Regency of the Fujiwara (A.D. 645–C.1100)

It was Fujiwara Kamatari who planned the introduction of a government on the T'ang model which would make the Japanese Emperor an absolute monarch, control the clans and replace the territorial power of their leaders by appointed officers administering the provinces under the orders of the throne. A civil service, modelled on the T'ang system, was to carry on the central government in the capital. But the reforms from the first met with a great and fatal obstacle. Land was controlled by the clan aristocrats, but land revenue was the only revenue then available to the government. Consequently, in order to make the new government completely effective, it would have been necessary to deprive the clan leaders of their lands. This was clearly politically impossible. From the first it was necessary to compromise, to appoint great landowners as provincial governors in the hope that some at least of the revenue would be remitted to the throne. By a clever use of new titles, official ranks and distinctions, to which a salary was attached, the court was able to build up a large class who were truly more courtiers than civil servants, but who none the less supported the central government and served its purposes. Yet even this class was always drawn from the aristocracy: the Chinese system of recruitment by public examination (introduced by the T'ang) never took root in Japan. It must be remembered that even in China it was at this time very new, and that the old system of recommendation – by which powerful people put their clients, relatives and followers into office – still continued for many years in diminishing force. But in Japan the power of the aristocracy, less disturbed by wars and invasions than it could ever be in continental China, was too strong to be broken.

One of the first needs for a new model, Chinese-style government, was a permanent capital city. Hitherto, the Japanese court had removed at the death of the reigning Emperor to a new site, in accordance with an ancient superstition that made the house of death unlucky. The palace was, consequently, a rather simple building, not expected to be used, or to endure, for very long. Although this need had been seen by the earliest reformers, it was not until A.D. 710 that the Japanese court was first permanently fixed at Nara, a new city which was designed and built in exact imitation of the Chinese capital, Ch'angan. About eighty years later (in A.D. 793), the capital was again moved, to the site of present Kyoto, where it remained until the Meiji Restoration in the nineteenth century. The reason for leaving Nara was that the city had become a stronghold of Buddhism (as it still is), and that the political power of the monks began to overshadow that of the throne. This problem was not in fact wholly solved by moving to Kyoto. The new capital was also copied from T'ang Ch'angan and named Heian, which is practically a synonym of the Chinese name Ch'angan.

In the first century of the Heian period, as it is called, from

A.D. 794 to 891, the actual reigning Emperors exercised some power, and the authority of the rising Fujiwara family was modestly displayed. But after the death of the Emperor Daigo, in A.D. 930, the Fujiwara acquired full power as Regents, and no subsequent Emperor for many years really ruled. This curious development deserves careful consideration, for it is the key institution of all Japanese history. The Japanese are rightly proud of the remarkable continuity of their single, unbroken imperial dynasty. From legendary times until the present no other family has occupied the throne. It was naturally customary, indeed recently compulsory, to attribute this stability to the divine character of the ruling house and the protection of the gods. Any study of recorded history will quickly show that the causes are more mundane. It is clear that for religious reasons, also sustained by the ancient clan system, the respect and reverence for the imperial family was real and lasting : but the capacity for government of this one family was no more enduring than in other countries and among other peoples. Among the early Emperors were men of ability, and also those who were incapable or foolish, children and idlers. In China or elsewhere, it would have been only a matter of time before some able family overthrew and replaced the dynasty.

But in Japan, for reasons which will probably always remain obscure, the example of China, so strong in every other field at this time, was not followed in the matter of dynastic succession. When Emperor Daigo died it was only a few years since the fall of the great T'ang dynasty, which had also in its decline been the plaything of military leaders. But the Fujiwara Regents who thenceforward monopolized power made no attempt to displace the Imperial Family. Instead they married into it. Only a Fujiwara girl could marry the Emperor, or if he had other consorts, only the children of the Fujiwara Empress had any chance of succession. Steadily, in this way, the Fujiwara established an unshakable control over the government of Japan which endured for fully four hundred years. It is interesting to notice that the term of Fujiwara power is approximately the length of the greatest Chinese dynasties. Behind the visible, but powerless, Imperial Family was another, which ruled but did not reign: and this family, and its successors in like office, was just as liable to decline and decadence as any enthroned dynasty of China or the West. There are really 'dynasties' in Japan – Fujiwara, Minamoto, Ashikaga and Tokugawa – but they did not sit on the throne. Instead they exercised power from outside the palace, in great offices created to legitimize their real usurpations.

The Fujiwara were the first, and the most enduring, of these controlling families. The later title Shogun – meaning generalissimo – had not come into use in the Heian period, or rather is first used, but not as a hereditary title, in the later Heian period. Counting the first prominent Fujiwara as the reformer of A.D. 645, the family remained in power, with brief intervals in the earlier times, until the last vestige of their authority disappeared in A.D. 1185. They had been declining since A.D. 1068, but if an analogy with any Chinese dynasty is drawn, the Fujiwara remained nominally Regents for five hundred and forty years, which considerably exceeds the length of any Chinese imperial dynasty. Yet although the Fujiwara maintained themselves for so long in power in Kyoto (Heian), they did so partly at the expense of allowing the rest of the country to slip from out of the control of the court. The Chinese system, which the Taikwa Reforms had tried to introduce, never worked properly, in the Chinese manner. It must also be said that in China itself the system of government, although always restored, had many periods of long decline and disorder. Yet the causes of the gradual breakdown in Japan were more deep-rooted and permanent.

There was firstly the important fact that as Japan was never for many centuries threatened by foreign invasions, the need for a central standing army to repel such attacks did not exist. Military power was dispersed among the landowning families, the great clans, and many new ones which arose in the course of time. They exercised their power against the Ainu of north Japan, and between A.D. 790 and 812 they had effectively conquered the Ainu and extended the area of Japanese control to the north coast of the main island, Honshu. As this conquest proceeded, the court nobles, field commanders and their followers were rewarded by large estates in the pacified country. The Ainu, although conquered, remained restive; the new landowners needed to protect their manors, and began to enlist men as hereditary soldiers in their own pay. This was the origin of the Samurai, the military followers of the later feudal lords, professional soldiers, but in the service of aristocrats, not of the throne. In consequence of this development the court always lacked a strong military force which could coerce insubordinate vassals or unruly distant landlords. The Fujiwara tended to control these elements by offering awards of titles, or depriving the troublesome of court rank, methods which were partly successful while the court was still strong enough to be respected and the country nobility too disunited to offer concerted opposition.

Secondly, the court never broke the power of the aristocracy based on landownership, whether this was the court aristocracy itself, or the provincial, rising, nobility. The Chinese system of appointed officials without local territorial interests never took hold. Court, that is to say civil officials, were themselves always aristocrats and landowners. They created a system of tax-free manors, awarded as favours, or for long and devoted service, so that more and more land was withdrawn from the revenue-producing area. The court began to be poor in resources, although the courtiers grew very rich. In the provinces the system soon took such hold that practically no revenue reached the capital from the distant regions of the east and north.

In China, the growth of the civil service system gradually replaced the power of the military aristocracy. In Japan, however, with a much stronger base in the old clan loyalties and a much more enduring connection with their lands, the aristocracy grew more powerful and the central government lost authority. The aristocracy were constantly strengthened by new families, all of whom had to be provided for. The Emperors had many sons: not all could remain as princes generation after generation – no system could have supported such a vast Imperial Family. So after two or three generations the grandsons of an Emperor, except the successor, were deprived of royal rank, but took new surnames, very often from some manor, and were established as new landowning lords, often in the new lands of the east and north, but also in the south and south-west. It was from such origins that the great families of later times took their rise. The Taira, Minamoto, Ashikaga and Tokugawa, as well as many others which never attained quite such importance, were all descended from the Imperial House. This fact goes far to explain why, however much such families might usurp power, they never sought to displace the dynasty itself.

The Heian court at Kyoto was rich, cultivated, very sophisticated, but an unwarlike society of aristocrats more occupied in refined pleasures than the business of government. It was protected by the guileful policy of the Fujiwara Regents, who had not only amassed huge landownings in all parts of Japan, but, by constantly intermarrying with the Imperial Family, kept control of the court and prevented any other clan from ousting them from power. The Fujiwara, mutiplying also, sent their younger branches off to eastern Japan to establish new lordships, which could, at least for a time, be relied upon to act as a check on the ambitions of other clans. It was not an efficient system. There was a vast difference between an oppressed peasantry, barely surviving under heavy taxation and rents, and the luxurious court society of Heian. Between the peasants and farmers of the north and east and their warlike lords there was less difference; no great luxury existed in these frontier regions, and the farmers were trained to arms to act as military followers of their lords.

The Taira Regency and the Gempei War
(A.D. C.1100–1185)

By the late eleventh century, four hundred years after the organization of the new imperial state and the Taikwa Reforms, the decline of the court and the rise of the military provincial nobles was already apparent. The court was harassed by near-by troubles as well. The Buddhist monasteries, grown enormously rich and become huge landowners, maintained great numbers of monks, and had armed some of these for their own protection. Presently, the monkish armies became a menace to authority, brawling in inter-monastic feuds in the streets, or engaging in political pressures and intrigues often accompanied by armed violence. The Fujiwara Regents were losing control, and inevitably they turned to the military nobility for support. In the middle of the twelfth century this situation came into the open when the new dominant eastern military clans, Taira and Minamoto, both of imperial descent, contested for supreme power, nominally in the service of this or that Emperor, this or that Fujiwara Regent. The Taira won the first round, and from 1156 to 1185 virtually ruled in Kyoto. At this time an extraordinary and devious system of government prevailed. There was the Emperor, often a child; his father, who had been Emperor, but had abdicated after a few years; his grandfather, also an abdicated Emperor. The last of these, the oldest abdicated Emperor, in reality exercised such powers as remained to the throne itself. Then there was the Fujiwara Regent, and theoretically below him, but actually the real source of power, the leader of the Taira clan, who might have some title such as prime minister, or merely general. The Taira owed their power to their soldiery and their following in the provinces; the Fujiwara owed their position to wealth and long tenure of authority; the Emperors, abdicated or reigning, were accorded almost divine honours, deep respect, but had virtually no power except that of legitimizing the authority of the Regent and the military overlord. Some of these abdicated Emperors did engage in the dangerous and intricate game of playing off Taira against Fujiwara, or against the temporarily defeated rival clan, the Minamoto.

It was a period of constant turmoil, very often in the capital itself, of treasons, revolts, mutinies and sudden *coups*. But all these disturbances, although destructive – for Japanese cities were built of wood, and setting fire to the opponents' mansions or palaces was a favourite act of war – engaged very few men. The armies of the Japanese military class were small, but consisted of highly trained warriors. They served their lord; no one else received their loyalty. The constant wars among them were small engagements, often not more than skirmishes. No clan had yet established a sufficiently advanced organization to win mastery, raise large forces and impose peace. In the country, the multiplication of new noble families had resulted in a confused situation which for a long time also prevented the domination of any one clan, or an orderly system of feudalism. Taira, Minamoto, Fujiwara and other clans did not hold large blocks of contiguous territory, but hundreds of manors intermingled with the holdings of their rivals. A war between the clans became a chaos of local actions, attacks, raids and reprisals, but from all this fighting no clear-cut decisions emerged. Victory at the capital, as when the Taira rose to power, might mean the exclusion of their rivals, the Minamoto, from offices, court positions and influence in Kyoto. It did not mean that the Minamoto had lost power in the provinces. On the contrary, retiring to their estates in the east, they nourished their strength, withheld revenues, enlisted more followers and made alliances, when possible, with other clans who were jealous of the Taira.

The chief figure of the Taira ascendancy at court was Kiyamori, born about 1118, died 1181. In 1153 he succeeded his father, already the ruling military figure, and for nearly thirty years he was supreme. Many plots, risings and intrigues to overthrow him were hatched. There were frequent violent and bloody battles in the city of Kyoto, but Kiyamori survived them all, and died in his bed. His successor was a less capable man, and the rival house of Minamoto saw its chance. Even before Kiyamori was dead, Minamoto Yoritomo had risen in the east, and with the appearance of this new leader the hopes of his clan were revived. Yoritomo is a key figure in the history of Japan, for where Kiyamori and the Taira failed, he succeeded. In a bitter war, called the Gempei War[1] (1180–5) from

1. The Chinese ideographs in which Japanese is largely written can be pronounced in Japanese in two ways – either by using the sound of the native Japanese word which is represented by the meaning of the ideograph, or by a Japanese version of the sound which attaches to the ideograph in spoken Chinese. Thus names

the shortened Sino-Japanese form of the two names Taira and Minamoto, Yoritomo conquered his foes, although the war was fought largely by his generals, rather than by himself.

These generals, including his own brother, Yoshitsune, and his cousin, Yoshinaka, were later hunted down and slain, for Yoritomo wanted no rivals of proved military ability close to the clan leadership. Yoshitsune had won the crowning victory at the naval battle of Dannoura in the straits of Shimonoseki, western Japan: it did not save him from being exiled, and then hunted to his death. His adventures during this period are a favourite theme of Japanese theatre and popular romance.

The Kamakura Shogunate and the Hōjō Regency
(A.D. 1185–1333)

Yoritomo visited Kyoto after his victory, but retained his military headquarters at Kamakura, not far from modern Tokyo, which now became the real centre of government. Before long the Emperor was induced to award him the high title of Shogun, which thenceforward became hereditary in his family, and was borne by those military rulers who followed in later centuries.

The real importance of the victory of Yoritomo was not the fall of the Taira and rise of the Minamoto, but the eclipse of the old Heian court system and the establishment of a feudal state organized round the supreme military figure, the Shogun, and governed from his headquarters, which were not at the capital but in eastern Japan. But, as was the Japanese pattern,

---

like Taira and Minamoto can either be sounded in this way, the Japanese sounds; or as Heike, the Sino-Japanese sounds for the ideographs with which Tairo is written; and Genji, the equivalent Sino-Japanese sounds for the ideographs with which Minamoto is written. The Japanese, like the Chinese, use the first two sounds only in combinations, so the Minamoto-Taira war becomes the Genji-Heike war, shortened to Gen-Hei, which, to add a further complication, is pronounced in combination Gempei.

no clean-cut break with the past occurred. The Emperor still reigned. There were still Fujiwara in high court offices at Kyoto; they retained great wealth, but their power was almost negligible. The real government was at Kamakura. This city had been Yoritomo's headquarters. The Minamoto had always been strong in the east, whereas the Taira had dominated in the west. It is perhaps significant that it was the eastern warrior, whose family had risen in the lands won from the Ainu, who won the struggle and created the new order of society. Yoritomo had spent much time and thought on the organizing of his support, and the institutions of Japanese feudalism derive in a great part from his work.

Until Yoritomo's victory Japan had never really had a government in control of the whole country. In the early Nara and Heian periods of the monarchy, a system copied from T'ang China had been hopefully instituted, but it had won only partial acceptance in the remoter provinces and soon decayed. Even in its heyday the Kyoto government never had any authority in north Japan, then still in Ainu occupation. When the Ainu were conquered in the early tenth century, great frontier lords replaced them, who paid little or no attention to the orders of the distant court. By the period of the Gempei War, the power of the court had declined much further. Thus the establishment of the feudal government at Kamakura is a most important landmark in the history of Japan. The Bakufu, as this institution was called (literally meaning 'Tent Government' or Military Headquarters), now for the first time really exercised authority over the whole country. The last great opponent, a Fujiwara who ruled the extreme north of Japan, was attacked and destroyed a few years after Yoritomo had overthrown the Taira. Although there were some stirrings of discontent here and there, swiftly and ruthlessly suppressed by the new Shogun, Japan was now at peace, and with only minor troubles remained so for a century.

In some ways the new régime thus resembled a new Chinese dynasty – the founder a strong ruthless general, his successors less able, or short-lived, but the stability of the institutions he had created or restored carried on for several generations. So it had been with the T'ang and Han in China. The Minamoto Shoguns, however, differ in several ways from Chinese patterns. For a start, they never attempted or desired to usurp the throne itself, although some of the Emperors and ex-Emperors intrigued against them, and one, Go Toba, went too far and was forcibly deposed and exiled. But a successor – a child of course – was found and the divinely descended dynasty retained the throne. After the opposition of ex-Emperor Go Toba had been repressed, the court lost more power, and also wealth, as the Bakufu confiscated many of the great manors of the court nobility who had supported the intrigue. By this time (1199) Yoritomo himself was dead, leaving no capable sons. After a short period of some confusion, assassinations and intrigues, a new system evolved, an even further extreme of indirect government. There was now an Emperor, almost always a child: an ex-Emperor, his father, and often a senior ex-Emperor, who had more influence than the junior one. Then there was the Minamoto Shogun, now also often a child, and behind him, the real power in the land, the Regent for the Shogun, always drawn from a family called Hōjō who were related by marriage – and constant remarriage – to the Minamoto Shoguns. This was the Fujiwara system transferred at one remove to the Shogunate. Strangely, too, the Hōjō were a family of Taira descent who had not supported their kinsmen, as the Hōjō lord was father-in-law to Yoritomo himself, and thus the grandfather of his sons. This fact serves to illustrate the true nature of the Taira-Minamoto quarrel, which was not so much a war of parties pledged to differing principles of government as a clan struggle between rival warlords.

Feudalism was thus formally established in Japan only a century or so after the Norman conquest in England, which also brought in the feudalism which had been developing on the continent of Europe. This parallel between English and Japanese history, like those noted earlier, was far from complete. Japanese feudalism was native, and, far from being under foreign influence or inspiration, drew nothing from China. It rather represented a national reaction against the Heian system which had copied China but had not fitted Japanese society.

The military class who now rose to power had defied and finally virtually destroyed the old imperial government, retaining only the throne itself in revered impotence. Moreover, Anglo-Saxon England was not a period of refined luxury, advancing literature and sophisticated art, as was Heian. The Normans brought in a more advanced culture; it could almost be said that the Shoguns represented a less civilized, but more virile class in Japan, coming from the less advanced parts of the country. Their great contribution was unity and peace, even though, as warriors, peace was not particularly agreeable to the mass of the new Samurai and feudal vassals.

Kamakura, the new working capital, in eastern Japan, was soon employing able civilian ministers from Kyoto, not usually the old court aristocracy, who disdained to serve the Shogun, but men of less noble origins who had found little opening in the imperial service, dominated by the aristocrats. Painters, artists, Buddhist monks and scholars came to Kamakura, where their talents also were appreciated, and the art of this period ranks high in Japanese achievement. Although nominally only a military headquarters, Kamakura was far from being a rough encampment. After 1252, when the direct descendants of Yoritomo failed, the Hōjō Regents filled the now purely ceremonial post of Shogun with a succession of young princes of the Imperial Family. These elegant young figureheads brought with them from Kyoto a large train of court nobles who still further modified the simple military manners of Kamakura. The Hōjō Regents were capable men who knew how to keep their military vassals in order, manipulate the curiously loose laws of succession both to the Shogunate and to the throne, and gain the goodwill of the ex-Emperor then in power, which greatly helped them to conciliate opponents and overawe possible enemies.

It was fortunate for Japan that they were, in the first and middle generations, men of ability, for Japan was soon to encounter the greatest danger that had ever threatened her. By the middle of the thirteenth century the Mongol conquerers of China were firmly established. The Southern Sung dynasty was being driven ever further south, to total destruction. Kublai

Khan reigned in Peking. Communications between China and Japan had much improved in the period of the Sung dynasty, which, since it was cut off from the old trade route across Central Asia, had developed an extensive seaborne trade both with Japan and also with western Asia. Chinese-built ships were then superior to those made in Japan, and the commerce between the Southern Sung and Japan was in the hands of Chinese merchants and shipmasters. It had brought many benefits to Japan, both material and spiritual. Among the former was the introduction of tea, and an extensive import of porcelain. Both products were before long to be naturalized in Japan.

Buddhist monks from south China were also frequent visitors, and it was at this time that the Ch'an sect, called Zen in Japanese, was introduced and spread very rapidly among the military class. From these sources a new wave of 'Chinese learning' reached Japan, but it was not copied with that indiscriminating admiration which the simpler age of Yamato had shown. The Japanese were now more mature, able to take things which suited them, but leave others aside. Moreover, the situation of the Southern Sung, pressed first by the Kin Tartars, then by the Mongols, was not one which the Japanese found valuable as a political model. The new influence was religious, literary and also commercial. The visiting monks, often refugees from the advancing hordes of the Mongols, brought news of this peril. Soon the Bakufu was made aware that a mighty and aggressive power had arisen on the mainland which planned to do what no Chinese dynasty, however strong, had contemplated – invade and subjugate Japan.

It was fortunate for Japan that she was now united under a strong government which could mobilize the resources of the whole Empire. In 1268 Kublai sent an ultimatum demanding that the 'King of Japan' acknowledge Mongol suzerainty and come to Peking to pay homage: otherwise Japan would be invaded. The court was deeply shocked. Accustomed to the unquestioned reverence paid to the Emperor, without regard to his political weakness, this demand, couched in scornful terms, was an outrage. While the Emperor, or rather the ex-Emperor then in power, had no intention of submitting to Mongol demands, he was, of course, quite unable to offer any resistance unless the Bakufu called up the manpower of its vassals. The Hōjō Regents were resolute, the Japanese military class ready to take arms, but money and organization were sadly lacking.

Six years of dilatory diplomatic negotiations followed. Kublai was building a fleet in Korea, but he had not yet quite finished the conquest of the Southern Sung: indeed, that final conquest was not achieved until 1278, after the first Mongol invasion of Japan. Perhaps on this account the first invasion was less formidable than the power of the Mongols gave cause to fear. Korea had been devastated by a Mongol conquest, the subservient, powerless king was unable, even if willing, to meet Mongol demands quickly. It was not until 1274 that a fleet carrying only fifteen thousand Mongol troops and eight thousand Koreans, much inferior as soldiers, set out for the coast of Kyushu. The Korean sea captains had no interest in the victory of their conquerors, the Korean soldiers no stomach for a fight. Soon after the invaders landed, meeting strong and brave resistance from the Kyushu vassals of the Bakufu, the weather turned stormy, and the Korean sea captains advised the Mongol generals that they would have to put to sea or be destroyed on the rocky coast, leaving the army cut off. The Mongols re-embarked, not without heavy loss both from Japanese attack and shipwreck.

The Japanese had been saved more by the weather and the inadequate preparations of the Mongols than by military success. Only the local vassals had been ready to resist – the main feudal army of the Regent had not yet arrived at this distant scene of war. It is probable that Kublai, convinced by long experience of the invincibility of Mongol armies, imagined that a small force would be sufficient to conquer Japan. A landsman, he had no understanding of the perils of sea warfare and what are now called 'combined operations' – the co-operation of a navy and army in an invasion. Moreover, the army was Mongol and the navy Korean. He did not profit by his experience, except to realize that much larger forces were needed. For these more ships were required, and as the war against the

Southern Sung, now being fought along the coasts of the far south of China, was a naval war also, he could not provide a sufficient fleet until that war was brought to a victorious end by the naval battle near Hong Kong in which the last Sung Emperor went down with his forces and his fleet (1278).

In 1281 the south of China had been conquered and pacified. Large numbers of former Sung soldiers were available, and to send them off to conquer Japan was one way of disposing of them. The fleet which had crushed the Sung was also now free for an invasion of the island Empire. This second invasion was launched in two prongs; one, in which the army was Mongol, and the fleet Korean, carried forty thousand men, mainly Mongols; the second, sailing from south China, was said to carry one hundred thousand Chinese (former Sung) troops. The fact that these would not be likely to feel much enthusiasm for the cause of their recent conquerors does not seem to have occurred to the Mongol Emperor. Both invading fleets made landings on the coast of Kyushu. The Japanese, in spite of their island country, had not yet developed real sea power; their ships were small, useful in confined waters, but apparently not sufficiently seaworthy to engage a hostile fleet in the open, rough waters of the Yellow Sea. Instead they had prepared an elaborate land defence, a stone wall several miles long, which had taken five years to build, running round the coast of Hakata Bay, the area where the Mongols had invaded the first time. No similar preparations had been made at the Gulf of Imari, which was where the Chinese invading force did in fact now land. But the Mongols, either because they knew too little of the Japanese coast to seek a fresh landing point, or because Hakata Bay seemed the best, came back to this place, and there encountered the main force of the feudal army.

Fierce fighting went on in this area for seven weeks, but the Mongols failed to break through, while farther south, the Chinese, only lightly opposed, but having no desire for battle, seem to have just landed and stayed where they were. The Mongols had again chosen summer for their invasion, sailing in the month of June. Had they gained swift success this might have been a wise choice, for the winter seas in these regions are rough and icy. But in August typhoons are common on the Japanese coast, and when the invaders had struggled on for seven weeks without a decision, the season was dangerously late. On 15 and 16 August 1281, a violent typhoon blew up. The Korean sea captains put out to sea to get off the lee shore, but many of the soldiers were left behind, and more than a third of the Mongol army perished either in shipwrecks or at Japanese hands. The losses of the Chinese were heavier yet. Most of their force was trapped in Imari Gulf and on neighbouring islands. The Japanese estimated that half the army was lost. Most of what remained, on shore, was taken prisoner or slain by the Japanese. The invasion was a total failure. The Japanese have ever since called this typhoon the Divine Wind (Kamikaze) sent by the protective gods to save Japan. (The term 'Kamikaze' had less pleasant connotations in the Second World War.)

If Japan was saved by these events, they were a first cause of the fall of the Hōjō Regency and the Minamoto Shogunate, thirty-three years later. The Bakufu had no reason to feel sure that Kublai, whose resources as Emperor – not only of China, but as overlord of the vast Mongol Empire stretching across the world to eastern Europe – were apparently inexhaustible, would not try again. Indeed he had every intention of doing so, and ordered the building of a new Korean fleet. So the government of Japan was forced to keep its preparations at full readiness. The army had to be fed, paid and maintained far from home. Feudal armies were never easy to retain in the field for long periods, for they were drawn from the farming population; their lords needed the services of the soldiers on their lands, and Japan had no experience of prolonged military stalemates such as now occurred. The Bakufu could for many years feel no assurance that the danger had passed: their information was scanty. The feudal vassals clamoured for rewards – which meant more land – the customary spoils of victory. But while in a Japanese civil war these spoils could be won and distributed from the property of the defeated party, the defensive victory in Kyushu had provided the Bakufu with no spoils to distribute, and certainly no new land. The feudal vassals, put to great expense and inconvenience by long service in the field far from home, grew discontented. It was twenty years before the Bakufu felt it was safe to demobilize, although, in fact, Kublai had died in 1298 and his successor, a weak ruler, had his own troubles and gave no further thought to invading Japan.

The last really competent Hōjō Regent had died in 1284, beset by these financial worries and still fearing a renewed invasion. His successors were at first incompetent, later vicious and foolish. The Hōjō 'dynasty' was clearly nearing its end. It never solved the problem of how to reward the discontented vassals, and gradually their loyalty cooled. When Kamakura was governed by men who won no respect, it was certain that the end was near. But it did not come, as might have been thought, by the rebellion of some great vassal aspiring to become Shogun, or Regent, himself. The crisis arose from a source which had long seemed powerless to oppose the Regents, the court of Kyoto. In its origin this crisis was not a movement against Kamakura, but a dynastic succession dispute between two branches of the Imperial Family, due to the strange workings of the system of ex-Emperors who ruled but did not reign. Emperor Go Saga (1220–72) had, as was usual, only reigned for four years, when he was a young man of twenty-two. He abdicated in 1246, and thenceforward, for twenty-six years until his death, dominated the court as ex-Emperor. He had two sons, Go Fukakusa and Kameyama, who both occupied the throne in turn, and both abdicated after a few years. The question arose, after the death of Go Saga, and the abdication of Kameyama two years later, which of these two ex-Emperors should dominate the court, and whose son should succeed. The elder, Go Fukakusa, claimed that as he was senior, he should rule, and his son follow on the now vacant throne. Kameyama had been his father Go Saga's favourite. It was claimed by his supporters that he should be senior ex-Emperor, and his son succeed to the throne.

In view of the fact that the government of Japan was carried on in Kamakura, and that all Emperors, reigning or abdicated, had little power, if much reverence, it might seem that the question did not matter very much. But the position of ex-Emperor, if only moderately important politically, had other compensations. The Imperial Family was enormously wealthy: the loss of power had not meant the loss of their huge estates, their manors and other property. All this was sacred, belonging to the throne. The feudal lords had never dreamed of touching it. Perhaps the idea that property was inviolable (as long as it did not belong to a defeated enemy) was welcome to feudal lords who owed their position to landed property. So the ex-Emperor, as the real head of the Imperial Family, controlled great wealth and great patronage. He could reward his courtiers with valuable stewardships, sinecure posts carrying large salaries, and all manner of profitable employment, or rather, posts which in so far as they had any function were left to underlings, while the court aristocrat drew most of the salary and did nothing.

The followers of the two ex-Emperors had thus much to gain or to lose if the rival claimant was preferred. They inflamed the dispute, which dragged on for years, the two families each in turn securing an Emperor, and for a time an ex-Emperor, but having to give way to their rivals at the next accession. The Bakufu seems at first to have switched support from one to another, no doubt thus hoping to keep the peace and also to keep the court weak. But in 1318 the grandson of the Emperor Kameyama, of the junior line, named Go Daigo, ascended the throne, but refused to abdicate, as by doing so the senior line would have come to power. He was not, moreover, a child or a young man; he was thirty-one years old, and he meant to rule as well as reign. The dispute grew more bitter, and the Bakufu, with its own troubles, and badly led by incompetent Regents, made many blunders. Go Daigo began to gather secret support among the feudal lords, who were now weary of the misgovernment of Kamakura. But it was not until Go Daigo, still refusing to abdicate, had reigned for thirteen years, that the crisis came to a head in 1331. Fearing that he would be deposed, Go Daigo fled from Kyoto by night, raised his followers, and started to assert his rule by force. He was at first defeated and captured, deposed and imprisoned. Next year, 1333, he escaped and once more took the field in western Japan. At this point, the general whom the Bakufu had sent against him, a member of the Ashikaga family (also of Minamoto descent from the Imperial Family) changed sides, joined Go Daigo, took Kyoto and brought Go Daigo back in triumph.

The defection of this great feudal lord was a signal for a general revolt against the Hōjō Regency. In conditions of the greatest confusion Kamakura was captured and set on fire, and the Hōjō Regency came to a violent end. This event proved not the end but the beginning of more troubles, known as the War of Succession, when for a time – the only time in Japanese history – there were two contending Emperors. Nearly a century was to pass before the consequences of the fatal quarrel between the sons of the Emperor Go Saga and the warfare between his grandsons were at length brought to an end. These events had a great influence on subsequent Japanese history, ushering in a new period and marking the end of the epoch of early Japanese history.

In the period of the Hōjō Regency there is again a rough, but very slight, parallel between the events of Japanese history and the course of English history. In Japan, the Mongol invasions are the only occasion before modern times when Japan was involved in war with the neighbouring continental power. Just as the Hundred Years War between England and France marked a great turning point in English history, so the Mongol invasions and their aftermath had similar influence in Japan. In both countries a time of civil wars between two branches of the royal house – York and Lancaster in England, the senior and junior houses in Japan – followed the continental war. But in Japan it was not the island Empire that invaded the continent, but the other way round; moreover, the Mongol crisis, including only two brief invasions, did not last more than thirty years in all. Yet the effects – the impoverishment of the nobility, the consequent weakness of the government, and the contentions of branches of the ruling house – were similar in both countries.

CHAPTER SIX

Japan : The Feudal Age

(A.D. 1333–1868)

IN the thirteenth century, after Minamoto Yoritomo had unified the country and set up the Kamakura Shogunate, it had seemed for more than a century that Japan would remain a relatively united if feudal state, under the rule of his able successors, the Hōjō Regents. It is possible that this might have been the outcome had not the long strain of the Mongol invasions and the economic troubles which followed them weakened the Kamakura government and bred increasing discontent with its rule. When it fell in 1333, there was a brief but significant attempt to return to the direct government of the Emperor, a movement known as the Kemmu Restoration (1334–6). The leader of this movement was the Emperor Go Daigo, who, succeeding at a mature age, refused to abdicate within a few years, as had become the custom, and aspired to rule as well as reign. He received at first the backing of the most powerful military figure of the day, Ashikaga Takauji, who had been the leading general of the Hōjō Regent, but changed sides and thus secured the downfall of Kamakura.

Thus the restoration of the Emperor was from the first the work of the military leader of the moment, and had no source of strength other than the support of the military class – or some part of it. Go Daigo does not seem to have appreciated this vital fact. He and his court immediately set about a paper restoration of the old Heian system, which had been ineffective for at least two hundred years. High offices were given to court nobles, but they had no power or experience. Princes were appointed as provincial governors, but as the provinces were in fact in the hands of warriors clans, all in arms against each other or the remnant of the Hōjō supporters, the new governors could not take office. A host of so-called supporters thronged Kyoto clamouring for rewards for their 'loyal' service to the throne. The rewards they wanted were, of course, landed estates. There was no possibility of meeting more than a fraction of such demands, for even the confiscated estates of the Hōjō were not often actually within the control of the court. Court nobles quarrelled with warriors, the numerous lesser warriors who had followed the restoration movement were discontented by their failure to win rich rewards, and the Emperor and his advisers were living in a dream world of Old Heian, which had virtually no contact with the harsh realities around them. Go Daigo was not unintelligent, nor was he a weak man. He firmly believed that the restoration of imperial rule was the solution of the nation's problems, he held unflinchingly to this aim, he showed great resource in maintaining his claim, in escaping from his enemies, and in winning the loyalty of partisans. But he had no real gift of statecraft, no willingness to compromise or understanding of the nature of the political situation which confronted him. In 1336 the Kemmu Restoration collapsed: Go Daigo fled before the power of Ashikaga Takauji, briefly regained Kyoto later the same year, but was captured and imprisoned by Takauji after the latter had won another victory and retaken Kyoto – all within one year (1336). Takauji set up a new Emperor from the senior line, and this event marks the beginning of the fifty-year civil war between the North and South Courts, as they were called.

More than five hundred years were to pass before the Emperor of Japan was once more the true ruler of the country; but after the Meiji Restoration in 1868 and the overthrow of feudalism, it became fashionable to remember Go Daigo and his brief bid for power as forerunners of the great Meiji Restoration. He was treated as a martyr and the Ashikaga execrated as traitors. This can only be taken as a very unhistorical view of the real facts of 1336. The fall of the Kamakura Shogunate had not heralded the end of Japanese feudalism, but rather begun a period of great disorder in which that form of society developed further, and finally emerged in a far more organized and effective form than had been the case under

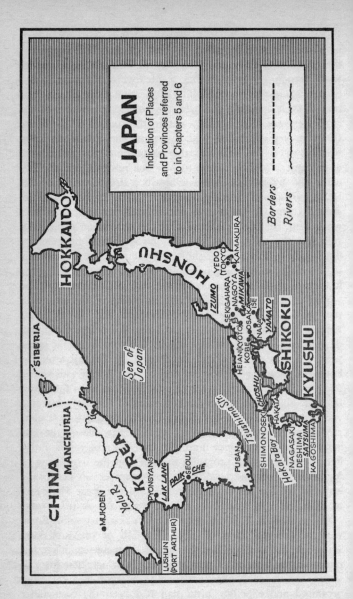

Map 4

Kamakura. Go Daigo was not a forerunner, he was a conservative looking back to a past age which could not be brought to life. Yet the fact that in this period of unbridled military disorder it was possible for an Emperor of strong character and determined opinions to strive, although unsuccessfully, to establish a central government by the throne, proves that the throne had still hidden sources of strength, reserves of reverence and respect, which were never lost, and which survived many calamities and centuries of military domination.

Go Daigo escaped next year from imprisonment, helped by many secret supporters. He at once set up his court in the mountainous region of southern Yamato, and there he and his successors for fifty years waged an inconclusive war against the Northern Court, in Kyoto, dominated and supported by the Ashikaga, who soon obtained the title of Shogun from their puppet Emperor. Go Daigo himself died in 1339, but his sons maintained the claim, and for a while with some success. They had the backing of one great patriotic and scholarly soldier, Chikafusa, a historian of great reputation, who came from the small landed gentry of the region not far from the capital. It is from the works of Chikafusa that most of the knowledge and understanding of this confused period is derived. The Southern Court (Go Daigo) had sent some of the Emperor's sons into the distant provinces to raise support, in which they were for a time successful, as many local lords expected to get their seizure of land legitimized by the Southern Emperor in return for supporting him. The main struggle was fought around the unfortunate capital city, Kyoto, which was between the years 1352–5 captured and retaken four times by the opposing sides. Each conflict meant prolonged street fighting, and the inevitable burning of large parts of the city. When the Ashikaga finally took and held the city, it was in ruins.

Even then the war continued for many years, sustained by the deepening chaos, the efforts of Southern Court partisans in the western island of Kyushu and the mountainous character of the region where the court held out. It was not until 1392 that it was at last brought to an end by some sort of compromise reuniting the two lines. This was a flimsy agreement, which the Ashikaga soon broke, but the Southern Court could no longer resist. The Japanese Imperial Family has always refrained from trying to decide precisely which line was really the legitimate successor; it has seemed best to leave this question unanswered. One of the reasons for the long inconclusive struggle was the nature of medieval warfare in Japan. The Japanese military had as yet no great experience in leading large armies, nor the resources to maintain them. Wars were carried on by relatively small bodies of the warrior-followers of a chief. The battles were haphazard encounters, poorly planned from a strategic point of view and fought by warriors as a series of single combats. Consequently defeats were rarely fatal and victories seldom conclusive. Defensive positions were as yet rudimentary. The cities were unwalled, 'castles' – the strongholds of the clan leaders – were only stockades, the art of stone walling had not yet been perfected.

The Ashikaga Shogunate and the Age of the Country at War
(A.D. 1336–1568)

The two centuries of the Ashikaga Shogunate are a strange contrast in social conditions. No effective government of the whole country ever emerged, for the new Shoguns were not sufficiently strong to impose order on the distant provinces; but in Kyoto they maintained a highly sophisticated and refined luxury which has left a heritage of famous works of art, beautiful buildings and great literature. Yet during this same period Kyoto itself was not infrequently the scene of disastrous struggles for power, and destructive fires. In 1467, for ten years until 1477, one such struggle called the Onin War was fought almost entirely in the streets of the capital, but at the very same time the Shogun Yoshimasa led a life of refined luxury and aesthetic cultivation of the arts within the security of his own palace. There was in truth only a bare fifty years of comparative peace between the end of the war between the two courts in 1392 and the decline of the Ashikagas, marked by the Onin War.

In that brief interval, the Shogun Yoshimitsu stands out as

the most capable member of his house. He strove to restore order in the country, and also to promote foreign trade with China, where the Ming dynasty was now in power. But the forces of change, expressed in terms of increasing disorder in the country, were too strong. One weakness of the Ashikaga was that they had established their rule in Kyoto itself, leaving the government of eastern Japan to deputies. But, ever since the rise of the Minamoto Shoguns at Kamakura, it had been clear that real power depended on the control of the eastern and northern provinces, once Ainu land, but now the home of the fighting clans and the best warriors. To leave this region beyond their immediate authority was a fatal mistake. Throughout these distant provinces and in those closer to the capital also, a new social class was rising. The small landholders, supplying the strength of the warrior class, were encroaching on the old manors of the great clans and court nobility, including those, some of the largest and richest, which were the property of the Buddhist monasteries. The manor system was breaking down, and from its collapse emerged, gradually, a new system of smaller independent landholders, unwilling to submit to the vague authority of the old clan leaders, and still more indifferent to the claims of Buddhist abbots or court nobles. They resisted taxation and defied the officers of the Shogun. who could only control them at all by inciting some to attack others.

One Japanese historian described this condition as due to 'unlimited numbers of men striving for a limited quantity of land'. Whether the population had really increased to the point where the pressure on the land was so serious is open to question, since it is certain that at a much later time the population was far larger though the area of cultivated land very little increased. It would seem more probable that the real cause of distress and strife was an antiquated system of land tenure; the old manor, which imposed upon the peasants a heavy load of duties, services, taxes, rents and all manner of charges, without giving real security of tenure on their plots. The breakdown of the manor system was also due to the growth of commerce: a self-contained agricultural unit, producing all it needed, manufacturing its own tools, and even weaving its own cloth, was no longer the best way to organize production when towns were growing, industries (of the handicraft type) springing up, and money coming into circulation and replacing payments in kind. The heavy import in these centuries of metal from China, including coined money, is a clear indication of the rapid growth of a money economy.

All these economic causes for the disturbances and changes were beyond the understanding of the warrior class who governed: their response to peasant unrest was repression, but the smaller gentry, who actually lived on the land, had more sympathy with and understanding of the grievances of the farmers. Numerous and violent peasant risings took place almost every year, it would seem, in some part of the country, during the fourteenth and fifteenth centuries. In very many cases small landholders, members of the warrior class, joined the farmers and provided leadership. To avoid taxation and oppression, peasants often enlisted as soldiers, for there was not at this period the rigid distinction between Samurai – warrior – and farmer, which was later imposed. Thus a new kind of fighting man came into existence, the foot soldier. The earlier warrior class had always fought on horseback (an interesting fact, since Japan is not a land of good grazing, and horses cannot be plentifully reared), but in the new conditions when there was much street fighting in Kyoto, in the war between the two courts and again in the Onin War, foot soldiers were essential for fighting in the narrow lanes and close-built streets of the city. Old class warriors disdained to fight on foot, so the new infantry were largely recruited from the absconding peasants from the manors.

The Shoguns, hoping to control the countryside, appointed constables for the provinces – great officers, nominally responsible to them – who were to keep the warriors in allegiance and stop the encroachment on landed property. The constables before long became the greatest encroachers themselves, and gathered in the manor lands, retaining their rents (always paid in rice) and raising forces at their own command. They came to be known as the Great Houses (Daimyo), a term which later stood for a great feudal lord. These new families soon gathered strength, and as they were often founded by men of more education than the usual country warrior, before long they took steps to consolidate their power. It is in this period that the castle and the castle town, characteristic features of later Japanese feudalism, began to appear. One of the most famous castles was founded by a newly-risen constable at a village called Yedo, a place which has now grown to be the largest city in the world – Tokyo. This castle was built in 1456. The castle towns, sheltering below the walls of the strongholds, developed from markets which were naturally held near these centres of military strength. At first small places, they gradually grew as merchants settled and artisans who worked for the lord and his followers set up their trades under his protection. This development, closely parallel with the rise of towns in continental Europe, came much later in Japan, and did not become general until the later sixteenth century.

The reason why social change in Japan, in wide terms not unlike the history of Europe, was so uneven and different in actual periods is in part due to the isolation of the country. While Japan had in the early Middle Ages a court and capital more luxurious, refined and, indeed, civilized, than Paris or London were to be until the seventeenth century, her rural organization and feudal society only began to reach full development at a period when this form of social order was declining and disappearing in Europe. Japanese feudalism reached its fullest development in the seventeenth century, but by that time it was in Europe already far gone in decay, or wholly superseded. Japanese social change was not in any way influenced by foreign contacts. Overseas trade was slight, confined to luxuries such as silk or porcelain, and some special imports such as copper coins and copper ingots, reserved for making coins. Japan exported such things as fans and swords, and this trade was almost confined to China and Korea. Firearms were as yet unknown in Japan, although the use of gunpowder in war had been developing in China since the early twelfth century.

The power of the Bakufu – the 'tent government' of the

Shogunate – decayed rapidly after the Onin War (1477). The next century is so chaotic that in Japan it is known as the Age of the Country at War, a welter of conflicts in all parts of the country, seemingly endless and fruitless, since no strong power emerged to dominate the country. These conditions lasted for a full century, but underneath the confusion new forces were shaping and new classes forming. Even the capital was no longer able to resist these changes. As the manors were seized by constables and other usurping military men, the court, and the Shogun also, grew poor. The Ashikaga treated the court with slight esteem, although never planning to dethrone the dynasty. One result of this impoverishment of Kyoto was that many refined and highly educated courtiers, unable to live on their dwindling stipends, removed to the seat of the new, rising powers. At the castles of the new Daimyos they were welcome and soon began to influence their hosts. At a time of deepening military disorder the warriors themselves were becoming better educated, patrons of the arts, and, as they had the wealth, promoters of skilled handicrafts and trades. The new lords were in fact gradually organizing the new feudalism. There were in 1500 about twenty very powerful Daimyos, governing one or more of the thirty-three provinces of Japan. The Shogun retained uneasy control of the provinces nearest to Kyoto; the rest of the country was parcelled out among approximately three hundred smaller lords, all of whom were in practice independent of each other, of the great Daimyos and of the Shogun. All were now busily building their castles, as strong points, family residences, arsenals and granaries. Soon they began to insist that their chief vassals should reside in the new castle towns, so that they could be supervised. Thus, although the Ashikaga period appears at first sight to be one of incompetent government and utter confusion on the political level, there was, on the level of social development, great and far-reaching change. Japan was not destroying herself, as an observer might well have believed, but confusedly building a new society.

Towards the end of the Age of the Country at War, in 1542, a new outside contact was made with Japan. In that year Portuguese mariners touched upon the coast of Kyushu. Within seven years the great missionary, and later saint, Francis Xavier, landed in Japan and was well received by the local Daimyo. Portuguese traders came back, in increasing numbers, and their visits were very welcome, for among other goods they brought firearms, which naturally appealed to the military masters of the country. The gun and the Bible, not for the last time, made rapid progress together. The story of the Catholic (there were no Protestant) missions in Japan is one which is of great interest, but perhaps more to Europeans than to Japanese. The total impact of Christianity on the country was not great, and later it was to be violently checked, but the response of the Japanese people, especially in the western part of the country, was none the less remarkable. Thirty years after St Francis Xavier landed in Japan there were estimated to be one hundred and fifty thousand Christians in Kyushu, although only some ten thousand in Kyoto, and, it would appear, very few, if any, in the eastern provinces. Kyushu, the nearest part of Japan to the mainland, was naturally the first area reached by foreign ships: moreover, the contacts with China in that island were old and had at times been close. Foreigners and foreign ways were not so strange in Kyushu. This was not the only explanation: the lords of western Japan, a relatively poor part of the country, needed trade to help their revenues, and, fearing conquest by neighbours, were anxious to acquire the new weapons brought by the Portuguese. They therefore welcomed the newcomers, both merchant and priest; and partly because they believed that conversion to the new religion would promote trade, partly because they had no strong religious ties with Buddhism, then much declined in influence, the feudal lords did not object to their followers and peasants accepting Christianity, indeed not a few of the lords themselves became converts.

There was thus a marked contrast between the Japanese reception of Christianity and the response of China. Japan, an island, and isolated, had always been interested in new things when they came, and that was rarely, from the outer world. It is still a national characteristic. Buddhism had been welcomed in much the same way, so had Chinese learning, and, later, Sung philosophy. There was thus nothing exceptional about Japanese willingness to accept Christianity. New Buddhist sects, such as Zen, also imported from China, had had great following in Japan, without ever driving all other Buddhist sects out of existence. So it might have been with Christianity. Had the period of confusion endured, it is certain that if one lord had persecuted the Christians, another one would, for that very reason, have protected them. But not very many years after St Francis Xavier began his mission, there came a great change in the political situation of Japan, a change which in the end proved unfavourable to Christianity. It must also be remembered that at this time many of the military leaders of Japan, hard and ruthless men, were not inclined to religion of any sort: while this favoured Christianity in the sense that there was not much attachment to Buddhism, or to Shinto, it also meant that the rulers came to regard Christians purely from the point of view of political advantage or loss. The fortunes of the faith depended on the character and whim of the feudal ruler.

Oda Nobunaga, born at an unknown date around 1530, was the son and heir of a small lord in the central provinces of Japan, the region near the modern city of Nagoya. He remained almost unknown until 1559, when, having inherited his family fief after a long and dangerous period as a hostage in the castles of rival houses, he embarked on a career of conquest, at first directed against the neighbouring fiefs and his nominal overlord, the head of a declining great house dating from early Ashikaga times. In 1560 he defeated these enemies in a battle which, although only small forces were engaged, was in its way decisive. Nobunaga secured a strong position and his rise was noted at Kyoto. The Shogunate was in full decline. Quarrels, jealousies, strife and treasons marked its last years. The Emperor, seeing that the Ashikaga were now nothing but a powerless nuisance, affording no protection to the capital, and disturbing such peace as it could hope for with their conflicts, appealed to Nobunaga, as a near-by and evidently competent commander, to come to his aid. This was in 1567. The next year Nobunaga, strengthened by this Imperial Command which removed from his actions any taint of rebellion, marched into Kyoto, from which the last Ashikaga Shogun fled.

The Rules of Nobunaga, Hideyoshi and Ieyasu
(A.D. 1568–1603)

In little more than ten years the unknown provincial lord had become the most powerful military leader in Japan. In 1573 he deposed the Shogun, but did not ask for that title for himself. His power grew rapidly: some Daimyos submitted, or joined him as allies, others were defeated and either reduced to vassalage or destroyed. The great Buddhist stronghold on the site of modern Osaka, which was also the headquarters of a militant sect, opposed him and was ruthlessly wiped out. This new type of warlord had no regard for things once held sacred. Yet he respected the throne, and restored to the Emperor much long-lost property. No doubt he realized how valuable the approval of the throne had been to him, but it is at least signifi-cant that this support was in fact of value. On the face of it, the Emperor was powerless: yet the most powerful military ruler in the country went out of his way to seek imperial favour, and profited much by obtaining it. This is one more striking example of the hidden but very real prestige which the Emperor, however politically powerless, continued to enjoy. Unless this fact is accepted, much of Japanese history appears almost unintelligible.

In 1582, when at the height of his power and fame, about to leave on campaign to crush the resistance of the great western Daimyo, Nobunaga was attacked by one of his generals when lodging in an undefended mansion in Kyoto, and after a des-perate defence by his bodyguard, slain. The reasons for this treachery are obscure. Adechi, who plotted it, profited very little, for within a short time he was hunted down and slain by other followers of Nobunaga, led by Toyatomi Hideyoshi, who was to be his great successor. It was certainly an age of treach-ery and bad faith. Lords and warriors pledged themselves by oaths, but easily broke their vows: the loyalty of the ancient nobility seemed to have been lost in the turmoil of strife and civil war. There appears to be no obvious reason why this plot was hatched. Nobunaga had shown no distrust of Adechi, and was clearly off his guard. Moreover, the conspirator had made no adequate arrangements to seize power, had acquired no important allies and was unable to resist for any length of time. He marched out of Kyoto immediately after the death of Nobunaga, took Nobunaga's great castle near by, but did not hold it, and in general seems to have acted without any certain or sensible plan.

Nobunaga was the first of the three great leaders who were at long last to impose peace and order on Japan. He was hard, cruel and merciless – but tremendously capable, a military commander of great ability and a far-sighted organizer. His work was only begun, and even the military unification of the country was not yet complete, but he had already thought out some of the broad lines of a new type of political organization which he intended to impose. It was the fate of Nobunaga to prepare the ground for others, while gaining for his own family no lasting prosperity. He left only a young son, who could not compete against the great leaders who now arose, and was set aside.

Toyatomi Hideyoshi is one of the great names in Japanese history, the man who completed the work of Nobunaga, banned Christianity, invaded Korea, and like Nobunaga, failed to found an enduring house. He was of very humble origin, and had enlisted as a soldier of fortune. This fact he afterwards tried to conceal, claiming to be from a remote branch of the Fujiwara family, but even in his lifetime this was known to be untrue. But the fact that a man of unknown family, a man of the people, could rise to supreme military power was as typical of the new age as it would have been impossible in any earlier one. Like Nobunaga, Hideyoshi made no claim to be Shogun, and never received that title. He was content with power. One of his first acts, reminiscent of another conqueror, the Norman William, was to order a kind of Doomsday survey of all the land in Japan. He was possibly carrying out an idea which

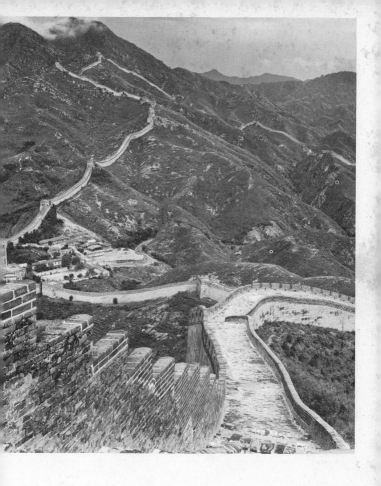

1. The Great Wall of China at the Nank'ou Pass. Built by the First Emperor in the third century B.C., it stretches for fourteen hundred miles along the northern frontier dividing China (on the right) from Mongolia.

2. The fifth-century Buddhist caves at Mai Chi Shan in Kansu province were hollowed out from a dome-shaped mountain. Fearsome statues guard entrances which were not rediscovered until 1952.

3. Hsia Kuei (*c*. A.D. 1180–1230): Talking with a Friend under Pines by a Precipice. By varying the brush strokes and leaving exposed parts of the silk on which it is drawn, Chinese painting achieves a quality of ethereal calm.

4 and 5. Cave dwelling in Yenan where the life style has remained little changed for centuries. To the villagers of Paichiachuang (*right*) in central China a new irrigation system will bring relief from summer drought.

6 and 7. Cat Street in the Chinese quarter of Hong Kong contrasts with the orderly stalls in the Nishiarai Temple, Tokyo. A genial old man wears the clothes of a devout Buddhist.

8. A young Shinto priest at the Meiji Shrine, Tokyo. He wears ceremonial robes and holds a shaku, a symbolic wand for waving away evil spirits.

9 and 10. The differing moods of Japan reflected by her bridges and motorways in Osaka, and (*below*) the Ritzurin Park in Takamatsu.

11. A farmer at the Kyongju Cattle Fair wears the traditional Korean horse-hair hat.

12. Buddhist monks descend the steep steps of the shrine at Angkor Wat, Cambodia. Dating from the twelfth century and surrounded by a moat 2½ miles in circumference, stepped pyramids and terraced levels lead towards the centre of one of the greatest monuments in Asia.

13. Brought from South America via Kew Gardens, rubber is a vital industry of the Malay Peninsula. On the plantation at Chud, Cambodia, a girl collects latex which has gathered in a cup since the tree was tapped early in the morning.

14. The home of a village chief in the Philippines. The far wall is decorated with Christian religious images and a wedding portrait. More traditional are their clothes and the tattooed arms of the chief's wife.

15. Jungle scene at Sarawak, North Borneo, where rivers are the main means of transport.

16. Cock fighting retains great popularity in Bali, contests often taking place in the temples.

17 and 18. The use of local building materials is reflected in the style of the thatched roofed pagoda at Kota Bangli, Bali, (*left*). The agrarian shrine to the Rice Goddess (*above*) gives a Balinese farmer hope for a rich harvest.

19. The floating markets of Bangkok. Traders prepare to sell local vegetables.

20. Built in the late eighteenth century, the temple of the Dawn commemorates the foundation of Bangkok. It was on this site that the royal army camped before taking the city. It is decorated with shells and pieces of pottery.

Nobunaga had already planned. This survey was exact and minute. Every rice field had to be recorded and measured (although the measurement must have been rather rough). It took fifteen years to complete, years during which by a series of swift campaigns Hideyoshi reduced all the Daimyos to obedience, forcing the great western lord of Satsuma to submit in 1587 and the northern lords of the main island in 1590. All Japan was now reduced to his obedience. This had not been known for three hundred years, since the best days of the Hōjō Regents at the time of the Mongol invasions.

Hideyoshi's new feudalism was far more thorough than the former unification achieved by Yoritomo. He had, in addition to the land survey (which permitted him to calculate the revenue and potential strength of every fief), conducted a 'Sword Hunt', a measure of general disarmament of the population. Henceforward only Samurai in the service of a lord, himself the vassal of Hideyoshi, might bear arms. The peasants were disarmed, agrarian risings made impossible and the strict division between classes was now imposed. On the other hand, the peasant, although tied to his farm, was now made the real tenant for life and could not be removed. The new system of taxation introduced after the land survey made the actual cultivator of a piece of land the man responsible for paying the tax. There was now no possibility of a landlord raising taxes and then failing to remit them to the government. The peasant had to pay his tax to the collectors sent by the government. The landlord might get the rent, and the warrior his stipend, but the government got the taxes. This change in itself, if still leaving the peasant harshly exposed to heavy taxation, gave the government an enormous new strength. No power could withstand it, and it became the main foundation of the new feudal system. That system was not yet fully perfected, and was the work of the first Tokygawa Shogun. Hideyoshi, like Nobunaga before him, laboured to achieve a mighty task from which others profited.

In the same year that the western Daimyo, Satsuma, whose fief lay in Kyushu, submitted, Hideyoshi banned Christianity in Japan. He had up to that time been on friendly terms with the

Catholic missionaries, and the reasons for his sudden change of policy are not wholly clear. It is true that in Kyushu the Christians were most numerous, and he had just completed the conquest of that island. But some of his own generals were Christians, and these he does not seem to have molested. It was the missionaries who were banned. There seems to have been at this time no general ban on Christian worship, nor persecution of Christian converts. It has been alleged that some missionaries, Spaniards, told the Japanese that their king was a great conqueror and boasted that he sent out missionaries to prepare the way for future invasions. But this well-known story is not documented from a contemporary source, and seems to be a later invention, of Tokugawa times, to justify the persecution of the Christians. Hideyoshi may have still doubted the loyalty of his western vassals and feared that they would use the missionaries as a channel of communication with foreign powers who would then give aid to them in a future rebellion. It was not invasion by foreigners that he feared, it was rebellion at home. As it is more than likely that the western lords had encouraged the missionaries with such ends in view, Hideyoshi had some grounds for his suspicions. At this time, flushed with power and success, and having, moreover, a huge army now idle, the dictator planned foreign wars to keep his troops employed and satisfy his ambitions.

Five years after the submission of Satsuma, Hideyoshi launched an invasion of Korea. He openly announced that this was to be the prelude and the way to an invasion of China with a view to the conquest of that country (1592). There was no doubt that as far as military power was concerned, Hideyoshi was fully strong enough to conquer Korea. His naval forces were, however, very inadequate. His belief that he could go on to conquer Ming China is more a proof of his ignorance of the outside world than of far-sighted planning. At this time the Ming dynasty had long passed its zenith, but it had still fifty years of power before it, and it was far from weak. The Manchu kingdom, which was to sap its strength, was only just beginning to rise. It is clear that Hideyoshi, and the Japanese leaders in general, had very imperfect ideas about the task they had rather lightly undertaken. They found Korea far larger than they had thought it to be; they had no conception of the vast extent of the Chinese Empire.

Although Hideyoshi planned to land a great army in Korea – one hundred and fifty-eight thousand men in the first attack, with a total of two hundred and twenty-five thousand for the whole campaign – he had virtually no war fleet. Japanese war vessels were small and far inferior to those of Korea. Had the Koreans intercepted the invasion while still at sea, the whole Japanese army would have been destroyed, the more so as the Japanese fleet had not even arrived, and the army set sail without it. It is clear that Hideyoshi had no experience or understanding of sea warfare. He was very lucky: the Korean court, which had given no offence, was unable to believe in the reality of the threat, and made no preparations. They reported the threat to their overlord, the Chinese Emperor, who paid no attention either. The Korean navy was not ordered into action, and the Japanese landed without meeting it. They took Pusan, and soon advanced rapidly northwards, meeting only light opposition. Seoul, the capital, was taken, and the king fled to Pyongyang, the northern capital (now the capital of North Korea). This place too was taken, and the Japanese advanced towards the Yalu River, the Chinese frontier.

It was then that things began to go wrong. The Korean army did not put up much resistance, but the people did. Guerrilla warfare started, the Japanese lines of communication were harried and cut; the Korean navy now also intervened and raided the sea communications with great effect. There was no great naval battle, but the Korean fleet constantly interfered with supply ships, and sank many. The Japanese army began to run short of supplies, and had to live on the country. This practice in turn roused the resistance of the Korean peasantry to a higher pitch: there was not enough food for both the people and the Japanese army, and soon a desperate struggle against the invaders spread far and wide. The Koreans were now led by the better men of their dispersed regular armies. The dilatory proceedings of the Chinese Ming government now also came slowly into action. They at first sent a small force, apparently heedless of the size of the Japanese army. This was repulsed.

In 1593 the Chinese re-entered Korea in great strength; the harassed Japanese could not withstand them, the Chinese retook Pyongyang and then Seoul, and the Japanese forces retreated towards the south. Hideyoshi, who had not commanded in person, seems to have had no realization that things were going against him: at this very time he was confidently proclaiming that China would soon be invaded and subdued. But the generals in the field now knew better. Negotiations with China were opened, while the Japanese army withdrew to its bridgehead at Pusan. The Chinese, apparently, thought the war was over and withdrew most of their forces. But the negotiations, pursued over a period of nearly four years, led to nothing. Hideyoshi, now undoubtedly afflicted with some form of mental disturbance, would take no account of the facts. He replied to the Chinese envoys as if he had won a clear-cut victory. In 1597, in spite of the doubts of his generals he ordered a new advance to the north. The Chinese then returned in great strength, forcing the Japanese to withdraw to Pusan again. Thereafter the Japanese defended this stronghold with great courage and success against repeated, but fruitless, Chinese attacks. It was obvious that the war was reaching a stalemate, and it was fortunate that at this moment, before some new turn came about, Hideyoshi died. His successors immediately negotiated peace with the Chinese, and the Japanese evacuated Korea. They were not to return to that country for more than three hundred years.

Some Japanese historians, noting the clear signs that in his last years Hideyoshi was becoming unbalanced, believe that the whole Korean invasion was no more than a symptom of this illness: but it seems at least more probable that the idea was conceived before the mental trouble had become pronounced, and was designed as a means of pacifying discontent at home, occupying the army abroad and employing potentially dangerous vassals in this war. It is also clear that Japanese information on continental Asia was defective at all points: they did not realize the strength of Korean sea power, they grossly underestimated the power of Ming China and they had only very inadequate knowledge of the extent and nature of the countries they invaded, or planned to invade. Under these circumstances it is not surprising that the invasion failed; it is a tribute to the fighting quality of the Japanese troops and their leaders that it did not end in a gigantic disaster.

Since early medieval times this was the first occasion on which Japan had intervened in Korea: the conditions of warfare, and the scale, had quite changed in the previous seven or eight hundred years. But the campaign of Hideyoshi has many interesting points of similarity with more modern campaigns in the Korean peninsula. The strength of China in a war along her Korean border was amply demonstrated – but quite forgotten four hundred years later in 1951. In 1894, on the other hand, the Japanese had fully learned the lesson that sea power was essential for a successful invasion and the only effective counter to Chinese land-bound intervention. Hideyoshi's dream of conquering China was unfortunately cherished by military men in Japan, and revived when, in a new age, Japan was once more in expansionist mood. It was to prove as unreal and disastrous in the twentieth century as it had been in the sixteenth. In these ways the relatively brief Korean campaigns, lasting only six years in all, foreshadow the prolonged intrusion of Japan into the continent of Asia in the first half of the twentieth century. Events at home, rather than those abroad, were to divert Japan from any such ambitions for a very long time, but the tradition of Hideyoshi's invasion lived on, although its lessons were forgotten.

When Hideyoshi was on his deathbed, he assembled all his greatest vassals and commanders and made them swear the most solemn oaths to protect and serve his young son, Hideyori. With the memory of the fate of Nobunaga's family in his mind, and many previous examples also, it seems strange that he can have believed that such oaths would bind men of the type then commanding the armies and holding the great fiefs. It was surely all too certain that the still recent unification of the country would not endure unless some powerful figure took the lead and completed the task. Within two years the inevitable clash occurred, from which emerged the third great founder of Japanese unity, Tokugawa Ieyasu. He had long been one of Hideyoshi's followers, and since 1561, when he first joined Nobunaga, he had played an important military role. A descendant of a minor branch of the great Minamoto clan (themselves descended at a remote degree from an early medieval Emperor), his original family name was Matsudaira. As a youth he had been a hostage, and it was not until Nobunaga defeated the clan – the Imagawa – who held him, that he was able to take charge of his own fief, and soon join the rising fortunes of Nobunaga. He was not involved in the murder of that commander, and was at the time far from his own fief, which was in the province of Mikawa, west of Kamakura and modern Tokyo. In the service of Nobunaga he spread his own influence, and the rule of his overlord, along the eastern sea coast provinces, the traditional home of the best warriors in Japan.

When Hideyoshi came to power, Ieyasu, who had now taken the more famous name of Tokugawa, from another branch of the clan, became his chief partner in the control of the Empire. He could hardly be described as a vassal, but more as the supreme commander in eastern Japan. Leaving Hideyoshi to rule at Kyoto, or rather from the great castle which he had built at Osaka, Ieyasu spent the years of Hideyoshi's power consolidating his position in eastern Japan. He took no part in the Korean War. At the time of Hideyoshi's death Ieyasu had a revenue more than double that of the greatest of the other Daimyos, and equal to half that of all the rest put together. There was thus already no doubt that he was the strongest power in Japan. Less than two years after the death of Hideyoshi the trial of strength between Ieyasu and his rivals came to a head, the pretext being accusations, no doubt well founded, that Ieyasu was not carrying out the will of Hideyoshi. The opposition consisted mainly of the western Daimyos, prominent among them being Satsuma and Choshu, whose fiefs were in the island of Kyushu and the extreme western end of the main island. Some of the Daimyos who had commanded in Korea were also in this party. The decisive battle (1601) was fought at a village called Sekigahara in the mountainous province of Mino, approximately half way between Kyoto and Yedo (Tokyo).

Ieyasu was somewhat outnumbered, but his enemies were a coalition of jealous Daimyos, some of whom were secretly planning to join whichever side seemed most likely to win. This was the factor which gave the Tokugawa the victory and settled the future of Japan. At the height of the battle one of the western Daimyos changed sides, or rather, having held off till this moment, now suddenly joined in against his supposed allies. The victory of Ieyasu was complete: the western Daimyos submitted to save their fiefs and safeguard the future of their families. Only the young Hideyori, son of Hideyoshi, still remained in the great castle of Osaka. Ieyasu left him alone there, no real threat for several years, while he built up his own now unassailable position.

The Tokugawa Shogunate (A.D. 1603–1868)

Two years after Sekigahara, Ieyasu was appointed Shogun, the first to hold that title since the fall of the Ashikaga. From this date (1603) the years of the Tokugawa Shogunate are counted, but in fact Ieyasu had been supreme since 1600, and the dominant figure since the death of Hideyoshi.

The battle of Sekigahara was the last field engagement fought in Japan between great armies: for more than two hundred and fifty years it was the last military operation in the country, except for the siege and capture of Osaka castle in 1615. In some ways this battle and its outcome bears a striking resemblance to the battle of Bosworth between Richard III and the future Henry VII (1485). Both battles ended an age of civil war and brought about a lasting peace under a new, firm and enduring government. Both battles were decided by the opportunist treachery of great feudal lords who watched and waited till they saw which side seemed to have the best chance of victory. But if these treacherous lords expected to profit from the result, in both cases they were disappointed. The new conqueror was strong enough to reduce them to a role of far less importance than that which they had hitherto played, and to deny them all chance of future triumph.

Fifteen years after Sekigahara the Shogun found it necessary to put an end to the latent threat of his former partner's son, Hideyori, son of Hideyoshi. Osaka was besieged, but none of the great western lords came to its rescue. It fell after holding out for six months with heavy slaughter on both sides, for Osaka was defended by a large garrison of the now masterless warriors who had followed the enemies of Ieyasu in the recent civil war. When the castle fell, Hideyori took his own life and his family were exterminated. This was the end of the civil wars in Japan: henceforward for two hundred and fifty years the Tokugawa Shoguns ruled the country in peace, until, in the middle of the nineteenth century, new forces pressing upon Japan disturbed their system and brought it down.

Ieyasu, although a cold, ruthless man – like many of his contemporaries and predecessors in power – was a political genius as well as a most able military commander. It is to the former quality that his family owed their long hold on power. Nobunaga, had he lived, might have achieved a similar result. But Hideyoshi, however able as a general, did not have the skill of Ieyasu in political matters. The new Shogun redesigned the entire feudal system of Japan on lines which made his own power almost beyond challenge. Many fiefs of his enemies were confiscated and allotted to his faithful followers, to collateral Tokugawa branches, or kept in his own hands. The rest were divided into two categories. Those who had fought for him at Sekigahara were called Fudai, and were direct vassals of the Shogun, holding fiefs close to the capital and to Yedo, which now became the Shogun's capital. Fudai fiefs were so placed that they separated the remaining fiefs from each other, and thus made combinations hostile to the Shogun very difficult. The great fiefs of the western Daimyos and some others who had not fought for Ieyasu (even if they did not fight against him) were called 'Tozama' meaning 'Outside Lords'. These were remote both from Yedo and from Kyoto, mainly in the west and north. They were reduced in size and wealth, but were not suppressed. Satsuma and Choshu, the two main western fiefs, remained among the greatest and were 'Outside Lords' – always suspected by the Shoguns, secretly hostile and ultimately after two and a half centuries the main instrument of the overthrow of the Tokugawa.

It must seem strange that Ieyasu, after winning complete military victory and full power, did not wholly abolish Japanese feudalism. In other parts of the world victories such as Sekigahara or Bosworth mark the end of the feudal system. But the Japanese warlords merely reformed the system, perfected it and maintained it unchanged until modern times. Their policy achieved complete peace and order in the country. Wars came to an end at home and they engaged in no foreign adventures either. Under these circumstances the maintenance of a warrior class, now protected by privileges from any loss of status, carefully marked off from the 'lower' classes, armed and forbidden to engage in commerce or agriculture, seems both unnecessary and dangerous. No wars occurred for the warriors to fight: no foreign invasions to keep them active: they were to some extent employed in the Shogun's government, but this opening could only provide occupation for a small fraction of the hordes of Samurai, who now attended on every Daimyo and the Shogun himself in picturesque idleness.

In addition to these thousands of Samurai,[1] whose numbers did not diminish with time since their rank and calling were hereditary, there were about five thousand small vassals called Hatamoto, direct vassals of the Shogun; about one hundred and forty-five Fudai, or 'loyal' great Daimyos, and some ten Tozama, who were often the greatest of all. It would now, it seems, have been possible to sweep away the whole feudal system, to organize a central government controlling every region and sending its officers out to govern the provinces. In China, as the Japanese well knew, this was the system, and at this very time, under the new Manchu dynasty, was once more in vigorous operation. It never seems to have been suggested or considered: the supreme warlord re-arranged the pieces on the feudal chess board so that he could checkmate any opponent, but seems to have had no desire to abolish the system itself.

1. Calculated to be one-twentieth of the whole population.

In every other respect his reforms were wide and deep. The whole population was rigidly divided into four classes, Soldier, Farmer, Artisan and Merchant. The court was aloof, remote, honoured, cared for, but kept outside all business of government; two hundred miles and more away the Shogun ruled from Yedo. His vassals, the Daimyos, were compelled to travel the length and breadth of Japan every year, or at best every second year, to Yedo, where they must attend the Shogun for four months. When they went home they had to leave their heirs and other members of their family in Yedo. No Samurai might work, no farmer might carry a sword, no artisan could do farm work, no merchant must engage in any occupation but trade. In these classes themselves were many minute subdivisions, and every class was hereditary. A man must work at his father's trade: he might not seek another. Peasants must remain bound to the soil they tilled: travel required a pass. These were no paper regulations, ignored in practice. They were carefully and rigidly enforced, punishments for any breach were severe, often capital. Daimyos who were suspect, or negligent, were dismissed, degraded, had their fiefs reduced or were transferred to worse fiefs in other parts of the country. This, it is true, did not apply to the Outside Lords, who had to be treated with more suspicion but greater courtesy.

The government was assisted by three councils of Great Elders, Elders and a Judicial Council. The Great Elders were very few, often only two, and acted as Regents when the Shogun was not of age to govern. The Elders acted as a kind of cabinet, engaged in the day to day business of government; the Judicial Council not only acted as a Supreme Court, but also had many administrative duties, for the 'separation of powers' between legislature, executive and judiciary, which is a principle of Western government, was not in force in Japan any more than in China. The Bakufu – the Shogun's government – also employed an elaborate system of intelligence officers, spies and informers, headed by great officers called Censors whose duty was to report any misdemeanour by any vassal, great or small. The Shogun could know everything that went on in the country, and it seems that for a very long time this system worked well. The whole system worked well – from the point of view of the Tokugawa. No risings occurred, no conspiracies went undetected, peace was preserved. The people may not have enjoyed the restrictions under which they were placed, but they did have security and slowly rising prosperity. Certainly they accepted the rule of the Shogun and for a very long time made no great opposition to it. Tokugawa feudalism was almost the 'perfect' totalitarian state. Whatever may be thought of such a system, it does not seem to have irked the people of Japan. The Tokugawa was a great age of art, literature and learning: an oppressive system of government did not stifle talent, although any scholar whose writings seemed critical or subversive was certain to get into dangerous trouble. This is one of the most interesting aspects of both Japanese and Chinese society. Liberty, or lack of authoritarian government, has always resulted in military anarchy, and has rarely produced creative art or literature. Firm, not to say oppressive and harsh, rule has produced peace and apparent content, and also a great flowering of the arts and literature. It is disturbing to observe this from the Western point of view, but the evidence that it was so throughout the history of these countries is overwhelming.

Ieyasu died only a year after the fall of Osaka, an old man of seventy-five. He was succeeded by an adult son, Hitetada, and within a few years by his grandson Iemitsu, also of age to govern, who then ruled Japan for nearly thirty years. These peaceful successions went far to establish the new régime. No regency, no infant reign, disturbed the transfer of power, and no opportunity was afforded to jealous rivals to grasp authority from a weak or child ruler. Among the enemies of Ieyasu the Christian Daimyo Konishi had been prominent, having also made a great reputation in the Korean War. Perhaps this fact was one reason why the first Tokugawas strongly persecuted the Christians, and in 1637–8 suppressed open Christian worship by force, massacring thousands of peasants in Kyushu and enforcing a most rigid search for hidden Christians. All missionaries were expelled, and those who tried to stay in hiding hunted out and slain. At the same time Iemitsu decided upon another remarkable policy, the total exclusion of all foreigners, and a ban on all Japanese travelling abroad. No ships large enough to cross the Yellow Sea were allowed to be built. The reasons for this drastic decision seem to have been, as with Hideyoshi's persecution of the Christians and expulsion of the missionaries, fear that the western lords, the Tozama, would gather strength from foreign contacts and gain power to challenge the Tokugawa.

In the time of Ieyasu there had been no suggestion that Japan would cut herself off from all contacts with the outside world. The first Tokugawa Shoguns promoted trade and intercourse with foreigners. In 1601, the year after the battle of Sekigahara, a Dutch vessel had been driven ashore on the coast of Japan. The pilot was an Englishman, William Adams, who was also an experienced shipwright. When Ieyasu learned of this castaway, he summoned him to his court, had a number of interviews with Adams in which he learned something of the Western world, and then employed Adams for several years to build modern ships for his fleet. During the next decade Dutch and also English ships touched at Japanese ports, and were welcomed to trade. The attitude of the new Shogun seems to have been pleasure at finding Westerners who were not Portuguese nor Spaniards and made no attempt to propagate their religion. The example of William Adams, the first English-speaking man ever to reach Japan, was followed by a number of Dutch scholars, who came out with their trading ships. It was not until nearly twenty years after the death of Ieyasu that the Exclusion Orders were brought into force, in the years 1637–8.

The exclusion was not in fact total: the Portuguese were forbidden to visit Japan, and all Japanese were forbidden to leave the country, and liable, if they did so, to summary execution on their return. But at Deshima, an island in Nagasaki Bay, the Dutch were allowed to call once a year, and maintain trade. Chinese were also permitted to call at Nagasaki. It seems that the British could have done so also had they wished to, but they left the slight trade with Japan to the Dutch. This system endured until the second half of the nineteenth century. Up to the date of the Exclusion Orders there had been flourishing Japanese colonies of traders in many parts of eastern Asia. Japanese were numerous at Manila, in the Malayan ports and in Siam and Burma. Some even travelled, in European ships, to western Europe. Those who did not return when the Exclusion Orders were issued, were never allowed, on pain of death. to come back. There is perhaps no other example of a nation which had already made considerable progress in establishing contact and trade with overseas countries cutting itself off from almost all such contact for two and a half centuries. The fact that the year before the Exclusion Orders were issued, the Shogun (Iemitsu) had had to face and suppress a great peasant Christian rising in Kyushu, called the Shimabara Rising, is the most probable explanation for this policy. With the suppression of this revolt, not only foreign trade and contact, but also any open showing of Christian belief, were absolutely banned.

The Shogunate deliberately rejected all possibilities of involvement overseas. Twenty years after the Shimabara Rising and the Exclusion Orders, in 1658, the government of Japan received an appeal for help from the Chinese Ming loyalist known to the Western traders as Coxinga, then master of the island of Formosa (Taiwan). This was the last stronghold of the Ming partisans. Coxinga (real name Cheng Cheng-kung; the corruption came from the southern way of pronouncing his title, Kuo Hsing Yeh, in Fukien dialect Kok Sing Ya – meaning Lord of the Imperial Surname, as he had been granted honorary membership of the Imperial Family of Ming) was now hard pressed by the conquering Manchus. He had strong naval forces which kept his base in Formosa safe, but he lacked any military strength to undertake campaigns on the mainland. It was this aid he asked for from Japan. But the Tokugawa did not share Hideyoshi's ambitions. They refused to meddle in Chinese affairs. Japan had turned her back on the outside world.

The Shogun had still many internal problems to meet. Some of these, such as the problem of the Ronin, might have been solved by foreign wars, but this was not the policy he decided to follow. The Ronin were masterless Samurai, men of the warrior class whose feudal lords had been deprived of their fiefs for fighting against Ieyasu, or had their fiefs and followers reduced. Ronin, as Samurai, were not supposed to engage in any trade: but they had no legal feudal lord to pay them their rice stipends and employ them. In Iemitsu's rule they were estimated to number not less than five hundred thousand, a formidable body of discontented and poor warriors. In 1651, despairing of any help from the Shogun's government, they plotted a rising which Tokugawa intelligence learned about and frustrated. This occurred during the minority of the next Shogun, Ietsuna. The Bakufu, although mastering this danger, realized that something must be done for the Ronin (the word means 'Wave Man', that is, one who wanders free as the waves of the sea). Those who were capable were taken into the government service, and the rules were relaxed – without open acknowledgement – permitting others to take up trades and other occupations. Many became masters of academies which were supposed to teach fencing, and other military arts – for many Ronin were experienced ex-soldiers, and most regular Samurai had never seen a sword drawn in battle. Gradually the Ronin faded out, through old age, and assumed other ways of earning a livelihood.

After a period of minorities and short reigns the Tokugawa produced in 1680 another memorable ruler, the Shogun Tsunayoshi (1680–1709). Although Japan was supposed to be a rigid class-bound society, Tsunayoshi's mother, the former Shogun's favourite, was a woman of the people, who had come to Yedo as the maid of a noble lady, was noticed by the Shogun, taken into his harem, and became his favourite and the mother of his heir. She continued during a long life to have a great influence with her son, who was able, eccentric and luxurious. Tsunayoshi's long reign was a curious period. The Shogun, influenced by his mother, a fervent Buddhist, tried to prevent the slaughter of animals, and particularly cared for dogs. Since he had been born in the Year of the Dog (the Japanese calendar, like the Chinese, designated the years by the names of the animals forming the cycle of the signs of the zodiac), he treated dogs with especial care. No dog might be killed: dogs had to be addressed as 'Mr Dog', and any person found ill-treating a dog was liable to the most severe punishment. The witty citizens of Yedo, now becoming a great city, nicknamed Tsunayoshi 'The Dog Shogun'. But although odd in many ways, Tsunayoshi was capable and effective as a ruler. Under his rule Japan grew very prosperous. This was the age when the culture of the new capital, Yedo, began to equal, if not to excel, the old civilization of Kyoto. It was different: based, for one thing, less on an aristocracy than on a wealthy bourgeoisie, the now rising class of merchants. They had money, they could not raise their social status, but they could enjoy themselves. The theatre, the print-makers, the whole world of pleasure and light art was open to them, and they entered wholeheartedly into it. They had no responsibility for the government or duty to society. They had the right to grow rich, and the opportunity to enjoy their wealth. It was this class which sustained the art of what the Japanese have called the 'Floating World' of Yedo, the actors, popular artists and many more questionable forms of entertainment.

Tsunayoshi is perhaps well remembered for these things more than for actual policy acts, and because in many ways he was the last of the great Shoguns. At his death the sure signs of decline began to appear. It was a full century since the rise of the Tokugawa, and Asian history has frequently shown that this period is about the limit of a ruling family's effective, active, authority. Power may be retained for much longer, but it is due to the loyal service of ministers who in effect take over the rule of the sovereign. So it was with the Shoguns of the Tokugawa house. One more effective Shogun, Yoshimune (1716 to 1745), grandson of Tsunayoshi can be reckoned, but in his time the state was increasingly troubled by economic ills. The prosperity and the luxury of Tsunayoshi's reign was now replaced by famines, violent fluctuations in the price of rice, and many natural disasters. These were, of course, no fault of the Shoguns. But the ruling philosophy of their régime was Confucianism, taken from Sung China, and this doctrine taught that the conduct of the ruler was reflected in the natural world. A good ruler would not be afflicted by droughts and floods: if these occurred, it meant that the government was failing in its duty. Such ideas therefore tended to weaken the prestige of the ruler when times were bad.

The Tokugawa had adopted Confucianism because they wanted a philosophy which justified absolute, total rule, and was not backed by a turbulent church, such as the Buddhist organization had been in the Middle Ages, nor yet a foreign creed with outside connections such as Christianity. Shinto was too closely associated with the now powerless but revered Imperial Family. Tokugawa patronage of Shinto would have revealed the Shogun in an awkward light, as a kind of usurper. It was in fact ardent students and scholars of Shinto who were to inspire the movement for the Restoration of the Emperor and the overthrow of the Shogunate in the early nineteenth century. So Confucianism, formal, ancient, orderly and authoritarian, suited the Shoguns very well. The history of this age is fully recorded by a great writer and historian, Arai Hakuseki, who served as minister for the Shogun who preceded Yoshimune, but did not long remain in the service of his successor. Hakuseki showed the nature of the financial troubles which now assailed the Bakufu; he related the earlier history of Japan with insight and profound scholarship. Himself originally a Ronin, who suffered poverty and hardship in this unemployed state, his learning won him a place as tutor in a great household, and from this vantage point he later rose to high rank in the Shogun's service. His career thus gives us a concrete illustration of how the late feudal society operated, and what chances lay open to the intelligent but poverty-stricken young Samurai.

The second half of the eighteenth century saw the Tokugawa decline. The successors of Yoshimune were long-lived but feeble men. Ieshige, who followed him, reigned from 1745 to 1788, but he was stupid, and stammered so badly that only his favourite Samurai could understand his speech. This man had to interpret the Shogun's words to his ministers. In consequence, the favourite acquired very great power; as he alone was supposed to know what the Shogun wanted, or said, he really ruled in his name. The next Shogun, Ieharu, was lazy, although intelligent. He could not be bothered with the affairs of government, not even taking time to listen to his ministers.

Government passed into the hands of his chamberlains, who, on pretence of conveying the Shogun's views to the ministers, really governed themselves. In this period there were more and severe financial troubles, rice riots by the starving people, both in the cities and the country, and a great number of famines, earthquakes and other disasters. The chief chamberlain of the idle Shogun, although able, was extremely corrupt. His example was widely followed, and the government was clearly losing its power and efficiency. Towards the end of the century there appear, in literature, and in the revival of Shinto studies, the first stirrings of the coming movement for Imperial Restoration.

It was in these circumstances that the bad effects of the policy of exclusion began to be felt. Outside Japan the world had changed: in the early seventeenth century the powers of Europe hardly intruded on the Asian scene. Some traders and missionaries made the long hard journey. Many more went out than ever came back. But by the end of the eighteenth century the advances in ship building, the growing technology of Europe, the conquest of large parts of Asia, had brought these European powers within close range of Japan. It is well known that it was an American squadron which in 1854 forced Japan to abandon her exclusion policy: it is not so often recalled that it was in fact Russian voyages and visitors who first breached that exclusion. The Russians in the second half of the eighteenth century had conquered the Tartar tribes of Siberia and reached the Pacific coast. Before long they constructed ports on this coast and built ships there, with which they began to explore the north Pacific. In 1792 one such ship touched upon the coast of the most northerly Japanese island, Hokkaido, or Yezo, and tried to open up trade. The Bakufu was alarmed and reluctant. The Russians were ordered to leave, and went, peacefully enough. But they returned, several times, and in this distant region it was hard for Yedo to prevent their visits. In 1804 an official Russian mission appeared in the southern port of Nagasaki, the only one open to any kind of foreign trade. The Shogun refused to receive the ambassador and ordered him to leave. After that the Russians felt themselves free to land in the north, the Yezo coast, as they pleased, and there were several clashes.

The policy of exclusion was breaking down not only from the attacks or intrusion of Western nations, but from internal reasons also. The main cause of the economic crises which shook late eighteenth century Japan, and continued into the nineteenth century, was a result of exclusion. The country was run as a rice economy; tribute, revenue, stipends and pay were in terms of so many bushels (Japanese 'koku') of rice. But no food could be imported, and there were no exports. If the rice crop was abundant, the price fell very low, and the Samurai and feudal lords, who had large expenses, got very little when they sold their rice allowances and revenues. When the crop was bad, the price skyrocketed, there was much hoarding by merchants, great distress among the poor and the peasants. So whatever happened, one class or another suffered, and all became increasingly discontented. The population had risen, but not very greatly. Unlike Manchu China, the long centuries of Tokugawa peace had not brought about a great rise in population. Whether this was due in part to the restrictive class system, or the constant famines, is a question which Japanese historians have spent much thought and research to discover, but have not yet a sure answer. By the end of the eighteenth century the Daimyo and Samurai were deeply in debt to the great merchants, the peasants were in dire distress, and the urban workers were often without the means to buy food. These were dangerous conditions for any government.

From the annual Dutch voyages to Nagasaki some Japanese scholars had acquired books and maps which showed them, as they slowly learned enough Dutch to read that language, that their ideas about the outside world were limited and wrong. Japan was not one of the great powers of this new world. The British, who were now masters of India; the Russians, who had occupied the northern half of Asia; the French, who were even then conquering most of Europe; and even the new United States, entering upon the heritage of a continent, were all greater powers than isolated Japan. When they learned, later, that even great China had, in 1842, been easily defeated by the

British in the Opium War, real consternation gripped the minds of intelligent Japanese. They began to realize that the blind policy of the degenerate Bakufu would bring the country to disaster. The movement for strengthening national defence, abandoning exclusion and restoring the Emperor, three linked policies, grew stronger.

Yet for another fifty years the Tokugawa Shoguns resisted these changes. In 1825 they ordered that foreign ships which approached the coast of Japan were to be fired upon, their crews, if they landed, captured and executed. This proved impracticable, for the western Daimyos, whose fiefs were most frequently visited by foreign vessels, neglected to carry out such dangerous instructions. In 1842 the Bakufu, now following inconsistent policies – a sure proof of increasing weakness – rescinded this order and instructed the coastal lords to give food and water to visiting ships, but 'request' them to sail away. And at the same time the government persecuted the scholars of the new Dutch learning, and tried to suppress it. Before long the problem grew more acute, American settlements on the Pacific Coast of the United States sent out many whalers to hunt for their catch all over the Pacific. Often they touched on the coasts of Japan, and there were difficulties, clashes and disputes. In 1845 the United States government sent a warship commanded by Captain Biddle to get redress: the Shogun refused to accept his letters or to deal with him. Communications were slow in those days. There was as yet no continental railway across the United States. It was not until eight years later that a United States squadron commanded by Commodore Matthew Perry arrived on the coast of Japan. He carried a letter from the President which he succeeded in having delivered to the Shogun. It requested, in firm language, that Japan open her ports, provide arrangements for the good treatment of shipwrecked sailors and permit trade. Perry sailed, saying he would come back in one year's time for an answer. It was clear that a further refusal would mean war (1853).

The Shogun and his advisers realized that they must yield. They had not the power to resist a well-armed modern squadron of warships, since Japan had built no sea-going ships for two hundred years. They feared to raise the feudal levies, since, once in arms, the great Daimyos might overthrow the Shogunate rather than fight the foreigner. When Perry returned in 1854 he got his treaty. Trade was permitted, the ports opened (not all of them) and an American Consul was to take up residence in Japan to look after his nationals. Within the same year Britain, Russia and Holland obtained similar terms. The policy of exclusion was abandoned.

As this change was so clearly the result of foreign pressure, it greatly damaged the prestige of the Shogun. The movement to Restore the Emperor was now linked with another cry, 'Expel the Foreigner.' It is an interesting fact that the forces which now gathered against the Tokugawa, and were soon to compass their downfall and inaugurate modern Japan, began as a reactionary movement aiming to return to the ancient rule of the Kyoto court and the total expulsion of all foreign influences. It was now, paradoxically, the hitherto stubbornly conservative Shogunate that wanted to move with the times, the court which inspired an opposition based on pure reaction.

As a result there was mounting trouble. Foreigners were attacked, sometimes killed by swashbuckling Samurai. The foreigners demanded redress; the Bakufu, if it consented, lost prestige and was accused of treachery and weakness by the opposition. But up to 1856, two years after Perry's second visit, there was no concerted movement to overthrow the Tokugawa. Opposition was concentrated on the 'weak' foreign policy of the Bakufu. In 1860, since this policy did not (indeed, could not) change, the court began to back a movement to overthrow the Shogun. The great Tozama – Outside Lords – gave support, particularly Satsuma and Choshu, although at first they were hindered by mutual jealousies and ambitions. In the same year, following the murder of an Englishman in Satsuma territory, and the failure to get any redress, a British squadron bombarded Kagoshima, the Satsuma capital, and won compliance with their demands. The Satsuma now seem to have realised that mere anti-foreign activity was not enough. Japan must be made strong, and to do this the Bakufu must be overthrown.

The Shogun was at his wit's end: he feared an invasion of

the country if he did not comply with foreign demands. In 1858 he had signed a new treaty with the foreign powers (United States, Britain, Russia, France and Holland) which was modelled on the treaties which these powers had recently exacted from China, giving them extra-territorial jurisdiction, a legal term which meant that foreigners were not subject to Japanese law but must be tried by their own consuls, both for civil and criminal cases. The Japanese customs tariff was also fixed, and at a low rate. It was this further sign of Bakufu weakness which had brought the Imperial court into opposition and stimulated the great western lords to revolt. The Shogun now made a fatal mistake. Hoping to rally support and explain the growing dangers of the country, he journeyed to Kyoto to put his case to the Emperor. No Tokugawa had made such a journey for two hundred years. It humiliated the Bakufu, and restored prestige to the Emperor such as his predecessors had not enjoyed since the fall of Go Daigo five hundred years before. In the same year the Shogun abandoned the rule of attendance by which the Daimyos had to spend part of each year at Yedo. The great lords retired to their fiefs to prepare for revolt. Next year (1864), as a result of some maltreatment of English visitors in the western province of Choshu, the Straits of Shimonoseki between Kyushu and the main island were forced by an English squadron, which landed men and demolished the forts that guarded this narrow passage. In the same year the Choshu leaders tried to bring off a *coup* in Kyoto against the Shogun, but were opposed by both Satsuma troops and those of the Shogun. Unwisely, the Shogun now thought he could use this as an excuse to destroy Choshu. But this did not suit Satsuma, who had opposed the Choshu leaders through unwillingness to let them get all the credit for an Imperial Restoration. The two great Daimyos made up their differences and allied in open revolt against the Bakufu.

After a year of vacillating negotiations and preparations the Shogun marched against them, calling on his other vassals for support; but most of them held back. In Osaka the Shogun Iemochi, twelfth of his line, died, to be succeeded by the thirteenth and last, Keiki, who rapidly lost what little support remained to the Bakufu. Next year, finding his régime collapsing, he resigned his office to the Emperor. Some of his forces resisted this surrender, but were easily defeated. In the year 1868 the government of Japan, after many centuries of domination by military leaders of several families, was returned to the Emperor Meiji. He was supported by the great Daimyos, and by many thousands of Samurai, but there was to be no restoration of feudal rule. The Satsuma and Choshu had at last avenged Sekigahara, but it was not the great Tozama Daimyos who were to succeed to power in the new Japan.

CHAPTER SEVEN

The Meiji Restoration and Modern Japan

(A.D. 1868–1945)

THE history of modern Japan, that is since the year 1868, divides into three clearly marked periods – the period of the Meiji Restoration and the modernization of Japan, lasting twenty-seven years from the Restoration itself in 1868 to the outbreak of the war with China in 1895; the period of military domination and expansion on to the continent of Asia, from 1895 to 1945, or just fifty years; and the post-war period of contemporary democratically-governed Japan, which has now endured for over twenty years. It is just over one hundred years since the fall of the Tokugawa Shoguns and the end of Japanese feudalism. Probably few nations in the world have gone through such a wide variety of experiences in so short a time, and few were so unprepared for such changes. Japanese institutions and way of life had remained very much the same for nearly one thousand years, since the decline of the Heian court. During all those centuries the country had been ruled, in one way or another, by a warrior class, which, with the exception of the small court nobility, alone enjoyed wealth and power. The peasants had remained an unarmed, helpless mass of near serfs. The merchants had been a despised class, easily despoiled of their wealth. Japan had only once engaged in a brief adventure on the continent of Asia, only once encountered, and repelled, an invasion from that continent.

In the next century Japan was to see the overthrow of the feudal system, the creation of a modern, centrally governed, but autocratic state, the enormous development of the economy and industry, the emancipation of the masses, military domination at home and rapid conquests and expansion abroad; ending in a national disaster of the greatest magnitude, the bombardment and destruction of most Japanese cities, the surrender of her armed forces, the foreign occupation of the country and the loss of all her overseas conquests. Thereafter Japan was to recover, under yet another form of government, this time capitalist-controlled democracy, still presided over by the Emperor, who, as before, reigned but did not rule. There are many elements of great change in this story, but also some of steady continuity with the past.

The Meiji Restoration (A.D. 1868–1895)

When the Shogun Tokugawa Keiki resigned his office to the Emperor, this event was the direct result of the virtual revolt of the four western fiefs, the Tozama, or 'Outside Lords', who had always been the objects of suspicion by the Shogun's government, and had originally been the enemies of the Tokugawa. They combined to support an Imperial Restoration, frustrated the feeble efforts of the Shogun to prevent this and thenceforward dominated and organized the new régime. This fact was long concealed, or denied, by current opinion and official history in Japan. The domination of the western clans was not exercised through their former Daimyos, in the feudal manner, but by able men of Samurai origin from these clans, who took over power from a feudal aristocracy no longer able to wield it. For this reason the 'clan government' of the Meiji period had the outward appearance of a true monarchical restoration in which the Emperor exercised personal power through his ministers. As has been seen throughout Japanese history, outward appearance and real facts in government rarely agreed. In the Meiji period the government of Japan was an oligarchy, the rule of a small group of able men, all of whom belonged to the two great western clans, Satsuma and Choshu. Very few men from other clans, or other parts of Japan, played really prominent parts, such exceptions as there were being some few members of the old court nobility. These men acted in the name of the Emperor: their decrees and revolutionary measures were sanctioned and recommended to the nation by the sacred character of the divinely descended Emperor, and an assiduous propaganda and system of education made sure that this interpretation of the character of the throne was spread deep and wide throughout the nation. The Meiji Restoration was a revolution, a profound revolution, but it was carried out by Imperial Decree, seemingly led by the Divine Monarch himself, and for this reason open opposition was stilled, or easily quelled. The real force and value of the Japanese reverence for the throne, never wholly obscured, was now harnessed to the overthrow of the social order and the recreation of a new society.

Intelligent and educated Japanese knew, no doubt, that the government of the Emperor was in fact the rule of the oligarchy: but they, on the whole, approved and accepted that rule. It was doing great things for the country, and it was almost impossible to oppose it without appearing to oppose the Emperor himself. It was this circumstance which distinguishes the history of Japan in the later nineteenth century from that of China at the same period. The men in control, or who could have controlled the government, were no more able in the one country than in the other, but the Japanese had what proved to be the vital asset, a sovereign, immensely respected, almost worshipped, heir to a dynasty which had reigned since record ran, completely identified with the national traditions and even with the national religion. The Manchu Emperor was an alien, scion of a conquering foreign people, who had been less civilized than the Chinese, and remained unpopular and disliked in a large part of the country. Moreover, the Emperor Meiji, although hardly more than a boy (sixteen) at his accession, was not subject to a Regency of reactionary women and old-fashioned courtiers, but ruled by himself. He was neither foolish, dissipated, nor unusually intelligent. He was sensible, shrewd, dignified and effective. He thus made an adequate leader in whose name the revolutionary ministers could carry through their sweeping reforms.

These oligarchs, the real makers of modern Japan, were of Samurai stock, drawn from the numerous class of feudal retainers, who for many years under the Shoguns had really governed the great fiefs. The Daimyos, forced to spend so much time in Yedo (Tokyo) or travelling to and from that city, had to leave the government of their territories to able retainers. A class of such men gradually became the actual policy makers in the great fiefs. It was rare to find a Daimyo who really ruled. Consequently it was these officials of the Daimyos who had impelled the western fiefs of Satsuma, Choshu, Tosa and Hizen into revolt, had guided them to restore the Emperor, and who now really exercised the power which had nominally been returned to the throne. Unless this understanding of what really went on at the Restoration is grasped, the history of modern Japan is unintelligible. The new oligarchy was not at first, nor from the first, pledged to modernize Japan. Far from it: their slogan had been 'Restore the Emperor, Expel the Barbarian' (i.e. the Western foreigners). They attempted at first to set up a form of government modelled on old Heian, and hoped to abrogate the treaties which the weakened Shogun had been forced to sign under foreign pressure.

But the new men were able and clear-headed: once in power they quickly realized that this programme was impossible, and would be disastrous if it were attempted. The foreign powers were too strong, the government must be modern to match that strength, the system of Heian would be quite unsuitable and archaic. Within a very few years of the Restoration the policy of the oligarchy was to overthrow feudalism and modernize the country. The very next year, 1869, the four great western feudal lords proposed to surrender their fiefs – in return for generous financial compensation – and thus give the lead to the abolition of feudalism. It was indeed in the interest of the great Daimyos to do this. They gave up their fiefs, but were given the equivalent of half the revenue of the fief as an income, later commuted to great sums in capital.

The former feudal lords ceased to be rulers but became millionaires. They were also now no longer expected to pay the stipends of their Samurai and all the other great expenses which their former state had required. They were much better off. Consequently in 1871 all the feudal lords surrendered their fiefs and the whole power of government was returned to the throne. This remarkable revolution amazed the world: that the great and powerful feudal lords, under no apparent compulsion, should abandon their status, titles and privileges, as well as their power, seemed truly a wonderful display of patriotism and loyalty. So it was long represented in official Japanese history. It was, in truth, almost inevitable once the ruling groups in Satsuma and Choshu had decided that such a plan was in the interest of the Empire – and their own. These clever men saw that the feudal top structure was merely an encumbrance to their plans: they knew that almost all the Daimyos were not the real rulers of their fiefs, and would welcome a cash settlement and a life of dignity, free from the varied and burdensome obligations of feudal lordship. Feudalism was in fact out of date, and the feudal lords were among the first to know it.

The Samurai presented a different problem. In 1871, at the surrender of the fiefs, there were two hundred and eighty Daimyos, but four hundred thousand Samurai, a mere hundred and fifty court nobles and a total population of about thirty-one million. The Daimyos and nobles could be easily satisfied with compensation and the prospect of future employment in the service of His Majesty the Emperor. But the new rulers did not want an army of unruly Samurai; they planned an army raised by national conscription, in which the peasants would provide the submissive and well-disciplined soldiers, and some selected men of Samurai origin (mainly from Choshu and Satsuma) would provide the officers. So the Samurai, too, had to be pensioned off, their feudal privileges discontinued, their right to wear two swords abolished. The prohibition on Samurai engaging in trade, agriculture or business was also abolished. The Samurai, on small pensions, or small cash compensation, were turned loose to sink or swim. It is a remarkable tribute to the discipline of the Japanese people that this harsh and unjust treatment did not cause more trouble than it did. It was, indeed, the direct cause of a rebellion in Satsuma itself, which was headed by Saigo, one of the leaders of the Restoration, but which was crushed without too much fighting by the new professional army and its modern firearms. This demonstrated to all that feudalism and the power of the old warrior class was indeed at an end (1877).

Nevertheless, the Satsuma rebellion had given the oligarchy a shock: thereafter they did more for the ex-Samurai, helping them to get new employment, very often in the lower ranks of the government and its ministries, and gradually absorbing them into new occupations, of which there were many open to intelligent men in the rapidly expanding, modernizing economy. Modernization went on at a headlong pace: railways were built to link up the cities and provinces of Japan. Cities were given a water supply, their streets paved, lit and drained. Ships were bought, and then soon built; banks were founded; great business enterprises came into being. But it is significant that the two greatest firms in Japan were Mitsui and Mitsubishi, whose ramifications were soon to penetrate every aspect of commercial and financial life. Both had risen in the Tokugawa period from rice merchants who traded the rice revenues of Daimyos and lent them ready money. The roots of the new capitalism were grown in feudal times.

The oligarchy which ruled Japan never numbered more than a dozen or so names, and some of these did not last very long in power. Kido and Okubo, the two chief architects of the Restoration, died – the latter assassinated – within two years of the Restoration. Their successors included fewer men from outside the two clans of Satsuma and Choshu, which now became completely dominant. Such men as Yamagata, the military leader, Ito, who was primarily a statesman, Kawamura the leading naval personage and others such as Okuma, were all from these two clans. They did not always agree: there were resignations, cliques which gained or lost advantage, a hidden world of political intrigue, all covered by the formal phrases of Imperial Decrees, accepting resignations, appointing new ministers, transferring and rewarding. The public neither knew, nor were to be permitted to know, what went on. All they had to do was pay their taxes, develop the country and serve in the armed forces. There was at first no pretence that modernizations should lead to democracy.

But when a nation borrows wholesale from a foreign culture

it is very hard to draw such firm lines. The Japanese were urged to study abroad, to come home as competent engineers, scientists, teachers or trained economists. They must read up these subjects in foreign books, in foreign languages. They could not fail to learn that foreign culture (mainly English and American) was also based on a system of government differing widely from their own. There were elected parliaments in the West. Within ten years of the Restoration, by 1877, an agitation for an elected assembly was in full swing. It was firmly repressed, even savagely persecuted, by the oligarchy. But it grew stronger. The rulers were not above criticism, even if the Emperor was. Ministers were sharply attacked in the new press; free, that is, to publish, but also to incur the wrath of the government, suffer fines, closings and imprisonments for the editors. The Japanese are a courageous people; they continued to criticize, to suffer and to go to prison. The oligarchy, or perhaps the Emperor himself, began to see that if they resisted this particular aspect of modernization, it not only exposed the throne to the risk of direct involvement in politics, but was also weakening Japan's prestige with the foreign powers. One of the great aims of the government, fully endorsed by the people as a whole, was to abrogate the 'unequal treaties'. In Japan, as in China, these gave foreign residents extra-territorial rights (they could not be tried in Japanese courts), concessions under their own rule in Yokohama, Kobe and Nagasaki and limited the Japanese rights to impose tariffs on foreign imports and exports. The government realized that the absence of any sort of democratic or elected body was a defect in foreign eyes, marking Japan as 'backward'. In that period, there was a universal faith in democratic systems, at least in the Western world.

The Meiji Constitution

In 1881 the Emperor made the momentous declaration that he would grant the people of Japan a Constitution and that this would provide for an elected assembly, which would come into being in 1889. So in twenty years Japan was to move from a medieval feudalism to a parliamentary system – at least outwardly. It must be remembered that this, to contemporaries, meant that every man of middle age had been brought up to manhood under feudalism. But the oligarchic government had no real intention of giving up power; the delay of nine years was to enable them to frame a Constitution which to outward appearance was modern and democratic – to a point – but would in reality conserve the power of the two great clans of Satsuma and Choshu.

Ito was sent on a prolonged tour of Europe to study the systems of government and find an appropriate model. He found it, in Germany. Germany was then the dominant military power in Europe. She had a few years earlier defeated France in the war of 1870, and had at that time unified herself under the rule of Prussia, and its king, who had become the German Emperor. There was much in modern Germany which seemed to agree with Japanese conditions. Here, too, was a newly-unified Empire which had formerly been divided among many feudal lords and princes. Here, too, was a military people who valued might and held their army in the highest esteem. There was also an autocratic government thinly disguised with some democratic institutions of no real power.

It was just what the oligarchy were looking for. The new Japanese system was thus to be based on German models. In 1885 the remains of the old 'Chinese model' Heian type institutions were abolished, and a government under the Emperor, Cabinet and ministries organized. There was no parliament as yet, but a Privy Council was created (really replacing the old imperial council) on which only the highest oligarchs and a very few of the court nobles closest to the throne ever served. This body, later to become the real secret organ of government, was from the first the inner defence of the oligarchy. It could advise the throne. No one was allowed to know if the advice was followed, but when the Emperor decided, all opposition must end.

In 1889, true to his promise, the Emperor proclaimed the Constitution, announced as a gift from His Majesty to the people of Japan. Gifts can be revoked. It first claimed in the most positive terms that the throne was divinely descended, and supreme. Government was the Emperor's government. The Cabinet was chosen by him, could be dismissed at his pleasure and was not responsible to the parliament, which in imitation of Germany, was called the Diet. The Diet had two houses, of Peers and Commons. The Peers, about five hundred in number, were made up of newly-created noblemen derived from the old Daimyos, the court nobles, the leading oligarchs, generals and admirals and some few others. It was therefore a safely conservative body. It had equal power with the lower house, neither could overrule the other, and if they disagreed the dispute was referred to the Emperor, who decided. This meant that the oligarchy reserved the right to make its own will prevail. The Diet could not initiate legislation, but could refuse to pass bills. If it refused to pass the money bills, the last year's budget remained in force. Thus the government could not be deprived of supply. The Diet could debate, and could send an address to the throne. These were the extent of its powers.

Yet, as it proved, they were more than enough to give the oligarchy a very rough passage for several years. The Diet clamoured for more power, and in particular for a Cabinet responsible to the political parties which had quickly formed. Refused this, it in turn refused to pass government bills. Deadlocks were frequent, dissolutions of the Diet almost annual events (it was supposed to sit for four years) and government began to get bogged down in an endless series of wordy and violent debates. The leading oligarchs disliked taking the thankless office of Prime Minister. A situation was arising which threatened the stability of the régime: if the government was to find itself in permanent conflict with the Diet, it was inevitable that public opinion, stimulated by a very active press, would turn against the régime, and thus involve the Emperor, in whose name it acted, in political strife.

The attempt to introduce a façade of democratic government, while denying it all substance, was failing. For one thing, the government was exposed to criticism for the failure of its foreign policy. This had been for years directed to treaty revision, that is, to the abolition of the 'unequal treaties' originally imposed on the Shogun in the last years of his power. But although the Western powers (who were the beneficiaries of these treaties) were willing to recognize that Japan had made great progress towards becoming a modern state, they were not willing to give up all the rights conferred in the treaties. Japan could have gained some modifications, which would have been important, but not everything. No faction within the oligarchy was willing to let rivals get the credit for a successful revision of the treaties, so whenever negotiations started, it was always easy to rouse the fierce chauvinism of the press, to decry the government's effort as weak, soft, almost treasonable, and hound any ministry out of office. No revision of the treaties was agreed upon, but the effect of successive failures in these negotiations was harmful to the prestige of an autocratic government.

Shortly after the Restoration, the capital of the country had been shifted to Yedo, the former Shogun's capital, which was now renamed Tokyo, meaning Eastern Capital. Kyoto still remained an alternative capital, but from this time onward Tokyo was the true centre of government. It is clear that this was a wise move. As the feeble rule of the Ashikaga Shoguns, compared with the relatively effective régime of the Hōjō Regents and the later Tokugawa, had proved, eastern Japan had become the main centre of power, and régimes which left this region in other hands were likely to regret it. The Restoration could have been particularly vulnerable in this respect. The régime was run and controlled by men of the western clans, Satsuma and Choshu. They came from the region of the country farthest from Tokyo and eastern Japan. Had they established the restored court in Kyoto, it would have been more than likely that some new force could have risen in Yedo, then already the largest city in the country, which would have challenged the western leadership. By establishing themselves, and the Emperor also, in the old capital of the Shoguns, this danger was avoided, and, with the growing unity of the country, has never recurred. It is often overlooked that the present Imperial

Palace in Tokyo is none other than the old Yedo Castle, seat of the Tokugawa Shoguns.

The Militarist Period (A.D. 1895–1945)

Four years after the opening of the first Diet, and in the midst of the stormy conflicts which had constantly followed since that date, Japan became involved in war with China, an event which really marks the end of the 'Restoration Period' and the beginning of a new age – the age of Japanese militarism and Asian expansion. The country was well prepared, psychologically, for this development. The warlike traditions of the Samurai were still cherished, but needed a new outlet, if civil wars were not to break out once more. The memory of Hideyoshi's invasion of Korea was kept alive, and the refusal of the Tokugawa to follow up this policy, and instead to close Japan, was now regarded as a selfish failure to perform their duty. China, moreover, was manifestly a declining power under the late Manchu Empire. She had been defeated by Britain in 1842, again by Britain and France in 1860 and still more recently by France in 1885. It is true that the French had not had it all their own way in Annam, but in the end China had yielded that kingdom to France. One reason for this was that already Japan and China were at loggerheads over Korea, and the Manchu government had realized that it certainly could not fight both France and Japan at the same time.

It was partly the hope of staving off the encroachments of Japan, much nearer to Peking than distant Annam, which made the Chinese willing to settle with France, although they had scored some military successes in that campaign. Korea was a decadent, helpless kingdom, nominally under Chinese suzerainty. It had completely failed to move with the times; its government was feeble and corrupt, the people ignorant and poor, the educated class ridden with factions. In the 'eighties of the nineteenth century Korea had been reluctantly opened up to the trade and commerce of the outer world, but this had meant a rapid rise of Japanese interests in the country. Soon

Japan was covertly challenging China as overlord, and when troubles broke out in Korea both sides sent in troops to maintain order in the capital.

This dangerous situation continued for some years, including a clash in which the Chinese force, commanded by the then young Yuan Shih-k'ai, came off best, and the Japanese had to leave Seoul. An agreement was then made between China and Japan by which both sides withdrew their forces from Korea, and agreed not to send in any troops without the prior knowledge and consent of the other party. This was a diplomatic victory for Japan, since it meant in effect that Chinese suzerainty over Korea was now shared by Japan, and also China's freedom of action weakened. But Ito, who had led the Japanese in this negotiation, was in those years busy with the preparation of the Constitution. The time for a collision with China was not ripe; China also wanted peace, so the crisis passed.

Ten years later it recurred. Korea remained in disorder, and the outbreak of a rebellion, which threatened to become a civil war involving the whole peninsula in confusion, clearly required foreign intervention. Japan claimed that China moved in first without consultation, thus breaking the treaty. The subject remains obscure, but there is no doubt that Japan wanted war – or rather the oligarchy was determined to go to war. The continual trouble with the Diet had convinced Ito that the only way to pacify the politicians and distract the attention of the public from this question of responsible government and cabinets subject to parliamentary control, was a foreign war. The mood of the country was favourable. Japan had made great advances, had now a modern army and a new, modern navy. For many years the radical opposition had clamoured for foreign expansion. For it is an interesting and significant point that the very parties and politicians who most vigorously opposed the oligarchy and clamoured for responsible cabinets were also the most active and vocal advocates of foreign wars, conquests and the acquisition of colonies. One reason for this was, no doubt, that it was the fashion. In the late nineteenth century imperialism was not only not condemned, it was admired, respected and approved. The Western nations were all engaged in the scramble for colonies in Asia and Africa. If Japan wanted to be recognized as a modern power – and all Japanese most ardently hoped to see that time – then she too must show herself to be an imperialist power, superior to her weak neighbours and able and willing to control them.

Japan was to prove an all too apt pupil of the Western imperial powers, and, as is often the case, the lessons she learned were not the ones they were most anxious to teach her. Japan invaded Korea and met with immediate and complete success. The Chinese fleet, with hardly any ammunition for its guns (the funds for this had been misappropriated by court eunuchs), was destroyed at the Battle of the Yalu, fought off the mouth of that river. The Chinese forces were driven from the country and the Japanese advanced triumphantly into south Manchuria. There seemed to be, and probably was, no obstacle to prevent them going to Peking itself. The Japanese public, in a frenzy of patriotic excitement and delight at the easy victories, was clamouring for advance; 'On to Peking' was the universal cry.

Ito and the oligarchy did not yield to this mass pressure. They now knew that if China was certainly weak and defeated, the Western powers had no intention of allowing Japan to reap all the harvest. Or, to change the metaphor, China was now a dish waiting to be carved up : the powers intended to take large shares for themselves, and were not going to let Japan have more than what they thought was her due. So Ito soon knew that 'on to Peking' would mean encountering the combined opposition of Britain, France, Russia and Germany. The disapproval of the United States was also clear. The Japanese public, in a mood of hysterical patriotism, would have taken on this combination and any other, but the oligarchy were shrewd men, and had no such foolhardy intention. Japan was not yet in the hands of its own military officers.

Peace was made. Japan gained the cession of Formosa, ended China's suzerainty over Korea – which was proclaimed a fully independent 'Empire' – and gained the lease of the tip of the Liaotung Peninsula in south Manchuria, including the good harbours called in Chinese Talienwan and Lushun. But even before he signed the treaty, Li Hung-chang, for China, knew that France, Germany and Russia had agreed, in return for other concessions, to prevent this clause coming into effect. No sooner was the treaty proclaimed than these three powers forced Japan to renounce the concession in Liaotung. This was almost immediately awarded to Russia, who proceeded to build a commercial port at Talienwan, called Dalny, and a naval base at Lushun, called Port Arthur. Japan had been tricked, or rather given the 'strongarm' treatment which was quite normal in the imperialist policies of that period. But it left a bitter sense of injustice in the Japanese people, and a determination to be avenged on those who had so treated her, particularly on Russia, who had got away with the spoils.

The effects of the Japanese victory in the China war were almost as important to Japan, and perhaps in the long run as disastrous, as they were immediately to China. In China the defeat destroyed the prestige of the dynasty and led before fifteen years had passed to revolution. In Japan victory consolidated the power of the oligarchy, but changed its nature. Henceforth it was the military side of that group which steadily rose to influence, and the civilian statesmen who lost power and control. The army and navy could point to Russia as the danger and the immediate foe of the future. But Russia was a great power; to fight her Japan must be strong, taxes must be raised, the forces increased and the Diet in some way induced to co-operate.

This was done by two devices. The oligarchy gave up its opposition to the participation of party politicians in the Cabinet, but they at the same time found that by lavish and open bribery they would win sufficient support in the Diet to get their bills passed, and government could carry on without too much trouble. The pattern soon became, and long remained, a regular cycle. The Diet sat for four years. In the first year the members were eager to co-operate with the government: they needed money to repay the heavy election expenses which they incurred to get elected. The government could thus win their support. In the second year, once more in funds, the members got more restive, and had to be bribed to support government measures. In the third and fourth years (there was very often no fourth year) the Diet became noisily critical of the government, demanded heavy outlay of funds on projects which would please the electors, decried 'clan government', abused the oligarchy and generally played to the gallery. They knew that dissolution was coming, and it was now more important to win electoral support by these tactics than collect bribes from the government. Once the election came, and was over, the need to recoup the expense produced the same pattern of behaviour.

It might have been thought that the real rulers of Japan would have wearied of this comedy: it was not a particularly entertaining spectacle, and it did the nation's name no good. But it had its uses. Under this system all real political agitation for reform of the Constitution died away, or was canalized into vain press campaigns only intended to boost the standing of some demagogic politician. He could always be bought when the time came to close down on these activities. The army and navy had meanwhile slipped a momentous provision into the workings of government. No law was passed, but by an Imperial Rescript it was laid down that only a serving general could act as Minister of War in the Cabinet, and likewise only a serving admiral as Minister for the Navy. These officers, being on the active list, remained subject to the orders of the commanders-in-chief of the two services. The head of the army during all this period was Yamagata, a Choshu leader of the oligarchy, the head of the navy, Kawamura, a Satsuma man, also dominant in the oligarchy. Thus the oligarchy, and in particular its military members, controlled any Cabinet. Their nominees, the two Ministers of War and Navy, obeyed their orders, not the policy of the Prime Minister, should this be different from that of the service chiefs. If these chiefs disliked the Cabinet's policy, or decided to change the Ministry, all they had to do was to order their Ministers of War and Navy to resign, and then refuse to nominate successors. Parliament was powerless to prevent this manoeuvre. From 1895 till 1945 this was the system by which the military party remained in real control, whatever surface changes might appear.

Except to the expert or the constitutional historian, seeking for the hidden roots of later changes, the political history of Japan from the beginning of the twentieth century until the end of the Second World War, is thus not important. It was always the same pattern of surface action covering the solid control of the military party through their two key ministers in any Cabinet. Elections might return this or that political party with a majority in the Diet; Cabinets were formed by these parties, but they always had to include the two service nominees, who could not in turn be controlled by their Cabinet colleagues, and obeyed only their own service chiefs. The main interest in internal Japanese politics in this long period of nearly half a century is the slow change in the nature of the oligarchy itself. Death took its toll of the original founders of the Restoration. Often it was not a natural death, for many of the best known leaders of the period died at the hands of assassins. Ito himself suffered this fate in 1909, at the city of Harbin in Manchuria. Almost always the assassins were fanatical youths, who could be induced to do these deeds in the belief that this or that prominent man was no longer truly serving the interests of the nation, or those of the Emperor.

There was an old tradition of such assassinations running through Japanese history, and there is no doubt that no such stigma attached to these crimes as was felt for ordinary, sordid murders for gain. The assassin never tried to escape; he met his death calmly and bravely, and everyone knew that he was only the instrument of some powerful figure who had judged the time ripe to remove a rival. Unfortunately this tradition is not yet dead, and a number of recent examples show that it is a real factor in Japanese political life today.

The surviving elder members of the Restoration leaders were grouped together in an informal, but very powerful inner ring, standing above the strife of the younger active oligarchs. These old men were called the Genro. They never numbered more than four or five at any time, and in the end the sole remaining Genro, who lived until the Second World War, was Prince Saionji, a man of ninety, a court noble by descent, scion of a house famous for its support of the Emperor Go Daigo in the fourteenth century. The Genro were not constituted by any formal decree or any clause of the Constitution. They simply acquired their position by age, and by retaining the trust and confidence of the Emperor, who always consulted them on great matters of policy. This was the position under the Emperor Meiji, but after his death, in 1913, and the succession of his son, who was soon incapacitated by illness, the Genro became in fact a kind of unofficial Regency advising the ailing Emperor, and later his young son the Crown Prince (the official Regent in the Emperor Taisho's later years), and in fact exercising the power of the throne. The Genro included men who were not from either the army or navy, or from Satsuma and Choshu. Saionji, a court noble, was an example of this. But if the presence of these men probably checked the more extreme policies of the military oligarchs, it was only a brake, not a control, which they exercised. Probably the military policies which Japan now followed had their approval and the whole-hearted support of the nation.

From the end of the war with China, Russia became the enemy of Japan; Russia not only was encroaching in Manchuria, which the Japanese coveted, but soon began to try to establish her influence in 'independent' Korea. That unfortunate country was now supposed to be an Empire (since the title of King, in the Far East, had come to mean a tributary monarch), but it remained only in the very first stages of modern progress, with only a tiny handful of trained administrators, educators or technologists. Japan intended to annex Korea, and Russian influence was thus obnoxious to her. The two countries drifted into almost open hostility. Meanwhile in 1902 the Japanese had won a great diplomatic success; the Anglo-Japanese Alliance, then concluded with Britain, not only made Japan the recognized ally of a Great Power, and thus gave her the status of one herself, but was preceded by the final and complete abrogation of the unequal treaties. After the victory over China, military power obtained what diplomacy had failed to win. No Western nation made any further objection to its subjects coming under Japanese law courts, all gave up the concession areas of foreign residence and control, and soon abandoned any hope of controlling the level of Japanese tariffs. China was to obtain the same result, and by the same means (military power) forty years later, when all other arguments had made no progress at all.

These and other experiences of the power politics of the early twentieth century convinced the Japanese people that their rulers were right to claim that only force mattered in international affairs. The military party had won a free hand in Asia, and they exploited this advantage to gain complete control of the nation's destiny and government. The war with Russia, opening in 1904, seemed to confirm their judgement. Japan was victorious by land and by sea. Having begun the war by an unannounced attack on Russian ships, the Japanese forces rapidly landed and occupied Korea, then advanced to besiege the Russian garrison of Port Arthur. Russia was at a great disadvantage from the point of view of geography. Her armies in Manchuria fought at the end of an enormous line of communications, the single track Trans-Siberian Railway, only recently completed.

Sea communications between Port Arthur and Russia meant going round the whole world and through the Mediterranean or Baltic seas to home ports. Yet the Russian Baltic fleet actually performed this great voyage, going round Africa, to the coast of China, and meeting the Japanese fleet in its home waters, the Straits of Tsushima separating Japan from Korea. There Admiral Togo won a complete victory over the Russian fleet, which was in poor seaworthy condition after so long a voyage. Japan obtained the mastery of the sea in her region, and before long took Port Arthur. Formidable Russian forces, which had fought well, though poorly equipped, still remained in Manchuria. Their commanders were still confident of ultimate victory, for they knew that Japan had gone to the limit of her strength, and could not sustain a campaign to conquer a huge region like Manchuria. But at home disasters and misgovernment had brought about the first, abortive Russian revolution of 1905. The Tsar wanted peace lest revolution gain strength. The President of the United States intervened with an offer of mediation, which both parties really gladly accepted, though feigning reluctance. A treaty was concluded at Portsmouth in the U.S.A. in September 1905.

By this treaty Russia gave up Port Arthur and Liaotung, which came to Japan. Japan also became the protector of Korea, and won the Russian rights in the railways of south Manchuria. China, the nominal sovereign of this territory in which the war had been fought, was supposed to be a neutral, and her rights were disregarded by both sides. Japan was now a major power: she had a colonial empire of Formosa, Korea (annexed outright five years later in 1910) and extensive leases and rights in south Manchuria which made that rich region virtually a Japanese possession. Had Japan stopped at this point, it is possible that she might have retained much, or all, and might have gradually developed a more liberal home government. But for the military in power this was but the first step, the step which would make possible an immense further advance into China, and perhaps into Siberia also.

Before long opportunity presented itself. Four years after the annexation of Korea, the First World War broke out, and this gave Japan chances for expansion which she was quick to seize. Britain and her allies invited Japan – an ally by virtue of the Anglo-Japanese Alliance – to join the war and take the German-leased territory and port of Tsingtao, in Shantung province. Japan did so, and had no intention of giving it back to China. Before the end of the war the Russian revolution broke out, and Japan was able to occupy northern Manchuria ('to maintain order') and also to occupy a large area of eastern Siberia: but from these regions she was later to withdraw, when the Russian Communist régime had gathered strength, driven the White Russian armies out of the country and was advancing to the Pacific.

During the war, in 1915, Japan presented to the President of China, then Yuan Shih-k'ai (who was planning to make himself Emperor), the famous Twenty-One Demands, which amounted to a claim to exercise a protectorate over China. Police powers, military missions and control, new concessions, railway rights and many other claims were asked for. Had they been accepted, Chinese independence would have been at an end and the country reduced to the position of Korea before annexation ended that country's independent existence. Aided by the protests of the Western powers, Yuan rejected the most severe demands, but had to accept many others, further strengthening Japan's hold on Manchuria, and rights in China proper. At the Versailles Treaty in 1919 Japan, in spite of China's protests, was awarded the former German port of Tsingtao on the coast of Shantung province. Japan also got all the German rights to build railways in that region, giving her a large measure of control over the whole province. It was already obvious that one strong faction in Japan planned to acquire still more powers in China, and ultimately might be aiming at the conquest of the whole country.

Japanese ambitions were now arousing the fears of the Western powers. The Washington Naval Treaty of 1921 not only compelled Japan to accept, most unwillingly, a ratio of 5:5:3 in naval power to America and Britain, but lost her the Anglo-Japanese Alliance, which was allowed to lapse. A Nine Power Treaty also guaranteed the sovereignty and independence of China. These treaties were highly unpopular in Japan. Liberal statesmen responsible for them were in danger of assassination, but the rising money power of the great capitalist firms acted as some check on the military party. War was now very expensive; and unless Japan could trade, she would not have the resources to compete with the military budgets of the greatest nations. Aggressive policies made these powers hostile, and roused Chinese nationalism, resulting in trade losses, boycotts and unfavourable legislation against Japanese imports in many countries. The new money power, as yet only influential, not really powerful, helped to give Japan and Asia an uneasy breathing spell, lasting from the end of the First World War until 1931, some ten or twelve years.

During that period the Japanese government had a more liberal character than ever before, the political parties won some real influence on affairs and the military power, though never diminished, was less active. Perhaps one reason for this was that the old leaders, the men who had won the reputation of heroes in the victorious wars against China and Russia, were now passing away. Military heroes must win battles; their influence dwindles when there is a long peace, and although there had been no peace which could be called long, there had equally been no war in which great battles could be won. Japan's ambitions in China and elsewhere were now facing difficulties which were very real, and some Japanese leaders at least knew this. The Russian revolution might have eleminated Tsarist Russia, the old enemy, but it had put in its place Communism, which soon proved to be a much worse danger. China was also in revolution which more and more took on a character alarming to Japan.

In the ten years between 1920 and 1930 the Chinese revolution had developed into an open contest between the Nationalist and Communist parties. Neither was pleasing to Japan. As an imperial monarchy, ruled by a form of parliamentary government which was strictly limited and largely subject to the control of bodies such as the Privy Council, responsible only to the Emperor, Japan could not be expected to see anything but menace in the prospect that a Communist Party might come to power in China. Such a government would be closely allied to Russia, and this combination would clearly be far too strong for Japan. A Communist China would be the end of Japanese power on the continent of Asia. We now can see that this has come about, but the Japanese military leaders could see the risk from the mid-twenties quite clearly.

The Nationalist Party (Kuomintang), on the other hand, although anti-Communist, had as its main programme the recovery of sovereign rights, the return of leased territories and concessions, the abolition of foreign privileges. These were all the fruits of Japanese conquests and military action. Japan had far larger stakes in China than any of the Western foreign powers; the success of Nationalist policy would thus strike away Japan's privileged position, and harm her commerce and industry. Not only the military, but also the great industrialists, feared the rise of China's power, be it Communist or Nationalist.

This fact largely undermined the opposition to militarist influence at home. The political parties, always dependent on money, had now found that the great industrial enterprises were good paymasters, and the interests of their directors coincided with those of most of the members of the Diet, who were usually landholders and businessmen themselves. In these years the political parties came to be at least partly controlled by the great industrial firms. One such government, in 1925, was commonly called the Mitsubishi Cabinet because of the close connection with that firm of the Prime Minister and some of his principal ministers. Partly as a result of this development, partly due to the death of some of the old leaders, such as Marshal Yamagata (for long the leader of the army, and later a Genro), the military party suffered a partial eclipse. There was no easy, obvious expedition which the armed forces could carry out without leading to unforeseen and large-scale consequences. Japan belonged to the League of Nations: an attack on China would provoke an international crisis. Korea was already annexed, most of the other countries of the Far East were colonies or protectorates of the Western powers. War was bound to mean major war, and that was a risk which the industrialists and the high civilian advisers of the throne did not wish to run. But in 1930 events at home precipitated Japan into this sort of venture, the end of which was the Second World War.

In 1930 a new naval conference, for the limitation of fleets of war, was called in London. After some negotiation the Japanese Cabinet approved a compromise by which Japan's claims, as formulated by the Navy Command, were somewhat reduced. The Cabinet authorized the signing of this treaty. But this result was brought about by the accident that as the Minister for the Navy, as usual an admiral, had been absent from the conference, the Prime Minister, Hamaguchi, was himself acting as Minister for the Navy, although a civilian. When the treaty was submitted for ratification by the Emperor, the Military Council – a kind of combined services high advisory body – criticized it strongly and advised rejection. The Privy Council, an even higher body, which was to some degree similar to the Genro (since the surviving Genro were members of it), after long debate unexpectedly advised the Emperor to ratify the treaty. A civilian Cabinet had taken the lead in a military matter and had had its policy approved by the throne. This was a severe blow to the power of the military faction, and seemed to foreshadow an important constitutional advance in the power of the Cabinet, and thus of the Diet.

It was said, later, that the Privy Council came to this conclusion on the advice of Count Makino, Keeper of the Privy Seal, and Prince Saionji, a Genro, and the most intimate adviser of the Emperor. Both these high court officials were civilians, and represented that vague but very powerful influence which the Emperor and his closest advisers could always exercise if they thought fit. The military were greatly disturbed, and there can be little doubt that this incident led them into that path of extra-legal military adventure which culminated in the Second World War.

The scene of the first action in the following year, 1931, was Manchuria. Japan's special position in that region had recently been affected by developments in Chinese politics. Chang Tso-lin, the Chinese warlord who had long ruled Manchuria, had been dead for three years, blown up in his train as he returned to Mukden (his capital) from his defeats at the hand of the Nationalists in China. It was said that his death was caused by the Japanese army, since he had failed them in giving way to the Nationalists. Since then, his son had ruled the province. However in 1930 Chang's son intervened in China, and occupied Peking in the Nationalist interest, suppressing a revolt against Nanking by the northern generals. This also was displeasing to Japan, who wished to check the growth of Nanking's power, which was now spreading over the whole country. There can be little doubt that the Japanese army had now decided that the Chang family were dangerous and must be removed, and that Manchuria, unless it were taken by Japan, would slip under the control of Nanking.

On the night of 18 September 1931, rather more than ten yars before Pearl Harbour, the Japanese army seized Mukden, alleging that Chinese forces had tried to blow up the South Manchurian Railway near that city. The railway was Japanese, taken from the Russians in 1905. It is quite certain now that no such 'incident' ever took place, and that it was invented as a pretext. The action of the army was rapid and effective. The Chinese were taken by surprise, and the best of their forces were south of the Great Wall, near Peking. In a few weeks the Japanese had occupied all the three provinces of Manchuria, including the northern one bordering on Russian Siberia.

The Japanese government at Tokyo was not really informed of these actions, nor consulted as they went on. The army had taken over. The next year the Japanese extended their occupation to the province of Jehol, in Inner Mongolia, north of Peking. By this time, a violent agitation had arisen in China, and even the Nanking government, though only anxious to pursue its war against the Chinese Communists, was forced by public opinion to oppose Japan. Early in 1932 Japanese forces in the concession at Shanghai clashed with Chinese forces, whom they had tried to drive away from the border of the concession. The Chinese fought back, and hard; the Japanese were pressed to the waterfront in some places, where their warships could give support. The eastern part of the Shanghai International Settlement (concession) was reduced to ruins and the fighting in it lasted two months.

Through the intervention of foreign powers, this outbreak was prevented from developing into a full-scale war, but it fatally prejudiced the prospects of lasting peace. Japan refused to withdraw from Manchuria, and later this same year, in September 1932, proclaimed Manchuria to be an independent state, for which they found an Emperor in the person of the ex-Emperor of the Manchu dynasty, P'u Yi, who had been driven out of his Peking residence six years before, and had been living in the Japanese concession at Tientsin. P'u Yi was enthroned as Emperor K'ang Te. But he never had the least power, being surrounded by Japanese advisers and 'experts' who ran the government of the new state. The Western and all other foreign powers refused to recognize Manchukuo, as the new state was called, and Japan withdrew from the League of Nations. But she suffered no sanctions, no interference in her accomplished act of aggression. This event marked the decline of the League of Nations, and the general deterioration of the prospects for world peace.

During the next five years there was increasing unease both in China and in Japan itself. The situation in the country was marked by the great economic depression which swept over the world in 1930–2, and perhaps as a consequence, the rise of new and violent-minded forces in Japan itself. There appeared at this time a movement among the young officers of the armed forces, which attracted much support from civilians also. It was anti-democratic, opposed the Diet and despised the parties, claiming that Japan must be renewed and return to her early virtues. In practice this meant that the young officers disliked the industrialists, distrusted the older statesmen as weaklings, despised the rich as worldly and decadent and violently opposed all political parties and politicians.

A number of assassinations of prominent people occurred, and in 1936 there was what came close to being a *coup d'état* against the government, most of whose members were shot down. The movement was with difficulty controlled – even Prince Saionji, the venerated Genro, had been attacked and wounded. The result was that although the leaders were condemned, the military party insisted on the suspension of parliamentary rule, as it was claimed that it was provoking the army into violence. In Japan the military were in control, but the control of the senior officers was actually threatened by the power and influence of their juniors, who were moved by a mixture of Fascist ideas, old-style Japanese ideals and hatred of the rich, which made them at times not far from Socialist in their thinking. Many of them came from relatively poor farming families, and the depression had brought great distress to the farmers and peasants. The Diet was largely representative of the landowning class: consequently the hostility of the young officers to the Diet was not merely a matter of political beliefs. It had a real economic basis.

Shortly after these events, a matter of a few months only, the war with China broke out once more. Japan had never really ceased to put on pressure and to achieve further penetration. In 1935, on one pretext or another, the Chinese had been compelled to accord Japan as much in the two northern provinces of Hopei and Chahar as she had formerly held in Manchuria before 1931. The local government was made autonomous of Nanking, the Chinese forces were reduced and very large Japanese forces were to be permitted to occupy points along the railways. Peking itself (not at this time any longer the capital) is located in Hopei province, and was virtually surrounded by Japanese forces. Japan, like other treaty powers, had had since the Boxer Rebellion in 1900 the right to station Legation Guards in Peking and along the railway to Shanhaikuan, on the coast. This gave her the ability to expand these originally small token forces into large formations virtually occupying Peking and holding the railway to the Manchurian border.

At Wanp'ing, a small town some twenty miles south of Peking, on the night of 7 July 1937, the Japanese army was engaged in night manoeuvres. They alleged that their forces were fired upon by the small garrison (Chinese) of Wanp'ing. It was another Mukden 'incident', either wholly fictitious or contrived. The Japanese forces attacked and took the town of Wanp'ing (strategically placed at the road crossing and railway bridge of the big Yun Ting Ho River) and in the next few days attacked and drove off the Chinese forces stationed throughout the province. Peking was occupied. The Chinese withdrew to the passes through the Great Wall to the north of the city. Heavy fighting soon broke out in this region, and in the southern part of the province along the railways leading to Hankow and Nanking on the Yangtze. To all intents the two countries were now at war. A few weeks later a new conflict broke out at Shanghai, where again the Chinese, better equipped than the northern forces, fought back with courage and success, holding the Japanese for three months. Once again the eastern part of Shanghai was destroyed by incessant street fighting and bombardment, and much damage was done by bombs to other parts of the city and concessions. The Western powers were helpless. They were themselves close to war in Europe, and quite unable to prevent Japanese action in eastern Asia. Their rights in China were now openly violated by the Japanese forces. An American gunboat, the *Panay*, was sunk by Japanese aircraft on the Yangtze, and the British Ambassador machine-gunned in his car by aircraft as he drove to Shanghai. Either of these outrages would have led to war in any earlier period.

It is hard to say with certainty what the Japanese army and navy expected to be the outcome of the attack on China in 1937. There is much evidence to show that they believed that the Nanking government would not really resist; that north China at least would be yielded to them, and that China would accept some settlement that would leave her weak and defenceless. The Japanese army leaders believed that Chiang Kai-shek and his Nationalist Party were more afraid of the Chinese Communists than of the Japanese army. They would prefer Japanese protection to Communist victory. It is possible that some, at least, might have made this choice, but it was not Chiang Kai-shek's nor that of the Chinese people as a whole. From the first the war got out of scale and beyond control. It spread far beyond the Hopei region, involving one province after another. Before the end of 1937 it was already obvious that Japan was embarked, unwillingly, unexpectedly, but inescapably, on an attempt to conquer China. No objective short of this could settle anything.

It was not called a war by either side. To avoid the operation of certain United States laws, which forbade trading with nations at war, both sides preferred not to declare war at all. Thus it was known as the Undeclared War. This phase lasted from July 1937 to December 1941. Japan made great advances in the early years. Nanking was taken in late 1937, and the city sacked with disgraceful atrocities. In the next year Canton and most of the coast were occupied, and the Japanese armies penetrated, aided by naval forces, far up the Yangtze, taking Hankow, the temporary capital, in late 1938. Meanwhile, operations in the interior of the northern provinces had met some setbacks. A Japanese force was heavily defeated in southern Shantung, and their advance westward by the central railway called the Lung-Hai was stopped by the Chinese taking the appalling step of breaching the Yellow River dykes. This let loose an immense flood in the path of the Japanese advance, led

233

to the river changing its course and devastating a vast region of eastern China. Many millions of people lost their lives, still more all that they possessed. This was indeed the policy which the Chinese named 'the scorched earth'. By the end of 1938 the Japanese advance had come to a stop. They had occupied coastal China, much of the eastern provinces and the middle Yangtze valley. But beyond these stretched another region, quite as large and nearly as populous, the mountain zone of western China, largely without communications of any modern sort, without navigable rivers, roads or railways. It stopped the Japanese advance.

Moreover, the occupied regions were but lightly held. The area was vast: a huge army would be needed to garrison every town, guard every railway and bridge. But soon it was plain that unless this was done such places would become bases of Chinese guerrilla resistance, such communications would be cut. The Japanese army had believed, when it was plain that China was going to resist, that the fall of Nanking, the capital, would bring the war to an end. It made no difference; the Chinese government retired to other cities, first Hankow, later Chungking. Then the Japanese thought that if the whole coast, all the ports, were occupied, China would be cut off from foreign supplies and forced to surrender. But this, too, led to no conclusion. China is vast, her resources are great, although at that time very little developed, and Chinese skill and energy rapidly improvised new bases and made new industrial centres. Heavy machinery was dragged by hundreds of men on rollers over the mountains, or poled up rivers in barges before the Japanese could seize it. It seemed that there was no end to this war. China was clearly too vast to occupy, and she would not submit. Guerrilla warfare, organized by the Communist Party, spread rapidly throughout the occupied zones of north China. Soon the Japanese found that large forces were tied down in this struggle, which never had any conclusive results.

The failure to win an outright victory in China, the prospect of a long war, would have been more disheartening to the military rulers of Japan had not, at this very time, the Second World War broken out, thus opening to Japan what seemed golden alternatives to the Chinese morass. Japan had been allied with Germany and Italy in what was called the Berlin–Rome–Tokyo Axis, ever since Germany and Italy, for other reasons, had also withdrawn from the League of Nations. But this alliance was rather superficial. It was more a matter of mutual diplomatic support against the Western powers, Britain and France, than one of joint military plans. The evidence is clear that Japan followed her own ambitions in Asia, while Germany had hers in Europe; there was no co-ordination. For example, Germany tried to mediate between China and Japan in 1939 and 1940: the Germans remained on good terms with the Kuomintang government till Pearl Harbour. Russia had been invaded by Germany in the summer of 1941: but Japan made no move against Russia for the whole duration of the war, until Russia attacked Japan in the last days of the struggle.

Thus, although Germany went to war with Britain and France in the first week of September 1939, Japan did not join her, and although relations between the Western powers and Japan were now hardly friendly, they continued to be at peace. Hard-pressed by the Germans, the British had no desire to engage Japan also, and sacrificed the interests of China and their own residents in that country to appease Japan (notably by closing the Burma Road, China's one supply line to the outer world, in 1940).

The fall of France (1940) altered this situation. When it became clear to the Japanese leaders that France was now powerless in the Far East, Holland also unable to defend her rich possessions and Britain fighting alone against triumphant Germany, it seemed obvious that the territories and colonies of these countries in eastern Asia were at Japan's mercy. The only possible obstacle was the United States. It was clear that America was sympathetic to the Allied cause, and opposed German Nazi and Italian Fascist aims. America also disapproved of Japan's invasion of China, and was applying some economic pressure upon Japan, by refusing the sale of scrap metal and oil.

Thus the reckless military party who now wholly dominated the Japanese Empire believed that the U.S.A. was a dangerous obstacle to their plans. To invade French Indo-China, the Dutch East Indies (now Indonesia) and Malaya would be easy : but if America opposed this move, she had bases in the Philippines, at Guam in the Pacific and above all at Pearl Harbour in Honolulu, Hawaii. Civilian counsel and diplomatic advisers were not listened to in Tokyo. They might have pointed out that under the elaborate Constitution of the United States it was very difficult for the President to declare war unless the territory of the United States was itself attacked. Had Japan invaded Malaya and the Dutch East Indies, President Roosevelt might have striven to get Congress to sanction a war with Japan, but it might have taken him six months or a year to arrive at that result. Long before, Japan would have been in consolidated possession of all these territories, and perhaps of Australia, or large parts of it, also. The military minds in Japan saw it otherwise. They saw that if Pearl Harbour and its great fleet were destroyed, America would be rendered powerless in the Pacific. If the Philippines and Guam were occupied, America would have no base on the western side of the ocean. So America could do nothing, and Japan would have a free hand. They miscalculated the immense power of American industry to recover from such a blow (which still left it quite intact), and the immense wave of indignation and patriotism which such an attack, unprovoked, would arouse in the American people. These two forces were to destroy militarist Japan.

The course of the Pacific War is well known and belongs to a wider field of history than that of Japan or even eastern Asia. At first all went well for Japan following the raid on Pearl Harbour, 7 December 1941, which crippled the American Pacific Fleet. The Philippines were invaded and occupied; Malaya was overrun and Singapore captured. French Indo-China, powerless and ruled by a German-dominated Vichy governor, surrendered to Japanese occupation. After the fall of Singapore, the Japanese army invaded the Dutch East Indies and in the course of 1942 occupied them. They pressed on into New Guinea, and also invaded Burma, which, too, was occupied. By the end of 1942 the Japanese Empire reached from the frontiers of India to the mountains in Papua, far out into the Pacific and covered half of China. Western rule was everywhere eliminated. Australia was in deadly peril.

That peril was averted by the Battle of the Coral Sea (1942), the first and, as it proved, the decisive check to Japanese advance. This had also been halted on the north-east frontier of India. By 1943 the Japanese tide was at slack water; by 1944 it was plainly on the ebb. She never received any significant help from Germany, who by 1943 was also being forced on to the defensive. Japanese resources were not sufficient for a war on this scale, and they had not the time to organize and utilize the resources of the many rich countries that their armies had overrun. The advance of General MacArthur's forces from island to island, bypassing those without strategic significance, striking down the resistance in those that mattered to his plans, became irresistible. By 1945 it had reached the territories of Japan herself, not only by the medium of devastating air raids which burned out the wooden cities of Japan (Kyoto, the ancient capital, with its wealth of art treasures was deliberately spared), but by the invasion and capture of the naval base of Okinawa in the Ryukyu Islands, just south of Japan itself. In August 1945, two atomic bombs were dropped, within a few days of each other, the first on Hiroshima, the second on Nagasaki. In each city more than two hundred thousand people were killed and the cities razed to the ground.

The Japanese government, it is now known, had already been brought to realize that surrender was inevitable, if Japan was not to be invaded and ruined. Tentative inquiries through Russia had been made, but as the terms seemed to the Japanese military too harsh, they were not followed up. The government was deeply divided, and there were now no Genro left alive to whom the Emperor could turn, and whose advice would be accepted by all. Whether, without the horrible holocaust of the atomic bombs, the rulers of Japan would have seen the necessity of unconditional surrender – the only terms offered by the Allied powers – cannot be known. It is certain that after those bombs had fallen, the Emperor saw that peace must be secured, and it was, as far as can be known, on his personal initiative that he broadcast to his people ordering them to cease

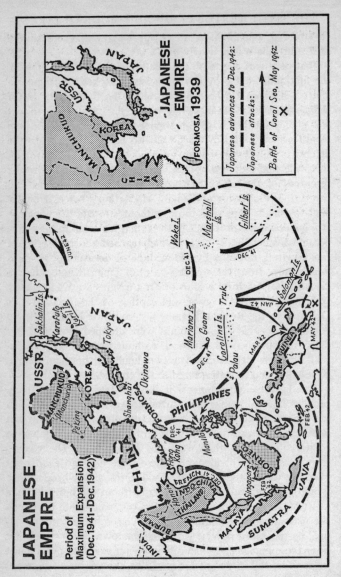

Map 5

fighting and accept the unconditional surrender, which was signed in Tokyo Bay on 2 September 1945. It must be recognized that at this moment the mystical prestige of the Japanese throne was the factor which saved not only Japan, but the lives of thousands of American and Allied soldiers also. No one else could have the authority to order such a disastrous end to Japan's dream of conquest. No one else would have been obeyed, as he was, by the huge Japanese armies then quartered in every country of eastern Asia. The last autocratic act of the Japanese Emperor was also the finest and the most valuable display of powers which he was henceforward no longer to wield.

CHAPTER EIGHT

Korea

It has been supposed that the basic population of the Korean peninsula came into that country at some unknown remote period from the neighbouring part of mainland Asia – the region today known as the north-eastern provinces of China, or Manchuria. There are linguistic relations between Korean and the Tungus languages still spoken by some small tribes in north Manchuria and eastern Siberia, but nothing is known of what can be called Korean history until the Chinese records become available. In 108 B.C. the Han Empire, then at its strongest, invaded north Korea and reduced that area – apparently very much the same region as the present 'North Korea' – to the status of a Chinese province, which was known as Lo Lang, or in Korean, Lak Lang, and had its capital at the city of Pyongyang, which is today the capital of North Korea. The Lak Lang colony was soon developed until it became a centre of civilization, but of Chinese civilization. The tombs of the ruling class, the Chinese officials, have been excavated in modern times and have yielded a truly remarkable collection of fine works of art, gold and silver ware, lacquer and many other products which show that Lak Lang was in touch with the finest products of Han culture. Yet it is equally clear that these luxuries were enjoyed only by a small class of Chinese ruling officials, and there is little in their tombs to show the level of civilization among their native Korean subjects.

Chinese rule endured as long as the Early Han remained strong, and there can be no doubt that the Lak Lang outpost had an immense influence upon the natives of Korea, not only among those who were under direct Chinese rule. Civilization, as it slowly came to the farther parts of the peninsula, was essentially, indeed exclusively, Chinese culture.

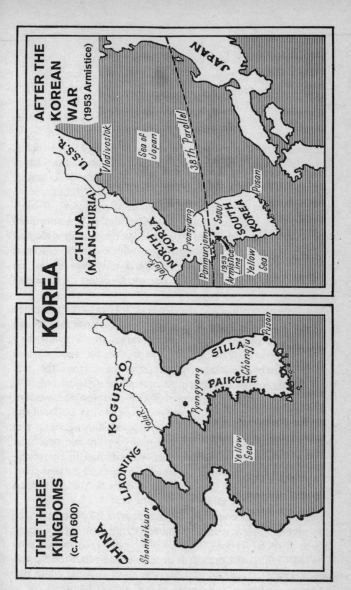

Map 6

The Three Kingdoms

In 57 B.C., at a time when the Early Han was entering into a period of internal strife, Chinese rule seems to have collapsed, and there soon emerged a tripartite division of Korea into three native kingdoms, all strongly under Chinese cultural influence. The most northerly, inheriting the former colony of Lak Lang, also extended beyond the limits of modern Korea into what is now south Manchuria, or the Chinese province of Liaoning. This, like Korea itself, is agricultural land, and suitable for a farming population, unlike the more northerly parts of Manchuria, which long remained pastoral country. This northern Korean kingdom was called Koguryo – a name which may be the first form of the later Koryo, from which our name 'Korea' is derived. Koguryo also made its capital at Pyongyang, which thus has the distinction of being one of the oldest capital cities in all Asia.

The Korean peninsula is divided lengthwise by a high range of mountains which follows close to the east coast; it is the valleys of the western side, running down to the sea, which provide the best farming land, until the far south-east is reached, where the range recedes somewhat from the east coast. This geographical fact determined the political boundaries of the other two kingdoms. Paikche occupied the western coast, below the border of Koguryo, probably not far from the present line of division between North and South Korea. It was smaller in area than Koguryo, but more fertile, and probably, therefore, almost as populous. Silla was situated in the south-east corner of the peninsula, a much smaller and weaker state, but protected by its isolated position and the wild eastern coast along the foot of the Diamond Mountains.

The history of these three kingdoms, which endured for the next seven hundred years, is known mainly through Chinese notices of such relations, whether of war or peace, as prevailed between China and Korea. It is at least evident that the Korean kingdoms steadily developed a civilization, which, while owing much to China, had yet local and native features. Literature, since the Chinese script (the only one in existence in eastern Asia at that time) was naturally borrowed, remained very strongly 'Chinese'; indeed it was little more than a provincial variant of the main culture. The Koreans learned to study the Confucian classics, and to model their governments more or less, on Chinese lines. In the fourth century A.D., during this long period, after the introduction of Buddhism to China, the new religion also reached Korea, where it was warmly welcomed, and soon became the national religion, ousting, or overlaying, the earlier polytheism, which mainly survives as country superstitions.

Archaeological evidence from Japan shows that during the period of the Korean Three Kingdoms there was an active and growing commerce with the Japanese islands, not yet unified into one state. Korean artifacts, weapons and other objects are found in large numbers in the mound burials of early Japan, and the quantity of these objects increases in the later burials, proving a growing commerce. Korea, as geography suggests, was the bridge by which much mainland culture – and probably immigrants also – reached Japan. The transmission of Buddhism by this route, which is a fully documented fact of Japanese history, was thus only a further step in a long-continuing process. Since the ideas and the culture which Korea passed on to Japan, had in turn been received by Korea from China, it is clear that contact with China in the long period of the Later Han and the following Six Dynasty Period must have been close. Chinese historical records, noting Korean embassies, provide some proof of this.

During the period of division between North and South in China, which did not end until the Sui dynasty reunited the Empire in A.D. 589, the Northern Empire of China, under the Wei or subsequent shorter, weaker dynasties, was not strong enough to coerce the Korean kingdoms. In general there seems to have been very little strife along the common frontier, which was in any case short. Koguryo reached down through what is now Liaoning (south Manchuria) to the Great Wall, but at the pass on the sea coast, Shanhaikuan, the coastal plain is reduced to a few miles (probably even narrower in antiquity) and the formidable range of the Yin Shan Mountains shuts off China proper from the lands beyond the wall.

After the Sui dynasty had come to full power over all China, in the reign of its second sovereign, the Emperor Yang Ti, the peaceful relations with Korea came to an abrupt end. The Emperor Yang Ti was a man of vast ambition, and inordinate vanity: he believed that, being now the master of all China, he had the right to reclaim the full territory of the former united Empire, that of the Han, which had once incorporated North Korea – the contemporary kingdom of Koguryo – in its Empire. He demanded the submission of the King of Koguryo, and when this was refused, set in motion a formidable invasion.

Yang Ti is no favourite of the Confucian historians of China, and they attribute his aggressive policy to dreams of glory and naked ambition for conquest. This may well be too simple an explanation. It would appear that the population of that part of Koguryo which is now the Chinese province of Liaoning was even then of mixed race, and probably had been largely settled by Chinese farmers who preferred the relative peace of Koguryo to the troubles of the failing Wei dynasty and its brief successors in north China. Yang Ti claimed them as his own, fugitive subjects. It is also more than probable that he was looking for a new territory in which to settle his own disbanded soldiery, since among the problems of all new Chinese dynasties were the swollen armies which had enabled them to win power, but which were unnecessary and even dangerous after the throne was theirs. But he was to find that Koguryo, the nearest Korean kingdom, was no easy prey. The Koreans fought a skilful delaying action, avoiding meeting the great Chinese armies in set battles, but defending their walled cities with great tenacity. The fact that they had so many such strongholds to defend is some proof of the advanced level of their culture.

Winter overtook the Chinese in the bleak climate of Liaoning, before they had reduced the strongholds or even penetrated beyond the Yalu River into the peninsula. They were obliged to retreat, with heavy losses from hardship, cold and the breakdown of supplies. Yang Ti failed to appreciate that the very size of his armies contributed to their defeat. It was almost impossible to supply so many men at such a distance from the more fertile regions of China: only a swift success could save them from being caught in the open country by the harsh Manchurian winter, when the land afforded no supplies. Yang Ti tried again (A.D. 612–13) and this time met with even greater disaster, through the same mistakes, and the same defensive tactics by the Koreans. The disaster caused grave unrest in China, where the continuance of a new dynasty was far from secure: when the obstinate Emperor determined to raise further armies for a third attempt, there was a general revolt, which, growing in complexity, finally overthrew the Sui dynasty in favour of the great T'ang dynasty.

Koguryo, and beyond her, all Korea, was saved. For several years there was no further war with China. It is indeed possible that the great T'ang Emperor T'ai Tsung, himself a master of warfare, was not anxious to repeat Yang Ti's errors and had no ambitions to conquer Koguryo. The renewal of the war was the consequence of Koguryo's own ambitions. Confident that, having defeated great China, she had little to fear from her small neighbour Silla, Koguryo started a campaign to force that country into submission. But Silla, far away from China, saw the T'ang as protectors rather than as enemies. The King of Silla sent an embassy to T'ang T'ai Tsung offering tribute and acceptance of Chinese suzerainty in return for protection against Koguryo. Not for the last time Korean internal quarrels were to open the road for foreign intervention. T'ai Tsung, for the sake of his own prestige, could not refuse. He could not admit that the T'ang were afraid to take the risk which had destroyed the Sui. He raised a large army, and once more invaded Koguryo by the land route. This no doubt saved Silla, but did not destroy Koguryo, which, using the same tactics as before, held up the T'ang advance by stubborn defence of the fortified cities. T'ai Tsung was not so unwary as Yang Ti; when winter approached he lifted the sieges and withdrew into China before his army could suffer from want and privation. But he was already a sick man and the rigours of the campaign, and its disappointing outcome, brought on his fatal illness (A.D. 649).

It is interesting to observe in the detailed description of T'ai Tsung's seige of the Koguryo city of An Shih Ch'ang, which lasted for sixty-three days, that the Koreans adopted very many of the same defensive devices which are described in the famous Persian siege of Plataea in Greece, more than a thousand years before. The Koreans, however, had a very close escape. Their field army, rashly engaging the full strength of the T'ang forces commanded by the Emperor, had been utterly routed; only the defence of An Shih Ch'ang and the approach of winter had saved them. The death of T'ai Tsung now brought the war to an end. It was several years before China was once more tempted to invade the peninsula. Then in the reign of T'ai Tsung's successor, in A.D. 655, it was the ambition of Koguryo – now in alliance with Paikche, and aimed at the destruction of Silla – which once more involved the T'ang. Silla appealed for help: many at the Chinese court were not in favour of sending any help, fearing more failures. At this time the weak and sickly Emperor Kao Tsung was under the influence of his remarkable wife, the Empress Wu. Chinese historians, who did not at all approve of the Empress Wu, refrain from attributing to her the new plan which proved successful, yet the fact that she is known at this time to have controlled policy makes it more than probable that it was her idea. It was also novel, unorthodox, untried and strange to Chinese tradition. It was to invade Korea by sea, avoiding the northern wastes and their inhospitable climate, and to direct the attack upon the weaker partner, Paikche, and then take Koguryo from the rear. This invasion was the first example of a Chinese sea-borne invasion in their history, and one of the very few ever recorded.

Chinese Suzerainty over Korea (A.D. 688–1895)

It was successful; not indeed immediately, or easily, but the Chinese won a foothold in Paikche, enlarged it, ultimately overcame that kingdom and then invaded Koguryo, which after a resolute defence was conquered. Silla co-operated with the Chinese. A Japanese force, invited by Paikche to save that kingdom, was destroyed by the Chinese in a land and sea battle on the west coast. This was the first time that Chinese and Japanese forces had ever met in war (A.D. 663). It was Silla which profited from the victory, becoming within a few years the ruler of all Korea, for the first time united in one kingdom, under Chinese suzerainty. The T'ang soon discovered that control of Korea in this way was easier and less costly than trying to impose direct Chinese rule on the conquered kingdoms. From A.D. 668, the date of the conquest, to A.D. 935, for three hundred and sixty-seven years the Silla Kingdom ruled Korea, and this is one of the greatest periods of Korean culture. The capital, located at Ch'ongju in the south-east, the old Silla capital, became a centre of arts and literature, which had a great and lasting influence across the seas in Japan, where the new empire set up at Heian was then at its most flourishing period.

The rule of Silla outlasted the T'ang, their protectors, by some thirty years, but when the T'ang had fallen and the power of China was weak under the turbulent Five Dynasties which followed, the old kingdom of Koguryo had its revenge. A rising in the north set up a new kingdom called Koryo, which overcame the declining power of Silla, and, free from Chinese interference, unified the whole peninsula under a new régime. It did not regain the former Koguryo territory of Liaoning (south Manchuria) which had by that time been incorporated in the border Empire of Liao, Tartar ruled, which also extended into the adjoining Chinese province of Hopei. Koryo set up its capital in the centre of the peninsula at Song-do, fifty miles north of modern Seoul. There was no revival of Paikche – nor of Silla either: from the foundation of Koryo the Korean kingdom remained united until the recent partition at the end of the Second World War, and whatever distinctive traits the old Three Kingdoms may have possessed disappeared. The Korean people are a unified race, speaking the same language and sharing the same culture in both North and South.

The Koryo period is regarded as less brilliant than the Silla epoch, but it was a highly civilized state. Its porcelain, developed under some Chinese (Sung) influence, is both beautiful and distinctive. Culture, especially literature, remained strongly tinged with Chinese influence and the government was also modelled on Confucian principles. But Korea was never a mere extension of China; it always retained a marked individuality, a strong national consciousness. The weakness of the Sung dynasty in China, which never controlled the border lands of the Korean peninsula, and the later division of China between the Kin Tartar dynasty in the north and the Sung in the south was no doubt the main reason why Koryo was able to live in peace and remain in control of the whole country. In the early thirteenth century, the conquest of north China by the Mongols, and later the conquest of the Sung also brought all China under Mongol rule, and in these circumstances Korea could not expect to escape. Invasion followed, but Koryo wisely submitted to the new power and was allowed to exist as a Mongol tributary state. This servitude involved the Koreans in assisting the Mongols in their abortive invasions of Japan, for which the Koreans had to provide the fleet, and lost very heavily when the expedition was destroyed by a typhoon (A.D. 1275).

Nevertheless, the kingdom of Koryo survived the Mongols, as Silla had outlived the T'ang. It was not until 1392 that the kingdom fell, after four hundred and fifty-seven years of rule. The long life of Korean dynasties is in sharp contrast to the much shorter duration of those which ruled China. Three hundred years is the extreme length of any Chinese dynasty, but since A.D. 668 Korea has been ruled by but three, Silla for three hundred and fifty-seven, Koryo for four hundred and fifty-seven and the Yi, the last, for no less than five hundred and eighteen years, from 1392 right down to the Japanese annexation of Korea in 1910.

Koryo fell through internal disorders, not foreign invasion. It was succeeded by a new native dynasty founded by a successful general, Yi T'aejo, and called the Yi dynasty from his surname. The Yi wisely acknowledged the suzerainty of the new, powerful Ming dynasty in China, which had driven out the Mongols only twenty-eight years before the Yi came to power in Korea, and were then at the height of their power. The Ming did not attempt to impose direct Chinese rule. Since T'ang times, indeed, the Chinese had clearly decided that Korea was best left to govern itself, in accordance with Confucian principles to be sure, and acknowledging the suzerainty of China – a situation which seems to have suited both nations, for it endured under many changes of Chinese and Korean dynasties for more than a thousand years, from A.D. 668 until in 1895 Japan supplanted China as the dominant power. It is as well to remember in considering the present state of Korea that this was the historic relationship between China and Korea, a long tradition which has only recently – and perhaps temporarily – been interrupted.

The Yi dynasty founded Seoul, the present capital of South Korea, and fixed their court in that city. In their early period Korea was an active centre of invention, art and highly developed crafts. One of the most interesting developments of this period was the invention, seemingly without any outside inspiration, of the Korean alphabet, which in modern times has largely replaced the use of Chinese characters. The Korean language, inflected and agglutinative, is much better suited to an alphabetic script than to an ideographic one (unlike Chinese). The new alphabet has been considered by linguists to be a remarkably perfect instrument for writing Korean, and it is surprising that these qualities took so long a period to mature. For under the Yi dynasty the new way of writing was confined to practical uses, letters, accounts and other 'non-literary' purposes. All literature continued to be written in Chinese ideographs and in practice in what amounted to a variant form of written Chinese. There was no popular education, consequently the simple practical alphabet, though never forgotten, was confined to very restricted uses.

At much the same time the Koreans also invented movable type for printing, an invention taken up in China also. But had the Koreans applied this valuable invention to their own alphabet, they could have developed an advanced culture much more independent of Chinese influence. That the Koreans of the earlier Yi centuries were an adaptable and ingenious people can be shown in other ways. When, two hundred years after the foundation of the Yi kingdom, the great Japanese invasion of 1592 disturbed the peace, the repulse and final retreat of Hideyoshi's armies was due more to the activity of the Korean navy than to that of the Ming armies sent to assist their tributary kingdom. Yi Sunsin, the Korean admiral, invented the ironclad ships – junks plated with iron – which could, and did, resist the attacks of the light Japanese ships, were not easily set on fire and successfully disrupted the Japanese communications. It is curious that this invention, preceding the later development of ironclads by nearly three hundred years, was never copied by other maritime nations, and allowed to fall into oblivion by the Koreans themselves. It may well be that the devastation of the Japanese invasions, which was great, permanently destroyed much of the strength and resilience of the Korean people. After the expulsion of the Japanese, Korea sank into a long decline, politically, socially and in the arts.

A few years after the Japanese invasion China succumbed to the Manchu conquest, and Korea passively changed masters. The (Manchu) Ch'ing dynasty now became the suzerains, but continued the Ming policy of non-intervention in internal affairs. On the other hand, the new Manchu Empire was too strong to tempt the Japanese to any further invasion, and Japan herself, under the Tokugawa Shoguns, adopted the policy of seclusion, cutting herself off from all but the most limited foreign intercourse. Korea tended to do the same. Under the later Yi, throughout the seventeenth and eighteenth centuries, Korea became known as the 'Hermit Kingdom'. No trade except a very limited exchange with China was permitted. Shipwrecked sailors were forbidden ever to leave the country, or were even put to death, and only tribute missions to Peking sustained a thin trickle of outside influence.

Yet in adhering to this policy of seclusion Korea was in some ways showing herself not uninfluenced by the outside world. Not only Japan, but also China under the Manchus, and such other east Asian states as Burma all at this period tended to seclude themselves to greater or lesser degrees. In sharp contrast to the relative accessibility of these countries in the

Middle Ages and up to the fifteenth century, there appeared this new tendency to regard any free intercourse with foreigners as dangerous and undesirable. In the case of Japan it was fear of the influence of Christian missionaries thought to be the agents of Spain, while in China the Manchu fear of their disloyal southern Chinese subjects was certainly one potent cause for restricting trade and commerce to one single port. But these considerations do not seem to be applicable to Korea. It may be that the underlying cause of all these seclusion policies was not so much the fear of the foreigner himself, as the jealousy of a landowning aristocracy against the rise of a native merchant class which could, by growing rich and influential, challenge the power of the long established feudal (in Japan) and bureaucratic landlord classes (in China and Korea). Trade had grown and the first signs of a wider, nascent capitalist development of handicraft industry had begun to appear in all these countries. In the view of many modern historians such authoritarian régimes as the Tokugawa Shoguns in Japan and the Manchu autocrats in China adopted the policies of seclusion to check the rise of new classes whose power would be based on non-agricultural sources of wealth.

Korea was an extreme case. No foreigner from the West had even so much as landed in the country until as late as 1653 when the shipwreck of the *Sparrow Hawk*, an English ship, was survived by a Dutch seaman named Hendrik Hamel. Hamel's life was spared, and after many years of captivity, or restriction, he returned to Europe to give the world the first authentic account of the Hermit Kingdom. It is true that already in 1609 it had been found necessary to permit a very limited trade with Japan through the port of Pusan, nearest to the Japanese islands. Neverthless the visit of Hamel proved an isolated example. Throughout the whole of the eighteenth century, and far into the nineteenth century also, Korea remained a sealed country. The internal consequences were disastrous. Such a policy might in a relatively large country such as Japan, or in a huge empire like China, have only slow, gradual, harmful consequences, offset by the fact that the very size of these nations gave a wide range of opportunity for all kinds of enterprise and varying careers at home. But Korea was much smaller. The shutting off of all outside influences led to a steady decline in all activities of the national life.

Art became monotonously repetitive, literature fossilized, craftsmanship and invention, the pride of the earlier periods, failed. Political and social life was dominated by the power of the Yangban, the landed aristocracy, who retained all power, filled every office and were bitterly divided into cliques and factions which incessantly intrigued against each other, paralysing all initiative and stultifying all possibilities of change or advance. The ruling dynasty produced no sovereigns of ability or energy. It became clear that no initiative from within could break this deadly spell: Korea needed the stimulus of some outside pressure, but when this came it was too late. A small country, whose mineral potential and resources were unknown to the outside world, Korea did not for many years interest the aggressive Western trader nor attract the intervention of the maritime powers. Trade was far more profitable with China, and later, after the opening of the country, with Japan. It was Japan herself who, a few years after the Meiji Restoration, moved to restore her old links with the peninsular kingdom, and persuaded the Korean court to conclude its first treaty with an outside power, in 1876. Such an innovation was significant and foreboding: hitherto, as the tributary of China, Korea had in theory at least no right to conclude treaties with outside parties, at least without the permission of Peking. But by 1876 China was hardly recovering from the T'ai P'ing rebellion, the Manchu court was still beset with other rebellions, and in no mood to look for trouble or assert half-forgotten rights. China made no move.

The example of Japan was followed by the U.S.A. a few years later, the treaty being signed in 1882. The 'most favoured nation' clause, by which other powers could demand similar treatment, then operated to permit Britain and other European powers to open relations with Korea. Korean isolation was at an end, but few of the Western powers took real advantage of their new rights. It was America which presented, at first, the main challenge in trade and mining enterprises to the Japanese.

But it was no part of American policy in the nineteenth century to back up by force the interests of her traders and entrepreneurs in distant lands. Japan soon found herself the virtually undisputed leader in the foreign commerce of Korea. This fact sharply differentiates the history of modern Korea from those of China or Japan herself. In those cases the pressure to open the country to trade, to engage in diplomatic relations and to enter into the full stream of modern commerce and industry came from the collective power of all the European trading nations and from the United States. Britain might take the lead in China, the U.S.A. in Japan, but all shared swiftly in the opportunities that were created.

Korea was increasingly left to Japan. This situation made her fate the concern of her two Asian neighbours, rather than that of the distant Western powers. In 1882 and 1884 the rising disorder and rivalry between China, trying to maintain her ancient suzerainty, and Japan, seeking a new empire, led to serious clashes in Seoul, in which the Chinese, under the energetic young Yuan Shih-k'ai, were not unsuccessful. The major clash was postponed by a compromise which amounted to a joint suzerainty over helpless Korea by the two rival empires a situation which already compromised China's ancient unique domination. This standstill agreement lasted uneasily for ten years, but during that decade the power of China was not increasing, while the might of a swiftly developing Japan was growing fast. In 1894 a serious rebellion broke out in Korea, called the Tonghak movement (Tonghak means 'eastern learning'). The character of this movement, a mixture of chauvinistic anti-foreign feeling, nationalist resentment at the weakness and incompetence of the government and unrest produced by worsening economic conditions, was similar to many such movements (notably the Boxers in China six years later) which tended to break out in these ancient Asian societies when put under the fierce stress of Western intrusion. The Korean government could not control the Tonghaks; Japan demanded the right to intervene to protect her traders; the Manchu court proclaimed the same rights. When the Japanese alleged that the Chinese by moving in troops without prior consultation had violated the agreement entered into in 1884, war followed, beginning with an attack by the Japanese navy on a Chinese transport, prior to any declaration of war.

The Sino-Japanese War of 1895 was fought in Korea, but without the helpless Korean government being in any way able to participate. It was brief, and ended with the complete defeat of the Manchu Empire. By the treaty of peace China had to renounce her suzerainty over Korea, which was promoted to the fictitious eminence of an 'empire'. The reason for this change of title was that in the Chinese (and thus also in the Japanese) language the ancient title 'wang', meaning king, had become the secondary title, with the equivalent value of prince, implying a higher sovereign over the 'Wang', that is, the Emperor of China. Japan had long assumed the full imperial status, and the 'King' of Korea thus implied a subordinate standing. So the king must now become an 'emperor' to mark his complete independence from China. Japan was not yet ready to assert her own total domination, and when she did so would not stop at any half-way stage of mere suzerainty.

Japanese Occupation and Annexation (1905–1945)

The rapid decline of China from the Sino-Japanese War onward soon encouraged Japan to go farther. The only obstacle to the complete control of Korea was now the ambition of Russia, the only country other than China to have a short land frontier with Korea. The rivalry of Russia and Japan for control of Korea, whose mineral wealth was now known, was one of the main causes of the Russo-Japanese War. The victory of Japan in this contest not only made her the heir of Russia's concessions in Manchuria, but eliminated Russian influence from Korea. In 1905 when the war was won, Japan proclaimed a protectorate over Korea. The Western powers raised no objection : they knew that the fate of Korea was sealed, and Britain had the Anglo-Japanese Alliance, regarded as a valuable bulwark of her eastern power, to provide an additional reason for letting Japan have her way.

In 1910 Japan took the final step; the annexation of Korea to the Japanese Empire was proclaimed. Korea could make no resistance. The royal – 'imperial' – family or the Yi were pensioned off with Japanese titles, but removed to Japan for permanent exile. In the last years of independence the Koreans had, too late, made some spasmodic efforts to organize their country as a modern state and stave off disaster. Young Koreans, many of high intelligence, had been sent overseas to study; a small diplomatic corps, formed from such men, had briefly appeared in the main Western capitals, but there was little scope for these returned students when they came home. There, all was either still sunk in the corrupt inefficiency of the old court aristocracy, or already controlled by the Japanese. When annexation came this small élite of Korean Western-educated men came under the strong suspicion and persecution of the new Japanese colonial authorities. Many spent their lives in more or less enforced seclusion, some as Buddhist monks. Others escaped abroad, to work in seemingly hopeless exile, in China, America or elsewhere for the lost cause of national independence. But it was from these few that the leaders of that cause, many years later, were to be derived.

The Japanese occupation and annexation produced in the early twentieth century many of the same consequences as had attended the Japanese invasion of 1592. In both cases the Korean regular forces made no effective resistance to the enemy, and in both cases a spontaneous rising of the people gave the Japanese much more trouble than they ever encountered from the Korean government. The Korean people resisted annexation fruitlessly, for they were unarmed, but sturdily and steadily. They were cruelly repressed, but the Japanese wholly failed to win their loyalty. When the first movement was crushed, the Koreans, heartened by the Wilsonian doctrine of 'self-determination' announced at the conclusion of the First World War, organized a very effective and sustained passive resistance movement against Japanese rule. In spite of all that the Japanese government could do, this movement gained the notice of the whole world and much sympathy (but little else) for the Korean people. It could not succeed, but it left its mark. Henceforward the world knew that the Koreans did not accept their fate. This could make little difference to their prospects of freedom at that time, for Japan was not only very strong, but no foreign power was willing to challenge or question her authority over Korea.

It would be a serious distortion of history to portray Japanese rule as wholly oppressive. Under their forceful authority the country was rapidly developed and modernized. Railways were built, harbours improved, cities given water, sanitation and lighting, public health greatly improved and literacy, at the lower level of education, became widespread. It soon exceeded fifty per cent of the population, which also increased rapidly. The Korean economy was rescued from stagnation and decline, and expanded to meet the demands of Japanese industry. Japan's investment in Korea was large and profitable; it was not foreseen that one day it would become the inheritance of the Koreans themselves. On the other hand, all this development was geared closely to the needs and profits of Japan: it was only to a secondary degree directly beneficial to the Koreans. No Koreans gained wealth, still less power. The old landlord class retained some of their property, but it was often now put under Japanese management, which may have been better for the peasantry, but equally barred them from any expectation of getting land for themselves. Business and industry were wholly controlled by the Japanese. The Korean merchant class, weak and old-fashioned before annexation, gained no better status under Japanese rule. Education taught the masses some degree of literacy, but was not extended to tertiary level, and Koreans were for the most part barred from employment in posts requiring high skills or advanced knowledge.

The government made no pretence of sharing power with the Koreans. The Japanese Governor-General, usually a high military officer, was supreme lord of the land. Apart from his staff of Japanese civil servants he was supposed to be assisted by a small sixty-five-member 'Central Advisory Council' consisting of hand-picked Korean aristocrats, who had no power to initiate discussion, and whose sole function was to approve the measures of the Japanese government. This body was so incon-

spicuous that most visitors were not even aware of its existence. The police, Japanese controlled and manned, were all-
powerful. As this was also very largely true of Japan itself in
these years, the Japanese can hardly have been expected to rule
a restless colony more liberally than they ruled themselves. Yet
there is a difference between the oppression of police of the
same race as the oppressed, and repression by an alien force.
There can be little question that Japanese rule in Korea exhibited all the faults of a colonial régime without the saving, or
mitigating, graces of stemming from a liberal democratic home
government.

In many ways it was quite unnecessarily vexatious and
wounding to Korean pride. The cities and towns were known
only by the Japanese form of their names. The official language
was Japanese; Korean was neglected. Imposing monuments
glorifying the Japanese Empire were erected in places which
were best calculated to offend Korean susceptibilities. Many of
the faults which marred Japanese rule when it was imposed by
conquest in South-East Asia and China during the Second
World War were glaringly apparent in pre-war Korea, but the
warning seems to have gone unheeded in other countries.
Korea had been the 'Hermit Kingdom' when independent; if it
did not now become the Hermit Colony there is little doubt
that many of the Japanese officials in Korea would have welcomed the virtual total exclusion of Western foreigners, whose
criticisms they resented. Tourists were admitted, but carefully
watched by the ubiquitous Japanese police. Conversation between them and Koreans of Western education was immediately followed by a police call to 'inquire the subject of the
conversation'.

The Korean people were sullenly resentful, but virtually
powerless. In the period of thirty-five years during which Japanese rule endured, the resistance of the Korean people could
only be limited. From 1935 there did appear a small guerrilla
movement in the mountainous region of north-east Korea adjoining Soviet Siberia. The guerrilla movement was led by
Communists who came from the Korean population domiciled
beyond the frontier and who had received Russian Communist

training. At that period it appeared insignificant, and was little noted outside the country. More account was taken of the exiles who made Shanghai their headquarters and formed there a Korean Government in Exile. This body was, unfortunately, racked by intrigues and feuds, reminiscent of the factions which had prevailed in the old Korean court. It received intermittent support from the Chinese, and, when the war with Japan ultimately broke out in 1937, was given some form of recognition by the Chinese government. Perhaps rather more significant was the presence with the Chinese Communist forces of several Koreans who returned to play a part in the government of Communist North Korea.

The early successes of the Japanese in the Second World War, after Pearl Harbour, seemed to offer the Koreans no hope of freedom. Japanese rule was spreading, not contracting. Large forces continued to garrison the country, but the strains of the war bore heavily on Korea, the resources of the country being exploited to the limit to sustain the Japanese war economy. Much of the progress and development were distorted or run down under these stresses. The Korean people were thus quite unprepared for the sudden end of the war, after the dropping of atomic bombs on Hiroshima and Nagasaki. Those who had in one way or another been able to follow the real course of the war, as opposed to what was officially disclosed by the controlled press, had expected massive American landings in eastern China as a preliminary to a later invasion of Japan. No one expected an invasion of Korea itself. It is probable that very few Koreans in the country were aware that at the Cairo Conference between the Allied leaders, Winston Churchill, President Roosevelt and Chiang K'ai-shek, these statesmen had included in their declaration of war aims a promise of independence for Korea 'in due course'. The precise meaning of this qualifying phrase was not defined.

Post-War Korea (1945–1950)

On 8 August 1945, when Japan was already preparing to surrender, Russia abruptly declared war and invaded 'Manchukuo' – the Japanese puppet state in Manchuria. The Russians at the same time announced their adherence to the Cairo pledge. The intervention of Russia radically altered the situation for Korea; within a very few days the Japanese resistance in Manchuria collapsed, Russian forces entered north-east Korea, Japan herself unconditionally surrendered (14 August 1945) and Korea was 'liberated'. A hasty negotiation between the major allies had decided that Russian forces should advance as far as the 38th parallel of latitude, while U.S. forces would occupy Korea south of that line. The sole purpose of this arrangement at the time was to define the sphere of operations of the respective armies, and to decide which should take the surrender of the Japanese forces in the respective zones. Yet this arbitrary division of a united country and people was to lead to fatal division, a destructive war and an apparently lasting partition.

The Japanese in Korea had a clearer idea of what the zone division might mean than had the Western allies. As the Russians advanced they fled *en masse* from North Korea, soldiers and civilians alike, officials, businessmen and police. They sought safety in South Korea, the American zone, where in common with the forces and officials of that region, they remained to surrender to the Americans when these landed on 8 September. The Russians thus had a month's start over the Americans, and this lead was never overtaken. The Koreans had, on 6 September, two days before the Americans landed, proclaimed a Republic of Korea in Seoul. But the American commander had no instructions to recognize any such government. As his forces were still few, he continued Japanese officials in office, under his supervision, until 6 January 1946, when all Japanese were repatriated to Japan. This co-operation with the hated oppressor greatly embittered the Koreans. It was, of course, not due to any American tenderness to the Japanese, but simply to the hasty and improvised character of the occupation, which had not been prepared with a long-range plan to deal with Korean government.

This situation, in any case difficult, was further complicated by a sharp division of opinion between Koreans of the Right and Left. The Republic proclaimed on 6 September was the work of men of Left Wing, but not Communist opinions. When the leader of the Korean exiles, Syngman Rhee, returned to Korea, he, a man of the Right, opposed this group. The American occupation authorities tended to favour Rhee, but were not yet ready to recognize any Korean administration. General Hodge explicitly declared that 'the military government [his own] is the only government in Korea'. Unfortunately, this was not the case. Neither the military government nor the Republic had any authority in North Korea. The Russians, following a different plan, set up no Russian military government in their zone, but installed an 'Executive Committee of the Korean People' manned by Communist Koreans, some of whom came with them from Russian Siberia, some from the small guerrilla movement which had long been active in the far north-east of the country. The Russians themselves took no open part in this régime, remaining in the background, ostensibly only a military occupying force.

Recognizing the manifest danger of a lasting division, the Allied powers tried to agree upon some plan for uniting the country. Neither side were apparently ready to entrust the Korean people with full powers of self-government – an attitude markedly in contrast to the readiness to hand over power to other, much less well equipped successors in colonies in Africa in later years. An agreement was made in Moscow by which Korea was to be reunited and governed under a trusteeship for five years before the Korean government was placed in full control. This did not in any way satisfy the Koreans. The strife between the Right and Left in South Korea grew more bitter, and the American military government leaned more and more towards the Right. In North Korea the Executive Committee began to function as a government, and clearly as a Communist government.

A conference to arrange reunion of the two zones met in

January 1946, but broke down without any agreement on 8 May 1946. The only result was a further consolidation of the division brought about by the zone arrangement. The Russian side opposed the membership of conservative Koreans in the proposed provisional government, the Americans opposed the inclusion of Communist Koreans. In May 1947 a second conference opened in Seoul. The Korean Right Wing leaders opposed and rejected the trusteeship agreement, the North Koreans rejected co-operation with the Right. The conference dissolved without accomplishing anything except added bitterness. Shortly after this the Left Wing leaders in South Korea were put under arrest. In August 1947 the United States proposed nation-wide elections to be held under United Nations supervision, perhaps the last hope for peaceful reunion. The Russian side rejected this suggestion. The U.S.A. then suggested mediation by the United Nations Assembly; the Russians countered with the suggestion that American and Russian forces should both withdraw simultaneously from Korea, leaving the Koreans to settle their problems themselves. This, they felt confident, would have resulted in the triumph of the now much better organized Executive Committee, which had functioned as the government in the north for over a year. The Americans rejected this proposal (23 September 1947).

Two days earlier the Americans had introduced a resolution in the U.N. Assembly for the establishment of a United Nations Territorial Commission for Korea, and this was accepted on 14 November by the General Assembly. It was proposed that elections should be held on 31 March 1948. Russia boycotted this meeting of the Assembly and recorded no vote. A stalemate ensued: feeling that the military government in the south could not continue without prejudicing all hope of reunion, the U.S.A. agreed to the proclamation of the Republic of Korea in Seoul on 15 August 1948. Syngman Rhee led this new régime as President. It was supported by the Right Wing Koreans. On 10 September, the Russians countered by allowing the Executive Committee in Pyongyang (North Korea) to proclaim the Democratic People's Republic of Korea. The country was now fatally and finally divided with two rival governments in power, one of the Right, the other openly Communist. In less then two years the Korean War began (end of June 1950) and all hope of peaceful reunion disappeared.

As had happened only too often in her past history, Korea was the sport of contending great powers, and her own people by their divisions and rivalry became the instruments of this contention.

The future of Korea is still obscure. The war, which devastated a country which had up to that time escaped the destruction of the Second World War, settled nothing, leaving the country as divided as before, but on a slightly more rational frontier than a mere parallel of latitude. The two halves of the country have diverged further. North Korea, possessing the great bulk of the mineral resources, has developed a modern heavy industry under Communism, but is less populous than the agricultural South, where industry is less developed. There is at present no basis for reconciliation between the two governments, even if the rivalry of the great powers, China now on the one side, and America on the other, could be sufficiently appeased to permit it.

Yet history has shown that the Korean people are a nation with a strong sense of unity, which produced a united kingdom more than fifteen hundred years ago, and which remained united under changing régimes down to the year 1945. In that long time the most stable system was the distant and lightly borne suzerainty of China, under which Korea governed herself – well or badly. The Japanese conquest was both brief and very unpopular. It would seem probable that in the course of time this old tradition, in a new form, will once more prevail, for it has been shown that the suzerainty of the continental power is more lasting, and seemingly more acceptable, than the authority of a power beyond the sea.

PART THREE

SOUTH-EAST ASIA

CHAPTER NINE

Early History

(TO A.D. 1500)

'SOUTH-EAST ASIA', a modern term growing increasingly popular, has come to mean all the countries lying between China to the north-east, India to the north-west and Australia–New Guinea to the south. These countries are: Vietnam, Laos and Cambodia, often called collectively Indo-China; the Philippines and Indonesia, Malaya (with Malaysian Borneo), Thailand and Burma. This is a vast area inhabited by a number of different peoples, and it falls mainly into three parts, from the historical point of view, parts which are not the same as the geographical division between mainland and island countries. There is first the region which received its civilization from China, Vietnam (both North and South); secondly, the countries which originally came under Hindu cultural influence, although never conquered by any Indian political state. These are Cambodia, Thailand, Burma and (in earlier times) Malaya and the western part of Indonesia, Bali, Java, Sumatra and part of Borneo. The third division is that area which received neither Chinese nor Indian civilization, and which consequently derives its present culture mainly from the much later penetration of Islam and Western Christianity. This includes the Philippines, and the eastern islands of Indonesia, the Celebes, Amboina and others.

There is thus no unity in the civilization of this region, nor in the languages, nor in the written scripts. The countries of Chinese civilization wrote in Chinese characters: those of Indian culture wrote in script derived from India, and originally in Sanskrit. These now include Cambodia, Laos, Thailand and Burma. Malaya and western Indonesia were also originally civilized by Indian contact, and wrote their sacred texts and early chronicles in Sanskrit or in scripts derived from it. Later they were converted to Islam, and their more recent literature is written in a script close to Arabic.[1] The Philippines had no written records before the Spanish conquest, and their language of culture became Spanish. Eastern Indonesia was only lightly penetrated by Islam, and large groups in the Celebes and almost the whole population of Amboina became Christian after Portuguese and later Dutch conquest.

There was therefore a wide difference between these various countries in the origin of their civilization and in their later history. Very little is known of the early history of the Philippines or of eastern Indonesia. Connected history for western Indonesia and Malaya is lacking before the seventh and eighth centuries A.D.: for Burma history really begins round about the year A.D. 1000; for Thailand not until the fourteenth century A.D.; but countries in the Indo-China area, Vietnam and Cambodia, have records and a connected story running back to the fourth century A.D. This situation is partly the result of the fact that for all these countries, whether under Chinese cultural influence or Indian, the earliest sources are Chinese, and for many centuries these are the only sources except some few evidences from archaeology. The countries the Chinese knew well are best recorded, those that were far off, and less frequently visited, get only slight, imperfect mention. In some of these countries inscriptions help to record the origins and rise of states, but this source is only really plentiful for Cambodia, which created the great cultural and political centre of Angkor. For long periods the contact between the various countries of South-East Asia was slight, their development uneven and unrelated to what was going on in the more distant parts of the region. It is therefore impossible to treat the history of these countries in the early period as a whole: in this chapter attention will be paid to the general character of their development, and more to the growth of civilization than to the history of dynasties, which is far from perfectly known.

All these countries lie in the tropics and their climate is governed by the monsoon winds which blow in the summer

1. Indonesia has now adopted the Latin alphabet.

(northern hemisphere) months from May to October from the south-west, bringing rain from the Indian Ocean; and in the winter months from November to April from the north, bringing dry weather from the great continental mass of Asia. Temperatures may vary only slightly, but the difference in humidity is much greater. The whole region grows rice as the main crop, wherever the land is flat enough or water sufficient. The mountains are covered with dense jungle, which for the most part was too impenetrable for pre-industrial man to clear or cultivate, except in small patches. Consequently, civilization and organized states were confined to the plateaux and river deltas – the mountains remained inhabited by sparse tribes of more primitive or backward peoples. This was also a major reason for the division of the region into separate countries inhabited by distinct peoples.

It is believed by archaeologists and historians that about the beginning of the Christian era the great migrations of neolithic peoples had come to an end, and that the countries of South-East Asia then were settled by the ancestors of the same peoples that now inhabit them. There are three main exceptions to this. The Vietnamese or Annamite people, Mongolian and closely related to the Chinese, did not reach southern Vietnam until historical times, driving out the previous inhabitants of the Mekong delta. The Burmese, a people related to the Tibetans, did not enter Burma until the eighth and ninth centuries A.D., driving south and east the previous inhabitants, a people called Mon, who were related to the Khmer or Cambodians. The Thai, the present dominant people in Thailand, only entered that country from south-west China in the thirteenth or early fourteenth centuries, and left large groups in eastern Burma (the Shan States) and west China (Yunnan). Malaya, Indonesia, the Philippines and Cambodia do not seem to have seen any large-scale immigration of foreign peoples in historic times, until the nineteenth century immigration of Chinese.

At some period, probably about the second century A.D., the countries of South-East Asia began to come under the influence of Hindu culture. There is no exact record of how this came about, but it is at least clear that it was not by military conquest. It is believed that at first Indian traders from the southern part of India visited the still barbarian lands of Malaya, Thailand, Indo-China, Sumatra, Java and Bali, and later Burma. There is no evidence that they reached the Philippines or eastern Indonesia. They were followed by Brahman priests who converted the ruling tribal chiefs to the worship of the Indian gods, and also set up kingdoms modelled on the ancient Indian system of kingship. There is at least some evidence (from Chinese sources) that some of these Brahmans intermarried with the local rulers and founded dynasties. There were events in contemporary Indian history which may have stimulated this migration of traders and priests, but there is no direct record of how it arose. The Indian influence was strong and continued for several centuries, later reinforced by the arrival of Buddhist monks, who left India when the Hindu revival against Buddhism gathered strength. In consequence the main countries of South-East Asia acquired a civilization derived from India, used Sanskrit as their sacred religious language, used scripts derived from Sanskrit to write for ordinary purposes in their own languages, and also created kingdoms in which Hindu ideas about kingship prevailed. Only northern Vietnam, adjacent to China, and for a long time part of that Empire, got its civilization from China and not from India.

What is known of the history of these countries up to about A.D. 1000 is almost entirely derived from Chinese historical records. These begin to describe the states of southern Indo-China as early as the third century A.D., in the Han period. There were then two kingdoms in the region now covered by South Vietnam and Cambodia. Both were under Hindu influence, but the names are only known in their Chinese form, and it is only in recent times that 'Fu Nan' has been shown to be derived from a Khmer (Cambodian) word Phnom, meaning mountain, and that the name of the other kingdom was probably Champa. There is good reason to believe that the people of Fu Nan were the ancestors of the Cambodians, and that the Champa people were closely akin. Both had linguistic and other connections with the Mon peoples, less advanced, who then inhabited Thailand and southern Burma. It is in fact probable that the ancient people of whom the Cambodians are the living representatives are the basic 'race' in continental South-East Asia. At much the same time, the late Han period in China (third century A.D.), the Chinese first mention states or kingdoms in Malaya, and in Sumatra. It is often very difficult to be sure just where these places mentioned really were. It is not, for example, certain whether Java is among them.

Sanskrit inscriptions dating from the fifth century A.D. have been found in Sumatra, Java and southern Indo-China, but these are invariably of a religious character, recording the foundation of a temple: sometimes a king is mentioned as a patron, but nothing else of a secular nature, so that apart from proving the spread of Hindu influence and the favour it received from the kings, nothing more is learned of the history of the country. During the disturbed times in China following the fall of the Han dynasty, contact with the south seems to have continued, but perhaps on a more limited scale. There was now no great Chinese Empire to overawe the little kings of the south and compel them to send 'tribute' to China. It is from such tribute-bearing missions that the Chinese historians obtained their information. It was the rise of Buddhism, following its introduction and spread in China, which stimulated a new contact in the sixth century A.D. Chinese monks, anxious to visit India to obtain the sacred Sanskrit texts of their faith, started to travel by sea, the land route being still more dangerous.

These monks therefore sailed south on the monsoon and landed at Sumatran ports, whence they sailed up the Straits of Malacca, across the Bay of Bengal or more probably along the coasts of Burma, until they reached the Indian ports near the mouth of the Ganges. They often recorded their travels, and the names of several are known. From their accounts it is clear that Sumatra and Java were by then both under strong Buddhist influence, which had not driven out the earlier Hindu religion, but lived with it. 'Fu Nan' had been a powerful state controlling most of the lower valleys of the Mekong and Menam (in Thailand) and having tributary kings in Malaya and even in lower Burma. It was constantly at war with its rival, Champa, occupying what is now South Vietnam. Chinese pilgrims to India, passing through these South-East Asian countries, were to continue and grow more numerous in the next century, when China was once more united under the T'ang dynasty. Diplomatic contacts with the southern regions also now became important, and consequently the sources for history are better. It becomes clear that two regions were already well in advance of the others, and long remained in the lead. They were the rising Khmer Kingdom of Kambuja (Cambodia) and the two islands of Sumatra and Java. The T'ang pilgrims and records also mention, for the first time, the existence of kingdoms in southern Burma, and notice the ports and trade of the cities on the west coast of Malaya. It is clear that these places were usually under the direct rule or overlordship of the Sumatran Kingdom.

There is a clear reason why south-east Sumatra should have risen to early importance. This coast controls the entrance to the only two passages by which the Indian Ocean communicates with the seas within the Indonesian archipelago, and the South China Sea to the north. All trade and traffic between India and the Far East must pass through these straits. It is the same reason that gives modern Singapore its importance and prosperity. But in earlier times ships did not need deep water harbours, such as Singapore. River estuaries, not now suitable for large ships, were then more convenient as they led directly to the main centres of population and the political capital of the country. This was why the east coast of Sumatra was then more important than the opposite coast of Malaya. Cambodia rose to power for rather different reasons. It is not a country with a long coast, and the mouth of the Mekong (where modern Saigon stands) was part of Champa, the rival state. But Cambodia was established on the middle reaches of the Mekong, a rich country, if irrigated, and the water was available from the river and from the great lake system of central Cambodia. This area could support a large population and produce a high revenue. It was also well situated to dominate the Mekong valley, and beyond it, that of the Menam in modern Thailand.

Cambodia thus rose to be the most advanced, cultivated and powerful state in continental South-East Asia.

Cambodia

The Chinese records of the early seventh century describe this Cambodia, in an age still two hundred years before the foundation of the great city of Angkor, by which it is so well known today. It had an advanced administration, with many ranks of officials, fine stone or brick buildings for religious purposes (but the people lived in timber houses), and this Chinese record is supplemented by a large number of stone inscriptions found on the ruins of the numerous temples and monuments which are earlier than Angkor itself. Cambodia has by far the richest archaeological heritage of any country in South-East Asia. The inscriptions are mainly concerned with religious matters, although they do provide a list of the kings, their relationship to each other and some outline of their deeds. Almost nothing is known of the people or their way of life from these sources, and what is known comes from the accounts of Chinese visitors. Cambodia seems to have taken over the Hindu concepts of kingship in their fullest form. The king was a living god: his function was not only to govern, but to protect religion, to embody the living community of the state. He was not only ruler but chief priest, interpreter of the sacred law and the 'essence' of the kingdom. His capital – when finally developed in the splendid city of Angkor Thom – was laid out to symbolize these ideas. The centre of it contained an immense temple rising tier by tier into a central tower which typified the mythological mountain of Hinduism, Meru, the centre of the world. This shrine was the personal temple of the king, and seems also to have been the mausoleum of the dead kings. The most famous of these temples of divine royalty are the Angkor Wat, just outside Angkor Thom, and earlier than the city, and the Bayon, which is the central shrine of Angkor Thom itself.

The Cambodians created in the centuries of their power, from about A.D. 550 to the middle of the fifteenth century, a great civilization and a magnificent art and architecture. It was wholly devoted to religion, at first Hinduism, especially the cult of Shiva, later Buddhism; but although this became the religion of the people, the court retained, and still retains, many Hindu ceremonies and rites. Cambodia today is the heir of the Angkor period, and the Khmer people are the descendants of the Khmer of that time. The mistaken belief that Angkor was the work of a 'vanished' people has no foundation in fact. The kingdom had its misfortunes: it was constantly at war with its neighbour, Champa, and the Chams at times were victorious; but gradually Champa had to yield ground to the constant pressure of the Annamites from the north, a pressure to which it finally wholly succumbed. Champa sheltered Cambodia from this danger, and thus Cambodia endured, and absorbed the remains of the Cham state. The Cambodians certainly had a large literature, and probably historical records, but owing to the later misfortunes and final fall of Angkor, most of this perished, except for the stone inscriptions. It is thus a difficult and laborious task to reconstruct the detailed history of the Khmer Empire. It is still far from complete.

The main known facts and dates of the Cambodian Empire centred on Angkor Thom are as follows. Between A.D. 800 and 850, under a king named Jayavarman II, the Cambodians or Khmer people (Khmer is the name of the people; Kambuja – latinized by early European missionaries as 'Cambodia' – is the name of the country) re-established their state in the middle Mekong valley, and made a city in the vicinity of later Angkor Thom, the capital. About one hundred and fifty years later, in A.D. 1001, another forceful ruler, King Yacovarman, settled the capital permanently at Angkor, but the early city of this date does not exactly correspond to the later Angkor Thom. In the ninth and tenth centuries Chinese historical records give accounts of Cambodia proving that it was an advanced and civilized state with an elaborate governmental organization. The earlier inscriptions on monuments at Angkor tell the same story, but have more to do with religious organizations and beliefs since they survive only on temples and shrines.

In Sung times, around A.D. 1128, the Chinese describe Cambodia as a powerful kingdom reaching the sea to the east (that is, in present South Vietnam) and to the west as far as the kingdom of Pagan, which was in Burma. All modern Thailand was under Cambodian rule. Cambodia was also overlord of the small states in Laos and on the east coast of the Malay Peninsula. In A.D. 1140, under the rule of a powerful king named Suryavarman II, the great temple of Angkor Wat was built to commemorate him. It survives as one of the most majestic architectural achievements of any people. In 1177, under feeble successors, the country suffered a great defeat at the hands of its neighbour to the east, the Kingdom of Champa, and the capital was taken. Some years later the Cambodians recovered their power and independence under their most famous king, Jayavarman VII (A.D. 1181–1218), who rebuilt the capital as the existing Angkor Thom (meaning Angkor the Great), surrounded it with a huge stone wall (which still stands) and built many of the most famous temples of the Angkor site, including the Bayon, his personal shrine temple, a huge monument in the exact centre of Angkor Thom. His architecture is strongly marked by Buddhist influence, and his reign is the period when Buddhism begins to overshadow the earlier Hindu cult of Shiva. All his monuments have great towers with faces of the Buddha on all four sides, of colossal dimensions. There is good reason to believe that these faces are portraits of Jayavarman VII himself.

It is probable that the great architectural works of Jayavarman VII exhausted the wealth of the kingdom, for the end of his reign marks a period of slow decline, or at least of no further advance. Later monuments at Angkor are few and slighter. By the middle of the next century (the thirteenth) the rise of the Thai people in modern Thailand began to challenge the Cambodian Empire. The Mongol invasions of Burma and Indo-China in 1282, although they did not directly affect Cambodia, overthrew other ancient states such as Pagan in Burma, and thus opened the road to new peoples, such as the Thai, who rose as the Mongol flood receded. In 1295 the visit of a Chinese embassy to Angkor is recorded in the work of one of the ambassador's staff, Chou Ta-kuan, and is the fullest account which exists of Angkor Thom at its prime. Much of what is known of the aspect of the city when still inhabited comes from this source, which also gives a very full account of the whole kingdom, and an accurate description of the great temples and shrines.

In the fourteenth century the decline of Cambodian power was swift. The old Sanskrit culture was being replaced by Buddhist influences coming from Ceylon and using Pali as the sacred language. The Thais had gained their independence in northern Thailand in 1220, and by the end of the century had conquered all that country. In 1352 they attacked and captured Angkor, but were later driven out (1357). In 1393 a new Thai invasion again captured the capital, which was once more recovered, but left the kingdom weak and unable to retain its distant provinces. Laos was still under Cambodian rule in the middle of the fourteenth century, but had become independent under Thai dynasties (more than one) by the second half of the century. Constant Thai invasion made Angkor so insecure that in 1450 the Cambodian kings abandoned the city and withdrew down the Mekong to the present capital, Phnom Penh. Thereafter Angkor rapidly declined until the jungle invaded the abandoned buildings and covered the whole site. Some of the temples, however, remained as places of pilgrimage until the site was discovered by French archaeologists in the nineteenth century, and was thereafter slowly cleared of the jungle. After the withdrawal from Angkor, Cambodia had little control over the upper Mekong, and remained a rather isolated state soon blocked off from the east coast by the Annamite advance into the delta of the Mekong.

Thailand

The decline of Cambodia meant the rise of Thailand which became in this period the most powerful continental South-East Asian state, challenged by Burma, but dominant in the northern part of the Malay Peninsula as well as in Laos and former Cambodian territory along the middle Mekong. Thai civilization owes much to that of the Khmer (Cambodia). It is something like the relationship between Greek and Roman art: the Khmer art is the classical, ancient and superior form of an art which, in Thailand, was modified by a warrior people of later civilization. This is at once clear to visitors who see first Angkor, then Bangkok. The art of Angkor is austere, strong and sophisticated: that of Bangkok, popular, light, colourful, but lacking the strength and purity of the Khmer masterpieces.

The earlier history of Cambodia, Thailand and Vietnam has left important consequences down to the present time. Cambodia continues to fear the encroachments of her old enemies and neighbours, who, for their part, continue to feel hostility to the heirs of Angkor. These attitudes play an important part in present-day policies. Another example of the relationship between Thai and Khmers, half enmity, half admiration, is the development of the Thai written language. In the earlier period, when the Thais were under Cambodian suzerainty, they had adopted the Khmer script, but somewhat modified it to suit a different language. In 1285 they deliberately invented a new script, taken from Pali, which was introduced by royal command, and is said on quite strong evidence to have been the invention of the King himself. Towards the end of the thirteenth century the Kingdom of Sukhot'ai, which was the first of the independent Thai states, declined, and was replaced by a more warlike competitor from the south, who established the capital at Ayudhya, a city, now abandoned, not far from modern Bangkok. The foundation of Ayudhya in 1347 heralded the intense pressure on declining Cambodia which the new Thai Kingdom now maintained.

Sumatra and Java

The T'ang Chinese pilgrims who made their way to India by sea have left plentiful accounts of the Kingdoms of Sumatra and Java, through which they usually passed on this route. Shrivijaya was now the main power in south-east Sumatra, and the Chinese describe it as a country under strong Buddhist influence with a well developed Sanskrit culture. One of the most famous Chinese pilgrims, Huan Tsung, recommended to his countrymen that those who wanted to go on to India to study Buddhist texts should spend a year or two in Sumatra learning Sanskrit, as it would be so much better for them if they arrived in India knowing that language. This suggests very strongly that there were established centres of Sanskrit studies in Sumatra. The leading power in Java was known to the Chinese as the Kingdom of Ho Ling, a name which has been equated with Sanskrit Kalinga. It is under this régime that the famous Buddhist shrine at Borobudur in west Java was erected, a vast monument rivalling Angkor Wat in size, and some centuries earlier. Java and Sumatra were thus rich and civilized kingdoms under strong Indian and Buddhist culture. They were also political rivals, engaging in frequent wars, the course of which is usually rather obscure, and the results mainly inconclusive. In the ninth century it would seem that Sumatra (Shrivijaya) was the more powerful, but conflicts continued throughout the tenth century. Shrivijaya was the more enduring of the two rivals. It remained the leading power, controlling the two straits until the middle of the thirteenth century, when it was dismembered by rivals, one of which was named Melayu, the first time this word, later to become attached to another country and a whole language group, appears in history.

Java had a less continuous history, for in the course of these centuries, the eighth to the thirteenth, several successive kingdoms rose to power and were replaced within a few generations by rivals. The more secure situation of Java, less involved in overseas contacts than Sumatra, may account for this difference. A Mongol invasion, sent out by the great Kublai, then Emperor of all China, in 1293, altered this situation and although it failed to conquer the island, produced a new pattern of power. By the end of the thirteenth century Shrivijaya was in full decline, and the King of the Java state had made himself overlord of south Sumatra and of part of the west coast of Malaya. The Mongol invasion, sent to punish this king for refusing tribute to the Emperor, found him already overthrown by a rebellion, but after some confused operations, and having made a rich booty, the commanders of the Mongol fleet (who were Chinese) decided that they had done enough, and withdrew. A new king quickly arose in Java, and, inheriting the conquests of the previous one, founded the Kingdom of Majapahit, which was long to remain the dominant power in the whole region.

Meanwhile, as a consequence first of the maritime contacts of the fallen Sumatran Kingdom, then of the fall of that state, a new influence had reached the Indonesian islands and Malaya which was to transform their culture. Marco Polo, returning by sea to Persia and then Venice, after seventeen years in the service of the Mongol Emperor in China, passed along the coasts of Sumatra, and notes that in 1291 the most northerly of the many small kingdoms into which the former Empire of Shrivijaya had disintegrated, had been converted to Islam by Arab merchants coming there to trade. Chinese records show that by 1281, ten years earlier, another Sumatran state was already converted, at least at the level of its rulers. A great change was in progress, and it is remarkable that the two waves of foreign culture which first civilized Indonesia, and later replaced that civilization with another, were the work not of foreign conquerors but of merchants from distant countries. The Indians who first brought Hinduism to the islands in the second century A.D. seem to have set a pattern which a thousand years later was followed, certainly unawares, by the Arabs. In the fourteenth century Islam made some progress in northern Sumatra, mainly along the coast, but the state of Melayu, in the centre of the island, remained under Hindu culture and offered strong resistance. The northern sultans, as they were now called, took up the task of converting their subjects and their enemies by more forceful means than the Indian merchants of antiquity or the first Moslem traders had dared to employ.

Java, under the Kingdom of Majapahit, which soon controlled south-east Sumatra also, was still unaffected by the Islamic movement. The new kingdom grew steadily stronger during the thirteenth and fourteenth centuries, at the same time as Thailand, under the kings reigning in the new city of

Ayudhya, was becoming the great power of the continental region, following upon the decline of Cambodia. It has been observed by modern historians that there is a relationship between the rise of strong states in South-East Asia and the decline of strong dynasties in China. This begins to appear, in Indo-China, as early as the T'ang period (seventh to tenth centuries). As T'ang China slowly declined, Cambodia grew strong on the continent and Shrivijaya in the islands. When the Sung were at the height of their power in China, they encouraged rivals to these strong powers, Champa on the one hand (against Cambodia) and Java against Shrivijaya (Sumatra). When the Sung declined, Cambodia rose again in the eleventh and twelfth centuries, and Shrivijaya attained its greatest power. The Mongol reunification of China coincides with the collapse of the new Burma power of Pagan, the decline of Cambodia and the fall of Shrivijaya. There is clear evidence that the Mongol Emperor Kublai sought these results, and it would seem that he was carrying on with a well established Chinese policy. After Kublai the Mongol dynasty declined: and Java in the islands (Majapahit) and Thailand on the continent, rose steadily to domination. This series is clearly no mere coincidence, but reflects a reality of power politics in South-East Asia, which the later European conquests long obscured and made forgotten, but which is once more clear enough today. It will be seen that when the Chinese Ming dynasty followed the Mongols, direct interference in the affairs of South-East Asia attained a new strength; when the Ming declined, in the sixteenth and seventeenth centuries, it was now the newcomers from the West – Portuguese, later Dutch and English – who profited and became the strong powers of South-East Asia.

Majapahit, the Javanese Kingdom, founded in 1293, prospered mightily for a century, and at its height controlled, for the first time in history, almost the whole of the modern Indonesia, except the northern arm of the Celebes; but, in addition, it was also master of the larger part of the Malay Peninsula, including the city of Tumasik, on the site of modern Singapore. Its decline was to begin late in the fourteenth century, with the death of the great King Rajasanagara (1350–89). Under a series of lesser successors the Empire of Majapahit shrank rapidly. In Malaya the foundation and rise of Malacca deprived it of the control of the straits, and of the rich revenues from the commerce which passed through them. Moreover, Malacca had become a centre of Islam, and a main source of the conversion of the Malay peoples to that faith. Majapahit was still Hindu; this was a certain cause of rivalry between the two states. When Islam gained a footing in Java itself, about the end of the fourteenth century, the struggle continued between the two religions until, by the end of the fifteenth century, the time at which the Kingdom of Majapahit finally collapsed (1513–28), Islam was everywhere triumphant, and the Hindu cults were restricted to the island of Bali, where they remain until the present day. It is fortunate that they did so, otherwise much, if not all, of the rich Hindu-Javanese literature and culture would have disappeared leaving only stone inscriptions.

Early in the fifteenth century the celebrated maritime expeditions of the Ming Emperor of China, Yung Lo, had touched upon Java, as well as Sumatra and other islands and countries of South-East Asia. The Ming purpose was to make the kings of the south acknowledge his suzerainty (which they for the most part did readily enough) and to subdue any who might be recalcitrant. This, also, was accomplished in a number of instances. This episode of Chinese maritime power, sustained for about twenty years under Yung Lo, but abandoned by his successors, has been already discussed in the chapters dealing with China. Here it is only necessary to recall that it was not so isolated an act of policy as it may appear to be. The Chinese, under Mongol rule, had already sent an expedition to Java in 1293, and earlier Chinese dynasties had exercised powerful indirect diplomatic influence in the islands to prevent the rise of any one dominant state.

The Ming Chinese sea-borne expeditions provide the first descriptions of the eastern islands of Indonesia, including Timor, which is the island nearest to Australia. These islands were visited by the Chinese fleets and their names recorded. It is interesting to observe that the island of Timor was already known by this name, since it is written in Chinese by characters which are read in most Chinese dialects as 'Ti Wen', but in that of Foochow alone as 'Ti Mo'. Now it is known that Foochow was the home base of the Chinese Ming fleets, and many, if not most, of the sailors and captains came from this famous seaport. It is clear evidence, therefore, that Timor was recorded as the name of the island by Chinese from Foochow, and in later times very few Chinese from that city settled in the Indonesian region. The inference is that it was the sailors of Cheng Ho's fleet which visited Timor who first recorded this name.

The Philippines

Chinese sources, more ancient than the Ming period, are also the only sources of knowledge of the Philippines prior to the Spanish discovery. Some Chinese porcelain has been found at various places in that country, proving that there was a trade carried on with the native inhabitants. But it is also clear from these Chinese accounts that no organized kingdoms had evolved, and the Indian influence which formed such states in other parts of the island region of South-East Asia did not reach the Philippines in sufficient strength to modify the native cultures. Some Sanskrit words have been identified in the languages of the Philippine Islands, but they are few in number and were probably introduced by traders from Majapahit as late as the tenth to twelfth centuries A.D. A very few Buddhist images have also been found at archaeological sites, and these, of Javanese origin, also date from the thirteenth and fourteenth centuries, although they may not have reached the Philippines until perhaps one hundred years later.

The south-west islands of the group were penetrated by Moslems, coming from the western Indonesian islands in the late fourteenth and fifteenth centuries. They introduced Islam and converted the tribes of Mindanao and Sulu to the new religion, and set up small Moslem states in this part of the country. Moslem influence had only just reached Luzon, the main island, prior to the Spanish settlement. Consequently the Moslem region of the Philippines had remained confined to the south-western islands. These islands were in touch with western Indonesia by the coastline voyage along the northern shore of Borneo, which had also been brought under Moslem Malay rule at much the same period. These countries were the farthest eastern outposts of Islam. They were far remote from the main centres of the faith and of Arabic civilization, and they were soon to be further cut off from such influences by the Spanish conquest of the Philippine Islands, which introduced the Roman Catholic religion to peoples who, apart from the small Moslem region in the south-west, had remained primitive pagans.

This fact makes the whole character of the Philippine Islands and the history of the country fundamentally different from that of the rest of South-East Asia. For the Philippines, civilization begins with the Spaniards, religion with the Catholic missionaries and history with the records of the Spanish administration. Although the Spaniards were not very numerous, and the bulk of the population is probably only very lightly mixed with Spanish ancestry (if at all), the culture of the country is of European, not Asian, origin. It does not share the Hindu substratum and later Buddhist culture which has either remained dominant, as in the continental states, or underlies the later Islamic culture in Indonesia and Malaya. It was little touched by Chinese civilization, apart from articles of trade, until much later immigration of Chinese under Spanish rule. The Moslem penetration of the south-western islands might, probably would, in time have covered the whole archipelago, had it not been checked and completely halted by the Spanish settlement when still in its early stages. This situation gives the Philippines their peculiar character; a country lying in the tropics, following the same patterns of agriculture as its neighbours, speaking languages (other than Spanish) which are akin to those of Indonesia, but in culture and religion, and in the way of life of the educated classes, wholly European. The Philippines under Spanish rule was a country largely cut off from close contact with the mainland of Asia: since independence the country has found itself involved in the affairs of a continent with which it has only very slight cultural ties.

It was in 1521 that the expedition commanded by Magellan, having rounded Cape Horn and crossed the immense width of the Pacific Ocean, touched at Cebu in the Philippines, only ten years after the Portuguese had taken Malacca. The Spaniards learned that Cebu, a port visited by ships from Asia, had very recently received a visit from Thai junks, which had probably sailed either from the northern part of the Malay Peninsula, or from the mouth of the Menam. Once again, the early sixteenth century was to be the turning point, or rather, in this case, the starting point of a new era in the history of a South-East Asian country.

The Malay Peninsula

The Malay Peninsula is mentioned in Chinese historical records from an early date, but for many centuries the states which existed there were small and weak, at first under the overlordship of the Kingdom of Fu Nan (ancient Cambodia), later under the Cambodian Kingdom of Angkor and later still divided in allegiance between the rising Thai Kingdom and the Indonesian Empire of Majapahit. Late in the thirteenth century, when Marco Polo passed through the Straits of Malacca, he did not even mention the existence of that city, nor is it recorded by other early European and Arab travellers. Yet Malacca was the first powerful state to rise on the peninsula, and for one century, the fifteenth, it dominated the commerce of the straits and became a powerful focus of the spreading religion of Islam. It was in 1403 that the first King of Malacca, still Hindu by religion, established himself in that city. and promptly accepted Chinese suzerainty. The Ming voyages were now in progress, and the friendship of the King of Malacca was useful to the Chinese since his city provided them with an advanced base in the southern seas. He was accorded the title of King by the Chinese Emperor.

From that date, until later in the century, the Ming Emperors withdrew their fleets from the southern seas; Malacca remained the Chinese base, and the successive kings the faithful vassals of the Chinese Emperor. In 1411, 1414 and again in 1419, the King visited Peking to perform personally the homage he owed to China. In return he asked for aid against the encroachment of the Thai Kingdom of Ayudhya which was already dominant in the northern part of the peninsula and constantly threatened Malacca. At this time the King was converted to Islam, and henceforward his city became the main centre of Islam in the Indonesian-Malayan area. This suited the Chinese, as the commanders of the great fleets sent south were also Chinese Moslems, and although the Emperor and his ruling civil service were, of course, Confucians, the Chinese had never felt any of the intolerance of alien religions so conspicuous in western Asia and in Europe. Later kings of Malacca kept up close relations with Peking, one of them visiting China twice and remaining nearly a year. By 1488 Malacca, under Chinese protection, had become a powerful state controlling the narrow straits, enriched by the commerce which passed through them. Its strategic position made it the forerunner of modern Singapore, and the fact that its harbour was too shallow for the shipping of later ages was not yet the fatal obstacle to further progress which it became in the nineteenth century.

It was, however, the position of Malacca controlling the straits, and as the centre of Islamic power in the region, which in the end attracted the enmity of a new power, and brought about its downfall. The Portuguese were already in the region, based on Goa, in India. They realized that unless they eliminated Malacca their expansion into the China Sea would be impossible: they also were determined to strike down the Islamic states, which they regarded as hereditary enemies. China by the end of the century had withdrawn from active participation in the affairs of South-East Asia, and thus Malacca had no powerful protector. In 1511, after a long siege, the city fell to the Portuguese, and this event marks the beginning of the 'Colonial Era' in South-East Asia. It is hardly in doubt that the withdrawal of Chinese sea power opened the way for the Portuguese, with consequences which were equally disastrous for China herself in later centuries.

Burma, the most westerly country of South-East Asia, had for many centuries a history which hardly impinged on the other countries of the region. The Burmese people descend from a tribe which migrated into Burma from Tibet in the eighth and ninth centuries. The earliest centre of their power was in the northern half of the country, round Pagan, a city not very far from modern Mandalay. The south was organized under the Kingdom of Pegu, a city in the delta of the Irrawaddy, and the inhabitants of this region were Mon, a people closely akin to the Khmers of Cambodia. The country was first unified by a great warrior, King Anoratha (A.D. 1044–77), who ruled in Pagan, conquered Pegu and expanded the Burmese Kingdom northwards to Bhamo, and westwards, at least for a time, across the mountains of Arakan to the coast of the Bay of Bengal. His conquest of the sea coast, including the Irrawaddy delta, had very important long-term results. For by opening up this 'window to the west' Burma was brought into relations with southern India and Ceylon, centres at that time of the form of Buddhism known commonly as Hinayana, but more correctly as Theravada. This is the older and (in the view of its followers) the purer form of that religion, now practised in Ceylon, Burma, Thailand, Laos and Cambodia. It is in many ways different in rites and beliefs from the Mahayana form which prevails in Vietnam, China, Korea and Japan. Burma became converted to Theravada, which was adopted as the national religion and became truly a popular one, not merely a court cult, as the Hindu religion in Java, Sumatra and elsewhere had very largely been.

The conversion of Burma thus provided Theravada Buddhism with a base from which in the twelfth and thirteenth centuries it spread throughout continental South-East Asia, except the Malay Peninsula, then under the domination of the Sumatran Kingdom of Shrivijaya. On the other hand, it made little headway in the islands, and did not penetrate the countries under Chinese cultural influence. This has had lasting consequences, evident to this day. The regions and countries which were converted to Theravada Buddhism proved impervious to the appeal of Islam: Burma, Thailand, Laos and Cambodia remain Buddhist to this day, and their form of Buddhism, Theravada, also marks their culture off in sharp contrast to that of Vietnam, China, Korea and Japan. Indonesia, where the old official royal cult was Hinduism, succumbed to the Islamic wave, with the sole exception of the island of Bali, which survives as a country of Hindu religion and culture. Malaya also became Moslem, a fact which prevented the Thai domination from achieving its full aim in the peninsula.

The Burmese Kingdom of Pagan flourished for two hundred years, until the Mongol invasions under the generals of Kublai Khan, already the master of China, destroyed it in 1287. Thereafter, Burma experienced a calamitous period of division and disasters for nearly two and a half centuries. The Mongol régime at first attempted to rule the country directly, as if it were a part of China. Distance, the climate, the differences in language and culture proved that this policy was impossible, and the Mongols then permitted Thai soldiers of fortune, nominally their tributaries, to control different parts of the country. These Thai rulers made war upon each other, were regarded as aliens by the Burmese and thus never gathered sufficient strength either to unite the country or throw off Mongol allegiance. When the Mongols were displaced by the Ming, that dynasty, following the traditional policy of China in her periods of strength, perpetuated the division of Burma, and gave no encouragement to any of the small rulers who might have reunited the country. But by the early sixteenth century the Ming had passed the zenith of their power: for some years Burmese nationalism had found a centre in the originally small principality of Toungoo in the Sittang valley (north and east of Rangoon). It was a king of this state, Tabinshweti, who in the years 1526 to 1539, by a series of rapid campaigns, overthrew the Thai and other local rulers and reunited the whole country under the Toungoo dynasty.

Conclusion

History is a continuous process, and the introduction of 'periods' can be both arbitrary and distorting. Yet there are times when some major change clearly marks off the centuries which follow from those that have gone before; and the last half of the fifteenth century, with the early years of the sixteenth century, is such a watershed in the history of South-East Asia. Up to the abandonment of Angkor in 1450 the ancient centres of culture were still the main centres of political power. By 1511, with the Portuguese capture of Malacca, all was changing, and new centres of power, and new, far-reaching cultural influences were transforming the character of large parts of the South-East Asia region. By the year 1500 Islam had made great progress in Malaya, Sumatra and Java, effacing the older Hindu culture, which survived only in Bali. The Empire of Majapahit, long dominant in Indonesia, and a stronghold of Hindu culture, collapsed in 1513. In 1539 the period of Thai domination over Burma ended with the reunion of the country under the Toungoo dynasty. In the same period, Thailand had consolidated into a powerful kingdom soon to be the rival of Burma, reaching out for dominion in the Malay Peninsula, and still pressing hard upon declining Cambodia, and replacing that kingdom as suzerain of the new, Thai Laotian principalities.

On the eve of the European expansion into eastern Asia, the South-East Asian area had thus acquired the basic political and cultural character which it continued to retain even under the later European domination. Burma, Thailand and Cambodia long survived as independent kingdoms, all of Theravada Buddhist faith and culture. Burma alone was finally conquered by the British, but remained a colony for less than one century. Cambodia was under French protection for little more than half a century; Thailand retained its independence. The former Majapahit Empire corresponded in its main regions to modern Indonesia, and to the heart of the Dutch colonial empire. Colonial rule and Christianity did not displace the relatively recent conversion to Islam, except in the most eastern islands where Islam had hardly made any headway. Nor did the Portuguese, later Dutch and finally British rule in Malaya alter the Islamic culture which the whole peninsula derived from the brilliant but short-lived kingdom of Malacca. The withdrawal of Chinese power under the middle Ming emperors preceded and perhaps opened the way for European penetration and was not reversed by the Manchu dynasty when it succeeded to the Ming. Thus the main structure of national power and the patterns of culture which existed under the coming European rule were already determined by the history of the region in the century before the Portuguese capture of Malacca. European rule tended to conform to this underlying pattern, with some exceptions. The British and French divided the continental area, the British ruling in Burma and Malaya, the French in Indo-China, with Thailand as a buffer state between them. The Dutch inherited the Empire of Majapahit and enlarged it to incorporate the distant eastern islands, and the largely uncivilized island of Borneo. When in due course European colonial rule passed away, it is still the pattern of nations and cultures formed in the fourteenth and fifteenth centuries which has re-emerged, like rocks long hidden by a high tide. It is for this reason that the complex problems of South-East Asia today cannot be understood without knowledge of the earlier period in which these nations acquired their distinct character and varying cultures.

CHAPTER TEN

The Age of European Penetration

(A.D. 1500–1900)

THE European penetration of the Far East was the work of four of the nations of Western Europe, all of which have seaboards on the Atlantic coast. The activity of Spain, a fifth nation with such a sea coast, was confined to the Philippine Islands as a consequence partly of her preoccupation with the empire she had built in the Americas. Also, in their world colonial competition with Portugal, the Spaniards travelled more slowly from America westward over the vast Pacific distances and, except near the Philippines, against unfavourable winds. The Portuguese moved more easily eastward from India into South-East Asia. Written agreements and earlier Papal blessing left the Portuguese supreme in the Indian Ocean and South-East Asia (except the Philippines). Spain retained the Philippines, the Pacific eastward and all the Americas except Brazil. Needless to say, the other nations of Europe later refused to accept this arrangement, but it did correspond very closely to the field of colonization in which they became active.

Portugal was the first to found a colonial empire in southern Asia. Holland followed, then Britain; France was last. The Portuguese had no serious competition for a full century; the Dutch then challenged and overcame them; the British did not really enter into the struggle until the beginning of the seventeenth century, and confined their main effort to India until the end of the eighteenth century. The French, having lost the contest for India, turned their attention to continental South-East Asia, and from the beginning of the nineteenth century concentrated on that region. Thus, in broad terms, the sixteenth century was the period of Portuguese power, the seventeenth century the era of Dutch domination, the eighteenth century the period of Anglo-Dutch and Anglo-French rivalry and the nineteenth century saw the rise of British and French power in the continental countries of South-East Asia, while the Dutch made no further conquests.

The Portuguese Empire was a purely maritime dominion, consisting of port strongholds strung along the great trade route from Africa to India, Malaya and so to China and Indonesia. Portugal never conquered large territories, nor established any great colony. Holland, and later Britain, began in the same way, but soon realized that such an empire was too dependent on sea power, and that in order to safeguard the seaports it was necessary to conquer their hinterland – the region or country in which these ports were situated. The French, last of all, having failed to establish an empire in India, immediately set about securing control over the whole country when they entered Indo-China. By the nineteenth century the superiority of European arms was so great that this policy, which would have been beyond the strength of Portugal two hundred years before, was easily accomplished. The fact that all the four powers began their conquests in the interest of trade, and at first shrank from trying to conquer large alien countries, accounts for another important difference in the history of the countries of the region in the period of European conquest. The islands were brought under Western control nearly one hundred years, in some cases more, before the main countries of continental South-East Asia became colonies or protectorates of the European powers. Malaya, Burma, Vietnam, Cambodia and Laos retained some part of their territories and independence until the latter part of the nineteenth century: Indonesia and the Philippines were fully under Dutch and Spanish control by the end of the seventeenth century. Thailand alone retained full independence, although in the second half of the nineteenth century she had to cede important provinces to both France and Britain.

This pattern of conquest and penetration makes it convenient to follow the fortunes of the invading powers, and the countries they assailed, in turn, and to leave the continental countries which were not at first involved in the struggle against the West to later sections.

The Portuguese

The Portuguese period of power began, as did the British later on, with establishments in India, but the history of that subcontinent is not the subject of this book. The great viceroy Albuquerque had seized Goa, on the west coast of India, in 1510. It was only one year later that he attacked and captured Malacca, thus opening the straits to Portuguese navigation and permitting trade and expansion into the Indonesian area. By 1521 the Portuguese had gained actual control over the small kingdoms of the Moluccas, islands in the eastern part of Indonesia, which were soon to be famous as the 'Spice Islands'. The trade in spices was the reason for the Portuguese interest. In the European Middle Ages, and for some centuries afterwards, methods of stock raising made it difficult to supply the market in winter with fresh meat. Once the pastures had thinned out with winter, cattle and sheep could not be fattened. Consequently meat was mainly dried or preserved, and not very palatable unless heavily spiced. The western and northern Europeans thus acquired a taste for spiced meat, and the spices came from the East.

The trade had for centuries been in Arab hands. They carried cargoes to Egyptian ports, whence the goods were taken overland to Mediterranean ports, and there bought by Venetian and other Italian merchants. The spice trade had long been most valuable to Venice, and also to the Moslem countries of the Near East through which it was sold to the Venetians. The Portuguese discovery and development of the sea route across the Indian Ocean and round the Cape into the Atlantic cut out the Moslem middlemen, and did great damage to the economy of these countries, then recently conquered by the new Turkish (Ottoman) Empire. It also caused the decline of Venice. The Moslem countries realized the danger, and after the capture of Malacca they made repeated efforts to oust the Portuguese. But

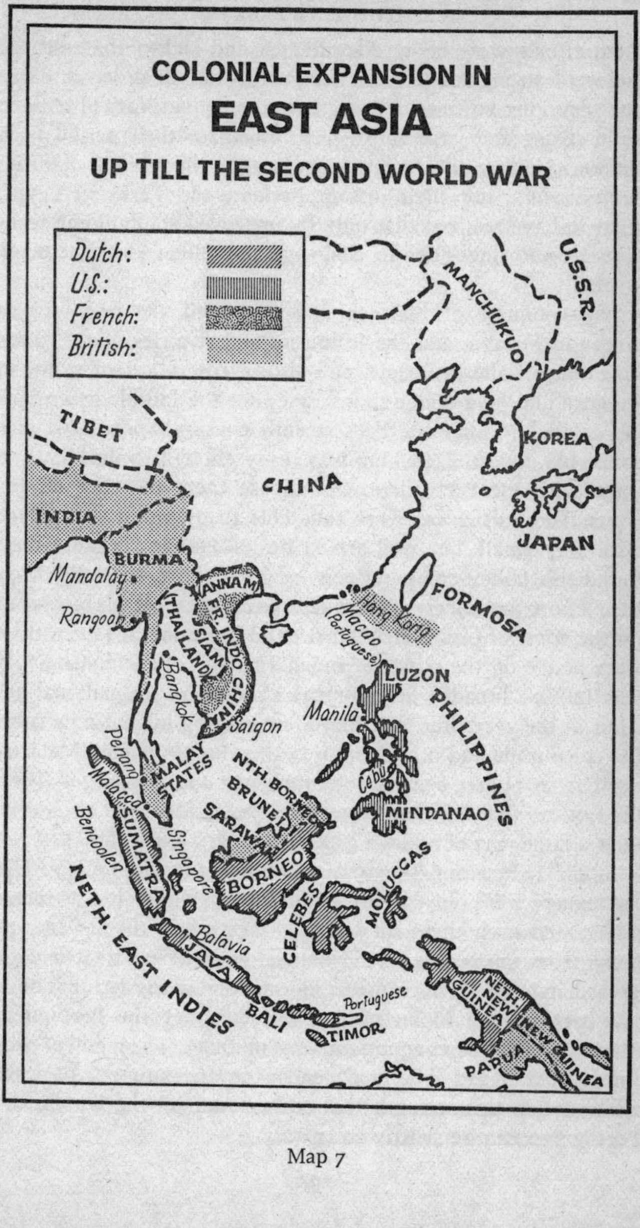

COLONIAL EXPANSION IN
EAST ASIA
UP TILL THE SECOND WORLD WAR

Dutch:
U.S.:
French:
British:

TIBET
INDIA
BURMA
Mandalay
Rangoon
CHINA
MANCHUKUO
U.S.S.R.
KOREA
JAPAN
FORMOSA
Hong Kong
Macao (Portuguese)
LUZON
Manila
PHILIPPINES
ANNAM
FR. INDO-CHINA
THAILAND
SIAM
Bangkok
Saigon
Penang
MALAY STATES
Malacca
SUMATRA
Bencoolen
Singapore
NTH. BORNEO
BRUNEI
SARAWAK
BORNEO
CELEBES
Cebu
MINDANAO
MOLUCCAS
Batavia
JAVA
BALI
Portuguese
TIMOR
NETH. EAST INDIES
NETH. NEW GUINEA
NEW GUINEA
PAPUA

Map 7

these efforts were badly co-ordinated and lacked the essential factor of strong sea power. The Portuguese, in order to carry out very long voyages across great oceans, had learned how to build strong and large ships, well armed for their period with cannon. Neither the Malay kingdoms of the islands, nor the Arab traders, nor their distant backers, the Turks in Egypt, seem to have realized that only by improved shipbuilding techniques could they hope to challenge and defeat Portuguese sea power.

The conquest of Malacca had destroyed the only strong power in Malaya, and the jealousies and rivalries of the petty kingdoms of the peninsula, and also of the successor states in Sumatra and Java which had arisen after the fall of the Empire of Majapahit (early in the sixteenth century), prevented any concerted action. Each king was ready enough to do lucrative trade with the Portuguese, and to use them to score off his rivals. The Portuguese were thus able to maintain themselves with very small, but well armed forces. Perhaps because they found this policy comparatively easy to follow, they dispersed their effort too widely. Portuguese posts were set up in Macao on the coast of China, they tried to do the same in Japan, they were active on the coasts of India, Thailand and Indo-China. It was far too broad a field for the strength of a small nation. Thus at the very time that they were reaping huge profits from the spice trade and other ventures, they had to defend Malacca itself from 1570–5 against determined attacks and sieges. They did not, on that account, concentrate their forces so as to conquer a large part of Malaya and make their base secure.

In the Indonesian islands it was much the same story. The Portuguese were only solidly established in the Moluccas themselves, and even there they had to face many revolts and attacks from the people of the islands, whom they treated with great harshness. Java, Sumatra, Borneo and many lesser islands lay between the Moluccas and Malacca, but the Portuguese made no effective conquests in any of them. Their power was thinly spread and wholly depended on the strength of their fleets; when this strength was outmatched by the Dutch, the Portuguese Empire swiftly collapsed.

There was another local reason for their failure in the Indonesian islands. The Portuguese arrived there just too late to introduce Christianity, for the Moslem conversion of the major islands had already occurred, only a short time before. The Portuguese were strongly opposed to Islam, the old enemy they had fought for centuries at home in the Iberian Peninsula. Their intolerance provoked very strong Moslem resistance, and this in itself was almost enough to prevent their penetration of any of the larger islands. St Francis Xavier, who visited the Moluccas, observed the results of Portuguese policy with despair, seeing that the greed of the merchants and the brutalities of the soldiers undid anything the Catholic missionaries might accomplish. He sailed away to China where, near Macao, he died. By the end of the sixteenth century, less than one hundred years after the fall of Malacca, Portuguese power was declining, mainly because it had not established any really consolidated base in the Far East.

The Dutch

Other Western nations were already looking with envy on the rich spice trade, and endeavouring to get their share of it. The Portuguese had to defend their rights, sometimes by force, against the Spaniards, who since the foundation of Manila in 1570 had a strong, expanding base in the Philippines, where no serious native power existed to oppose them. Sir Francis Drake, on his round the world voyage (1578), had touched at Ternate in the Moluccas, and obtained some spice. Consequently the English desire to share in this trade was also sharpened. England had still too much to contend with nearer home, including the great danger of the Spanish Armada (1588), to take active steps to challenge Portugal in the East; when, a few years later, they were able to devote money and resources to overseas conquests, the Dutch had already taken the lead in the Indonesian islands, and English effort was diverted to India.

The first Dutch voyage to the islands occurred in 1595. It brought great profits, and immediately encouraged Dutch merchants to invest in the trade. In 1602 the Dutch East India Company was formed, two years after the formation of the English East India Company. ('East India' meant to the men of this age the countries of Asia beyond the Indian Ocean, as against 'West India' which meant the islands and coasts of Central and South America.) For some years the two countries were rivals in their efforts to secure the trade of the Spice Islands, but the Dutch gained an important advantage by occupying in 1619 the Javanese city then called Jacatra, which they renamed Batavia, and made the future capital of their empire. This is the modern Jakarta, capital of Indonesia. England was soon to be involved in her Civil War, and her effort in the East was limited. The Dutch had now no real rival, for they were superior at sea to the Portuguese, and, since they made no effort to convert the Moslems to Christianity, got along rather better with the local kings. They had no ambition to seize these kingdoms, only to obtain a monopoly of their foreign trade.

The second half of the seventeenth century therefore saw the very rapid rise of Dutch power. Their capture of Malacca from the Portuguese in 1641 was decisive. This meant that the control of the vital straits was now in Dutch hands, and Portuguese eastern trade and navigation choked. The Dutch did not, for their part, rely so much on the straits for their own communication. They followed another route: after rounding the Cape of Good Hope where, at Capetown, they had a station, they sailed across the Indian Ocean by the southern route (the 'roaring forties'), and with these constant westerly winds occasionally made landfall on the coast of Australia. Normally they followed northward till they entered the Indonesian islands by the Sunda Straits, between Sumatra and Java. Thus, though they knew of Australia, the largely desert coasts of Western Australia did not appeal to them, since there were no advanced natives to trade with. They merely used the continent as a sailing mark. The Portuguese had followed the northern route, crossing the Indian Ocean from south-east Africa to Goa in India, thence through the Bay of Bengal to the Straits of Malacca. The names of 'Delagoa Bay' and 'Algoa Bay' in southeast Africa perpetuate this old route, the one being the port

(Delagoa = 'from Goa') used on the homeward voyage, the other (Algoa = 'To Goa') used when taking the south-west monsoon to cross to India on the outward voyage. In later times the English also used this route, as it led to their establishments in India.

In 1667 the Dutch conquered the island of Celebes, which was too close to the Moluccas to be left independent and hostile. By 1682 they had used their power in Java to such effect that they really dominated the weak kingdoms into which the island was then divided. It was perhaps partly the fact that, after Majapahit fell, no powerful state united Java and Sumatra – or indeed any large part of either island – which enabled the Dutch to obtain such rapid success. The fate of Indonesia was, at least to some degree, the consequence of the divisions, rivalries and short-sighted policies of the kings of the Indonesian states. By the end of the century the Dutch were in complete control of Java and had reduced the remaining kingdoms to the position of vassals. Their progress in Sumatra was less rapid; in the north of that island the strong and fanatically Moslem state of Acheh continued to block their path, and long remained a formidable power.

In spite of their conquests, Dutch power declined in the eighteenth century due to the falling off of the trade in spices. Better agricultural methods were producing a change of taste in Europe, and the cultivation of the spices in other lands cut into the market. Cloves, nutmeg and mace had been the spices most prized in Europe. Some of these were now being produced in other parts of the world, and the Dutch did not in this period seek to introduce new crops into the islands they governed or controlled; on the contrary, they harshly limited the cultivation of the spices, to keep the price up. 'Buying cheap and selling dear' meant that the trade declined slowly, while the native cultivators sank into poverty. The British were now in the general field of the Eastern trade and taking an increasing share of it; at the beginning of the eighteenth century the Dutch had superior resources in finance and shipbuilding, but the English rapidly overtook them in this century. The equality between the two sea powers, often tipped in favour of the

Dutch in the reign of Charles II, was now altered overwhelmingly in favour of the British.

The Napoleonic wars seemed at one time likely to end Dutch rule and influence in the East. Holland was occupied by the French, and as a satellite state of the French Empire was legally enemy territory for England. The Prince of Orange, former head of the Netherlands state, had taken refuge in England. He authorized the Dutch authorities in all overseas possessions to admit British forces and accept British rule for the duration of the war, Britain promising to return these territories when peace was made. The British thus took control of Java from 1810 until the final defeat of Napoleon. Sir Stamford Raffles was the British Governor, and in many ways he reversed the trade policy of the Dutch administration which had been based upon the principle of monopoly for the Dutch East India Company (which had been wound up in 1799 in a bankrupt condition). When the war was over the British Government, in spite of Raffles's unwillingness, did hand back Java to the Netherlands, but the affairs of the two countries in the Far East were not finally settled until the Anglo-Dutch Treaty of 1824, which ended the very considerable friction between them. By this treaty Holland ceded Malacca to Britain and agreed to seek no territory or base in the Malay Peninsula. Britain gave up her port of Bencoolen on the west coast of Sumatra, and agreed to seek no other settlement in the islands. It was agreed to liberalize trade.

The Dutch had lost their trade during the long Napoleonic wars, and it had passed almost entirely to Britain, who had the command of the sea. Holland found it difficult to recover, and for this reason was forced to turn to a new policy in her island empire, that of exploiting the resources of the interior, rather than monopolizing the foreign trade of the country. This new policy inevitably met with resistance from the semi-independent sultans who ruled over the remaining, diminished kingdoms of Java. From 1825 to 1830 Holland had to fight a hard war against the Indonesian patriot Prince Dipo Negoro (now a national hero in Indonesia), who seems to have been one of the first leaders of Asian resistance to adopt guerrilla warfare rather than try to face trained armies with inadequate, ill-armed regular forces of his own. He failed in the end, and died an exile. The crushing of this resistance and the reduction of the former kingdoms to complete impotence enabled the Dutch Government to put into effect a new policy, called the Culture System, which certainly had the result of reviving the Dutch economy and bringing great profits to their merchants.

Governor-General Van den Bosch invented this system and enforced it. It was designed to produce large export crops which would be bought by Dutch companies, shipped to Holland in Dutch vessels and marketed in Europe through Dutch firms. It made Amsterdam the centre of the European trade in many commodities which were winning large markets. Every Javanese farmer was compelled by law to set aside part of his land to raise these crops which were bought at fixed prices. The production of rice on which the food supply of the country was dependent thus decreased, sometimes to danger point, and there were famines. But very large crops of coffee, tea, tobacco, pepper, sugar, cinnamon and cotton were raised and exported. The country was developed as a huge Dutch estate on which the Javanese toiled for low wages while the Dutch made large profits. It is true that the country was also developed, pacified and improved. Roads, and later railways, were built to move the crops to the ports. The population increased, but it had no share in the government, and perhaps no other European colony was more completely under the rule and control of the alien governing people than Java. It is the memory of this period, which endured for most of the nineteenth century, which has so greatly embittered the Indonesians against 'Colonialism'.

In the later nineteenth century, under the pressure of more liberal opinion at home, the government of the Netherlands East Indies slowly modified the system, but more in response to the changing demands of trade than for any other reason. Coffee, which continued to be the main valuable crop far into the modern period, was raised under the culture system as late as 1917. One other result of this system was that the Outer Islands were neglected, as rich Java produced all that was needed. The spice trade had fallen away to small proportions. Northern Sumatra was not under Dutch control, Bali was resentful and defiant of that control, Borneo still mainly jungle. The discovery of oil in Borneo and later in Sumatra had not yet made these islands valuable. The continuing hostility to Dutch influence of the north Sumatran state of Acheh, fiercely Moslem in religion, led to a long colonial war, starting in 1873, but still continuing at the end of the century and only finally brought to an end in 1907. The resistance of Acheh for so long a time, and the difficulty the Dutch found in pacifying this region, left a lasting result: hardly had the Moslems of Acheh been brought under Dutch rule before the Indonesian people as a whole, particularly the Javanese, began to stir to the first movements of modern nationalism.

In the late nineteenth century and first decade of the twentieth century, the heyday of Western colonial imperialism, few Europeans thought that any change was imminent. The period had seen the extinction of the last of the old independent states of South-East Asia (Thailand excepted) and the tightening of control over peoples who had remained at least partly self-governing in the earlier period. The idea that Asian nationalism would soon arise to prove a far more formidable enemy than the old kingdoms had ever been was quite outside the thinking of European rulers and merchants in this period. Yet in retrospect it can be seen that by destroying the old régimes the Europeans really made it inevitable that new forces would be freed which would generate much greater opposition to Western control. This happened in all the Western colonies, whatever internal policy they followed. Another cause of the comparative ease with which the Western powers held and extended their colonies in the second half of the nineteenth century was that the three major colonial powers were always at peace with each other. The long quarrel between the French and English ended with the Napoleonic wars; Britain and Holland had no disputes; Holland and France were on good terms. There was thus no war between the colonial powers themselves to open an opportunity for revolt among their subjects. It was not until a new, Asian, power arose to challenge their rule that the artificial nature of their power could be demonstrated.

The British

Britain had been too occupied by the expansion of her Indian Empire in the eighteenth century to play a major part in South-East Asia. By the end of that century the growing trade with China, and the naval strategy of the Napoleonic wars, made it important to secure control over the Straits of Malacca in order to safeguard the trade route to the Far East. The wars between France and England in the eighteenth century, which all had their repercussions in India, were also important factors. It was in 1786 that Captain Light established British rule in the island of Penang near the northern end of the straits. This was the first British foothold in Malaya, and it was originally as a naval base that this island was occupied. It did not prove to be a suitable place for such a base, but it rapidly prospered as a trading station. The occupation of the Dutch possessions during the war with Napoleon increased British interest in the region. At the end of the war, when Malacca had to be given back to the Dutch, Sir Stamford Raffles secured the island of Singapore as an alternative, and far superior, harbour to Malacca. The treaty with Holland in 1824 returned Malacca to the British, and these three cities, Penang, Malacca and Singapore, at first a dependency of Bengal for governmental purposes, were later withdrawn from the Indian Empire and made into a separate colony known as the Straits Settlements.

The situation in the Malay Peninsula in the first half of the nineteenth century certainly invited the intrusion of some strong power. Thailand exercised an intermittent but oppressive suzerainty over the four northern sultans, of Kedah, Perlis, Kelantan and Trengganu, with vaguer pretensions over the more southerly states of Selangor and Pahang. Jahore, once the most powerful, had declined; all the states were a prey to constant disorder, and hardly controlled more than the rivers on which their sultans had their capital towns. The Sultan of

Kedah had ceded Penang to the British in the expectation that they would defend him against Thailand. But when in 1821 the King of Thailand sent an army to invade Kedah, the British in Penang, governed by distant Calcutta, were told not to intervene. This made a bad impression on the Malays, and in later years was one cause why the sultans began to look for some other protector. Meanwhile, Singapore rose rapidly to become one of the great ports of the world. It was mainly inhabited by Chinese, whom Raffles had encouraged to settle there, finding the island almost uninhabited when he took it over. The population of the whole peninsula was then very small, and shortage of labour was its main problem for more than a century.

Tin had been found in many parts of the peninsula, and was mined by Chinese from south China who flocked into the country. They soon controlled this industry on which the sultans depended for such revenues as they possessed. The tin mining areas thus became a new cause for contentions between the Malay states, and the Chinese miners, tough and hardy, soon joined in these little wars, first on one side, then on another. The chaos deepened, trade was impossible, the merchants of Singapore, both Chinese and English, clamoured for British intervention.

It is a matter of record that the governments in London, whether Liberal or Conservative, were most unwilling to undertake any such obligations. India was one thing, but the indefinite extension of British rule in other parts of Asia was opposed by many influential men. But the logic of power could not be avoided. Malaya was a chaos of warring predatory chiefs and Chinese mining societies; Singapore, Malacca and Penang were well governed, rich trading centres, ruled by a great sea power. It was impossible to tolerate such conditions on their doorstep. Then it became probable that other European powers were ready to rush in where England feared to tread. The Governor of the Straits Settlements, Sir Andrew Clarke, who had rather imprecise instructions from the home government to 'use his influence' to bring peace to the warring princes of Malaya, decided that these words covered him if he took firm action. Making use of one of many incidents of piracy and plunder of merchants under British protection, he summoned the sultans of the west coast to a conference on the island of Pangkor, and there obtained from them the famous agreement to accept British Residents at their courts, whose 'advice must be asked for and acted upon in all questions other than those touching Malay religion and custom' (1874).

Whatever Sir Andrew expected, these words became a charter which put the British into control over Malaya. The sultans received, and were compelled to carry out, 'advice' which brought about a complete reform of their turbulent states. They, in fact, soon lost all but nominal power. British officials took charge of the revenue system, the customs, the police, the defence and the development of these countries. In 1895 a further step was taken by bringing about the federation of the four central states of Perak, Selangor, Negri Sembilan and Pahang, under a unified administration presided over by a British High Commissioner, who was at the same time Governor of the Straits Settlements. The northern four states had remained under nominal Thai suzerainty until 1909, when a treaty between Britain and Thailand transferred suzerainty to the British Crown in return for the renunciation of extra-territorial rights for British citizens in Thailand. Johore also remained outside the Federation, but the powers of the British advisers to the courts of the unfederated states were in practice no less than those of the Residents in federated states. In effect, all Malaya was a British colony, with some variations in local government.

It prospered exceedingly. Tin continued to be a major industry, but the planting of rubber seeds, brought from Brazil and first matured at Kew Gardens, gave Malaya the great source of her wealth and attracted a large number of new immigrants into the country. British rule was not concerned with racial questions: labour was short, so it was brought in from where it was over-abundant, south China and south India. The Chinese arrived by shiploads, brought in by contractors who paid their fares and recouped their money from the wages these men earned. In spite of the obvious ease of exploiting such poor and illiterate labourers, very many of them rose in one lifetime from complete poverty to great wealth, and not a few died millionaires.

The Indians, who were British subjects, were brought by agreements with the Government (British) of India, and had to be repatriated after fixed terms of service, unless they obtained other employment. They worked the rubber plantations, and a certain number stayed in the country, but the majority returned to India. For this reason the Indian element in the population today is not more than about ten per cent, whereas the Chinese (excluding Singapore) is nearly forty per cent. Indians and Chinese in the peninsula equal together the number of Malays; in Singapore the Chinese are eighty per cent of the population. The Malays also increased by a large immigration from Sumatra across the straits. It is often said that the Malays are the true inhabitants of the country, and the Chinese and others only foreign immigrants. In reality a high proportion of the Malay population is also recent, derived from the Sumatran immigrants, and some at least of the Chinese, especially in the cities of Penang, Malacca and the tin mining towns of Taiping and Ipoh, have been there for much more than a century. The Chinese temple in Malacca dates from the Ming dynasty and is dedicated to Cheng Ho, the great navigator of early Ming times.

The British had also in the nineteenth century come into possession, or control, of northern Borneo. The suppression of piracy, a scourge of the seas at the beginning of the nineteenth century, was the original cause of such intervention. British naval squadrons attacked and destroyed pirate lairs on the coast of Borneo to clear the trade routes to China and the Philippines. In 1841 a British subject, James Brooke, helped the Sultan of Sarawak to suppress rebels, and later his services to the Sultan were so much appreciated that the childless monarch made him his heir and successor. So began the rule of the 'White Rajas' of Sarawak; independent, but seeking and obtaining British protection, their kingdom prospered and continued until the Japanese invasion of 1942. Soon afterwards the British Government took the Sultanate of Brunei under protection, and established a colony called British North Borneo in the north-eastern end of the island. This country had been under the vague authority, not extending farther than the coast, of weak Malay sultans, themselves at the mercy of the pirates. Except for a thin belt of Malay colonization along the coast and rivers, all of these countries were primitive, inhabited by tribes who had neither come under Moslem nor earlier Indonesian Hindu culture. Here also, following British rule, there was a considerable immigration of Chinese, who now form about one-third of the inhabitants, and control the economy and the skilled professions.

Burma and Thailand

The advance of British power in South-East Asia, apart from the influence which command of the sea gave to her in every region of the Far East, was otherwise confined to Burma. Here the problem was different in many ways from those which had been met in Malaya or in Borneo. Burma was an old and, in a pre-industrial sense, civilized kingdom. It was a centre of Buddhism, and had for many centuries been a leading power in the continental region of South-East Asia. It will be recalled that after the Mongol invasions Burma had suffered a long period of chaotic rule under Thai princes, none of whom controlled any large part of the country. In the first half of the sixteenth century the Burmese threw off this yoke, and under the Toungoo dynasty recovered their unity and freedom. In the middle of the century from 1551 to 1581 the country was ruled by a forceful warrior king named Bayinnaung who spread the power of Burma far and wide. First taking control over the Shan States, a number of Thai principalities along the China–Burma border, he next invaded Thailand, and in 1564 took the capital, Ayudhya, and imposed his suzerainty on the whole country. The Thais soon revolted, but Bayinnaung returned, took Ayudhya again in 1569, and next invaded Laos. There he found the country and the situation too much for him. He did not succeed in incorporating Laos in the new Burmese Empire.

This indeed did not prove to be enduring. After the death of Bayinnaung, the Thais rose and drove out the Burmese (1587), and a few years later it was their turn to invade Burma in 1592, and, after gaining a complete victory, leave it in chaos. Once more the Burmese found a new warrior, King Anaukpetlun (1605–29), who restored the kingdom. The ding-dong wars with Thailand continued, but neither side won decisive advantage, and the struggle gradually subsided. The restored Toungoo dynasty ruled for another hundred and fifty years until 1752. During this comparatively peaceful period the kingdom developed rather exclusive and conservative trends, similar in many ways to the exclusive policies which the Ming and Manchu dynasties in China, and the Tokugawa in Japan, were following at the same period. There seems to have been a general tendency to shut out foreign contact in all these countries, but it is not possible to show that the Burmese policy was adopted in imitation of China, although it would seem probable. Foreign efforts – Portuguese, British, Dutch and lastly French – to open up the country for trade, or to establish trading posts (called 'factories' in those days) at the ports, were never welcome to the Burmese court. Travellers visited the country, but trade did not become important.

Towards the middle of the eighteenth century the Toungoo dynasty began to lose control. Revolts in various provinces weakened the court, until the great revolt of the southern provinces, still inhabited by the old people named Mon, led to the fall of Ava, the capital, and the end of the dynasty. Mon rule was, however, short. Within a few years a new Burmese king, Alaungpaya by name, swept the Mons out of power, took Pegu, their capital (1757) and reunited the whole country under a new dynasty, the Konbaung. It was this king who, in 1755, shortly before the final victory over the Mons, founded a new city at Rangoon, a name which he gave to it because he hoped this foundation meant the end of war; and that, 'End of Strife', is the meaning of the name Rangoon.

It would seem that in the countries of South-East Asia the arrival of a new dynasty to power immediately led to a war with the neighbouring kingdom. Whether the Burmese or the Thai kingdom was revived by a new rule, the result was always the same, the new conquering king attempted to seize his neighbour's kingdom. So it was with Alaungpaya; he had hardly established himself supreme in Burma (1757) than he invaded Thailand (1760), but at the siege of the capital of that country, Ayudhya, he was killed by the explosion of a cannon. His successor took up the task and in 1766 captured Ayudhya and destroyed the city. The Thai dynasty was overthrown, and the general who founded the next one set up his court at Bangkok, lower down the Menam, where the capital of Thailand has since remained.

Burma was now a formidable power, controlling not only her homeland but also Thailand: this did not suit the Manchu dynasty, which under the Emperor Ch'ien Lung was then at the height of its power. It had always been Chinese policy to prevent any one king in South-East Asia becoming dominant. Consequently, Ch'ien Lung now intervened. But although the Chinese diversion enabled Thailand to throw off the Burmese rule, the Burmese themselves actually defeated the Chinese invading army and drove it back into Yunnan. The court of Peking, apparently satisfied that the object of their intervention – to get the Burmese out of Thailand – had been achieved, made no further attempt to carry on the war against Burma itself (1770). A few years later another warrior king, the third son of Alaungpaya, came to the Burmese throne. Perhaps because it was clear that China would intervene in further attempts to conquer Thailand, King Bodawpaya (1782–1819) turned his attention elsewhere, with consequences which were ultimately fatal to his house and country.

Arakan, the west coastal region of Burma, had long been independent under its own kings. It is cut off from the interior valley of the Irrawaddy by a range of rugged mountains which has favoured this separation. During the tenth century this region had been settled by the Burmese, but owing to its isolated position and sea connections across the Bay of Bengal it received successive waves of Indian influence, Buddhist first, later Moslem, although the basic population remained Burmese and predominantly Buddhist. In the sixteenth and seventeenth centuries Arakan became a strong state, especially at sea, and was the first part of Burma to be visited by and to trade with the European merchants. In the late seventeenth century the country fell into disorder and was also under strong pressure from the Mughal Empire in India, since northern Arakan has a common border with East Bengal (now part of Bangladesh). Conditions in the eighteenth century went from bad to worse; the kingdom became the haunt of pirates, and soon the leaders themselves were petitioning the court of Burma to intervene. King Bodawpaya did so in 1784 and incorporated the whole of Arakan in the Kingdom of Burma. From the point of view of the Arakanese this was no doubt a change for the better, but it had momentous consequences. East Bengal was now no longer ruled by the viceroy of the Great Mughal in Delhi; it was ruled by the British.

King Bodawpaya did not realize how dangerous his new neighbour might become; instead of cultivating good relations with the English authorities in East Bengal he allowed considerable disorder to continue on the frontier, due to smuggling, piracy and banditry. He himself in 1786, like so many of his predecessors, went off to try to conquer Thailand, but was unsuccessful. He then once more turned his attention to the northern region of his kingdom, and in 1817 invaded and occupied Assam, the most easterly province of India, not yet under British rule. Bodawpaya himself died in 1819, and his successor, a far less competent soldier and king, was soon to find that the prestige of Burma, built up by conquests over weak and disorganized small states, was not equal to the power of the English East India Company, now rapidly becoming the real masters of India. Continual trouble in Assam, on the border of British India, and on the Arakan frontier also, provoked the English into taking strong action. The Burmese expected war, if it came, on the northern borders; all their preparations were made in that area. But the British, using their unchallenged sea power, simply landed at the mouth of the Irrawaddy, took Rangoon and were in a position to advance up the Irrawaddy to the capital unopposed.

Burma had to make peace, cede Arakan and also the southern province of Tenasserim, in the peninsular part of the kingdom. Assam had to be evacuated and came under British rule. Events now began to follow the familiar pattern of Western expansion in South-East Asia during the nineteenth century.

Burma did not learn quickly enough that the whole power system in the region had fundamentally altered. The prestige of Bodawpaya and his predecessors for more than two hundred years, when Burma had been the most warlike and powerful kingdom, blinded their successors to the changed situation. In 1852 the British, on rather slight pretexts, invaded again and this time occupied and annexed the whole of the delta region including Rangoon and Pegu. The Burmese simply refused to recognize this act, the British proclaimed annexation, but no treaty was ever signed. Under a wise and gentle, fervently Buddhist, ruler, King Mindon, Burma still retained her main central and northern provinces for another thirty years. But Mindon, although he knew that the British were too strong to resist, was unable, owing to the conservative character of his court, to effect any lasting reforms or strengthen the kingdom. His son and successor, Thibaw, the last King of Burma, was foolish, and under the influence of his ruthless Queen, Supayalat (whom the British Tommies, when the inevitable war came, nicknamed 'Soup Plate'). The Burmese court, now cut off from the sea, under strong British pressure to open the country, yield mining and other concessions and denied the status of a sovereign state (the British dealt with Burma through the India Office, not the Foreign Office, which caused great offence), began to intrigue with France in the hope of playing off French rivalry with Britain. This led, in 1885, to a new invasion and the conquest and annexation of the whole kingdom.

In the light of subsequent history it can easily be seen that British policy was quite unnecessarily aggressive and uncompromising. Burma is a distinct country having very little relation with India, and inhabited by a wholly different people, with a different religion and a social system unlike that of India whether Hindu or Moslem. But Britain made it into just another province of the Indian Empire. It would have been very much wiser to continue the Kingdom of Burma under British protection rather than to destroy it, for the Burmese people, without their traditional leadership, proved unruly, hostile and resentful. It is a strange irony that the Burmese were a people whom the British administrators found sympathetic, and that only in Burma, of all the British colonies of the late nineteenth and early twentieth centuries, did British and Burmese mix as equals, intermarry without prejudice and enjoy good personal relations. But on the level of government the British showed little or no comprehension of the Burmese situation. Resistance after the annexation was prolonged and fierce. The campaign had been a walk-over, but it took five years to pacify the country.

British rule in Burma endured just half a century, from the fall of Mandalay in 1885 to the Japanese invasion, and the subsequent independence of Burma after the end of the Second World War. Already by 1921 it was obvious that the annexation had been a mistake, and the incorporation into the Indian Empire a worse one. It was then proposed to separate the two countries, and this was finally achieved in 1935, when Burma obtained a measure of self-government. This, however, did not permit the Burmese government to apply the policies which almost all Burmese favoured, above all the limitation of immigration from India.

The British after annexation had disestablished the Buddhist Church, applying the rule of Indian policy that the British Raj would not discriminate in favour of any one religion. In India this was wise, in view of the bitter divisions between Moslem and Hindu. In Burma it was folly, for the Burmese Buddhist Church had been the great organ of social stability, the main institution for education and had the respect and support of all social classes. Kings might misgovern, but the monasteries and monks, leaders of a national religion, maintained a degree of order, discipline and learning which had sustained Burmese civilization. The Buddhist Church played in Burma almost exactly the role of the Catholic Church in the European Middle Ages, taming the excesses of the warriors, holding the kings in check, educating the people. The disestablishment was perhaps the most unfortunate example of the consequences of annexing Burma to the British Indian Empire. All too often, especially in the earlier years of British rule, the officers administering the country did not speak Burmese; and as the country was now only a province of the Indian Empire, the most part of their careers was passed in India. For them a knowledge of the main Indian languages was far more important, and of lasting value, than learning the language of Burma, unlike any Indian tongue, and spoken only in a country where they expected to serve for very few years. This was also a major cause of the lack of understanding of Burmese affairs shown by the government in Delhi. For these reasons, when independence came after the war, Burma alone refused to remain in the British Commonwealth: she insisted on complete and total independence.

The history of Thailand in the seventeenth and eighteenth centuries is intimately related to that of the rival Kingdom of Burma. Throughout these two hundred years the two kingdoms were engaged in a duel for supremacy in the region of continental South-East Asia, but the contacts of Thailand with other states were more extensive than those of the comparatively isolated Burmese Kingdom. Thailand had, for more than a century, encroached upon Cambodia and Laos: the centre of the kingdom, first at Ayudhya, later at Bangkok, was much nearer to the sea than the successive capitals of Burma, all located in the middle valley of the Irrawaddy. Consequently Thailand had from an early date active relations with the sea powers of Europe, and came to realize their strength. King Naresuen had in 1592 not only freed his country from the Burmese, but carried out a counter-invasion which destroyed the first Toungoo dynasty. He also encouraged Dutch traders, and employed a large number of Japanese mercenary soldiers, themselves refugees from the Tokugawa Shogunate, who could not return to Japan. Shortly after King Naresuen's death in 1605 his successor, in 1609, sent an embassy to Holland, the first ever dispatched by a king in South-East Asia to a European country.

King Narai, who reigned for thirty years from 1657 to 1688, entered into close relations with France, under Louis XIV, in order to check the pretensions of England and Holland. At this time he gave his confidence to a European minister, a Greek named Phaulkon, who, originally in the service of the English East India Company, had left it, under a cloud, and become bitterly anti-English. Phaulkon promoted the interest of France;

a Thai embassy went to Versailles in 1680, and in 1687 French troops were sent to Thailand to secure the kingdom against possible English attack. That at least was how Phaulkon represented the case, but in reality he was now plotting with the French to gain control of the kingdom. This was the first French venture in South-East Asia, and like the later and more successful attempts, it aimed at the control of the whole of a kingdom, not the establishment of trading ports or sea coast colonies. Thus from the first French colonial policy had different aims, and was 'continental' rather than 'maritime'.

Phaulkon's designs were frustrated by a Thai revolt, when many of the princes and ministers at court became suspicious of the intentions of the French. He was put to death, the King died in the troubles and the French were compelled to withdraw from the country (1688). In the eighteenth century France turned her attention to India rather than to South-East Asia, engaging in a long contest with England for supremacy in the declining empire of the Mughals. Thailand, freed from foreign fears, turned to the perennial war with Burma, which swayed to and fro, each side scoring successful invasions, neither side achieving a lasting conquest. Thailand in this period was dominant in Cambodia and Laos, whenever Burmese pressure permitted her to turn her arms in this direction. The Cambodian Kingdom continued to exist, but it had lost much territory to Thailand and was reduced often to a situation little better than that of tributary to Ayudhya. The Thai dynasty founded by the king who drove out the French, Pra Petraja, lasted until the great Burmese invasion of 1767, when Ayudhya was taken and destroyed. A few years later the Thais recovered their independence, moved the capital to Bangkok, where, after the rule of the liberating King Pya Taksin had ended in his lunacy, the present dynasty of Thailand was founded by General Chakri, who ruled as Rama I.

The last years of the eighteenth century saw the end of the long wars between Burma and Thailand. After King Bodawpaya of Burma had failed in his invasion of Thailand in 1786, he was soon to turn his attention to Assam, and his successors became involved in a fatal series of disputes with the growing power of Britain in India. Thailand thus was left in peace and could engage in other policies. For several centuries the Thais had disputed the control of the narrow part of the Isthmus of Kra, in the Malayan Peninsula, with Burma, and with the Malay sultanates farther south. When, in 1826, the British took Tenasserim, the Burmese province in the north of the peninsula, they were at first inclined to offer it to Thailand with the port of Mergui, which had been under Thai control in the seventeenth century. Thailand wisely refused; but she continued to claim suzerainty over the four northern states of what is now Malaya, as well as more direct sovereignty over other Malay sultans ruling in the narrow isthmus of the peninsula. These claims led to a series of disputes with the British, as they gradually spread their power and influence in the Malay Peninsula. Thailand's claims were vague. The whole question of what was meant by 'suzerainty' was confused by the very different ideas which prevailed in Europe and those to which Asians were accustomed.

To the Westerners a suzerain power was a supreme authority, protecting the weaker state, ordering its affairs, especially its relations with other countries, but allowing it some measure of self-government. The Asians did not see it that way at all. To them, a powerful state exacted from a weaker neighbour a symbolic act of obedience, or deference: the sending of a customary tribute, usually a gift of value, but not in itself worth great sums of money. In return, the vassal state received often larger gifts as marks of the bounty of the suzerain power. Neither party had any other obligations. The vassal was free to make war or peace with his neighbours, to govern or to misgovern at home as he pleased. The suzerain undertook no responsibility. This situation was mystifying and exasperating to the early European governors; if Kedah behaved outrageously, they thought Bangkok should intervene. If Bangkok replied that it was not the king's business, then why should he claim to be suzerain? When Kedah, which had ceded Penang to the English in the hope of backing against Thailand, was left to fend for itself when the Thai King exacted retribution for some slight, the Malays were disillusioned, and the British shocked at the severity of the Thai reprisals. As we have seen, the question of what Thai suzerainty meant in north Malaya dragged on throughout the nineteenth century and was only finally settled by the renunciation of all Thai claims in 1909. Nevertheless, the ghost was not really laid: in the Second World War the Japanese, after occupying Malaya, gave the four northern states back to Thailand, and they were administered on behalf of the Thai Government by Malay rulers throughout the Japanese occupation.

The first half of the nineteenth century saw a peaceful period for Thailand: the Western peoples came to trade, concluded some treaties regulating such commerce, but made no attempts to gain more control over the country. The Thais could observe the fate of Burma with some relief: there would be no more Burmese invasions. Thailand was fortunate in that in the crucial second half of the century, when the European advance was so decisively resumed in all parts of South-East Asia, they were governed by two successive kings of outstanding ability, Mongkut, 1851–68, and his son Chulalongkorn, 1868–1910. Before Mongkut's reign there was every indication that Thailand might be about to follow the path which Burma was marking out. In 1831 an attempt to dominate Cambodia failed, and was followed by ten years in which Cambodia fell under the rule of Vietnam (the Empire of Annam, as it was then called). In 1841 the Cambodians revolted, the Thais joined in, and an uneasy compromise was arrived at for joint suzerainty between Thailand and Vietnam. This was only a few years before the French began to exert their influence and power in Vietnam, and already they had their eyes on other countries also.

Mongkut's reign coincides with the period in which the French established themselves in Indo-China. He was thus faced with very much the same threat which the Burmese kings failed to meet when it came from Britain in India. His reaction was very different. Mongkut is the 'King of Siam' (Siam is the old name for Thailand, not used by the Thais themselves, but the name their neighbours gave to the country) who has become well known to the West by both books and musical comedies, as the employer of Mrs Leonowens ('Anna') as governess for his children, one of whom was later King Chulalongkorn. In these popular accounts he is often shown as a reactionary tyrant – an old-style Oriental despot. Nothing could be more inaccurate. He was a scholarly man who had renounced his rights to the throne to become a Buddhist monk, which he remained for twenty-five years. Called to the throne against his will at the failure of other heirs, he spent his spare time on Buddhist theology, of which he was a well-known master; and devoted his reign to a courageous and largely successful effort to modernize his country and avert the threat of Western conquest. The employment of an English lady as governess for his children was only one relatively small matter in which this policy was displayed. It was, none the less, important, since King Chulalongkorn learned English (although the way he expressed himself in that language was often more picturesque than grammatical), and thus was in touch with Western thought in a way which was not paralleled by any other Asian monarch of the period.

Mongkut had a keen interest in science and technology. He introduced many reforms, sent the sons of the nobility, and his own, to England for their education, and gradually built up respect for the independence of Thailand as a more progressive state than its neighbours. He had accepted a treaty introducing extra-territorial jurisdiction for British subjects (this meant that they were not subject to the Thai courts of law) in 1855. He then used the goodwill of Britain to check French ambitions. His reforms were neither so far-reaching nor so fast as those which were introduced into Japan at the Meiji Restoration, which occurred in the year of his death, 1868, but this does not detract from a monarch who could see the need for changes even before the ardent modernizers of Japan had undertaken that task. Mongkut died in characteristic fashion: he had invited a large number of European scientists to view an eclipse of the sun, only visible from a rather unhealthy part of Thailand. The occasion was a great success, and the fact that an Asian monarch had so contributed to world science made a deep impression on European public opinion. Unfortunately, the King contracted malignant malaria in the swampy region, and died shortly after he returned to his capital.

Chulalongkorn was only sixteen when he succeeded to the throne. He immediately announced that during the regency which was set up, he would travel abroad until he took over the government, to improve and complete his education. When he returned five years later after what amounted to a world tour, he at once started a series of reforms which were based upon what he had seen on his travels. The first effort was to send students abroad to acquire the skills and knowledge of the West. The opening up of the country by building railways followed; but the royal government did not feel that Thailand had any need for the democratic forms of government then prevailing in Western countries. Perhaps Chulalongkorn was right: Thailand was certainly not ready for democracy, and the enlightened rule of a progressive monarch was much more in accord with the real needs of the country. The history of the nineteenth century kings of Thailand is a rare example of progress and real reform carried out by absolute monarchs, at their own will and pleasure, without any form of democratic institutions. It may well be that one reason why the King felt that such innovations would be unwise was the fact that during his reign he witnessed the rapid, and to him, menacing spread of French power in all the neighbouring kingdoms; while in Burma, the old rival, Britain extinguished the kingdom by annexation. Thailand lived dangerously, poised between two imperial powers; it was her fortune to be a buffer state, and her merit to be a progressive and orderly one.

The French

In the Empire of Annam, which comprised North and South Vietnam, the opposite policies had been in favour. Annam had had a chequered history: sometimes a Chinese province, at others under Chinese suzerainty, and at all times under strong Chinese cultural influence, it stood apart from the realms of former Hindu and later Theravada Buddhist, and Moslem

culture. In the eighteenth century French Catholic missionaries had penetrated Annam and made considerable progress.
But from 1800 to 1848 the country was ruled by the Emperor
Tu Duc, who was firmly opposed to all foreign influence and
strongly Confucian in outlook. He followed the contemporary
Chinese policy of restricting foreign intercourse and banning
missionary activity. Disorders followed: the missionaries continued to enter the country, to make converts, and to suffer
martyrdom. The French people and government, recovering
from the collapse of the Napoleonic Empire, were less and
less inclined to tolerate these outrages. In 1857 intervention
was decided upon, not entirely for reasons of religion. Britain
had recently won the Opium War against China and just taken
most of southern Burma in the Second Burmese War (1852).
France was not going to be left out of the scramble for Asia. In
1859 the French captured the southern capital of the Annamite
Empire, Saigon, and in 1862 forced the Emperor to cede the
whole southern province of Cochin China (as the Europeans
called it) to France. This roughly corresponds with the delta of
the Mekong, and much of what is now South Vietnam. It was
one of the richest areas, a great rice-producing basin. Advancing up the Mekong, whose mouth they now controlled, the
French imposed a protectorate on Cambodia in 1864.

The King of Cambodia was at that time a harassed and almost powerless monarch. Thailand was demanding his allegiance, and the terms seemed likely to be hard. He was threatened
with invasion unless he went personally to Bangkok to pay
homage. At this moment, the arrival of a French expedition
demanding that he accept the protection of France offered a
way out. King Norodom accepted the French terms, in return
for which he was relieved of his fear of Thailand, even if he
was also soon to be relieved of any real responsibility for the
government of his ancient kingdom.

The French Protectorate over Cambodia lasted until the general French withdrawal from Indo-China in 1954 after the vain
attempt to recover control when the Japanese – who had occupied the entire region – surrendered. It is clear that for Cambodia this loss of real independence was not so serious a

catastrophe as the loss of all freedom for Burma or for Java. The country was weak and threatened: France saved it. The ancient culture of Angkor was preserved and virtually rediscovered by the French, who in turn came to have a high regard for the civilization of the oldest of the South-East Asian kingdoms. France did much for the country in the development of roads and modernization, education and health services. Until the overthrow of Prince Sihanouk in 1969 Cambodia was the best governed and most peaceful of the states of South-East Asia; much of the credit is certainly due to the French, and French-educated Cambodians formed under the Protectorate.

From 1870 disorders in the northern part of Annam (Tongking) gave the French reason for intervention in that part of the declining Empire of Annam. Their activity, interrupted by the Franco-Prussian War of that year, was resumed in the early 'eighties when France proclaimed a Protectorate over the Empire of Annam. China protested against this invasion of her rights, and war followed. In this contest China was by no means without some victories in Tongking. But the threat of French naval power on her coasts and the danger of a concurrent war with Japan in Korea compelled the Manchu court to agree to terms by which France acquired full suzerainty over Annam, and China abandoned her claims. It only remained for France to advance into the fragmented and weak principalities of Laos, which had been once under Cambodian, later under Thai, suzerainty. Using the former historical fact for a pretext, and in addition claims made by Annam to such suzerainty, France occupied Laos in 1890 and the following years. In 1907 pressure was put upon King Chulalongkorn of Thailand. He was compelled to yield the two districts of Battambang and Siemreap (the latter of which contains the site of Angkor) nominally to Cambodia, but actually to French control. It must be said that these areas are Cambodian in race, speech and historical record, and had only been taken by Thailand in the latter centuries of Cambodia's decline.

Conclusion: South-East Asia in 1900

Thus at the beginning of the twentieth century the expansion of the European colonial empires in South-East Asia had all but wiped out the independence of these ancient kingdoms. Only a reduced Thailand, shorn of all her imperial claims, remained wholly free. It was very generally believed in the West that this was the natural sequence of history, the weak yielding to the strong; and the assumption that the West would always be strong enough to hold what it had taken was unquestioned. Yet even before these last stages in the advance had been reached, the tide was elsewhere on the ebb. It was in 1905 that Japan had defeated Russia and ousted her from south Manchuria: six years later, the Chinese revolution of 1911 was to start a great process of change of which we are only now seeing the full range. In India the agitation for Swaraj – Home Rule – was already active. In Burma it was smouldering; in the Netherlands East Indies resentment of foreign rule was building up to danger point. The assumption that the rule of the West in South-East Asia must be more enduring than the domination of the Portuguese, or of the many preceding empires which had risen and fallen in the region, was soon to be proved baseless; and when the Western colonial empires had collapsed, it was perhaps not surprising that the landscape which emerged was so remarkably similar to that which they had submerged a hundred years earlier.

Burma, Thailand, Cambodia, Vietnam (still, as often before, divided into rival northern and southern states), Java and Sumatra dominating, uneasily, the Outer Islands, just as Maja-pahit had done before the Portuguese came – these ancient states are once more the leading powers on the South-East Asian stage. There are also some new ones. Malaysia is more than the old kingdom of Malacca ever was, the Republic of the Philippines has arisen in what were then primitive islands. In the background, now as then, looms the immense enigmatic power of China, sometimes exercised with decisive force, more often left unused for long periods at a time.

*

A Case Apart—The Philippines

It has been pointed out in the last chapter that the story of the Philippines stands apart from that of the rest of South-East Asia. Too far east to receive the Hindu cultural influence which first brought civilization to the islands and to continental South-East Asia, the Philippines remained in the tribal state until the late fourteenth century, when Moslem settlers from the western islands of Indonesia brought their faith to the most southerly Philippine islands, Sulu and Mindanao. Chinese trade with the islands was older : it is proved by the discovery of shards of Chinese porcelain in archaeological sites, and also by mention in the Chinese historical and geographical literature. Apart from some earlier references to overseas islands which have been conjecturally identified as the Philippines (but could equally well be the Celebes and the Moluccas), the first clear Chinese mention of the country dates from A.D. 1209–14, the dates between which the famous Sung scholar Chao Ju-kua composed his 'Record of all the Barbarians' – a comprehensive account of all the foreign overseas countries known to the Chinese either by visits or by hearsay. This book deals with the Philippines and Japan to the east, and with Spain, northwestern Europe and also Africa to the west. Chao records that Chinese traders visited the Philippine Islands regularly.

Between 1380 and 1475 Malay settlers from Sumatra established themselves in Sulu, Panay, and lastly the larger island of Mindanao, where they set up small sultanates, and spread the religion of Islam. This was the foundation of the modern 'Moro' people of these islands, strong Moslems, and inveterate enemies of the Spaniards, who were never able to subdue them. 'Moro' is simply the Spanish word for 'Moor', meaning Moslem, as was the common usage in all Western European countries in the sixteenth century (for example, Shakespeare's Othello, the Moor of Venice). The Moro kingdoms kept some records of their history and introduced the use of the Arabic script into the region they colonized. By 1570, on the eve of the Spanish conquest, the Moro had established outpost sultanates in Luzon

Island, on the shores of Manila Bay. Meanwhile, for a brief time, it had seemed possible that the Philippines would fall under the lasting dominion of another culture and people – the Chinese. The Ming Emperor Yung Lo was sending his great fleets throughout the South Seas and Indian Ocean in the first years of the fifteenth century. From 1405 to 1417 the fleet of the great navigator Cheng Ho repeatedly called in at the Philippines and a Chinese governor was appointed. Unfortunately there does not appear to be a clear enough indication of what ports the Chinese used or where they made their main base. It was no doubt one of the ports most frequented by the Chinese traders, who would be familiar with the coast. If the subsequent experience of the Spaniards is a guide, and the contemporary expansion of the Moslems in the southern islands an example, the Chinese would have found little difficulty in establishing a lasting and strong colony in the Philippines, and it would no doubt soon have grown very populous. The native peoples were not hostile to foreigners, there was ample land for development, and, as was shown in Spanish times, the Chinese from the south-eastern provinces were eager to settle and to trade in the Philippines. The consequences of such a settlement by the Ming would have been profound.

But, as was the case elsewhere in South-East Asia, some thirty years after the first voyages of Cheng Ho, the Ming court under the successors of Yung Lo reversed their policy and withdrew their fleets. The Philippine colony, in so far as it ever existed, was abandoned. Thus when Magellan found the islands in 1521, the Chinese were no longer in the country, except for the seasonal voyages of their traders. Magellan touched at Cebu in 1521 on his famous voyage round the world – the first time this feat of navigation was ever performed. He himself was killed in a skirmish with the natives, but one of his ships returned to Spain in 1522.

The news of the discovery raised high hopes in Spain, and during the next fifty years several expeditions were sent out, but failed either to arrive or to establish themselves. It was not until after the Spanish pacification of Mexico gave Spain a base on the Pacific side of the American continent that the successful occupation of so distant a land as the Philippines was possible. The Mexican ports made it unnecessary for the expeditions to cross the Atlantic and round Cape Horn: all communications with the Philippines were henceforward routed via Mexico, and made the sea voyage to the Atlantic coast of that country, then by land to the opposite coast, whence they sailed in locally built ships for the Pacific crossing to Guam and the Philippines. The Spanish, in accordance with the agreement with Portugal, did not use the Indian Ocean route to reach the Philippines.

In 1565 the Spanish founded at Cebu their first permanent settlement. Five years later they discovered Manila Bay, attacked and defeated the local Moslem sultans, and the next year, in 1571, founded the city of Manila, which was to be and remain the capital of the country. The Spanish occupation of the island of Luzon, on which Manila is situated, and which is the largest of the Philippine group, was from their point of view only just in time. The Moslems were already there, but not in strength. The Spanish drove them away, and thus secured the main part of the Philippines for themselves, and for Christianity. Had Spanish settlement been delayed another few years, perhaps less than fifty, it can hardly be doubted that the Moslem religion would have become the dominant creed of the native peoples, as it did in Indonesia; and the Philippines, even if conquered, would have become an Islamic country. The history of Sulu and Mindanao goes to show that once Islam had been introduced and taken root, no subsequent attempt to change the religion of the people would prevail. The destiny of the Philippines was thus decided by the small skirmishes around Manila in 1570–1.

The Spaniards met very little opposition to their occupation and conquest of the main island of Luzon and all the islands other than those in which the Moros were already dominant. A Japanese pirate lair in northern Luzon gave them some trouble, but was overcome and the pirates were driven out of the country. The closing of Japan by the Tokugawa Shoguns not long after removed this threat – for four hundred years. The native peoples not only made very slight resistance, they actually often welcomed the Spanish rule and readily accepted Christianity. It has been said with great truth that the Spanish conquest of the Philippines was effected by the Cross rather than the Sword. The monks of the Catholic monastic orders provided a large number of intrepid and devoted missionaries who penetrated into every island and rapidly converted the people, who had not previously been in touch with a higher religion or an advanced civilization. What had happened with Hinduism and Buddhism in Indonesia and continental South-East Asia centuries earlier was now repeated in favour of Catholic Christianity in the Philippines; the peaceful conversion of simple pagan peoples, their ready acceptance of a new civilization.

Spanish military power, although in itself superior in arms to any native force, was numerically very small indeed. The distance, the climate, the ignorance of hygiene and of tropical diseases, contributed to keep the number of Spaniards low. In the first century of Spanish rule the number of soldiers available to the Governor-General was usually not more than three hundred or four hundred: even in 1707, nearly one hundred and fifty years after the foundation of Manila, the number was only two thousand. Without the conversion of the people and their acceptance of Spanish rule, no Spanish settlement would have been possible with such limited forces, and the fate of Spain in the Philippines would have been the same as that of Portugal in Malaya. As it was, the attacks of the Dutch were more of a danger than the hostility of any unsubdued native people, and Manila was more than once in peril from these Protestant adversaries. The other peril, or so the Spaniards thought, was the danger of a Chinese uprising.

Large numbers of Chinese came to Manila and settled to trade, and to conduct handicraft industries. They were a problem for the Spanish. Without them, the country could hardly prosper, since they supplied almost all the skilled craftsmen and retail traders. But they did not convert to Christianity very readily, and they were suspected of planning to seize the country. There was probably no foundation for this fear: Chinese beyond the seas were of little interest to their home government, and the Ming Court had now long abandoned its expansionist policy. The Spaniards, on the other hand, were greedy and rapacious: they taxed the Chinese traders, imposed all manner of vexatious restrictions upon them and goaded them to desperation. In 1603 the Manila Chinese did resist in arms; the Spanish thought their worst fears had come to pass, and in the subsequent strife massacred almost the entire Chinese community of over twenty thousand people.

Soon it was found that without the Chinese, Manila and the whole country went short of many necessities: the Chinese came back, and then, once more, in 1639, provoked by Spanish oppressions, they rose, and another massacre of twenty-four thousand Chinese ended for a time all Chinese settlement in the country. Once again the Chinese were allowed to return: in 1662 the Ming loyalist, Coxinga (Cheng Cheng-kung), lord of Formosa, sent an ultimatum to the Spanish Governor-General, demanding his submission. The Spanish were outraged, and for a time there seemed likely to be a third wholesale massacre of the resident Chinese. It was averted by the sound sense of the Governor and the Archbishop of Manila. Coxinga died next year, and this peril, if it ever was very real, passed away. Thereafter Spanish policy towards the Chinese swung to and fro between the fears of the settlers and the needs of the economy. Orders for the expulsion of all Chinese were made by the King of Spain, notably in 1766, but the damage which such expulsion would cause to the life of the colony, always brought about a change of policy, either before the order was actually enforced, or as in 1778, two years later when the disastrous consequences were all too clear.

The last serious attack upon the Chinese had occurred in 1764, after Spain recovered Manila which, in 1762, had been occupied for two years by the English. The Chinese had co-operated with these new rulers, and when Manila was returned to Spain the Spanish authorities took revenge on those whom they regarded as traitors, or as we would now say, 'collaborators'. It was this last massacre, on a smaller scale than those of the seventeenth century, which caused the King to order the expulsion of all Chinese, an order which had to be revoked two years later. The Chinese were then left at least alive, if still oppressed. Their numbers consequently grew rapidly.

In the early years of Spanish rule there had been only some three or four thousand Chinese in Manila and the neighbouring districts of Luzon. It is uncertain how many there really were at the time of the massacres of 1603 and 1639, the main evidence being the number the Spanish claimed to have put to death. In 1740 the number of Chinese in the Philippines is given as twenty thousand: in 1850, a century later, it was fifty thousand. But when the American administration was set up after the Spanish-American War, the census of 1903 gives only forty thousand Chinese. It is believed that many concealed their nationality, for only thirty years or so later, in 1939 on the eve of the Second World War, the returns give one hundred and seventeen thousand Chinese, and in 1947, after the devastation and slaughter of the Japanese invasion, the numbers are about one hundred thousand. The Chinese have continued to dominate retail trade, the handicrafts and, in later times, the professions also. A very large number of modern Filipinos, by some estimates more than one million, have Chinese blood, but the vast majority of these have become Christians, speak Spanish and have no close relations with their ancestral race.

In the late sixteenth and early seventeenth centuries several of the Spanish governors entertained rather grandiose ideas about future conquests on the mainland of Asia. Plans to invade China were submitted to the King of Spain, and were even more unrealistic than the almost contemporary schemes of the Japanese warlord, Hideyoshi. Either because Madrid realized this, or because he had too many preoccupations nearer home, such wild adventures were never sanctioned by the King. The Spanish did make some small expeditions to the coasts of Vietnam, and became involved in the revolutions of declining Cambodia. These incursions left no lasting foothold for Spain on the mainland, and seem to have been abandoned and forgotten in the next century.

The Philippine colony had in reality much closer relations with distant South America than with near-by Asia. Mexico and Peru were the Spanish dominions on the Pacific coast of

America which traded with Manila: almost all the Philippine trade was conducted with these countries, and the Viceroy of Mexico was the actual superior of the Governor of the Philippines. The Philippines were not profitable to Spain: the restrictions on trade which Spanish policy imposed, based on the false economics of the Mercantile Theory,[1] reduced the prosperity of naturally rich islands. The land system was also a grave handicap.

The Spaniards, coming into the country in the sixteenth century, brought with them a form of feudal land tenure which they had evolved at home in lands taken from the Moors of Spain. The Encomienda was a feudal land holding granted to Spanish settlers, giving them extensive rights over the native inhabitants, who became the bondsmen of the landlord. He could enforce labour and collect rent, had jurisdiction over the native tenants, and in effect they were little better than his serfs. They therefore remained extremely poor, the more so as all natives had to pay a 'tribute' to the Spanish authorities – whether they were Christians or still pagan. The Catholic churchmen frequently exposed the evils of this system, and several of the archbishops and higher clergy attempted to reform it. Their efforts had no great effect, for the lethargy of the home government and the interest of the local grandees combined to thwart them. Thus until the very end of Spanish rule the feudal system endured, depriving the mass of the population of any purchasing power, depressing prices and retarding the economy. Its after-effects still hamper the development of the Republic.

The Spanish Government made repeated attempts to subdue the Moros of Sulu and Mindanao, who engaged in piracy, raided the Christian settlements and refused to acknowledge the rule of Spain. Throughout the whole Spanish period this problem recurred. Treaties made with the Sultan of Jolo, the chief Moro power, were broken: punitive campaigns had no

---

1. According to this theory, a country should conserve its gold and silver. It was believed to be harmful to buy foreign goods with payments of hard cash.

lasting effect. Late in the nineteenth century the Spanish were still trying to conquer the Moros and still met with determined and successful resistance. It was never overcome: when the American occupation followed Spanish rule, the Moros fought the Americans with equal determination until 1913, when the power of American modern arms finally overcame the Moro tribes. Then a treaty was made giving them the right to practise the Moslem religion and preserve their own culture. This measure, which should have been taken centuries earlier, at last brought the Moros into peaceful relations with the rest of the Filipino nation.

The loss of South America in the early nineteenth century, when the colonies of Spain in that continent revolted against the king and became independent republics, made a great change, but not for the better, in the Philippines. The islands were now an isolated colony, the last Spanish possession of any importance, at the ends of the earth, and economically a drain on the resources of the Spanish state. The nineteenth century was thus a period of decline and decay in the economy, and increasing unrest among the people. When the war of 1898 with the United States broke out (for causes which had nothing to do with the Philippines), the American fleet destroyed the Spanish squadron at the Battle of Manila Bay, and the islands were ceded to the United States in the subsequent peace treaty. Spanish rule, from the foundation of Cebu in 1565 to the fall of Manila in 1898, lasted exactly three hundred and thirty-three years; the longest European dominion in any part of the South-East Asian region, and the one which for the reasons which have been shown made the most lasting impression on the people of the country. In another way the experience of Spain was different from that of the other colonizing powers. Spain was displaced not by any uprising of the native population, nor by a nationalist movement, but by conquest by another Western power. America was not normally an imperialist power, and the seizure of the Philippines presented her with problems which were very unfamiliar. A long campaign of pacification, resisted by Philippine nationalists such as Aguinaldo, was necessary. Before many years had passed, the question of the Philippines was to vex the Congress of the United States as much as the rising national movements in India, Indonesia, Indo-China and Burma were to trouble the governments of Britain, Holland and France.

CHAPTER ELEVEN

The End of the Colonial Era

(A.D. 1900–1960)

AT the beginning of the twentieth century the might of the European colonial powers overshadowed South-East Asia. They had never seemed so strong, so irresistible, so secure. American rule had just replaced in the Philippines the decaying authority of Spain; China was in the last days of the failing Manchu dynasty, unable to play any part in the destinies of the region: Japan, the one strong Asian power, was the ally of Britain and was herself learning quickly how to become a colonial power. Thailand alone retained independence as a buffer between France and Britain, countries which up to the close of the century had been far from friendly rivals for colonial power, even if they had avoided fighting each other for it. Less than half a century later, most of the European colonies were independent states, and those that remained under foreign rule were in the course of wars for liberation destined to expel the rule of the colonialists. Probably no great political change affecting so many peoples and different countries has taken place so quickly, for the fall of the colonial empires affected not only the political rule, but also the social system in almost every one of these states. In some respects, the disappearance of the European ruling power meant the reappearance of the ancient, pre-colonial states, but only very few of these regained their freedom under forms of government in any way resembling those under which they had lost it.

Kingdoms such as Burma, Java, Annam, became republics very much inclined to the Left when freed. Thailand is still a monarchy, but no longer an absolute one. In more than one of these countries the prospect of a further turn to the Left and the advent of a Communist régime is very real; thus the long-term effects of the colonial régimes have been to promote very extreme political systems in countries which, when taken over by the colonial powers, were generally regarded as backward and archaic. The South-East Asians, once again, learned a great deal from their European masters, but the lessons they took to heart were not those which the Europeans wished to teach them.

European rule had degraded or destroyed the authority of the ancient kings: no doubt they often governed cruelly and stupidly, but none the less the court in almost every one of these countries was the real and only centre of its culture, the focus of the national life, the patron of religion, the foster mother of its art. Once it was gone, these things decayed rapidly. The art, the literature and the traditions of the people withered when no king remained to patronize them. Religion survived, but grew conservative, withdrawn and no longer offered a constructive leadership to the people. The European rulers had not foreseen these consequences, and when they began to be all too evident it was realized that something must be created to fill the gap in the intellectual and spiritual lives of the people. The answer seemed to be Western education, which would train them to be useful civil servants, professional men and modern citizens. It did not occur to the colonial rulers that if these results were achieved, such people would very soon ask why they should remain subject to an alien rule.

The young men were sent to study in the homelands of the colonial powers: later, universities were set up in the major colonies themselves, but usually very much later, when a whole generation had been formed by study abroad. In Paris, London or Amsterdam, the Asian students, picked for their ability, quickly realized that these home countries were ruled in a quite different way to the colonies from which they themselves had come. Democratic systems of government prevailed: there were Left Wing parties, Socialists, and already, on the continent, Communists, who seemed to attract many of the best writers and some of the most renowned university teachers. The Asian students discovered that these parties and men professed to deplore the existence of colonial régimes. which

PRESENT DAY
EAST ASIA

Indonesia:
Malaysia:

USSR

CHINA

Peking

Pyongyang
KOREA
Seoul
Pusan

Nanking

JAPAN

BURMA

Dien Bien Phu
Hanoi
LAOS
Canton
TAIWAN

Rangoon
THAILAND
NTH.
VIETNAM
HAINAN
Hong Kong

CAMBODIA
STH. VIETNAM
PHILIPPINES

Saigon
LUZON

Manila

MALAYSIA

BRUNEI
SABAH
MINDANAO

SUMATRA
SARAWAK
Singapore
BORNEO

Bandung
Jakarta
CELEBES
MOLUCCAS

INDONESIA
JAVA
Jogjakarta

TIMOR
W. IRIAN
TERRITORY
OF PAPUA &
NEW GUINEA

Map 8

were supported by their political opponents of the Right. It therefore seemed probable that if Left Wing parties could be formed in the colonies, their friends in the homelands would support them, and would help the colonies to recover their independence or, at least, home rule.

The Asian students returning home found, very soon, that the colonial governments did not at all welcome the formation of Left Wing Nationalist parties, and suppressed them. Many returned students were soon in gaol. Some of them, like Sukarno of Indonesia became the leaders of their nations. Thus was born the nationalist movement in all the countries of South-East Asia. It was contemptuous of the past (of which its members were usually very ignorant), scornful of the antiquated monarchies, if these still had any remaining vestige of power, but inspired with a fierce patriotism and a determination to rid the country of foreign domination. Almost all these parties and their followers were well to the Left in political ideals. If few were yet Communist, hardly any party or leader really supported the ideals of the Right. In their own countries no true conservative movement came into existence, for what was there to conserve which patriots would wish to perpetuate? The old régimes of pre-conquest days could not be revived, and were in any case undesirable and backward in the eyes of Western-educated reformers: no one was prepared to defend colonial rule as more desirable than independence. The Europeans in these countries were for many years strangely unable to understand this attitude. Reformers must be 'agitators' who had failed to observe the great benefits which the Western colonial government had brought to their country. The belief that the people of the country would ruin everything if put in control was held by almost all Europeans: the fact that history has often shown that people would rather misgovern themselves than submit to good government by foreigners was ignored, although the history of the homelands of the colonial powers showed many examples of just such a stubborn attitude.

The First World War and its Aftermath

The movements for independence or self-rule were greatly stimulated by the rise of Japan and the results of the First World War. Japan in 1905 had defeated a European power, Russia, in a major war. This had not happened in Asia for centuries, and in eastern Asia it had never previously happened at all. The ancient story of the Arab reaction against the Crusades, or even the later advance of the Turks and Mongols into Europe, was little known to the peoples of South-East Asia, and would have seemed irrelevant to most of them if they had heard about it. But the victory of Japan was another matter. What Japan could do, others should be able to do also. The First World War exhibited the European powers in a poor light. They were fighting each other, and, moreover, recruiting Asians to take part in the war. If Asian troops could be used to fight Germans, why should they not be able to fight English, French or Dutch just as well. The myth of the invincible European army began to fade. In the post-war years all the European powers found themselves faced with a clamorous demand for reforms, home rule or even independence.

The powers reacted to these demands in different ways. Britain, with India as her main preoccupation, soon realized that some promise of political advance was essential if that vast empire was to be held in peace, and then discovered that Burma, a province of India by British conquest, was determined both to separate from India and achieve her own self-government. Rather reluctantly, when the agitation had become very serious, the British Government recognized this fact: Burma was promised both separation and home rule, and achieved the first in 1935, with a limited grant of home rule also. In Malaya Britain did not have to face the problem. That country had been developed very rapidly since British control over the sultanates was established in 1874. Very great numbers of Chinese had come into Malaya, grown rich and now formed the business community and the professional class. But most of them were not British subjects, were still closely connected with their homeland and did not seek political power in a foreign colony. The older settled Chinese were British subjects, but much preferred that status to the prospect of being citizens of an independent Malaya. Such a prospect was not then a reality. There was no 'Malaya', only a federation of Malay sultanates and a colony of the Straits Settlements. The Malays had local feeling of loyalty to their separate sultans, but no common national feeling. The resident Chinese had no part in these loyalties, and would not have been welcome to the Malays if they had sought such allegiance.

Malaya was in this sense a 'new' country, the majority of the population recent immigrants of different races, different religions and without a common culture except in so far as the educated class had learned English. It was to be many years before the nationalist movement arose in Malaya. The Malays were conservative and as yet very little touched with the new nationalism: they were also, as a whole, of a lower educational standard, not forward in commerce or the professions and thus less affected by the foreign influences which were stirring other Asian peoples. The Chinese who were to the fore in business and professional life were educated mainly in their own Chinese schools, which they paid for and supported: they learned English for business reasons, not as a cultural language; their political interests were concentrated on the reform of the falling Empire of China, or, later, on the fortunes of the new Republic. They were not in the least concerned with the government of Malaya, in which they had no part, provided it made conditions suitable for making money and developing commerce. This the British Raj most certainly achieved, and the Chinese were well content with it.

The Dutch were slow to move: the pressures of the First World War were less noted in a country which had been a neutral. The dominance of business and finance made the colonial government very unwilling to interfere with a system which suited these interests, for even if the culture system was now falling into disuse, the marketing of Indonesia's rich exports was entirely in Dutch hands. Retail business was usually Chinese; the Indonesians, denied any share in government, had equally little part in commerce or industry. It was for these reasons that the Indonesian students abroad so readily embraced Socialist views, while their closely related cousins, the Malays of Malaya, who were employed in the minor and also in the ceremonial offices of the government, remained conservative and indifferent to the nationalist movement. This difference between the two communities of Malay-speaking peoples still persists, and underlies the present disagreements concerning Malaysia. The Dutch granted no real reforms, no democratic institutions of any authority and did not train Indonesians for the higher ranks of the civil service. It might be said that the British system in its last years opened a safety valve in limited democratic assemblies and local government, resulting in a great deal of political agitation which the colonial régimes opposed but did not crush. The Dutch system opened no safety valves: it sat tight, the pressure rose, but silently, since it had no means of expression. Outward calm hid greater danger.

The French had another variant of colonial policy. Much more liberal than the British in race relations, they concentrated on education, not to make civil servants and efficient clerks, but to make Asian intellectuals in the image of French intellectuals. They took the view that men formed in France would follow French ways and accept French policies. By treating their colonial subjects with real social equality they largely took the bitterness out of the clash of races. But they were rather more authoritarian in political matters than the British, granted no democratic institutions to the colonies but employed capable men in all ranks of their service. French culture took real root in the countries ruled by France, and still flourishes there after French rule has passed away. In pre-war Indo-China there was indeed an active movement for independence, but it was more prominent in Tonking and Cochin China, the former provinces of the Empire of Annam, than in the protected Kingdom of Cambodia or the Annamite Empire in central Vietnam, which still retained some vestiges of royal government. The tendency was also for the movement in the French territories to be more Left Wing than in Burma, or even in Indonesia. One reason for this was the strength of the Socialist and Communist parties in France itself, where the Indo-Chinese students came into contact with men of these views.

Thailand was an independent kingdom. On the death of King Chulalongkorn in 1910 he was succeeded by King Vajiravudh, his son (one of thirty-four sons), who continued to govern as an absolute monarch. The new king had not the ability, as a monarch, of his father and grandfather. He was more interested in art and literature, in which he excelled. But he did not develop any new institutions, even allowing the Cabinet, which Chulalongkorn had established, to fall into disuse, merely seeing individual ministers from time to time. He did abolish a number of antiquated social customs, including polygamy, and other practices which did not appeal to the taste of a king who had been educated at an English university. He gave his favour to a group of officials and courtiers who abused it by indulging in many corrupt practices, and he also maintained his numerous brothers in high offices, which blocked the promotion of men of merit. In his foreign policy he was careful to keep in line with the two great powers, Britain and France, now allies, who dominated the South-East Asian scene. In 1917, when the First World War was in progress, he declared war on Germany, and a small Thai force was sent to fight in France. King Vajiravudh died in 1925, to be succeeded by his younger brother (he had no sons), King Prajadhipok, the last of the absolute monarchs of Thailand.

The new King was fond of travel and spent much time in Europe. A few years after his accession, the great economic depression of 1929–31 struck Thailand as it did all the world, and brought acute financial troubles. Salaries were cut, and the army and civil service, feeling that they were made to bear the brunt of these economies while the court and princes suffered much less, grew restless and discontented. In Thailand also a younger generation of men educated in the West, or in Western ways, had now grown to manhood and found the absolute rule of the King irksome and out of date. Led by a young and able lawyer, Pridi Banomyong, the young officers and civil servants carried out a bloodless revolution in 1932 when the King was absent from Bangkok. A constitutional monarchy was proclaimed by which the King was shorn of almost all his powers. King Prajadhipok accepted this situation, although in the next few years he endeavoured to reshape the constitution more to his liking. The Young Thai Party, as it was called, rejected such changes, and in another *coup* overthrew the Cabinet which had favoured them. In 1935, the King, feeling that the new movement was repugnant to him, abdicated and retired to England. He was succeeded by a boy of ten, King Ananda Mahidol, then at school in Switzerland. Thailand was under the effective authority of a soldier, Pibun Songgram, who was long to dominate its government.

Thus, on the eve of the Second World War, all South-East Asia was stirring with nationalist movements, extremist and moderate, but all equally inspired by new political and social ideas acquired from the Western countries themselves.

The Second World War

Whatever the outcome of the pre-war nationalist movement might have been, the Japanese invasion violently disrupted the pattern, and swept away, for a time, all European rule in South-East Asia. When the preoccupations and hostile attitudes of the European powers to each other in the years just before the Second World War are recollected – Germany, under Hitler, asserting claims which could only be satisfied if the whole Versailles Treaty settlement were upset, Italy making similar demands in the Mediterranean – it is surprising that the real weakness of the colonial powers in the Far East was not more apparent to their subjects. With war threatening in Europe, neither Britain nor France could spare forces to maintain their position in the Far East, and both powers were mortally afraid that the ambitions of Japan would lead to a conflict there which they could neither avoid nor hope to win. Japan was already riding roughshod over the rights and concessions of these powers in China : if they made no attempt to stop this encroachment, would they be any better able to defend their own colonies? The question seems hardly to have been asked by either the average European living in the Far East, or by all but a few Asian nationalists.

Consequently when Japan struck in 1941 with the raid on Pearl Harbour, followed immediately by the invasions of Malaya and the Philippines, and already preceded by the Japanese occupation of Indo-China (to which defeated France had been forced in July 1941 to agree, neither the resident Europeans nor the Asian peoples were in any way prepared for the catastrophe which now befell them. The first four months of the year 1942, with the last three weeks of December 1941, saw the complete Japanese conquest of all the colonial empires in South-East Asia. What had taken nearly four hundred years to acquire was lost in four months. On 15 February 1942, the Japanese took Singapore, completing the conquest of Malaya; on 7 March they took Rangoon and within nine weeks had overrun the rest of Burma; all resistance in the Netherlands East Indies (Indonesia) ceased on 9 March 1942; the fall of Bataan marked the end of resistance in the Philippines on 9 April 1942. So rapid, extensive and complete a victory had never been seen in the history of the world.

As is well known, these events marked the high water mark of Japanese success: in June 1942 the defeat of their fleet at the Battle of Midway in the Pacific Ocean, only six months or so after Pearl Harbour, showed how far they had miscalculated the real strength of America; for Midway was not only a defeat, it inaugurated the new kind of naval battle in which the two rival fleets never came within the range of each other's guns, but decided the issue by the attacks of their aircraft upon the aircraft carriers of the other side. America's immense resources enabled her to build aircraft and carriers far faster than Japan could hope to do; with this change in the character of naval warfare Japan's powerful navy was put out of date, and although it won some local actions, as at Guadalcanal, it never thereafter won a major encounter, and lost at the Coral Sea, and later at Leyte and Lingayan Gulf in the Philippines, the effective command of the seas.

These strategic changes, which were to bring victory to the United States and her allies, were not at all obvious to ob-

servers cut off from news, such as were the populations of the
fallen colonial empires. What they saw was that the rule of the
Europeans had collapsed suddenly, without warning, and at
once: therefore they had clearly been much weaker than anyone supposed. Where any resistance to the Japanese occupation was continued, it was the work of local, Asian peoples,
such as the Chinese of Malaya. Later, the Burmese Anti-Fascist
People's Liberation Front, first organized as the Burmese
National Army, changed sides. In the Philippines also, the local
resistance was the work of Filipino nationalists, with a strong
Communist element. The same situation was developing in
North Vietnam, where also resistance was organized by Communist leadership, even though the following was at first
mainly nationalist.

The reaction of the leaders of South-East Asian nationalism
to Japanese occupation thus went through two phases: at first,
deeply impressed by the magnitude of the Japanese victory,
they naturally assumed that the Japanese had in effect won the
war, and that all future political settlements would have to
deal with Japan as the real military master of the region. The
nationalist leaders therefore tended to co-operate with the Japanese, while striving to win from them recognition of their
own hopes for independence under the inevitable Japanese protection. This was also the policy of Japan herself. The 'East
Asian Co-Prosperity Sphere' which she attempted to set up
planned to establish a number of so-called independent states in
the former European colonies, all of which would look to
Japan for guidance and protection, and all of which would be
economically bound to Japanese industry and commerce.

The plan comprised three categories of states and territories.
First the 'fully' independent states; these were to be Burma, the
Republic of the Philippines and the Empire of Annam with the
Kingdom of Cambodia. Next the protected states, which were
to include Laos, Java and the eastern islands, and a new state
comprising Sumatra and Malaya. The northern sultanates of
Malaya, formerly under Thai suzerainty, were returned to
Thailand, who had been forced to become an ally of Japan.
Singapore and Penang, with possibly some other bases such as

Amboina in the Moluccas, made up the last category; these were to be Japanese colonies (as was Hong Kong).

These arrangements were never fully carried out. The progress of the war prevented the fulfilment of the plan, and the final details had not been settled when the Japanese surrender brought all to an end. But the plan, though never put into effect, has left an often unacknowledged consequence behind it: when Malaysia and Indonesia were at odds, underlying President Sukarno's hostility to Malaysia was the fact that the Japanese planned to take Sumatra out of Indonesia and combine it with Malaya, a plan in which they had the co-operation of most of the now leading Malay statesmen of Malaya and also of some of the Indonesian leaders who come from Sumatra. The consultations which General Count Terauchi, supreme Japanese Commander in South-East Asia, held at Ipoh with leaders such as Dato Onn bin Jaafar of Malaya and Hatta of Indonesia, were proceeding to establish 'Mahamalaya', the new state of Sumatra combined with most of Malaya, when the war ended. This would have been a revival of the ancient Sumatran Empire of Shrivijaya, and had thus good historical and racial basis.

The plans of the Japanese, since they failed, have often been wholly ignored by writers and politicians of the West dealing with post-war South-East Asia, but unless they are known and understood, much of what has happened since is not easily grasped. The Japanese occupation not only destroyed the prestige of the European colonial rulers, it also called in question the rather arbitrary boundaries which the colonial powers had imposed on the whole region, as a result more of chance than of thought-out design. The idea that there is no sanctity in the boundaries of the former colonies was implanted, and has not been removed by post-war changes. For example, the old quarrel between Cambodia and Thailand was revived and strengthened by the Japanese agreement that Thailand should take back the two districts of Battambang and Siemreap (including Angkor) which Thailand had taken from Cambodia in the eighteenth century, but had been forced to restore to Cambodia when the French dominated Indo-China. Cambodia got these territories back in 1945, but still fears that Thailand has ambitions to regain them. There has been no friendship between the two countries since the war.

In the second phase of the Japanese occupation, from the end of 1942 to the surrender, the nationalist leaders in South-East Asia soon became disillusioned with Japanese rule. The Co-Prosperity Sphere turned out to be shared misery rather than co-prosperity. Japan, losing command of the seas, could not implement her promises. The military occupation was oppressive, harsh and unintelligent. Japan lacked trained administrators who knew the languages and customs of these nations. The brutal persecution of all resisters and non-sympathizers by the Japanese military police alienated much opinion, even if the victims of this persecution were more often Chinese than natives. The leaders of the nationalist parties began to see that Japan might lose the war after all, and their main worry was that if this happened, they themselves would be regarded as enemies by the victorious Western powers. What they now aimed to do was to establish the independence of their countries before the Japanese were forced out, and thus confront the Western powers with an accomplished fact, which they hoped would be impossible to ignore.

The Colonial Powers Return

Burma

In Burma, Aung San, now styled General, had organized an army which at first co-operated with Japan. He had been an 'agitator' – or patriot – before the war, had fled to Japan and returned to Burma with their invading army. He was made head of the Burmese Army under the government of Burma, set up by Japan, which had proclaimed its independence in 1943. But by 1945 Aung San could see which way the wind was blowing: he had no love for the Japanese, who had misgoverned Burma grossly under an occupation which was never secure, since war continued against Britain, America and China in the northern provinces bordering upon India. When the last

Japanese offensive to conquer Assam and so cut the communications of the British forces trying to advance into Burma failed, the Japanese were soon losing ground before this advance. In April 1945, after long and secret negotiations with Lord Mountbatten, British Supreme Commander in the Indian Ocean war zone, Aung San revolted against the Japanese and joined the Allies with his Burmese Army. During the final phase of the Burma campaign, which ended in the Allied capture of Rangoon on 2 May 1945, the Burmese Army under Aung San performed valuable service to the Allied cause. Thus at the surrender of Japan, Aung San stood in a strong position to demand British agreement to Burma's total independence.

Britain granted full independence to Burma in October 1947, following an agreement concluded the previous year by which the British Government agreed to accept the result of the Burmese general election held in April 1947. That election gave overwhelming victory to Aung San and his party. Tragically, the modern hero of Burma did not long outlive his success. In July 1947, Aung San and all his Cabinet were assassinated by armed men hired by his rival, a former pre-war Premier of Burma, U Saw. U Saw, however, failed to profit from this crime, and had to flee the country. The government of Burma was taken over by U Nu, with whom the British, later in the year, concluded the formal renunciation of British sovereignty. 4 January 1948 saw the legal establishment of Burma as a fully independent state, not a member of the British Commonwealth. Burma has had many troubles to cope with since independence, for there were Communist and other insurrections against the government, but there has been no suggestion that Britain was behind these movements, nor did the British ever attempt to foment separatist movements in different parts of the country, the error made by both France and Holland, which so greatly and fatally embittered the struggles in Indonesia and in Indo-China.

Malaya

The British never re-invaded Malaya. Plans for this operation were ready, and it was timed for the late autumn of 1945, but the Japanese surrender on 14 August 1945, anticipated the need. The British re-occupied Malaya on the surrender terms, and found there the Chinese guerrilla force, which had opposed the Japanese, under Communist leadership. This force was disarmed, and its leaders (later to be the leaders of the Communist insurrection in Malaya) rewarded with decorations, but it became a political party which before long was opposing the British rule. The Malay sultans had remained in the country, and had to varying degrees co-operated with the Japanese occupation. They had felt their duty to their subjects required them to stay. But the position was delicate, and it was clear that the former system of government could hardly be restored without change. The Chinese had suffered appalling cruelties and massacres from the Japanese; they had befriended British prisoners and opposed the enemy; they could no longer be treated as if they were not there at all, denied all political rights and treated as an immigrant group with no stake in the country. Some of the Indian population had been recruited by the Japanese into an Indian National Army, and had fought against the British in Burma. They, too, presented a delicate problem, in view of the rising agitation for Indian independence in their homeland. The restored colonial régimes were from the first faced with problems which had not existed before the war, and made great changes inevitable.

Furthermore, the British returned to Malaya to find the country in a desperate economic condition. Malaya did not at that time support itself on home-grown food, since much of the country is not suitable for rice growing, and the economy has depended on the rubber industry and tin mining. The Japanese, losing control of the seas, had not been able to keep up imports of rice from Burma and elsewhere, and in any case the Irrawaddy delta, the great granary of the region, had been devastated by war and partly gone out of cultivation. The economic problem was tackled by the British with skill and determination: food was imported, the rubber plantations weeded and renewed, industry restarted. But there were grave political problems in a country which had hardly known them before the war. To escape Japanese persecution and also to grow food to live on, many thousands of the poorer Chinese, losing their employment in the cities, had fled to the fringes of the jungle where they cleared land and made small farms. The Japanese had turned a blind eye on this development, as it helped to feed a population which they could not supply. But in pre-war Malaya the ownership of farm land had been reserved for Malays, as this land was in the sultanates, where Chinese had no rights of citizenship. The Malays began to demand that the Chinese squatters be driven off their land.

On the other hand, the Chinese community, comprising nearly forty per cent of the population and eighty per cent of the people of Singapore, had opposed the Japanese both in a clandestine resistance movement and in an open guerrilla war. The Malay sultans had not taken an open stand against the Japanese. It was realized in London that it was impossible to return to the pre-war political situation in which the Chinese had no political rights, and the federated and unfederated Malay states formed two units, while the Straits Settlements made a third. The country was too small for this division, and its problems had to be settled as a whole. The British therefore proposed to set up (January 1946) a Malayan Union, in which, while Singapore would be detached as a colony later to get self-government, the rest of the country would become a unified state. The powers of the sultans and the autonomy of their states would be reduced to empty titles and local government; the citizens of all races born in the country would have full political rights; those born elsewhere could become citizens after five years' residence and a clear determination to make the country their home.

This plan met with the sudden, unexpected and violent opposition of the Malays. The sultans had been reluctantly compelled to sign the agreement, but the Malays found a leader in Dato Onn bin Jaafar (who had played a prominent part in the Japanese plans for 'Mahamalaya', the combined Sumatra–Malaya state). Dato Onn organized the United Malay National Organization (U.M.N.O.) to fight the plan for the Malayan Union. The separation of Singapore also displeased the Chinese, as it cut off the chief city of the country from the rest of the state, and left them in a minority in the new Malayan Union. This, indeed, was the purpose of separating Singapore, to appease Malay feeling and make the Union acceptable. It failed to do this, and the British Government, strongly influenced by senior officers of the Malayan civil service, who were in a majority in favour of the Malays, and little acquainted with the Chinese point of view, bowed to the storm and abolished the Malayan Union. After long and obstinate negotiations a new scheme, the Federation of Malaya, was proclaimed in 1948, by which some of the Malay objections were met. Chinese right to citizenship in the Federation was greatly reduced, and several clauses of the new constitution guaranteed the predominant position of Malays in the civil service and in political life. The Chinese population resented these changes, and for some years it appeared likely that the new system would break down on the racial issue.

Another complication perhaps both prevented this development while at the same time plunging the country into new troubles. The guerrilla movement against the Japanese had been led by and largely consisted of Chinese of Communist views. After the war the guerrillas had been disarmed and disbanded, with rewards, but had concealed many of their arms, and at once organized a Communist Party which rapidly gained great power in the trade unions. For two years, 1946–7, the Communists attempted to disrupt the economy by strikes and agitation, helped by the strong feelings which the various plans for a political settlement aroused among the Chinese, and the fears of the farmer squatters for their lands. In 1948, following repression of Communist activities in the cities, the party went underground and suddenly started a full-scale insurrection, based on the jungle, in which the tactics were to slay European planters and officials, disorganize the administration and hope to seize control of a base area, following the pattern of the rise of the Communist Party in China.

The Communist insurrection was called in Malaya 'the Emergency' and lasted for over ten years: even at the present time, a small remnant of the rebels still hangs on in the jungles along the Thai–Malaya frontier, but the insurrection as a threat to the country was virtually brought to an end by the declaration of Malayan independence in 1957. The British Government waged a long anti-guerrilla war against this movement, with growing success, which had to be based on sweeping measures of reform. The Chinese squatter farmers, who supplied most of the food for the guerrillas, through either fear of reprisals or fear of losing their land to the Malays, were resettled in new villages with permanent land title, farther from the fringes of the jungle. This greatly diminished both their ability to supply the guerrillas and their fears. But there is no doubt that it was the British decision to give Malaya full self-government, and independence if she chose it, which brought the mass of the population into support for the government, and indifference, or opposition to, the guerrillas. As long as the Communists could claim to be fighting for Malayan independence as well as for Communism, they won either support or at least toleration from many anti-Communist people. When self-government was established, they lost this support and tolerance.

Meanwhile the prospect of self-government and independence, if the two communities, Malays and Chinese, could work together, and the fear that if they continued divided the grant of self-government would be withheld, brought them into a working agreement. An Alliance Party was formed between the U.M.N.O. (Malay), now led by men more moderate than Dato Onn, and the Malayan Chinese Association (M.C.A.), which represented the more substantial part of the resident Chinese population of the Federation, led by the wealthy bankers, merchants, tin miners and rubber planters. The Alliance won a sweeping victory at the general election of 1955 and in August 1957 Malaya became an independent federated kingdom under an elected king, always one of the sultans. Singapore remained separate, but obtained full self-government in 1959 and was soon ruled by the People's Action Party (P.A.P.), which was a party of moderate socialist outlook. The new system worked well: the Communist rebellion was mastered, and after a few years the difficulty which the separation of Singapore involved was met by the ingenious plan of creating

Malaysia (1963), which would include the Federation of Malaya, Singapore and the former British protectorates and colonies in North Borneo in one new federated state. This state had a population in which Malays and non-Chinese Borneans were a slight majority, even when Singapore was taken in. This alleviated the fears of the Malays. On the other hand, it restored to Singapore her natural hinterland and her dominant economic position as the greatest city of the region, and thus helped her to overcome her problems of rising population and the need for increasing development to provide more jobs.

The Constitution of Malaysia provided for the gradual grant of political rights to all the inhabitants, to all born in the country. As massive Chinese immigration ceased just before the last war, the growing majority of the Chinese were now people born in the country, and it was hoped that the old problem of the status of the immigrants would soon fade out of existence as they passed away.

Malaysia's immediate problem was not the internal racial question so much as the external threat posed by the policy of Indonesia, which under President Sukarno threatened to 'crush' Malaysia and to carry on guerrilla warfare in the new Borneo states of Malaysia. The British abandoned sovereignty over these Borneo countries in 1963: Sarawak (which was ceded to Britain by the last Raja Brooke after the war) and North Borneo, now called Sabah, which had been a colony. The small Sultanate of Brunei, a British Protectorate, and rich in oil, refused to join Malaysia, hoping for better terms. It is more than probable that some of the roots of the quarrel between Malaysia and Indonesia lay in the war period, when Japan tried to detach Sumatra from Indonesia and combine it with Malaya in a new state, a circumstance which neither side, in Malaysia or in Indonesia, has forgotten.

In the new Malaysian parliament, the Government was formed by the predominantly Malay Alliance Party and led by Tunku Abdul Rahman. The Singapore-centred and predominantly Chinese People's Action Party, led by Singapore premier Lee Kuan Yew, formed the main opposition. For some time a

Western-style democracy seemed possible, but racial tensions re-asserted themselves. The Tunku accused Mr Lee of attempting to become Prime Minister – a reasonable aim for the leader of the opposition in a true democracy, but a sinister threat when seen, as the Tunku saw it, as an attempt to assert Chinese hegemony over the confederation.

Even so, the world was surprised and shocked when, on Monday, 9 August 1965, it was announced that, by agreement of both parties, Singapore had separated from the Federation. For Mr Lee, it meant the failure of a great experiment in multi-racialism which he had helped to create as an example for the world to follow. For the Tunku, it was seen as a political necessity if further racial trouble was to be avoided.

The future of Malaysia continues to be uncertain, despite moderation in Indonesia's policy.

Indonesia

Indonesia in 1945 presented the Dutch with even greater difficulties. Between the situation of the British in Burma particularly and the Americans in the Philippines, on the one hand, and the Dutch in Indonesia and the French in Indo-China on the other, there was a wide difference. The British had reconquered Burma; the Americans had won the Pacific War and liberated all these countries by forcing Japan to surrender. The French had been defeated and occupied by Germany until late in 1944; Holland was only freed from the German occupation by the total defeat and surrender of the German forces in May 1945. Neither France nor Holland had the ships, nor the men, nor the aircraft to recover their former colonies unless aided by their allies. Britain had been about to mount a great offensive to recover Malaya, and had no difficulty in occupying the country; America had already re-occupied parts of the Philippines in the course of the war, and could enter the whole country when Japan surrendered.

Consequently, while the Burmese and, later, the Malayan peoples could only bargain with a former colonial power already re-instated, the Indonesians and the Indo-Chinese peoples saw no reason why the former colonial power should be brought back at all. Both countries had been declared independent before the Japanese surrendered, both refused to annul this act and claimed that it was valid. The Japanese, as we have seen, had not quite made up their minds about Indonesia until very late in the war. They clearly doubted that the Indonesians would prove willing and submissive allies, and they had planned to divide the country, an idea repugnant particularly to the Javanese. It was thus only on 17 August 1945, three days after the Japanese surrender, but before this event had been made public in Indonesia, that the Japanese Commander in that country hastily summoned Sukarno and other leaders, and conferred independence upon Indonesia. The Indonesians proclaimed a Republic and began as quickly as possible to organize an armed force, and establish organs of government. All this, of course, had no sanction from the Allied High Command in South-East Asia.

Holland had no forces available. The country had only just been liberated, it had not had time to reconstitute its forces, except to a very slight degree. Nor were they in the Far East zone. Consequently it fell to the lot of the British to send in a small force to take the Japanese surrender, disarm the large Japanese forces and arrange for their shipment back to Japan. When General Christison arrived at Jakarta he found the Republican government already installed and operating as the legal government of the country. He had very small forces, for the Japanese surrender, the result of the atomic bombs, had not been foreseen, and no large force was ready for an invasion of Indonesia, which it had been expected would be strongly defended by the Japanese. British plans had envisaged the conquest of Malaya first, as a necessary step before Indonesia could be invaded. It had taken time to collect even the small force under General Christison. It did not arrive at Jakarta till 29 September, more than five weeks after the proclamation of the Republic of Indonesia. General Christison had to co-operate with the Republic to carry out his task; this he was careful to say did not mean British recognition, but it did in practice amount to something like it. Dr Van Moek, the newly appointed Dutch Governor-General, arrived within a few days, but although he opened negotiations with the Republicans, he could do nothing to enforce his authority.

Dutch troops were soon arriving in the Far East, and the British force was then withdrawn. It became necessary to decide the future of Indonesia before trouble broke out. The Dutch Government refused to accept Dr Sukarno as the President of any régime, on the grounds that he had collaborated with the Japanese. Sukarno therefore resigned, and his place was taken by Sutan Sjahrir. The leaders of the Indonesian movement had divided themselves into two groups during the Japanese Occupation, one remaining to co-operate with the Japanese, the others going into hiding in the mountains, the idea being that in any eventuality some of them would remain at liberty to carry on their movement. There was no difference of view between the two groups, but this was not realized by the Dutch authorities. Negotiations dragged on. The Dutch reoccupied the Outer Islands, which the Republic had not had time to control, while the Republic expanded its army in Java, the essential key island. A Communist attempt to seize control of the Republic was defeated in June 1946, and, following mediation by the British, the Republic and Holland agreed late in 1946 to a new arrangement. There was to be a federation called the United States of Indonesia, which was to form a part of a Netherlands Indonesian Union. This agreement was accepted by both sides and signed on 25 March 1947.

It did not work. The Dutch suspected the Indonesian side of bad faith, the Indonesian parties were reluctant to forgo complete independence. It proved impossible to get the new system started. In May 1947 the Dutch presented an ultimatum, which was rejected, and the Dutch forces then went into action against the Republic in what was called the 'First Police Action'. Their troops occupied some of the most important towns and cut off the forces of the Republic from each other. This Dutch action roused great resentment throughout Asia, and before long, as a result of the diplomatic intervention of India (newly independent) and Australia, the United Nations Security Council set up a Good Offices Committee to arbitrate between the two sides. A truce was called in January 1948.

But this attempt to find a solution also failed. In December 1948 the Dutch once more resorted to force in the 'Second Police Action', seizing the Republican leaders and putting them into gaol, while occupying most of the Republican territory. Once more, following a violent agitation in Asia, and at the United Nations, the Security Council intervened and imposed a cease-fire, the Dutch having to evacuate Jogjakarta, the Republic's temporary capital, and free the imprisoned leaders. Negotiations were resumed. It was now clear that Holland could not reconquer the country in the face of the hostility of other Asian powers, the trend of world opinion at the United Nations and the determination of the Indonesians to resist. In August 1949 a conference was called at The Hague to arrange for the transfer of sovereignty from Holland to Indonesia. On 27 December the independence of Indonesia was formally proclaimed and accepted by Holland. The question of West Irian, or West New Guinea, which Holland retained on an ambiguously worded clause of The Hague Treaty, remained to vex relations until this territory was finally passed to Indonesia in 1962.

Indo-China

The end of Dutch rule, or rather the failure to re-establish it, might have proved a warning to France, which was endeavouring to recover Indo-China, but although the course of events was at first similar, the French situation was complicated by the nature of the independence movement in Vietnam, which led to a long war, and has not yet found a final solution. In March 1945 the Japanese, who had occupied the whole of the French territories in Indo-China since July 1941, leaving administration to the French colonial service (which acknowledged the Vichy Government in France), proclaimed the independence of the three kingdoms into which the country was nominally divided: Annam, under Emperor Bao Dai, Cambodia under its own King and Laos under the King of Luang Prabang, a ruler who had had vague title to overlordship of other, smaller Laotian principalities. But in the North of Annam, Tongking, Ho Chi Minh, the leader of the Communist resistance in the country, refused to acknowledge Emperor Bao Dai's government, seized the northern capital, Hanoi, when the Japanese surrendered and proclaimed a provisional Republic. Meanwhile British forces under General Gracey had been sent to Saigon, in the south, to take the Japanese surrender there. They were able to hand over this city and some others to the returning French, but neither the British nor these French troops could occupy the southern countryside which was soon in the hands of nationalist guerrillas. The Chinese (Nationalist) Government had been authorized to take the Japanese surrender in northern Vietnam, down to the 16th parallel of latitude. They moved in, leaving Ho Chi Minh in control of Hanoi.

In February 1946 the Chinese and French made an agreement by which the Chinese withdrew, but left Ho in control. The French then made an agreement with Ho recognizing the Republic of Vietnam as a free state forming part of a proposed Indo-Chinese Federation, to which Cambodia and the rest of Annam were to belong, while Cochin China (the most southerly part of Annam, now South Vietnam) was to decide by referendum whether it would join the Republic. But the new French Governor-General, Admiral d'Argenlieu, had his own interpretation of these agreements; he proposed to create a new state of Cochin China, which was clearly intended to be a French puppet. A conference called at Fontainbleau failed to get agreement and the pattern of the Dutch interventions in Indonesia was clearly being repeated. The conference failed, and in November the French air force suddenly bombed the North Vietnam port of Haiphong, with great loss of life. Next month the Vietnamese made surprise attacks on the French garrisons, and a full-scale war began.

This war lasted for nearly six years, until in 1954, after the defeat of the French at Dien Bien Phu in Tongking, a conference of the major powers was called at Geneva, at which Communist China, America and Britain were represented (Chou En-lai for China, John Foster Dulles, Secretary of State, for the U.S.A., Sir Anthony Eden for Britain). This conference partitioned Vietnam into North and South. It also recognized the full independence of Cambodia and Laos, and arranged for the evacuation of all French forces. South Vietnam was organized as a Republic under a Right Wing leader, Ngo Dinh Diem, protected by the United States. North Vietnam became a Communist Republic under Ho Chi Minh. But as is well known, this solution has not provided peace. The pro-Communist guerrillas who had fought the French in the south soon started to fight the South Vietnam Republic. The war still continues. The attempt to recover Indo-China for France thus failed, and with more disastrous consequences than the attempt to recover Indonesia for the Dutch.

Thailand

Before the war Thailand was the only independent state left in South-East Asia. When Japan struck in December 1941, the country was under the dictatorial control of a general, Pibun Songgram, and the young King Ananda Mahidol was a school-boy in Switzerland. There he remained until after the war was over, the royal powers being exercised by a Regency. Pibun could not resist the Japanese, so he joined them. During the war the co-operation of the Thai Government with Japan was not very close, but Thailand was given back suzerainty over the four northern unfederated states of Malaya, and also recovered the Battambang and Siemreap districts of Cambodia, the French being forced by the occupying Japanese to yield these provinces of their protected Kingdom of Cambodia. Meanwhile, Pridi Banomyong, the original leader of the anti-absolute monarchy revolution of 1932, was still in power, acting as Regent for the absent King. Pridi was not in agreement with the pro-Japanese policy of Pibun, and made use of his position as Regent to co-operate secretly with the Allied powers. The United States, taking the view that Thailand had acted under Japanese constraint, refused to admit that a state of war existed between Thailand and America. This made it easier for Pridi to communicate with the Allied Supreme Commanders.

In July 1944 the Japanese were clearly losing the war: Pridi and his followers were then able to put Pibun out of power and negotiate the surrender of Thailand to the Allies without internal opposition, and this was peacefully arranged at the right

SOUTH-EAST ASIA

moment when Japanese intervention was no longer possible. Thailand had to give up the four northern Malay states, and Battambang and Siemreap once more went back to Cambodia, but Thailand suffered no other loss of territory. Internal policies were, however, disturbed. The King had returned from Switzerland at the end of the war, having now attained his majority. In July 1946 he was found dead, with a bullet through his head. There has never yet been a fully satisfactory answer to the problem of this tragedy, whether murder, suicide or accident. The Thai Government, when later Pibun returned to power, claimed that it was a murder, and executed some of the King's guards as accomplices, but few people in Thailand credited this particular version of the crime. The dead King was succeeded by his younger brother, the present King Phumiphon Adulet, and in 1947 Pridi Banomyong was driven from power by a *coup d'état* organized by Pibun Songgram. Pridi left Thailand and soon after disappeared: it was believed that he later went to Peking, when the Communist government in China came to power. Pibun, who had collaborated with the Japanese, was none the less accepted by the Western powers, because he was openly and actively anti-Communist, and by 1947 the rise of the Chinese Communist Party was already evident.

The Philippines

The American rule in the Philippine Islands was from the first intended to be a temporary phase. America did not believe in colonies, but realized that after three hundred years of Spanish rule the Filipinos were unready to govern themselves. The United States therefore set up democratic institutions which exercised limited powers under the supervision of the American Governor, while the United States armed forces pacified the country, and undertook its protection and defence. Manila, with the island fortress of Corregidor, became a major American base. It was no doubt expected that when the Philippines became fully independent, they would agree by treaty for the continuation of this base under American control. The American administration imposed the Chinese exclusion laws, then operating in the U.S.A., on the Philippines when they annexed the country. Chinese immigration thus virtually came to a stop fifty and more years ago, leaving over one hundred thousand Chinese resident in the country, and many more people of mixed descent. In 1934 the U.S. administration was withdrawn and the Philippines became a free 'Commonwealth' still under American protection and military power, but wholly self-governing in internal matters. The Filipino people were not fully satisfied with this stage of their progress, and a continued agitation for full independence continued.

The Japanese invasion in 1941–2 rapidly overran the whole country, in spite of the heroic defence of Corregidor and Bataan by the American forces. It was not until 1944 and early 1945 that the armies and fleets of the United States were able to return to the country. The Japanese had followed their usual plan. The Philippines were declared an independent Republic, and a collaborating President assumed office. But Japanese occupation was just as harsh and intolerable in the Philippines as in Burma, Malaya or Java, and the mass of the Filipino population resisted, either openly or secretly sympathizing with the Allies. A guerrilla movement, the Hukbalahap movement (the word means 'freedom fighters' in the Tagalog language) arose under Communist leadership. Thus when Japan surrendered, the Philippine situation was closely similar to that prevailing in Burma, Indo-China, Java and Malaya: a ruined country, a weak nationalist government and a well-trained and experienced Communist guerrilla movement. The Philippines, by the Japanese invasion, were for the first time in their history brought into the main stream of South-East Asian history and shared the same problems as their mainland and island neighbours.

The policy of the American Government, that of a country now militarily supreme in the area, was wise and far-seeing. Independence, full and complete, was at once granted to the Philippines (4 July 1946). American military advisers and some combat units helped the Philippine regular army to fight the Hukbalahap Communist insurrection. In this way, America avoided the mistakes of the Dutch and French, and followed, or rather went hand in hand with, the British policy in Burma, and later Malaya. The 'Huk' movement, as it came to be called, was eventually suppressed: after a period of weak and inefficient government, the Philippines have found increasing stability under presidents who have made a serious effort to reform the archaic land tenure system, a legacy of Spanish rule, which nourished rural discontent and sustained movements such as the Hukbalahap rebellion. But instability still continues, due to corruption, and the Hukbalahap movement is still active.

Nomenclature and Orthography

THERE are many scripts in use in eastern Asia: Chinese, the Japanese modification of Chinese ideographs, Pali, Sanskrit and their derivations, the modern Burmese, Thai and Cambodian script and the Arabic derivatives used in Malaya and formerly in Indonesia. These have no exact equivalent with the Latin alphabet, and various systems of romanization exist. The policy adopted has been to use the system most widely current, which will be found in use in the largest number of books on these countries and their culture.

For Chinese the Wade-Giles system is used, except for such accepted variants as the names of the cities, Canton, Nanking and Peking, and a few very well-known individuals who spelt their names in dialect form, i.e. Sun Yat-sen, Chiang K'ai-shek, and the latinisms, 'Confucius' and 'Mencius'.

For Japanese the Hepburn system of romanization has been used throughout.

There is no universally accepted system for the countries and languages of South-East Asia, where not only are Sanskrit words pronounced in the local manner, often differing from the apparent sound of Latin transcriptions (i.e. 'Pibul Songgram' is pronounced 'Pibun Songgram'), but also the transcriptions tend to reflect the spelling habitual to the foreign colonial people who formerly ruled in these countries. Thus the Dutch 'oe' sounded similarly to the English 'u' appears frequently in names, such as 'Soekarno'. 'Sukarno' now seems to be more frequently used. 'Djakarta' is also a Dutch form, and the 'd' is unnecessary in English: 'Jakarta' gives the correct sound. In general, the practice adopted for South-East Asia follows the forms used by Professor D. G. E. Hall in his well-known and authoritative *A History of South-East Asia* (Macmillan and Co., London, new edition, 1964).

Chinese surnames come first; the given name, sometimes of two words, sometimes of only one, comes second. In 'Mao Tse-tung', 'Mao' is the surname, 'Tse-tung' the given name. In 'Li Yuan', 'Li' is the surname, 'Yuan' the given name. It is sometimes customary among modern Western-educated Chinese to write their surnames last preceded by initials for the given name, as 'C. K. T'ang' in the Western manner, but this cannot be employed in writing in the Chinese language, which in non-alphabetic.

The surname also comes first in Japanese; i.e. in 'Tokugawa Ieyasu', 'Tokugawa' is the surname. Japanese given names appear as one word in romanization, as do the surnames, but these are often written in Japanese with two or even more Chinese ideographs.

Korean names follow the same rules as Chinese, surname first, given name second.

The peoples of South-East Asia, whether Moslem or Buddhist, did not in pre-modern times use surnames. In East Asia this appears to have been a Chinese invention, adopted by the Japanese and Koreans. Names such as 'Alaungpaya' (Burmese) are personal, and do not indicate the common name of a family. Persons of the same family do not have names in common.

General Bibliography

China

W. Eberhart, *A History of China* (California, Berkeley, 1950).

C. P. FitzGerald, *China: A Short Cultural History* (Cresset Press, London, 3rd rev. ed., 1961; paperback ed. 1965).

L. C. Goodrich, *A Short History of the Chinese People* (Harper & Bros., New York, 3rd rev. ed., 1959; Allen & Unwin, London, 1962).

O. Edmund Clubb, *Twentieth Century China* (Columbia Press, New York, 1964).

Jerome Ch'en, *Mao and the Chinese Revolution* (Oxford University Press, 1965).

China, Japan and Korea

Edwin O. Reischauer and John K. Fairbank, *A History of East Asian Civilization* (Houghton Mifflin Co., Boston, 1960–4; Allen & Unwin, London).
  Volume One *East Asia: The Great Tradition*.
  Volume Two *East Asia: The Modern Transformation*.

Japan

G. B. Sansom, *A History of Japan* (three volumes) (Cresset Press, London, 1964; Stanford University Press, Stanford).

G. B. Sansom, *The Western World and Japan* (Cresset Press, London, 1950).

Korea

S. McCune, *Korea's Heritage; A Regional and Social Geography* (Charles E. Tuttle Co., Rutland, Vermont and Tokyo, 1956).

C. Osgood, *The Koreans and Their Culture* (Ronald Press, New York, 1951).

South-East Asia

D. G. E. Hall, *A History of South East Asia* (Macmillan and Co., London, new edition, 1964).

BIBLIOGRAPHY

Victor Purcell, *The Chinese in South-East Asia* (Oxford University Press, 1952).

H. J. Benda, *The Crescent and the Rising Sun* (Van Hoeve, The Hague, 1958).

C. A. Fisher, *South-East Asia: A Social, Economic and Political Geography* (Methuen, London, 1965).

See also Reischauer and Fairbank, op. cit., Volume Two, Chapters 6 and 9.

Index

359

Ho Chi Minh, 349–51
Hodge, General, 260
Hōjō, 163, 172
Hōjō Regency, 164–9; end of, 171, 172, 185, 216
Hokkaido (Yezo), 147, 201
Holland, see Dutch
Honan, 5, 86, 90, 101
Hong Kong, 87, 115, 167
Honolulu, 236
Honshu, 149, 156
Hopei, 5, 82, 232–3, 247
Hōryūji, 153
Hsi Hsia, 83, 87
Hsia dynasty, 4–5
Hsiang Yu, 29
Hsien Feng, 122
Hsiung Nu, 44–7, 49
Hsuan Tsung ('The Brilliant Emperor'), 75–6, 80
Hsuan T'ung (P'u Yi), 128, 131
Hsua Ta, 96
'Hu', 24
'Huai-Hai', 144
Huai River, 144
Huang Ti ('The Yellow Emperor'), 4
Huang Tsao, 78–9, 116
Hui Tsung, 85
Hukbalahap movement ('Huks'), 353–4
Huan, 18, 46, 116, 119, 142
Hundred Years' War, 171
Hung Hsiu-ch'uan, 115–20
Hungary, 89
Hung Wu (Chu Yan-chang), 92, 96
Huns, 44
Hupei, 142
Imagawa, 190
Imari, Gulf of, 167

Imperial Family (Japan), 151–5, 158, 164, 170, 176, 200; Restoration, 207–17; Prestige of Emperor, 239
Imperial Rescript, 221
India, 35, 48, 56, 64–5, 68, 79–80, 89, 93, 114, 144, 202
Indian Ocean 93, 97, 267
Indians, in Malaya, 302
Indo-China, 236; after the Second World War, 349–51; see Vietnam
Indonesia, 93, 148; after the Second World War, 346–9
Inner Mongolia, 91, 120, 122, 142, 230
'Innovator' group, 85
Ipoh, 338
Iraq, 9
Ise, 151
Ito, 214, 219, 222
Izumo, 151

Jacatra, 294
Jakarta, 294, 347
Japan, 33, 64, 81, 106; 1894 war with China, 125; First World War, 133; war with China, 1937–45, 143–4; cf. with England, 147; trade with China and Korea, 177–9; growth of commerce, 177; contacts with China, 181; expansionist policy (Hideyoshi), 186–9; cf. with 19th century China, 209; militarist period, 217–39; annexation of Korea, 247, 254–8; occupation policy in Pacific War, 336–9
Japanese, 97, 196; militarism, 207, 217–39

INDEX

Romans, 35, 41
Ronin, 197–8, 200
Roosevelt, Franklin D., 236, 258
Russia, 44, 82, 89, 125, 128, 136–7, 201, 204, 220, 223–7, 254, 261
Russian Turkestan, 48
Russo–Japanese War, 224, 254
Ryukyu Is., 237

Sabah, 345
Sages, 3–4, 16, 85
Saigo, 211
Saionji, Prince, 222–3, 229, 231
Samarkand, 47
Samurai, 157, 178, 185, 193–4, 197–8, 200–204, 208–12, 217
Sanskrit, 57, 64–5, 103, 265–6, 268–9, 276
Sarawak, 302
Satsuma, 185–6, 190, 192, 204–6, 208–12, 214, 216, 221, 223
Scandinavia, 84
School of the Law, 17, 22, 26
Script, 6–8, 12, 19, 34, 150, 243, 249, 318, 355
Sea power: Ming, 92–5, 279–80; Manchu, lack of, 106
Sea routes (to China), 51, 92–3
Seclusion, policy of (Korea), 250–52
Second World War, 143, 222, 228–9, 234–9, 247, 257–8, 262; its effect in South-East Asia, 335–9
Sekigahara, Battle of, 191; cf. with Bosworth, 191, 196, 206
Seoul, 187, 247, 249, 253, 259, 261
Shang, 3–6, 9–13, 35
Shanghai, 137, 140–43, 144, 232–3, 258
Shanghai International Settle-

ment, 139, 230
Shanhaikuan, 102, 128, 232, 243
Shansi, 24
Shantung, 13, 100, 127, 225–6
Shensi, 12, 13, 20, 90, 142
Shikoku, 148
Shimabara Rising, 197
Shimonoseki, 161, 205
Shinto, 151, 182, 200–201
Shogun(s), 156, 161–2, 164, 169, 177, 192
Shōtoku, Prince, 152–3
Shrivijaya, see Sumatra
Shu, 20
Shun, 4, 33
Shun dynasty, 101–3
Siam, 106; see Thailand
Sian (Ch'angan), 13, 61, 79, 127, 142
Siberia, 92, 128, 136, 201, 230, 257, 260
Siemreap, 316, 351
Silla, 242, 245–7
Singapore, 236, 278, 283, 299; population of, 342; separation from Malaysia, 346
Sinkiang (Chinese Turkestan), 45, 47, 49, 92, 106
Sino–Japanese War, 217–19, 223, 254
Sjahrir, Sutan, 348
Soga, 152
Songdo, 247
South Court (Japan), 173, 175–6
South-East Asia, 93, 257; definition of area, 265; general introduction, 266–73; colonial structure, 287–8; European penetration, 288–326; 20th century, 317, 327–30
South Korea, 259–62

INDEX

MORE ABOUT PENGUINS
AND PELICANS

Penguinews, which appears every month, contains details of all the new books issued by Penguins as they are published. From time to time it is supplemented by *Penguins in Print*, which is a complete list of all titles available. (There are some five thousand of these.)

A specimen copy of *Penguinews* will be sent to you free on request. For a year's issues (including the complete lists) please send 36p if you live in the United Kingdom, or 60p if you live elsewhere. Just write to Dept EP, Penguin Books Ltd, Harmondsworth, Middlesex, enclosing a cheque or postal order, and your name will be added to the mailing list.

In the U.S.A.: For a complete list of books available from Penguin in the United States write to Dept CS, Penguin Books Inc., 7110 Ambassador Road, Baltimore, Maryland 212.

In Canada: For a complete list of books available from Penguin in Canada write to Penguin Books Canada Ltd, 41 Steelcase Road, Markham, Ontario L3R 1B4.

ASIA AWAKES

DICK WILSON

'A vividly-written survey of a whole continent' – *Asia and Africa Review*

Until the middle of this century the area bounded by Pakistan, China, Mongolia and Borneo lay dormant. Since then countries with hierarchical societies and little or no modern industrial technology (with the important exception of Japan) have struggled to telescope the achievements of centuries in Europe into a single lifetime. The disruption of traditional forces in Asian life has made the present a time of unprecedented turmoil.

Dick Wilson, author of *A Quarter of Mankind*, uses a wide variety of sources, including his own fifteen years of travel in Asia, to expose the ideological, cultural, social and economic problems which face both individual countries and Asia as a whole.

'He handles an enormous mass of disparate materials with skill and finesse' – *New Society*

'Mr Wilson has a great deal of knowledge, his prose is lucid and unaffected. The structure of the book is clear and inviting' – *The Times Literary Supplement*

Not for sale in the U.S.A.

THE CHINESE ROAD
TO SOCIALISM

E. L. WHEELWRIGHT AND
BRUCE MCFARLANE

It is only recently that it has become possible to extract information about modern China's internal social, political and economic policies – and what information there has been is not always believed.

In this Pelican, however, Wheelwright and McFarlane make one of the first comprehensive investigations of the struggling economic policy of an overpopulated and under-developed nation, of the ideology behind the Cultural Revolution, and of the theories underlying the Chinese brand of socialism.

The two authors of this book are working from first-hand information. Both have visited China on separate occasions; they have seen large and small enterprise in cities and towns, and have examined agricultural communes in the more remote rural areas. By amalgamating their individual experiences they have contrived to produce an authoritative and deeply absorbing account of the Chinese road to socialism.

Not for sale in the U.S.A. or Canada